EFFECTIVE
SUCCESSION
PLANNING

THIRD EDITION

EFFECTIVE SUCCESSION PLANNING

THIRD EDITION

Ensuring Leadership Continuity and
Building Talent from Within

William J. Rothwell

American Management Association

New York • Atlanta • Brussels • Chicago • Mexico City • San Francisco
Shanghai • Tokyo • Toronto • Washington, D.C.

Special discounts on bulk quantities of AMACOM books are available to corporations, professional associations, and other organizations. For details, contact Special Sales Department, AMACOM, a division of American Management Association, 1601 Broadway, New York, NY 10019.
Tel.: 212-903-8316.   Fax: 212-903-8083.
Web site: www.amacombooks.org

Library of Congress Cataloging-in-Publication Data

Rothwell, William J.
      Effective succession planning : ensuring leadership continuity and building talent from within / William J. Rothwell.— 3rd ed.
          p.   cm.
      Includes bibliographical references and index.
      ISBN-10: 0-8144-0842-7
      ISBN-13: 978-0-8144-0842-1
      1. Leadership.   2. Executive succession—United States.   3. Executive ability.   4. Organizational effectiveness.   I. Title.

HD57.7.R689 2005
658.4'092—dc22

                                                                    2004024908

Printing number

10   9   8   7   6   5   4

To my wife Marcelina, my daughter Candice,
my son Froilan, and my grandson Aden

CONTENTS

LIST OF EXHIBITS

PREFACE TO THE THIRD EDITION

A colleague told me over the phone the other day that "there have been no new developments in succession planning for decades." My response was, "*Au contraire*. There have been many changes. Perhaps you are simply not conversant with how the playing field has changed." I pointed out to him that, since the second edition of this book was published, there have been many changes in the world and in succession planning. Allow me a moment to list a few:

Changes in the World

▲ *The Aftereffects of 9/11*. When the World Trade Center was destroyed, 172 corporate vice presidents lost their lives. That tragic event reinforced the message, earlier foreshadowed by the tragic loss of life in Oklahoma City, that life is fragile and talent at all levels is increasingly at risk in a world where disaster can strike unexpectedly. In a move that would have been unthinkable ten years ago, some organizations are examining their bench strength in locations other than their headquarters in New York City, Washington, or other cities that might be prone to attack if terrorists should wipe out a whole city through use of a dirty nuclear weapon or other chemical or biological agent. Could the organization pick up the pieces and continue functioning without headquarters? That awful, but necessary, question is on the minds of some corporate and government leaders today. (In fact, one client of mine has set a goal of making a European capital the alternative corporate headquarters, with a view toward having headquarters completely re-established in Europe within 24 hours of the total loss of the New York City headquarters, if disaster should strike.)

▲ *The Aftereffects of Many Corporate Scandals*. Ethics, morality, and values have never been more prominent than they are today. In the wake of the scandals affecting Enron, Global Crossing, WorldCom, and many other corporations—and the incredible departure of Arthur Andersen from the corporate world—many leaders have recognized that ethics, morality, and values do matter. Corporate boards have gotten more involved in succession planning and management owing, in part, to the requirements of the Sarbanes-Oxley Act. And corporate leaders, thinking about succession, realize that future leaders must model the behaviors they want others to exhibit and must avoid practices that give even the mere appearance of impropriety.

▲ *Growing Recognition of the Aging Workforce.* Everyone is now talking about the demographic changes sweeping the working world in the United States and in the other nations of the G-8. Some organizations have already felt the effects of talent loss resulting from retirements of experienced workers.

▲ *Growing Awareness that Succession Issues Amount to More Than Finding Replacements.* When experienced people leave organizations, they take with them not only the capacity to do the work but also the accumulated wisdom they have acquired. That happens at all levels and in all functional areas. Succession involves more than merely planning for replacements at the top. It also involves thinking through what to do when the most experienced people at all levels depart—and take valuable institutional memory with them.

Changes in Succession Planning

▲ *The Emergence of "Talent Management" and "Talent Development."* As is true in so many areas of management, these terms may well be in search of meanings. They have more than one meaning. But, in many cases, *talent management* refers to the efforts taken to attract, develop, and retain best-in-class employees—dubbed *high performers* (or HiPers) and *high potentials* (or HiPos) by some. Talent development may refer to efforts to groom HiPers or HiPos for the future. Think of it as selective attention paid to the top performing 10 percent of employees—that's one way it is thought of.

▲ *The Emergence of "Workforce Planning."* While some people think that succession planning is limited to the top of the organization chart—which I do not believe, by the way—others regard comprehensive planning for the future staffing needs of the organization as *workforce planning*. It is also a popular term for succession planning in government, rivaling the term *human capital management* in that venue.

▲ *Growing Awareness of Succession Planning.* More decision-makers are becoming aware of the need for succession planning as they scurry to find replacements for a pending tidal wave of retirements in the wake of years of downsizing, rightsizing, and smartsizing.

▲ *The Recognition that Succession Planning Is Only One of Many Solutions.* When managers hear that they are losing a valuable—and experienced—worker, their first inclination is to clutch their hearts and say "Oh, my heavens, I have only two ways to deal with the problem—promote from inside or hire from outside. The work is too specialized to hire from outside, and the organization has such weak bench strength that it is not possible to promote from within. Therefore, we should get busy and build a succession program." Of course, that is much too limited a view. The goal is to get the work done and not replace people. There are many ways to get the work done.

▲ *Growing Awareness of Technical Succession Planning.* While succession planning is typically associated with preparing people to make vertical moves on the organization chart, it is also possible to think about individuals such as engineers, lawyers, research scientists, MIS professionals, and other professional or technical workers who possess specialized knowledge. When they leave the organization, they may take critically important, and proprietary, knowledge with them. Hence, growing awareness exists for the need to do technical succession planning, which focuses on the horizontal level of the organization chart and involves broadening and deepening professional knowledge and preserving it for the organization's continued use in the future.

▲ *Continuing Problems with HR Systems.* HR systems are still not up to snuff. As I consult in this field, I see too little staffing in HR departments, poorly skilled HR workers, voodoo competency modeling efforts, insufficient technology to support robust applications like succession, and many other problems with the HR function itself, including timid HR people who are unwilling to stand up to the CEO or their operating peers and exert true leadership about what accountability systems are needed to make sure that managers do their jobs to groom talent at the same time that they struggle to get today's work out the door.

Still, my professional colleague was right in the sense that the world continues to face the crisis of leadership that was described in the preface to the first and second editions of this book. Indeed, "a chronic crisis of governance—that is, the pervasive incapacity of organizations to cope with the expectations of their constituents—is now an overwhelming factor worldwide."[1] That statement is as true today as it was when this book was first published in 1994. Evidence can still be found in many settings: Citizens continue to lose faith in their elected officials to address problems at the national, regional, and local levels; the religious continue to lose faith in high-profile church leaders who have been stricken with sensationalized scandals; and consumers continue to lose faith in business leaders to act responsibly and ethically.[2] Add to those problems some others: people have lost faith that the media like newspapers or television stations, now owned by enormous corporations, tell them the truth—or that reporters have even bothered to check the facts; and patients have lost faith that doctors, many of whom are now employed by large profit-making HMOs, are really working to "do no harm."

A crisis of governance is also widespread inside organizations. Employees wonder what kind of employment they can maintain when a new employment contract has changed the relationship between workers and their organizations. Employee loyalty is a relic of the past,[3] a victim of the downsizing craze so popular in the 1990s and that persists in some organizations to the present day. Changing demographics makes the identification of successors key to the future of many organizations when the legacy of the cutbacks in the middle-management ranks, traditional training ground for senior executive positions, has begun to be felt. If that is hard to believe, consider that 20 percent of the best-known companies in the United States may lose 40 percent of their senior executives to retirement at any time.[4] Demographics tell the story: The U.S. population is aging, and that could mean many retirements soon. (See Exhibits P-1 and P-2.)

Amid the twofold pressures of pending retirements in senior executive ranks and the increasing value of intellectual capital and knowledge management, it is more necessary than ever for organizations to plan for leadership continuity and employee advancement at all levels. But that is easier said than done. It is not consistent with longstanding tradition, which favors quick-fix solutions to succession planning and management (SP&M) issues. Nor is it consistent with the continuing, current trends favoring slimmed-down staffing, outsourcing, and the use of contingent workers, which often create a shallow talent pool from which to choose future leaders.

In previous decades, labor in the United States was plentiful and taken for

Exhibit P-1. Age Distribution of the U.S. Population, Selected Years, 1965–2025

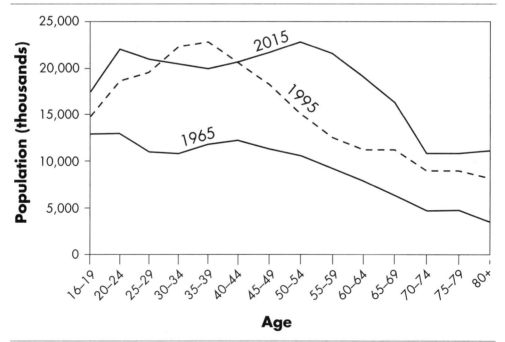

Source: Stacy Poulos and Demetra S. Nightengale, "The Aging Baby Boom: Implications for Employment and Training Programs." Presented at http://www.urban.org/aging/abb/agingbaby.html. This report was prepared by the U.S. Department of Labor under Contract No. F-5532-5-00-80-30.

Exhibit P-2. U.S. Population by Age, 1965–2025

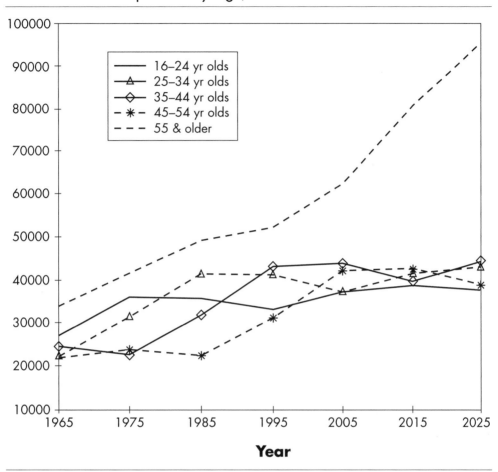

Source: Stacy Poulos and Demetra S. Nightengale, "The Aging Baby Boom: Implications for Employment and Training Programs."
Presented at http://www.urban.org/aging/abb/agingbaby.html. This report was prepared by the U.S. Department of Labor under
Contract No. F-5532-5-00-80-30.

granted. Managers had the leisure to groom employees for advancement over long time spans and to overstaff as insurance against turnover in key positions. That was as true for management as for nonmanagement employees. Most jobs did not require extensive prequalification. Seniority (sometimes called *job tenure*), as measured by time with an organization or in an industry, was sufficient to ensure advancement.

Succession planning and management activities properly focused on leaders at the peak of tall organizational hierarchies because organizations were controlled from the top down and were thus heavily dependent on the knowledge, skills, and attitudes of top management leaders. But times have changed. Few organizations have the luxury to overstaff in the face of fierce competition from low-cost labor abroad and economic restructuring efforts. That is particularly true in high-technology companies where several months' experience may be the equivalent of one year's work in a traditional organization.

At the same time, products, markets, and management activities have grown more complex. Many jobs now require extensive prequalification, both inside and outside organizations. A track record of demonstrated and successful work performance, more than mere time in position, and leadership competency have become key considerations as fewer employees compete for diminishing advancement opportunities. As employee empowerment has broadened the ranks of decision-makers, leadership influence can be exerted at all hierarchical levels rather than limited to those few granted authority by virtue of their lofty titles and management positions.

For these reasons, organizations must take proactive steps to plan for future talent needs at all levels and implement programs designed to ensure that the right people are available for the right jobs in the right places and at the right times to meet organizational requirements. Much is at stake in this process: "The continuity of the organization over time requires a succession of persons to fill key positions."[5] There are important social implications as well. As management guru Peter Drucker explained in words as true today as when they were written[6]:

> The question of tomorrow's management is, above all, a concern of our society. Let me put it bluntly—we have reached a point where we simply will not be able to tolerate as a country, as a society, as a government, the danger that any *one of our major companies will decline or collapse because it has not made adequate provisions for management succession.* [emphasis added]

Research adds weight to the argument favoring SP&M. First, it has been shown that firms in which the CEO has a specific successor in mind are more profitable than those in which no specific successor has been identified. A possible reason is that selecting a successor "could be viewed as a favorable general signal about the presence and development of high-quality top management."[7] In other words, superior-performing CEOs make SP&M and leadership continuity top priorities. Succession planning and management has even been credited with driving a plant turnaround by linking the organization's continuous improvement philosophy to individual development.[8]

But ensuring leadership continuity can be a daunting undertaking. The rules, procedures, and techniques used in the past appear to be growing increasingly outmoded and inappropriate. It is time to revisit, rethink, and even reengineer SP&M. That is especially true because, in the words of one observer of the contemporary management scene, "below many a corporation's top two or three positions, succession planning [for talent] is often an informal, haphazard exercise where longevity, luck, and being in the proverbial right place at the right time determines lines of succession."[9] A haphazard approach to SP&M bodes ill for organizations in which leadership talent is diffused—and correspondingly important—at all hierarchical levels and yet the need exists to scramble organizational resources quickly to take advantage of business opportunities or deal with crises.

The Purpose of This Book

Succession planning and management and leadership development figure prominently on the agenda of many top managers. Yet, despite senior management interest, the task often falls to human resource management (HRM) and workplace learning and performance (WLP) professionals to spearhead and coordinate efforts to establish and operate planned succession programs and avert succession crises. In that way, they fill an important, proactive role demanded of them by top managers, and they ensure that SP&M issues are not lost in the shuffle of fighting daily fires.

But SP&M is rarely, if ever, treated in most undergraduate or graduate college degree programs—even in those specifically tailored to preparing HRM and WLP professionals. For this reason, HRM and WLP professionals often need assistance when they coordinate, establish, operate, or evaluate SP&M programs. This book is intended to provide that help. It offers practical, how-to-do-it advice on SP&M. The book's scope is deliberately broad. It encompasses more than *management* succession planning, which is the most frequently discussed topic by writers and consultants in the field. Stated succinctly, the purpose of this book is to reassess SP&M and offer a current, fresh but practical approach to ensuring leadership continuity in key positions and building leadership talent from within.

Succession planning and management should support strategic planning and strategic thinking and should provide an essential starting point for management and employee development programs. Without it, organizations will have difficulty maintaining leadership continuity—or identifying appropriate leaders when a change in business strategy is necessary. While many large blue-chip corporations operate best-practice SP&M programs, small and medium-sized businesses also need them. In fact, inadequate succession plans are a common cause of small business failure as founding entrepreneurs fade from the scene, leaving no one to continue their legacy,[10] and as tax laws exert an impact on the legacy of those founders as they pass away. Additionally, nonprofit enterprises and government agencies need to give thought to planning for future talent.

Whatever an organization's size or your job responsibilities, then, this book should provide useful information on establishing, managing, operating, and evaluating SP&M programs.

Sources of Information

As I began writing this book I decided to explore state-of-the-art succession planning and management practices. I consulted several major sources of information:

1. *A Tailor-Made Survey.* In 2004 I surveyed over 500 HRM professionals about SP&M practices in their organizations. Selected survey results, which were compiled in June 2004, are published in this book for the first time. This survey was an update of earlier surveys conducted for the first edition (1994) and second edition (2000) of this book. While the response rate to this survey was disappointing, the results do provide interesting information.

2. *Phone Surveys and Informal Benchmarking.* I spoke by phone and in person with vendors of specialized succession planning software and discussed SP&M with workplace learning and performance professionals in major corporations.

3. *Other Surveys.* I researched other surveys that have been conducted on SP&M in recent years and, giving proper credit when due, I summarize key findings of those surveys at appropriate points in the book.

4. *Web Searches.* I examined what resources could be found on the World Wide Web relating to important topics in this book.

5. *A Literature Search.* I conducted an exhaustive literature review on SP&M—with special emphasis on what has been written on the subject since the last edition of this book. I also looked for case-study descriptions of what real organizations have been doing.

6. *Firsthand In-House Work Experience.* Before entering the academic world, I was responsible for a comprehensive management development (MD) program in a major corporation. As part of that role I coordinated management SP&M. My experiences are reflected in this book.

7. *Extensive External Consulting and Public Speaking.* Since entering academe, I have also done extensive consulting and public speaking on the topic of SP&M. I spoke about succession planning to sixty-four CEOs of the largest corporations in Singapore; conducted training on succession in Asia and in Europe; keynoted several conferences on succession and spoke on the topic at many conferences; and provided guidance for a major research study of best practices on the topic in large corporations. Most recently, I have focused attention on best practices in government succession at all levels—local, state, federal, and international.

The aim of these sources is to ensure that this book will provide a comprehensive and up-to-date treatment of typical *and* best-in-class SP&M practices in organizations of various sizes and types operating in different industries.

The Scheme of This Book

Effective Succession Planning: Ensuring Leadership Continuity and Building Talent from Within, Third Edition, is written for those wishing to establish, revitalize, or review an SP&M program within their organizations. It is geared to meet the needs of HRM and WLP executives, managers, and professionals. It also contains useful information for chief executive officers, chief operating officers, general managers, university faculty members who do consulting, management development specialists who are looking for a detailed treatment of the subject as a foundation for their own efforts, SP&M program coordinators, and others bearing major responsibilities for developing management, professional, technical, sales, or other employees.

The book is organized in four parts. (See Exhibit P-3.) Part I sets the stage. Chapter 1 opens with dramatic vignettes illustrating typical—and a few rivet-

Exhibit P-3. The Organization of the Book

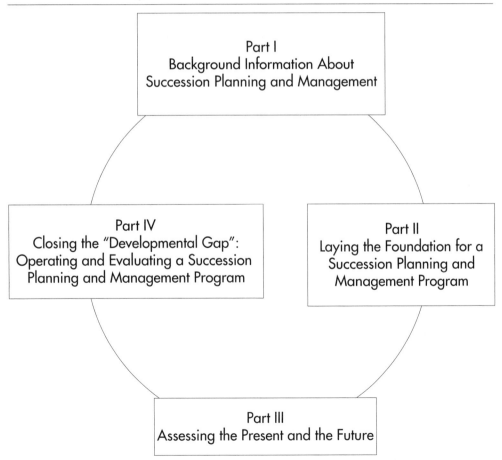

Part I
Background Information About
Succession Planning and Management

Part IV
Closing the "Developmental Gap":
Operating and Evaluating a Succession
Planning and Management Program

Part II
Laying the Foundation for a
Succession Planning and
Management Program

Part III
Assessing the Present and the Future

ingly atypical—problems in SP&M. The chapter also defines succession planning and management. It also distinguishes it from replacement planning, workforce planning, talent management, and human capital management. Then the chapter goes on to emphasize its importance, explain why organizations sponsor such programs, and describe different approaches to succession planning and management.

Chapter 2 describes key trends influencing succession planning and management. Those trends are: (1) the need for speed; (2) a seller's market for skills; (3) reduced loyalty among employers and workers; (4) the importance of intellectual capital and knowledge management; (5) the key importance of values and competencies; (6) more software available to support succession; (7) the growing activism of boards of directors; (8) growing awareness of similarities and differences in succession issues globally; (9) growing awareness of similarities and differences of succession programs in special venues: government, nonprofit, education, small business, and family business; and (10) managing a special issue: CEO succession. The chapter clarifies what these trends mean for SP&M efforts.

Chapter 3 summarizes the characteristics of effective SP&M programs, describes the life cycle of SP&M programs, identifies and solves common problems with various approaches to SP&M, describes the requirements and key steps in a fifth-generation approach to SP&M, and explains how new approaches to organizational change may be adapted for use with SP&M.

Chapter 4 defines competencies, explains how they are used in SP&M, summarizes how to conduct competency studies for SP&M and use the results, explains how organizational leaders can "build" competencies using development strategies, defines values, and explains how values and values clarification can guide SP&M efforts.

Part II consists of Chapters 5 through 7. It lays the foundation for an effective SP&M program. Chapter 5 describes how to make the case for change, often a necessary first step before any change effort can be successful. The chapter reviews such important steps in this process as assessing current SP&M practices, demonstrating business need, determining program requirements, linking SP&M to strategic planning and human resource planning, benchmarking SP&M practices in other organizations, and securing management commitment. It also emphasizes the critical importance of the CEO's role in SP&M in businesses.

Building on the previous chapter, Chapter 6 explains how to clarify roles in an SP&M program; formulate the program's mission, policy, and procedure statements; identify target groups; and set program priorities. It also addresses the legal framework in SP&M and provides advice about strategies for rolling out an SP&M program.

Chapter 7 rounds out Part II. It offers advice on preparing a program action plan, communicating the action plan, conducting SP&M meetings, designing and delivering training to support SP&M, and counseling managers about SP&M problems uniquely affecting them and their areas of responsibility.

Part III comprises Chapters 8 and 9. It focuses on assessing present work requirements in key positions, present individual performance, future work requirements, and future individual potential. Crucial to an effective SP&M program, these activities are the basis for subsequent individual development planning.

Chapter 8 examines the present situation. It addresses the following questions:

▲ How are key positions identified?
▲ What three approaches can be used to determining work requirements in key positions?
▲ How can full-circle, multirater assessment be used in SP&M?
▲ How is performance appraised?
▲ What techniques and approaches can be used in creating talent pools?

Chapter 9 examines the future. Related to Chapter 8, it focuses on these questions:

▲ What key positions are likely to emerge in the future?
▲ What will be the work requirements in those positions?
▲ What is individual potential assessment, and how can it be carried out?

Part IV consists of Chapters 10 through 14. Chapters in this part focus on closing the developmental gap by operating and evaluating an SP&M program. Chapter 10 offers advice for testing the organization's overall bench strength, explains why an internal promotion policy is important, defines the term *individual development plan* (IDP), describes how to prepare and use an IDP to guide individual development, and reviews important methods to support internal development.

Chapter 11 moves beyond the traditional approach to SP&M. It offers alternatives to internal development as the means by which to meet replacement needs. The basic idea of the chapter is that underlying a replacement need is a work need that must be satisfied. There are, of course, other ways to meet work needs than by replacing a key position incumbent. The chapter provides a decision model to distinguish between situations when replacing a key position incumbent is—and is not—warranted.

Chapter 12 examines how to apply online and high-tech approaches to SP&M programs. The chapter addresses four major questions: (1) How are online and high-tech methods defined? (2) In what areas of SP&M can online and high-tech methods be applied? (3) How are online and high-tech applications used? and (4) What specialized competencies are required by succession planning coordinators to use these applications?

Chapter 13 is about evaluation, and it examines possible answers to three simple questions: (1) What is evaluation? (2) What should be evaluated in SP&M? and (3) How should an SP&M program be evaluated?

Chapter 14 concludes the book. It offers eight predictions about SP&M. More specifically, I end the book by predicting that SP&M will: (1) prompt efforts by decision-makers to find flexible strategies to address future organizational talent needs; (2) lead to integrated retention policies and procedures that are intended to identify high-potential talent earlier, retain that talent, and preserve older high-potential workers; (3) have a global impact; (4) be influenced increasingly by real-time technological innovations; (5) become an issue in government agencies, academic institutions, and nonprofit enterprises in a way never before seen; (6) lead to increasing organizational openness about possible successors; (7) increasingly be integrated with career development issues; and (8) be heavily influenced in the future by concerns about work/family balance and spirituality.

The book ends with two appendices. Appendix I addresses frequently asked questions (FAQs) about succession planning and management. Appendix II provides a range of case studies about succession planning and management that describe how it is applied in various settings.

One last thing. You may be asking yourself: "How is the third edition of this classic book different from the second edition?" While I did not add or drop chapters, I did make many changes to this book. Allow me to list just a few:

▲ The book opens with an Advance Organizer, a new feature that allows you to assess the need for an effective SP&M program in your organization and to go immediately to chapters that address special needs.

▲ The survey research cited in this book is new, conducted in year 2004.

▲ The literature cited in the book has been expanded and updated.

▲ New sections in one chapter have been added on specialized topics within succession, including: (1) CEO succession; (2) succession in government; (3) succession in small business; (4) succession in family business; and (5) succession in international settings.

▲ A new section has been added on using assessment centers and work portfolios in potential assessment.

▲ A new section has been added on the use of psychological assessments in succession, a topic of growing interest.

▲ The section on competency identification, modeling, and assessment has been updated.

▲ A new section has been added on planning developmental strategies.

▲ A new section has been added on the CEO's role in succession.

▲ The book closes with a selection of frequently asked questions (FAQs) about succession planning and management, which is new.

▲ A CD-ROM has been added to the book—a major addition in its own right—and it contains reproducible copies of all assessment instruments and worksheets that appear in the book as well as three separate briefings/workshops: one on mentoring, one as an executive briefing on succession, and one on the manager's role in succession. (The table of contents for the CD is found at the back of this book.)

All these changes reflect the many changes that have occurred in the succession planning and management field within the last few years and since the last edition was published.

William J. Rothwell
University Park, Pennsylvania
January 2005

ACKNOWLEDGMENTS

Writing a book resembles taking a long journey. The researching, drafting, and repeated revising requires more time, effort, patience, and self-discipline than most authors care to admit or have the dedication to pursue. Yet no book is written in isolation. Completing such a journey requires any author to seek help from many people, who provide advice—and directions—along the way.

This is my opportunity to thank those who have helped me. I would therefore like to extend my sincere appreciation to my graduate research assistants, Ms. Wang Wei and Ms. Yeonsoo Kim, for their excellent and able assistance in helping me to send out and analyze the survey results, and for helping me to track down and secure necessary copyright permissions.

I would also like to thank Adrienne Hickey and other staff members at AMACOM, who offered numerous useful ideas on the project while demonstrating enormous patience with me and my busy schedule in consulting and presenting around the world.

ADVANCE ORGANIZER
FOR THIS BOOK

Complete the following assessment before you read this book. Use it to help you assess the need for an effective succession planning and management (SP&M) program in your organization. You may also use it to refer directly to topics in the book that are of special importance to you now.

Directions: Read each item below. Circle **Y** (yes), **N/A** (not applicable), or **N** (no) in the left column next to each item. Spend about 15 minutes on this. Think of succession planning and management in your organization as you believe it is—not as you think it should be. When you finish, score and interpret the results using the instructions appearing at the end of this Advance Organizer. Then be prepared to share your responses with others in your organization as a starting point for planning. If you would like to learn more about one item below, refer to the number in the right column to find the chapter in this book in which the subject is discussed.

Circle your response in the left-hand column for each response below.

			Has your organization:	**Chapter**
Y	N/A	N	1. Clearly defined the need for succession planning and management (SP&M)?	1
Y	N/A	N	2. Distinguished succession planning and management from replacement, workforce planning, talent management, and human capital management?	1
Y	N/A	N	3. Made the business case by showing the importance of succession planning and management?	1
Y	N/A	N	4. Clarified the reasons (goals) for the succession planning and management program?	1
Y	N/A	N	5. Investigated best practices and approaches to succession planning and management?	1
Y	N/A	N	6. Considered the drivers of change and the trends that may influence succession planning and management?	2

1

Y N/A N	7.	Clarified how trends, as they unfold, may influence succession planning and management in your organization?	2
Y N/A N	8.	Investigated the characteristics of effective succession planning and management programs?	3
Y N/A N	9.	Thought about how to roll out a succession planning and management program?	3
Y N/A N	10.	Set out to identify, and try to avoid, common problems with succession planning and management?	3
Y N/A N	11.	Considered integrating whole-systems transformational change into the succession planning and management program?	3
Y N/A N	12.	Considered integrating appreciative inquiry into the succession planning and management program?	3
Y N/A N	13.	Planned for what might be required to establish a state-of-the-art approach to the succession planning and management program?	3
Y N/A N	14.	Defined competencies as they might be used in your organization?	4
Y N/A N	15.	Considered how competency models might be used for your succession planning and management program?	4
Y N/A N	16.	Explored new developments in competency identification, modeling, and assessment for the succession planning and management program?	4
Y N/A N	17.	Identified competency development strategies to build bench strength?	4
Y N/A N	18.	Specifically considered how values might impact the succession planning and management program?	4
Y N/A N	19.	Determined organizational requirements for the succession planning and management program?	5
Y N/A N	20.	Linked succession planning and management activities to organizational and human resource strategy?	5
Y N/A N	21.	Benchmarked best practices and common business practices in succession planning and management practices in other organizations?	5

Y	N/A	N	22.	Obtained and built management commitment to systematic succession planning and management?	5
Y	N/A	N	23.	Clarified the key role to be played by the CEO in the succession effort?	5
Y	N/A	N	24.	Conducted a risk analysis?	6
Y	N/A	N	25.	Formulated a mission statement for the succession effort?	6
Y	N/A	N	26.	Written policy and procedures to guide the succession effort?	6
Y	N/A	N	27.	Identified target groups for the succession effort?	6
Y	N/A	N	28.	Set program priorities?	6
Y	N/A	N	29.	Addressed the legal framework affecting the the succession planning and management program?	6
Y	N/A	N	30.	Established strategies for rolling out the program?	6
Y	N/A	N	31.	Prepared a program action plan?	7
Y	N/A	N	32.	Communicated the action plan?	7
Y	N/A	N	33.	Conducted succession planning and management meetings?	7
Y	N/A	N	34.	Trained on succession planning and management?	7
Y	N/A	N	35.	Counseled managers about succession planning problems in their areas?	7
Y	N/A	N	36.	Identified key positions?	8
Y	N/A	N	37.	Appraised performance and applied performance management?	8
Y	N/A	N	38.	Considered creating talent pools?	8
Y	N/A	N	39.	Thought of possibilities beyond talent pools?	8
Y	N/A	N	40.	Identified key positions for the future?	9
Y	N/A	N	41.	Assessed individual potential for promotability on some systematic basis?	9
Y	N/A	N	42.	Considered using assessment centers?	9
Y	N/A	N	43.	Considered using work portfolios to assess individual potential?	9
Y	N/A	N	44.	Tested bench strength?	10
Y	N/A	N	45.	Formulated internal promotion policy?	10
Y	N/A	N	46.	Prepared individual development plans?	10
Y	N/A	N	47.	Developed successors internally?	10
Y	N/A	N	48.	Considered using leadership development programs in succession planning?	10

Y	N/A	N	49. Considered using executive coaching in succession planning?	**10**
Y	N/A	N	50. Considered using mentoring in succession planning?	**10**
Y	N/A	N	51. Considered using action learning in succession planning?	**10**
Y	N/A	N	52. Explored alternative ways to get the work done beyond succession?	**11**
Y	N/A	N	53. Explored innovative approaches to tapping the retiree base?	**11**
Y	N/A	N	54. Investigated how online and high-tech methods be applied?	**12**
Y	N/A	N	55. Decided what should be evaluated?	**13**
Y	N/A	N	56. Decided how the program can be evaluated?	**13**
Y	N/A	N	57. Considered how changing conditions may affect the succession planning and management program?	**14**

Scoring and Interpreting the Advance Organizer

Give your organization one point for each Y and zero for each N or N/A. Total the number of Ts, and place the sum in the line next to the word *TOTAL*.

Then interpret your score as follows:

50 or more Your organization is apparently using effective succession planning and management practices.

40 to 49 Improvements could be made to succession planning and management practices. On the whole, however, the organization is proceeding on the right track.

30 to 39 Succession planning and management practices in your organization do not appear to be as effective as they should be. Significant improvements should be made.

28 or less Succession planning and management practices are ineffective in your organization. They are probably a source of costly mistakes, productivity losses, and unnecessary employee turnover. Take immediate corrective action.

PART I

BACKGROUND INFORMATION ABOUT SUCCESSION PLANNING AND MANAGEMENT

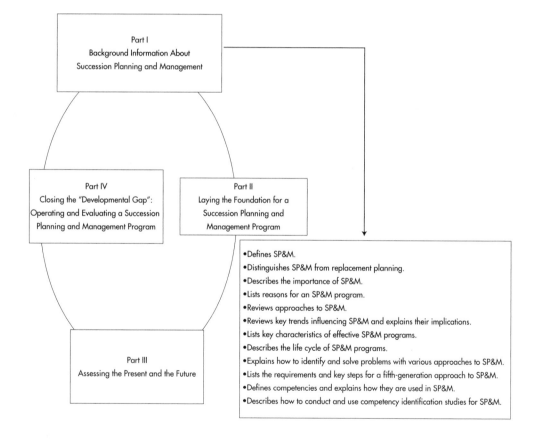

Part I
Background Information About
Succession Planning and Management

Part IV
Closing the "Developmental Gap":
Operating and Evaluating a Succession
Planning and Management Program

Part II
Laying the Foundation for a
Succession Planning and
Management Program

Part III
Assessing the Present and the Future

- Defines SP&M.
- Distinguishes SP&M from replacement planning.
- Describes the importance of SP&M.
- Lists reasons for an SP&M program.
- Reviews approaches to SP&M.
- Reviews key trends influencing SP&M and explains their implications.
- Lists key characteristics of effective SP&M programs.
- Describes the life cycle of SP&M programs.
- Explains how to identify and solve problems with various approaches to SP&M.
- Lists the requirements and key steps for a fifth-generation approach to SP&M.
- Defines competencies and explains how they are used in SP&M.
- Describes how to conduct and use competency identification studies for SP&M.

WHAT IS SUCCESSION PLANNING AND MANAGEMENT?

Six Ministudies: Can You Solve These Succession Problems?

How is your organization handling succession planning and management (SP&M)? Read the following vignettes and, on a separate sheet, describe how *your* organization would solve the problem presented in each. If you can offer an effective solution to all the problems in the vignettes, then your organization may already have an effective SP&M program in place; if not, your organization may have an urgent need to devote more attention to the problem of succession.

Vignette 1

An airplane crashes in the desert, killing all on board. Among the passengers are top managers of Acme Engineering, a successful consulting firm. When the vice president of human resources at Acme is summoned to the phone to receive the news, she gasps, turns pale, looks blankly at her secretary, and breathlessly voices the first question that enters her mind: "Now who's in charge?"

Vignette 2

On the way to a business meeting in Bogota, Colombia, the CEO of Normal Fixtures (maker of ceramic bathroom fixtures) is seized and is being held for ransom by freedom fighters. They demand 1 million U.S. dollars in exchange for his life, or they will kill him within 72 hours. Members of the corporate board are beside themselves with concern.

Vignette 3

Georgina Myers, supervisor of a key assembly line, has just called in sick after two years of perfect attendance. She personally handles all purchasing and production scheduling in the small plant, as well as overseeing the assembly line. The production manager, Mary Rawlings, does not know how the plant will function in the absence of this key employee, who carries in her head essential, and proprietary, knowledge of production operations. She is sure that production will be lost today because Georgina has no trained backup.

Vignette 4

Marietta Diaz was not promoted to supervisor. She is convinced that she is a victim of racial and sexual discrimination. Her manager, Wilson Smith, assures her that that is not the case. As he explains to her, "You just don't have the skills and experience to do the work. Gordon Hague, who was promoted, already possesses those skills. The decision was based strictly on individual merit and supervisory job requirements." But Marietta remains troubled. How, she wonders, could Gordon have acquired those skills in his previous nonsupervisory job?

Vignette 5

Morton Wile is about to retire as CEO of Multiplex Systems. For several years he has been grooming L. Carson Adams as his successor. Adams has held the posts of executive vice president and chief operating officer, and his performance has been exemplary in those positions. Wile has long been convinced that Adams will make an excellent CEO. But, as his retirement date approaches, Wile has recently been hearing questions about his choice. Several division vice presidents and members of the board of directors have asked him privately how wise it is to allow Adams to take over, since (it is whispered) he has long had a high-profile extramarital affair with his secretary and is rumored to be an alcoholic. How, they wonder, can he be chosen to assume the top leadership position when he carries such personal baggage? Wile is loathe to talk to Adams about these matters because he does not want to police anyone's personal life. But he is sufficiently troubled to think about initiating an executive search for a CEO candidate from outside the company.

Vignette 6

Linda Childress is general manager of a large consumer products plant in the Midwest. She has helped her plant weather many storms. The first was a corporate-sponsored voluntary early retirement program, which began eight years ago. In that program Linda lost her most experienced workers, and among its effects in the plant were costly work redistribution, retraining, retooling, and automation. The second storm was a forced layoff that occurred five years ago. It was driven by fierce foreign competition in consumer products manufacture. The layoff cost Linda fully one-fourth of her most recently hired workers and many middle managers, professionals, and technical employees. It also led to a net loss of protected labor groups in the plant's workforce to a level well below what had taken the company ten years of ambitious efforts to achieve. Other consequences were increasingly aggressive union action in the plant; isolated incidents of violence against management personnel by disgruntled workers; growing evidence of theft, pilferage, and employee sabotage; and skyrocketing absenteeism and turnover rates.

The third storm swept the plant on the heels of the layoff. Just three years ago corporate headquarters announced a company-wide Business Process Reengineering program. Its aims were to improve product quality and customer service, build worker involvement and empowerment, reduce scrap rates, and meet competition from abroad. While the goals were laudable, the program was greeted with skepticism because it was introduced so soon after the layoff. Many employees—and supervisors—voiced the opinion that "corporate headquarters is using Business Process Reengineering to clean up the mess they created by chopping heads first and asking questions about work reallocation later." However, since job security is an issue of paramount importance to everyone at the plant, the external consultant sent by corporate headquarters to introduce Business Process Reengineering received grudging cooperation. But the Business Process Reengineering initiative has created side effects of its own. One is that executives, middle managers, and supervisors are uncertain about their roles and the results expected of them. Another is that employees, pressured to do better work with fewer resources, are complaining bitterly about compensation or other reward practices that they feel do not reflect their increased responsibilities, efforts, or productivity. And a fourth storm is brewing. Corporate executives, it is rumored, are considering moving all production facilities offshore to take advantage of reduced labor and employee health-care insurance costs. Many employees are worried that this is really not a rumor but is, instead, a fact.

Against this backdrop, Linda has noticed that it is becoming more difficult to find backups for hourly workers and ensure leadership continuity in the plant's middle and top management ranks. Although the company has long conducted an annual "succession planning and management" ritual in which standardized forms, supplied by corporate headquarters, are sent out to managers by the plant's human resources department, Linda cannot remember when the forms were actually used during a talent search. The major reason, Linda believes, is that managers and employees have rarely followed through on the Individual Development Plans (IDPs) established to prepare people for advancement opportunities.

Defining Succession Planning and Management

As the vignettes above illustrate, organizations need to plan for talent to assume key leadership positions or backup positions on a temporary or permanent basis. Real-world cases have figured prominently in the business press in recent years. (See Exhibits 1-1 and 1-2.)

Among the first writers to recognize that universal organizational need was Henri Fayol (1841–1925). Fayol's classic fourteen points of management, first enunciated early in the twentieth century and still widely regarded today, indicate that management has a responsibility to ensure the "stability of tenure of personnel."[1] If that need is ignored, Fayol believed, key positions would end up being filled by ill-prepared people.

Succession planning and management (SP&M) is the process that helps ensure the stability of the tenure of personnel. It is perhaps best understood as any effort designed to ensure the continued effective performance of an organization, division, department, or work group by making provision for the development, replacement, and strategic application of key people over time.

Succession planning has been defined as:

> a means of identifying critical management positions, starting at the levels of project manager and supervisor and extending up to the highest position in the organization. Succession planning also describes management positions to provide maximum flexibility in lateral management moves and to ensure that as individuals achieve greater seniority, their management skills will broaden and become more generalized in relation to total organizational objectives rather than to purely departmental objectives.[2]

Succession planning should not stand alone. It should be paired with succession management, which assumes a more dynamic business environment. It recognizes the ramifications of the new employment contract, whereby corporations no longer (implicitly) assure anyone continued employment, even if he or she is doing a good job.[3]

An SP&M program is thus a deliberate and systematic effort by an organization to ensure leadership continuity in key positions, retain and develop intellectual and knowledge capital for the future, and encourage individual advancement. Systematic "succession planning occurs when an organization adapts specific procedures to insure the identification, development, and long-term retention of talented individuals."[4]

Succession planning and management need not be limited solely to man-

Exhibit 1-1. How General Electric Planned the Succession

Good news, bad news.

The idea that the hard-nosed CEO of a major corporation would lose sleep over giving bad news to two executives takes a bit of swallowing.

It happens to be true. The CEO in question was Jack Welch, boss of General Electric (GE). The bad news he had to impart was that James McNerney, head of GE's aircraft-engine business, and Robert Nardelli, chief of the business making turbines and generators for electric utilities, would not be succeeding Welch as CEO.

Welch had delivered bad news any number of times before, but the circumstances here were different. He said: "I've fired people my whole career—for performance. Here I've got three guys who've been great."

The third guy was Jeffrey R. Immelt, head of GE's medical-system's business and the ultimate winner. Later this year he will become chief executive of the world's most valuable company.

The process of choosing Welch's successor, throughout shrouded in the utmost secrecy, had taken six years, five months and two days. The story that has now emerged is curious in many ways. Most significantly, Welch and the board broke what are considered to be the rules in corporate-succession planning.

No Room for Outsiders

Traditionally, approaches might include naming a chief operating officer or other heir apparent. An outsider might be considered or some common template used for measuring candidates.

These possibilities were eschewed and the time factor was remarkable, too. Best-practice guidelines for boards suggest use of fewer than 100 director-hours to go through the succession processes. GE's board spent thousands of hours over several years.

Two factors make GE's approach worthy of further examination. First, many major U.S. companies have recently failed in their choice of a new CEO, which suggests something is wrong with the way that the boss is picked. Second, Welch has, in his 20 years at the top, proved himself to be a CEO with a very sure touch.

The succession process began formally in June 1994, when Welch was 59. During a board management development and compensation committee (MDCC) meeting, 24 candidates were discussed in three groups. "Obvious field" covered the seven men running GE's largest businesses. "Contenders" were four executives just below the top tier, and 13 others admired by Jack Welch were included under "broader consensus field." This was the list that produced the three "finalists."

(continues)

Exhibit 1-1. (continued)

Welch has said that the process was about "chemistry, blood, sweat, family, feelings" not simply mechanics, and what happened from 1994 onwards backs that up.

Getting to Know Candidates

Every candidate was tested for his ability to grow and Welch also wanted directors to get to know the leading candidates. Directors and candidates mixed socially, for example at the Augusta National Golf Club before the U.S. Masters tournament, and played golf together at GE's headquarters in Fairfield, Connecticut. Welch also encouraged candidates to call directors directly, bypassing him, when they thought it would be useful.

More formally, regular board events provided the opportunity for hundreds of director-hours each year devoted to discussing potential successors.

A couple of years after the process began, Welch and the MDCC decided that committee members needed to know more about leading candidates. The committee spent a year or so visiting several GE businesses. It was a highly unusual practice in the corporate world and one smokescreen involved taking in more visits than were necessary for the succession process.

By December 1997, the field was down to eight. Gradually several men effectively dropped out of the running. When head of lighting, David Calhoun, left to run the Employers Reinsurance business within GE Capital, he was correctly viewed as an ex-candidate. Finally, it was down to three: McNerney, Nardelli and Immelt.

Welch continued to buck convention. At this point he might have brought the top contenders to jobs at GE headquarters where he and the board could have had them under intense scrutiny. But what he wanted to avoid was the "political and poisonous" atmosphere created 20 years earlier when he had been a contender at HQ himself. Then, as he jockeyed for pole position, he had at lunch to "sit across from the guys you were competing with."

McNerney, Nardelli and Immelt continued therefore, hundreds of miles apart, to run their own businesses.

If everyone at GE is to be believed, six years of discussion took place before a name was put forward as the proposed winner. Director Frank Rhodes, Professor Emeritus at Cornell University, was the first to break ranks. He opted for Immelt; other directors agreed and, though the announcement was four months away, it was clear which way the wind was blowing.

Skeptics Confounded

In late October, GE announced its biggest ever acquisition—Honeywell for $45 billion in stock. This delayed announcement of the succession but the skeptical view that Welch was reluctant to give up power proved unfounded: Immelt will take over in December, eight months later than originally scheduled.

Welch flew to Cincinnati and Albany to give McNerney and Nardelli respectively the bad news. Both men are now CEOs elsewhere. Welch says he will never reveal the reasons that Immelt emerged triumphant, but his youth—he is 44—his popularity and the perception that he has the greatest capacity to grow must all have been factors. Frank Rhodes said that he demonstrated "the most expansive thinking."

If he is to survive and flourish like his predecessor, Immelt will need to continue to develop that quality.

The General Electric approach to finding Jack Welch's successor as CEO was thorough to the point of overkill. On the other hand, we are talking about the world's most valuable company. Welch was absolutely determined to succeed, where many major companies have failed recently, in finding the right man for the job. It will be fascinating to see whether Jeffrey Immelt fits the bill.

Note: This was a precis of an article by Geoffrey Colvin, entitled "Changing of the Guard," which was published in *Fortune,* January 8, 2001.

Source: "How General Electric Planned the Succession," *Human Resource Management International Digest* 9:4 (2001), 6–8. Used with permission of *Human Resource Management International Digest.*

agement positions or management employees. Indeed, an effective succession planning and management effort should also address the needs for critical backups and individual development in any job category—including key people in the professional, technical, sales, clerical, and production ranks. The need to extend the definition of SP&M beyond the management ranks is becoming more important as organizations take active steps to build high-performance and high-involvement work environments in which decision making is decentralized, leadership is diffused throughout an empowered workforce, and proprietary technical knowledge accumulated from many years of experience in one corporate culture is key to doing business.

One aim of SP&M is to match the organization's available (present) talent to its needed (future) talent. Another is to help the organization meet the strategic and operational challenges facing it by having the right people at the right places at the right times to do the right things. In these senses, SP&M should be regarded as a fundamental tool for organizational learning because SP&M should ensure that the lessons of organizational experience—what is sometimes called *institutional memory*—will be preserved and combined with reflection on that experience to achieve continuous improvement in work results (what is sometimes called *double loop learning*).[5] Stated in another way, SP&M is a way to ensure the continued cultivation of leadership and intellectual talent, and to manage the critically important knowledge assets of organizations.

(text continues on page 16)

Exhibit 1-2. The Big Mac Succession

Jim Cantalupo's sudden death brought out the best in McDonald's board. At his first annual meeting as chief executive, Jim Cantalupo faced an angry shareholder displaying photos of a filthy McDonald's toilet and demanding action. "We are going to take care of it," he pledged. And he did. His strategy of ending the rapid expansion of the world's biggest fast-food company and refocusing it on providing better meals in cleaner restaurants with improved service was starting to produce encouraging results. Then, on April 19th, he suddenly died. The death of a leader at such a critical time can ruin a company. But, thanks not least to Mr. Cantalupo, it will probably not ruin McDonald's.

Mr. Cantalupo was a McDonald's veteran. He joined the company in 1974, as an accountant in its headquarters near Chicago. As head of international operations, he presided over much of the globalization of the Big Mac: McDonald's now has more than 30,000 restaurants in 119 countries. Although promoted to president, he was passed over for the top job when Jack Greenberg was appointed chief executive in 1998.

Then McDonald's began to stumble badly. Service levels came in for increasing criticism, sales began to fall and the company suffered its first quarterly loss. It also became embroiled in the debate about obesity and the role of fast food. McDonald's was even sued by some parents for making their children fat. (Although this failed, a future lawsuit may yet succeed.) Mr. Greenberg put a recovery plan into action and vowed to stay on to execute it, only to be forced out by worried investors. The board turned to Mr. Cantalupo, who came out of retirement to take over as chairman and chief executive in January 2003.

Mr. Cantalupo, who was 60, died of a suspected heart attack at a huge convention in Orlando, Florida, for more than 12,000 employees, suppliers, owners, and operators of McDonald's restaurants worldwide. It was the sort of big meet-the-troops event that the affable Mr. Cantalupo enjoyed.

Those members of the board already in Florida quickly assembled and others joined by phone. Within six hours, Charlie Bell, a 43-year-old Australian who had been appointed chief operating officer by Mr. Cantalupo and had been working closely with him, was made chief executive. Andrew McKenna, 74, the board's presiding director and also the boss of Schwarz, which supplies McDonald's with lots of packaging materials, was appointed non-executive chairman.

The speech that Mr. Cantalupo was due to give to welcome the delegates was later given by Mr. Bell, who joined the McDonald's empire when, aged 15, he got a part-time job in an outlet in a suburb of Sydney. So he knows how to flip a burger. The delegates were clearly saddened, but they gave Mr. Bell, the first non-American to lead the company, a resounding reception. Mr. Cantalupo would have approved.

So did Jeffrey Sonnenfeld, head of the Chief Executive Leadership Institute at Yale University. "It was a board operating at its finest," says Mr. Sonnenfeld, author of "The Hero's Farewell," a book about the contentious job of selecting a new boss.

Concerning Mr. Cantalupo, the McDonald's board has twice acted impressively, he says. First, it acted decisively in reversing course and turning to Mr. Cantalupo when things went wrong. Second, it acted swiftly to execute a succession plan that Mr. Cantalupo himself had put into place, even though he was expected to remain in the job for several more years. Mr. Bell had been widely acknowledged as Mr. Cantalupo's heir apparent.

Succession planning can be fraught with difficulty, and is all too often neglected. Vodafone had no succession strategy in place when, in December 2002, Sir Christopher Gent, its chief executive, said he would leave. A search for a replacement led to Arun Sarin, a non-executive director, being given the job. Now Vodafone operates a succession-planning process in every country where it has a business. But more formal procedures, though on balance superior, can cause difficulties, especially if an officially anointed heir starts to get restless (i.e., Prince Charles syndrome). And it takes a trusting, well-disciplined board to stick to a succession plan, as the General Electric board did when Jack Welch groomed three potential contenders for his job.

A sudden death can be the toughest kind of succession to deal with. Some bosses are said to leave a sealed envelope holding the name of a preferred successor in the event of a fatality. Yet the succession at McDonald's, forced on it by tragic circumstances, contrasts sharply with that now under way at Coca-Cola. Ever since Roberto Goizueta, Coke's pioneering boss, died of lung cancer in 1997, the firm has been beset by troubles. Douglas Ivester was appointed quickly to replace Mr. Goizueta, but two years later was forced to step down. In February, his successor, Douglas Daft, suddenly announced that he would retire by the end of this year. Coke is said to want James Kilts, the boss of Gillette, for the top job—but he may not want it. Publicly looking outside its ranks for a leader is interpreted by some analysts as evidence of management weakness within.

McDonald's could not be accused of that, although Mr. Bell still has to prove his worth. New menus, featuring smaller portions and such healthier things as salads and bottled water, are reviving the company's image. But at the same time the company cannot afford to drive away its many fans of burgers and fries. Simply getting them to come back more often could do wonders for McDonald's profits. There are valuable lessons to be learned from successful markets, such as Australia and France—both places where Mr. Bell has worked. But there remains a long way to go, and things could yet become extremely difficult. Even planning well ahead and having a chosen successor ready and waiting, though better than not doing so, is no guarantee that the successor will actually be a success.

Source: "Business: The Big Mac Succession: Face Value," *The Economist* 371:8372 (2004), 74. Used with permission of *The Economist*.

Distinguishing Succession Planning and Management from Replacement Planning, Workforce Planning, Talent Management, and Human Capital Management

Terminology can be confusing. And that fact is as true with succession planning and management as it is with anything else. So, how can succession planning and management be distinguished from replacement planning? Workforce planning? Talent management? Human capital management?

Succession Planning and Management and Replacement Planning

Succession planning and management should not be confused with replacement planning, though they are compatible and often overlap. The obvious need for some form of replacement planning is frequently a driving force behind efforts that eventually turn into SP&M programs—as Vignettes 1 and 2 at the opening of this chapter dramatically illustrate. That need was only heightened by the 1996 plane crash of U.S. Secretary of Commerce Ron Brown, which also claimed the lives of over thirty other top executives.

In its simplest form, replacement planning is a form of risk management. In that respect it resembles other organizational efforts to manage risk, such as ensuring that fire sprinkling systems in computer rooms are not positioned so as to destroy valuable computer equipment in case of fire, or segregating accounting duties to reduce the chance of embezzlement. The chief aim of replacement planning is to limit the chance of catastrophe stemming from the immediate and unplanned loss of key job incumbents—as happened on a large scale when the Twin Towers of the World Trade Center collapsed and on an individual level when the CEO of McDonald's was stricken by a heart attack.

However, SP&M goes beyond simple replacement planning. It is proactive and attempts to ensure the continuity of leadership by cultivating talent from within the organization through planned development activities. It should be regarded as an important tool for implementing strategic plans.

Succession Planning and Management and Workforce Planning

Workforce planning connotes comprehensive planning for the organization's entire workforce.[6] To some people, *succession planning and management* refers to top-of-the-organization-chart planning and development only. However, in this book, succession planning and management refers more broadly to planning for the right number and right type of people to meet the organization's needs over time.

Succession Planning and Management and Talent Management

"Talent management is the process of recruiting, on-boarding, and developing, as well as the strategies associated with those activities in organizations."[7]

Like so many HR-related terms, "the phrase *talent management* is used loosely and often interchangeably across a wide array of terms such as succession planning, human capital management, resource planning, and employee performance management. Gather any group of HR professionals in a room and you can be sure to have a plethora of additional terms."[8] Some organizational leaders associate talent management with efforts to devote special attention to managing the best-in-class talent of the organization—the upper 1 to 10 percent. Not limited to top-of-the-house planning, it may refer to investing money where the returns are likely to be greatest—that is, on high-performing or high-potential talent at any organizational level. Hence, efforts to develop talent that is strategically important for the organization's future means the strategic development of talent.[9]

Succession Planning and Management and Human Capital Management

Human capital management (HCM) theory is all about individuals and their economic value. Unfortunately, HCM has been (too broadly) interpreted to mean that individuals are calculating players who act out of self-interest only, that the only value of individuals is as economic commodities (and thus the saying that "people are our greatest assets"), and that the social value of developing human resources resides only in summing the total value of individual development efforts.[10] Like talent management, HCM is also a term in search of meaning. Indeed, "out of 49 organizations surveyed, just 11 said they attempted to measure human capital—and many of these confessed to being unsure what the term meant."[11]

But a key point about human capital management is that people are valuable for more than the labor they can produce. Human beings are enormously creative—a key thing that sets them apart from machines, gizmos, and gadgets—and this ability to think creatively has economic value. Individuals, not computers, discover new ideas that can be turned to profit. As entrepreneurs, they found companies. They also discover new ways to serve customers, find new customers or markets for old products, and discover ways to improve work processes to increase productivity.

A key issue in HCM, then, is that creativity has value. So does the institutional memory that individuals carry in their heads. While more will be written about that later in this book, it is worth emphasizing at this point that succession planning can mean more than just finding warm bodies to fill vacancies. Additional issues should be considered—such as the value of institutional memory and creativity.

ASTD has published an important white paper on HCM that is worth reviewing, since it describes best practices in the area.[12] The U.S. General Accounting Office has also done work to emphasize the importance of HCM in U.S. government work.[13]

Making the Business Case for Succession Planning and Management

Many requirements must be satisfied if organizations are to survive in a fiercely competitive environment. One key requirement is that replacements must be available to assume critically important positions as they become vacant. Indeed, "succession planning, like a relay race, has to do with passing on responsibility. . . . Drop the baton and you lose the race."[14]

Numerous surveys over the years have emphasized the importance of SP&M. Chief executives consistently cite the issue as one of their major concerns. Leadership succession has also surfaced as an issue of concern to corporate boards[15]: A survey of corporate board member policies and practices by Korn/Ferry International asked chairpersons to assess the importance of issues facing their companies in the next five years. Those typically seen as trendsetters—the billion-dollar companies—rated management succession as the *third most important issue* [emphasis added], on the heels of financial results and strategic planning. According to Lester Korn, CEO of the search firm, boards are beginning to realize that they have "the same obligations to protect the human resource asset base for the shareholders as they do to protect the balance sheet of the corporation."

There are several reasons that both CEOs and corporate boards are so interested in SP&M. First, top managers are aware that the continued survival of the organization depends on having the right people in the right places at the right times to do the right things. Strategic success is, in large measure, a function of having the right leadership. Leaving the development of those leaders to chance, and hoping for the best, may have worked at one time. Ignoring the development of leaders and depending on headhunters to find replacements for key people may also have worked at one time. But these approaches are not working now. Some effort must be made to ensure that the organization is *systematically* identifying and preparing high-potential candidates for key positions.

Second, as continuing downsizing and other cost-containment efforts have led to reductions in the middle management ranks—a traditional training ground and source of top management talent—there are simply fewer people available to advance to the top ranks from within. That means that great care must be taken to identify promising candidates early and actively cultivate their development. Individuals who are both high performers on their present jobs and high potentials for future leadership positions should not be taken for granted, especially in a seller's labor market, where exceptionally talented workers, like star athletes, can barter their abilities to the highest bidders.

The reason is that slimmed-down organizations have reduced their absolute numbers. Worse yet, members of this group are differentially affected by downsizing because, as work is redistributed after a downsizing, high performers end up shouldering more of the burden to get the work out while (in most cases) the rewards they receive are held constant. They are thus more likely to become dissatisfied and leave the organization than will their less productive peers. To avoid that problem—which can be disastrous for the leadership continuity of the organization—top managers must take active steps to identify, reward, and advance high performers through vertical and horizontal career moves in a manner commensurate with their increased contributions.

Third, when SP&M is left informal and thus unplanned, job incumbents tend to identify and groom successors who are remarkably like themselves in appearance, background, and values. They establish a "bureaucratic kinship system" that is based on "homosocial reproduction."[16] As Rosabeth Moss Kanter explained:

> Because of the situation in which managers function, because of the position of managers in the corporate structure, social similarity tends to become extremely important to them. The structure sets in motion forces leading to the replication of managers as the same kind of social individuals. And the men who manage reproduce themselves in kind.[17]

As a consequence, white males tend to pick as successors other white males. (It is worth noting that white males are not the only ones guilty of picking people like themselves because people of other sexes, races, and backgrounds will do likewise.) That practice, of course, perpetuates such problems as the so-called glass ceiling and other subtle forms of employment discrimination. To avoid these problems and promote diversity and multiculturalism in the workplace, systematic efforts must be made to identify and groom the best successors for key positions, not just those who are clones of the present key job incumbents.

Succession planning and management is important for other reasons as well. Indeed, it "forms the basis for (1) communicating career paths to each individual; (2) establishing development and training plans; (3) establishing career paths and individual job moves; (4) communicating upward and laterally concerning the management organization; and, (5) creating a more comprehensive human resources planning system."[18]

As I have toured the country—and other countries—to do public speaking and consulting about succession, I am often asked, "How do we make the case for succession in our organizations?" To answer that, I ask whether the questioners face supportive or skeptical CEOs. If the CEO is supportive, then the most important customer has already been convinced. But if the CEO is skeptical, then some effort should be made to analyze the risks that the organization may face. (This is called *risk analysis*.)

One way to do that is to request from the payroll department the projected retirement dates for the organization's entire workforce. That should also be done for three-year rolling periods to assess what percentage of the workforce is eligible to retire at various points in time. Then the percentage of workers eligible to retire can be assessed by location, job code, or level on the corporate hierarchy. The goal is to see if some areas, levels, or regions will be more at risk than others. If the results are shocking (and sometimes they are), then the data may convince a skeptical CEO that something must be done to develop talent—and preserve the specialized knowledge, gained from experience, of those who are about to leave—in areas deemed particularly at risk.

Reasons for a Succession Planning and Management Program

Why should an organization support a systematic SP&M program? To answer that question I updated a survey that I sent out in 1993 for the first edition of this book. (The first survey was mailed to 350 randomly selected members of the ASTD in October 1993.) The survey for the second edition of this book was mailed in December 1999 to 742 members of the Society for Human Resources Management (SHRM). A follow-up mailing was sent in January 2000 to SHRM members, and a second follow-up mailing went out in February 2000. The survey for the third edition of this book was sent out in early 2004 to members of the International Society for Performance Improvement (ISPI), and the results were compiled in July 2004. Exhibit 1-3 presents demographic information about the respondents' industries from the 2004 survey; Exhibit 1-4 charts the sizes of the respondents' organizations; Exhibit 1-5 presents information about the respondents' job functions; and Exhibit 1-6 summarizes the respondents' perceptions about the chief reasons their organizations operate systematic SP&M programs. These reasons are discussed further, in order of their importance, in the sections that follow. Each reason corresponds to a possible goal to be achieved by the SP&M program.

Reason 1: Contribute to Implementing the Organization's Strategic Business Plans

Succession planning and management should not be conducted in a vacuum; rather, it should be linked to, and supportive of, organizational strategic plans, human resource plans, human resource development plans, and other organizational planning activities. Perhaps for this reason, my survey respondents

Exhibit 1-3. Demographic Information About Respondents to a 2004 Survey on Succession Planning and Management: Industries

Question: In what industry is your organization classified?

Industry	Frequency	Percentage
Manufacturing	2	9.09%
Transportation/ Communication/ Electric/Gas	1	4.55%
Retail Trade	1	4.55%
Finance/Insurance/Real Estate	5	22.73%
Healthcare	1	4.55%
Government/Armed Forces	6	27.27%
Other	6	27.27%
Total	22	100.00%

Note: Not all respondents chose to answer this question.

Source: William J. Rothwell, *Results of a 2004 Survey on Succession Planning and Management Practices.* Unpublished survey results (University Park, Penn.: The Pennsylvania State University, 2004).

Exhibit 1-4. Demographic Information About Respondents to a 2004 Survey on Succession Planning and Management: Size

Question: How many people does your organization employ?

Organization Size	Frequency	Percentage
0–99	2	9.09%
100–249	2	9.09%
250–499	2	9.09%
500–1999	5	22.73%
2000–4999	5	22.73%
5000 or more	6	27.27%
Total	22	100.00%

Note: Not all respondents chose to answer this question.

Source: William J. Rothwell, *Results of a 2004 Survey on Succession Planning and Management Practices.* Unpublished survey results (University Park, Penn.: The Pennsylvania State University, 2004).

indicated that the most important reason to sponsor systematic SP&M is to "contribute to implementing the organization's strategic plan."

Strategic planning is the process by which organizations choose to survive and compete. It involves formulating and implementing a long-term plan by which the organization can take maximum advantage of its present internal organizational strengths and future external environmental opportunities

Exhibit 1-5. Demographic Information about Respondents to a 2004 Survey on Succession Planning and Management: Job Functions of Respondents

Question: What is your job function?

Job Function	Frequency	Percentage
Trainer or Training Manager	10	45.45%
Human Resource Manager	7	31.82%
Other	5	22.73%
Total	22	100.00%

Note: Not all respondents chose to answer this question.

Source: William J. Rothwell, *Results of a 2004 Survey on Succession Planning Practices.* Unpublished survey results (University Park, Penn.: The Pennsylvania State University, 2004).

while minimizing the effects of present internal organizational weaknesses and future external environmental threats.

To implement a strategic plan, organizations require the right people doing the right things in the right places and at the right times. Without them, strategic plans cannot be realized. Hence, leadership identification and succession are critical to the successful implementation of organizational strategy. Particularly at top management levels, as Thomas Gilmore explains, "performance criteria are rarely cut and dried. They often flow from a strategic plan which the chief executive is responsible for developing and carrying out."[19] At least five different approaches may be used to integrate strategic plans and succession plans[20]:

1. *The Top-Down Approach.* Corporate strategy drives SP&M. Leaders identified through a systematic SP&M process support the successful implementation of strategy.

2. *The Market-Driven Approach.* Succession planning and management is governed by marketplace needs and requirements. As necessary talent is required to deal with competitive pressures, it is sought out.

3. *The Career Planning Approach.* Succession planning and management is tied to strategic plans through individual career planning processes. In consultation with their organizational superiors and others, individuals examine their own career goals in light of the organization's strategy and make decisions about how they can best contribute to emerging organizational needs while also improving their own chances for eventual advancement.

4. *The Futuring Approach.* Succession planning and management becomes a vehicle for anticipating talent needs stemming from corporate strategy. It is viewed as a way to scan external environmental conditions

Exhibit 1-6. Reasons for Succession Planning and Management Programs

Question: There are many reasons decision-makers may wish to establish a Succession Planning program in an organization. For each reason listed in the left column below, please *circle a response code in the right column* indicating *how important you believe that reason to be for your organization.* Use the following scale: **1** = Not at all important; **2** = Not Important; **3** = Somewhat Important; **4** = Important; **5** = Very Important.

Reasons for Sponsoring Succession Planning	Importance in Your Organization (Mean Response)
Contribute to implementing the organization's strategic business plans.	4.56
Identify replacement needs as a means of targeting necessary training, employee education, and employee development.	4.44
Increase the talent pool of employees.	4.33
Provide increased opportunities for high-potential workers.	4.22
Tap the potential for intellectual capital in the organization.	4.11
Help individuals realize their career plans within the organization.	3.89
Encourage the advancement of diverse groups —such as minorities or women—in future jobs within the organization.	3.67
Improve employee morale.	3.33
Improve employees' ability to respond to changing environmental demands.	3.22
Cope with the effects of voluntary separation programs—such as early retirement offers and employee buyouts.	2.78
Cope with effects of downsizing.	2.44
Decide what workers can be terminated without damage to the organization.	2.22
Reduce headcount to essential workers only.	2.00

Source: William J. Rothwell, *Results of a 2004 Survey on Succession Planning and Management Practices.* Unpublished survey results (University Park, Penn.: The Pennsylvania State University, 2004).

and match the organization's internal talent to the demands created by those conditions.

5. *The Rifle Approach.* Succession planning and management is focused on solving specific, identifiable problems confronting the organization, such as higher-than-expected turnover in some organizational levels or job categories. (One trend is to single out and track the turnover of high potentials in the organization, which is called *critical turnover*.)

Consider what role SP&M should play in supporting the strategic plans of your organization. In doing that, realize that "there is no one universal approach that works well across all companies; rather, effective companies match their succession strategies to their business strategies."[21]

Related to strategic planning is human resource planning (HRP), which is "the process of analyzing an organization's human resource needs under changing conditions and developing the activities necessary to satisfy these needs."[22] HRP is comprehensive in scope, examining an organization's workforce and work requirements. One result of HRP should be a long-term plan to guide an organization's personnel policies, programs, and procedures.[23]

Few authorities dispute the growing importance of HRP. As Manzini and Gridley note, "The need for people with increasingly specialized skills, higher managerial competencies, and commitment to new levels of excellence, with professional qualifications in disciplines that did not exist a few decades ago—at costs commensurate with their contribution to organizational objectives—is and will continue to be the overriding 'business' concern of the organization."[24] Succession planning and management is integrally related to HRP, though SP&M is usually focused more on leadership needs and leadership skills. Many techniques and approaches that have evolved for use in HRP may also be applied to SP&M.

Succession planning and management should focus on identifying and developing critically important leadership talent. Moreover, SP&M may rely on means other than planned learning or promotion from within to meet talent requirements. For instance, critical succession needs may be met by external recruitment, internal transfer, or other means.

Reason 2: Identify "Replacement Needs" as a Means of Targeting Necessary Training, Employee Education, and Employee Development

The second reason cited by survey respondents for organizations to sponsor systematic SP&M is to "identify 'replacement needs' as a means of targeting necessary training, employee education, and employee development." In other words, SP&M becomes a driving force to identify justifiable employee training, education, and development needs. Training helps employees meet their current job responsibilities; employee education prepares them to advance to future responsibilities; and employee development can be a tool for individual enlightenment or organizational learning.

Reason 3: Increase the Talent Pool of Promotable Employees

Respondents in organizations sponsoring systematic SP&M cited the third most important reason as to "increase the talent pool of promotable employees." Succession planning and management formalizes the process of preparing people to fill key positions in the future. Of course, the term *talent pool* may mean a group of individuals—rather than one identifiable successor—from which possible successors for key positions may be selected.

Reason 4: Provide Increased Opportunities for "High Potential" Workers

My survey respondents indicated that the fourth important reason to sponsor systematic SP&M is to "provide increased opportunities for 'high potential' workers.'" Although definitions of high potentials (HiPos) may differ, they are usually regarded as those employees who have the potential for future advancement. Hence, a very important reason for SP&M is to identify appropriate ways to accelerate HiPo development and improve the retention of talented people with potential.[25] A few important retention strategies are summarized in Exhibit 1-7.

Reason 5: Tap the Potential for Intellectual Capital in the Organization

Intellectual capital refers to the value of the human talents in an organization. Tapping the potential for intellectual capital was cited as the fifth most important reason for an SP&M program in an organization. SP&M is thus important in making and realizing investments in intellectual capital in the organization.

Reason 6: Help Individuals Realize Their Career Plans Within the Organization

Organizations make a substantial investment in the training of their employees. Employee performance may improve with experience as individuals advance along a learning curve in which they master organization-specific and job-specific knowledge. When individuals leave an organization, their loss can be measured.[26] If they remain with one employer to realize their career plans, then the employer benefits from their experiences. In this sense, then, SP&M can serve as a tool by which individuals can be prepared for realizing their career plans within the organization. That reason was cited by my survey respondents as the sixth most important for organizations to sponsor systematic SP&M.

Exhibit 1-7. Strategies for Reducing Turnover and Increasing Retention

Possible Causes of Turnover People leave the organization because they:	Possible Strategies for Increasing Retention
Are dissatisfied with their future prospects in the organization or believe they have better prospects for the future in another organization.	△ Assess the extent of this problem by using attitude surveys (paper-based or online), by using exit interviews with departing workers, and by running selected focus groups to gather information. △ Give people hope by establishing and communicating about a succession planning and management program. △ Establish or improve job posting programs, job rotations, and other efforts to give people more exposure and visibility within the organization. △ Improve communication about the future of the organization and what that might mean for individuals in it.
Dislike their supervisors and/ or their supervisors' approach to supervision.	△ Assess the extent of this problem by using attitude surveys (paper-based or online) and by using exit interviews with departing workers. △ Improve supervisory training, with special emphasis on addressing sources of dissatisfaction that influence turnover. △ Establish or improve job posting programs, job rotations, and other efforts to give people more exposure and visibility within the organization.
Dislike the kind of work that they do or the kind of assignments that they have been given.	△ Assess the extent of this problem by using attitude surveys (paper-based or online), by using exit interviews with departing workers, and by running selected focus groups to gather information. △ Establish or improve job posting programs, job rotations, and other efforts to give people more exposure and visibility within the organization.

Dislike their wage or salary level, believe it is not competitive, or believe they are not compensated in a way commensurate with their contributions.	△ Assess the extent of this problem by using attitude surveys (paper-based or online), by using exit interviews with departing workers, and by running selected focus groups to gather information.
	△ Conduct regular wage and salary surveys outside the organization.
	△ Clarify the organization's philosophy of rewards ("Do we want to pay only at competitive levels? If so, why?").
	△ Make use of innovative reward and compensation practices that go beyond mere considerations of wages to include alternative reward and alternative recognition programs and "cafeteria rewards" tailored to individual needs.
Are stressed out or burned out from too much work or too little personal rest and recreational time.	△ Assess the extent of this problem by using attitude surveys (paper-based or online), by using exit interviews with departing workers, and by running selected focus groups to gather information.
	△ Take steps to add a component on work-life balance in descriptions of high-potentials and high performance and communicate that change to the organization.
	△ Add to the social life of the organization by stepping up social activities and re-examining to whom and how work is allocated.

Reason 7: Encourage the Advancement of Diverse Groups

The workforce in the United States is only becoming more diverse, reflecting the nation's increasingly diverse population. Unfortunately, not all workers have historically been treated equally or equitably. Discrimination, while prohibited by federal and state laws, still occurs. Indeed, the realization of that prompted Supreme Court Justice Thurgood Marshall to explain that, as a black in America in 1991, he did not feel free.[27] While reactions to that view may vary, there is increasing recognition of a need to promote multiculturalism, which involves increasing the consciousness and appreciation of differences associated with the heritage, characteristics, and values of many different groups, as well as respecting the uniqueness of each individual. In this approach, *diversity* has a broad meaning that encompasses sex and ethnic groups along with groups based on such attributes as nationality, professional discipline, or cognitive style.[28]

Perhaps as an indication of increasing recognition that organizations have a responsibility to pursue diversity at all levels, respondents to my survey indicated that "encouraging the advancement of diverse groups" was the seventh most important reason for organizations to sponsor systematic SP&M. Many organizations build in to their SP&M programs special ways to accelerate the development of protected labor classes and diverse groups.

Reason 8: Improve Employee Morale

Succession planning and management can be a means by which to improve employee morale by encouraging promotion from within. Indeed, promotions from within "permit an organization to utilize the skills and abilities of individuals more effectively, and the opportunity to gain a promotion can serve as an incentive."[29] Once that goal is achieved, the promoted employee's example heartens others. Moreover, particularly during times of forced layoffs, promotions from within and "inplacement" (movements from within of individuals otherwise slated for layoff) can boost morale and can help offset the negative effects of "survivor's syndrome."[30]

Reason 9: Improve Employees' Ability to Respond to Changing Environmental Demands

A ninth reason to sponsor systematic SP&M is to "improve employees' ability to respond to changing environmental demands," according to the respondents to my survey. "One role of the leader," writes Gilmore, "is to shield the organization from ambiguity and uncertainty so that people can do their work."[31] Organizations sponsor SP&M as one means by which to prepare people to respond to—or even anticipate—changing environmental demands. People groomed for key positions transform the ambiguity and uncertainty of changing external environmental demands into vision and direction.

Reason 10: Cope with the Effects of Voluntary Separation Programs

My respondents identified "coping with the effects of voluntary separation programs" as the tenth most important reason that organizations sponsor systematic SP&M. Voluntary separation is closely related to forced layoffs and is often a preliminary step to it. In a voluntary separation, employees are offered incentives to leave the organization—such as prorated pay by years of service or years added to retirement. Like a forced layoff, a voluntary separation requires work to be reallocated as productive employees leave the organization. That requires some effort to identify "successors." Hence, SP&M can be valuable in identifying how—and to whom—work should be reallocated after workforce restructuring.

Reason 11: Cope with the Effects of Downsizing

An eleventh reason cited by survey respondents for organizations to sponsor systematic SP&M is to "cope with effects of downsizing." Downsizing has been—and continues to be—a fact of life in corporate America. While not as widely publicized as it once was, downsizing, the evidence suggests, has continued unabated since before the first edition of this book was published in 1994. Middle managers and professionals have been particularly affected. While jobs may be eliminated, work does not go away. As a consequence, there is often a need to identify those who can perform activities even when nobody is assigned special responsibility for them. Succession planning and management can be a tool for that purpose.

The respondents to my survey confirm that organizations have continued to undergo radical workforce restructuring in recent years, a trend first pinpointed in the 1994 edition of this book. (See Exhibit 1-8.)

Reason 12: Decide Which Workers Can Be Terminated Without Damage to the Organization

When making hiring decisions, employers have long considered an individual's potential for long-term advancement, as well as his or her suitability for

Exhibit 1-8. Workforce Reductions Among Survey Respondents

Question: In the last 5 years, has your organization experienced organization change? *Circle all responses in the right column below that apply.*

Organization Change	Frequency	Percentage
A Layoff	11	21.57%
An Early Retirement Offer	8	15.69%
A Reduction in Force	11	21.57%
A Hiring Freeze	13	25.49%
Reduction by Attrition	17	33.33%
Others	2	3.92%
Total	51	100.00%

Source: William J. Rothwell, *Results of a 2004 Survey on Succession Planning and Management Practices.* Unpublished survey results (University Park, Penn.: The Pennsylvania State University, 2004).

filling an immediate job vacancy. Perhaps for this reason, then, survey respondents cited "deciding which workers can be terminated without damage to the organization" as the twelfth most important reason for organizations to sponsor SP&M.

Reason 13: Reduce Headcount to Essential Workers Only

The thirteenth reason for organizations to sponsor succession planning and management, as cited by my survey respondents, is to "reduce headcount to essential workers only." In an age of fierce competition, processes must be reengineered to decrease cost, reduce cycle time, and increase quality and output. Processes must be reexamined in light of results required, not activities that have traditionally been performed. In such environments, "companies don't need people to fill a slot, because the slot will only be roughly defined. Companies need people who can figure out what the job takes and do it, people who can create the slot that fits them. Moreover, the slot will keep changing."[32] Headcount will also shift to keep pace with shifting requirements.

Best Practices and Approaches

Numerous studies have been conducted of SP&M in recent years.[33] Exhibit 1-9 summarizes some of the key best practices identified from those studies.

There are numerous approaches to SP&M. They may be distinguished by direction, timing, planning, scope, degree of dissemination, and amount of individual discretion.

Direction

Who should make the final decisions in SP&M? The answer to that question has to do with *direction*. A *top-down approach* to succession planning and management is directed from the highest levels. The corporate board of directors, CEO, and other top managers oversee program operations—with or without the assistance of a part-time or full-time SP&M coordinator, a leadership development specialist, or a human resource generalist assigned to help with the program. The highest-level leaders make decisions about how competence and performance will be assessed for present positions, how future competence and potential will be identified, and what developmental activities—if any—will be conducted with a view toward preparing individuals for advancement and building the organization's bench strength of leadership talent.

In contrast, a *bottom-up approach* to SP&M is directed from the lowest levels. Employees and their immediate supervisors actively participate in all activities pertaining to SP&M. They are also on the lookout for promising people to assume leadership positions. Decisions about SP&M are closely tied to

Exhibit 1-9. A Summary of Best Practices on Succession Planning and Management from Several Research Studies

Based on several research studies of SP&M programs, best practices are:

Best Practices According to Robert M. Fulmer

Deploying a Succession Management Process

△ Best-practice organizations make succession planning an integral corporate process by exhibiting a link between succession planning and overall business strategy. This link gives succession planning the opportunity to affect the corporation's long-term goals and objectives.

△ Human resources is typically responsible for the tools and processes associated with successful succession planning. Business or line units are generally responsible for the "deliverables"—i.e., they use the system to manage their own staffing needs. Together, these two groups produce a comprehensive process.

△ Technology plays an essential role in the succession planning process. Ideally, technology serves to facilitate the process (make it shorter, simpler, or more flexible) rather than becoming the focus of the process or inhibiting it in any way.

Identifying the Talent Pool

△ Best-practice organizations use a cyclical, continuous identification process to focus on future leaders.

△ Best-practice organizations use a core set of leadership and succession management competencies.

Engaging Future Leaders

△ Best-practice organizations emphasize the importance of specific, individualized development plans for each employee.

△ Individual development plans identify which developmental activities are needed, and the "best practice" firms typically have a mechanism in place to make it simple for the employee to conduct the developmental activities. Typically, divisional human resource leaders will monitor employee follow-up in developmental activities.

△ Best-practice partners rely on the fundamental developmental activities of coaching, training, and development most frequently and utilize all developmental activities to a much greater extent than the sponsor organizations.

△ In addition to traditional executive education programs, best-practice partners increasingly use special assignments, action learning, and Web-based development activities.

(continues)

Exhibit 1-9. (continued)

Key Best Practices According to William Rothwell

△ Use a "big picture roadmap or model" to guide the effort.

△ Ensure hands-on involvement by the CEO and other senior leaders.

△ Use competency models to clarify what type of talent the organization's leaders want to build.

△ Develop and implement an effective performance management system.

△ Lead the target by clarifying what competencies will be needed for the future if the organization is to achieve its strategic objectives.

△ Use individual development plans to narrow developmental gaps.

△ Develop descriptions of the values and ethical standards required and assess people relative to those as well as competencies.

△ Build a viewpoint that high-potential talent is a shared resource rather than owned by specific managers.

△ Use leadership development efforts to build shared competencies needed for the future.

Source: William Rothwell, Ed., *Effective Succession Management: Building Winning Systems or Identifying and Developing Key Talent* (Lexington, Mass.: The Center for Organizational Research [A division of Linkage, Inc.]). See http://www.cfor.org/News/article.asp?id=4. Used with permission.

Four Key Best Practices According to Chief Executive *Magazine*

1. *Identify.* Find HiPo candidates in the organization by using consistent, objective criteria.

2. *Diagnose.* Assess individual candidates' strengths and weaknesses compared to the organization's needs.

3. *Prescribe.* Provide the right development to build competencies in the organization.

4. *Monitor.* Make sure that the succession process works to build leaders over time.

Source: "Succession Management: Filling the Leadership Pipeline," *Chief Executive*, April 2004, pp. 1, 4. Used with permission.

individual career-planning programs, which help individuals assess their present strengths and weaknesses and future potential. Top managers receive and act on decisions made at lower levels.

A *combination approach* attempts to integrate top-down and bottom-up approaches. Top managers are actively involved in establishing SP&M procedures, and remain involved in the SP&M program. Employees and their immediate supervisors are also actively involved in every step of the process. Some effort is made to integrate SP&M and individual career planning. Often, a succession plan without a career plan is a wish list because designated HiPos may not aspire to the career goals to which managers think they should aspire. A career plan without a succession plan is a road map without a destination.

Timing

How much time is devoted to SP&M issues—and when is that time devoted to it? The answer to that question has to do with *timing.* Succession planning and management may be conducted fitfully, periodically, or continuously. When handled fitfully, systematic SP&M does not exist because no effort is made to plan for succession—with the result that every vacancy can become a crisis. When handled periodically, SP&M is carried out on a fixed schedule—usually quarterly or annually. Often it distinctly resembles an employee performance appraisal program, which is typically part of the SP&M effort. Managers complete a series of forms that may include a performance appraisal, an individual potential assessment (or full-circle, multirater assessment), an individual development plan (IDP), and a replacement chart for their areas of responsibility. This information is then turned over to the human resources department and/or to an individual assigned responsibility for SP&M.

When handled continuously, SP&M requires ongoing decision making, information gathering, and action taking. Less attention is devoted to forms than to results and developmental activities. Employees at all levels are expected to contribute to the continuous improvement of themselves and others in the organization through mentoring, networking, sponsorship, coaching, training, education, development, and other means.

Planning

How much planning is conducted for succession? The answer to that question has to do with the *planning* component of an SP&M program. Succession planning and management may be a systematic effort that is deliberately planned and is driven by a written, organization-wide statement of purpose and a policy. On the other hand, it may be an unsystematic effort that is left unplanned and informal. An unsystematic effort is driven by the idiosyncrasies of individual managers rather than by a deliberate plan and strategy for developing individuals for advancement and for ensuring leadership continuity.

Scope

How many—and what kinds—of people in the organization are covered by succession plans? The answer to that question has to do with program *scope.* Succession planning and management may range from the specialized to the generalized. A specialized program targets leadership continuity in selected job categories, job levels, functions, or locations. Often, such programs grow out of crises—such as excessive turnover in selected areas of the organization. On the other hand, a generalized program aims to prepare individuals for advancement in all job categories, job levels, functions, and locations. It is often a starting point for identifying individualized training, education, and development needs and for meeting individual career goals.

Degree of Dissemination

How many people participate in SP&M processes? The answer to that question has to do with the program's *degree of dissemination.* It is a philosophical issue that stems from—and influences—the organization's culture. The degree of dissemination may range from closed to open. A closed SP&M program is treated as top secret. Managers assess the individual potential of their employees without the input of those affected by the assessment process. Decisions about whom to develop—and how to develop them—are limited to a "need-to-know" basis. Individual career goals may—or may not—influence these decisions. Top managers are the sole owners of the SP&M program and permit little or no communication about it. Secrecy is justified on two counts: (1) succession issues are proprietary to the organization and may reveal important information about strategic plans that should be kept out of the hands of competitors; and (2) decision-makers worry that employees who are aware of their status in succession plans may develop unrealistic expectations or may "hold themselves hostage." To avoid these problems, decision-makers keep the SP&M process and its outcomes confidential.

On the other hand, an open SP&M program is treated with candor. Work requirements, competencies, and success factors at all levels are identified and communicated. The SP&M process—and its possible outcomes—is described to all who ask. Individuals are told how they are regarded. However, decision-makers do not promise high performers with high potential that they are guaranteed advancement; rather, they send the message that "you must continue to perform in an exemplary way in your current job and take active steps to prepare yourself for the future to benefit from it. While no promises will be made, preparing yourself for the future will usually help you qualify for advancement better than not preparing yourself."

Amount of Individual Discretion

How much say do individuals have in assessing their current job performance and their future advancement potential? The answer to that question has to do with the *amount of individual discretion* in a succession planning and management program. There was a time in U.S. business when it was assumed that everyone wanted to advance to higher levels of responsibility and that everyone was willing to relocate geographically whenever asked to do so. Such assumptions are no longer safe to make: not everyone is willing to make the sacrifices that go with increased responsibility; not everyone is willing to sacrifice work-life balance; not everyone is willing to relocate due to the complexities of dual-career families and situations where elderly parents require care.

Mandated succession planning and management ignores individual career goals. Decision-makers identify the best candidates for jobs, regardless of individual preferences. Whenever a vacancy occurs, internal candidates are approached first. While given right of refusal, they may also be pressured to accept a job change for the good of the organization. *Verified succession planning and management* appreciates the importance of the individual in SP&M. Decision-makers identify desirable candidates for each job and then verify their interest in it by conducting career planning interviews or discussions. When a vacancy occurs, internal candidates are approached, but decision-makers are already aware of individual preferences, career goals, and interests. No pressure is exerted on the individual; rather, decision-makers seek a balance in meeting organizational succession needs and individual career goals.

Ensuring Leadership Continuity in Organizations

There are two main ways to ensure leadership continuity and thereby fill critically important positions. These may be generally classified as traditional and alternative approaches. Each can have important implications for SP&M. Hence, each warrants brief review.

Traditional Approaches

In 1968, Haire noted that people can make only six types of job movements in any organization: *in* (entry), *out* (termination), *up* (promotion), *down* (demotion), *across* (lateral transfer), or *progress in place* (development in the current position).[34] Any one—or all—of these traditional approaches can, of course, be used as a means to meet succession needs for key positions.

Moving people into an organization (entry) is associated with recruitment and selection. In short, "hiring off the street" is one way to find successors for key positions. However, people hired from outside represent a gamble. They have little stake in the organization's status quo, though they may have valuable knowledge in which the organization is otherwise deficient. They may generate conflict trying to put new ideas into action. That conflict may be destructive or constructive. Top managers may be reluctant to hire more than a certain percentage of outsiders for key positions because they do represent a gamble. Their track records are difficult to verify, and their ability to work harmoniously in a new corporate culture may be difficult to assess. If they fail, outsiders may be difficult to terminate both because managers can be reluctant to "fire" people and because wrongful discharge litigation is an issue of growing concern.

Moving people out of an organization (termination) is associated with layoffs, downsizings, reductions in force, firings, and employee buyouts. It is generally viewed negatively, continuing to carry a social stigma for those "let go" and to be a public relations concern for organizations that regularly terminate individuals with or without cause. Yet, if properly used, termination can be an effective tool for removing less-than-effective performers from their positions, thereby opening up opportunities for promising high-potential employees with proven track records.

Moving people up in an organization (promotion) is associated with upward mobility, advancement, and increased responsibility. Succession planning and management has long been linked with this approach more than any other. Indeed, replacement charts—while increasingly outdated—remain tools of SP&M in many organizations. They usually imply an upward progression from within the organization—and often within the same division, department, or work unit. Career maps show the competency requirements necessary for advancement and are often substituted now for replacement charts. Job-posting programs can also be paired with replacement charting or career maps so as to communicate vacancies and provide a means of allowing movement across functions, departments, and locations.

Promotion from within does have distinct advantages: it sustains (or improves) employee morale, and it smoothes transitions by ensuring that key positions are filled by those whose personalities, philosophies, and skills are already known to others in the organization. However, experts advise limiting the percentage of positions filled through internal promotion. One reason is that it tends to reinforce the existing culture. Another reason is that it can end up perpetuating the racial, sexual, and ethnic composition already present in the leadership ranks.

There are other problems with strict promotion-from-within approaches to succession planning and management. First, exemplary job performance in one position is no guarantee of success in a higher-level position. Requirements at different organizational levels are not identical—and that is particularly true in management. Effective promotion from within requires planning and rarely occurs by luck.

Moving people down in an organization (demotion), like terminating them, is commonly viewed negatively. Yet it, too, can be an effective source of leadership talent on some occasions. For instance, when an organizational unit is being disbanded, effective performers from that unit may fill vacancies in other parts of the organization. Individuals may even accept demotions voluntarily if they believe that such moves will increase their job security or improve their long-term career prospects.

Moving people across an organization (lateral transfer) is becoming more common in the wake of downsizing. (It is sometimes linked to what has come to be called *inplacement*.[35]) That, too, can be a valuable means by which to cross-fertilize the organization, giving new perspectives to old functions or activities. Job rotations, either temporary or permanent moves from one position to others as a means of relieving ennui or building individual competencies, are a unique form of transfer that can also be used in succession planning and management.[36]

Finally, *progress in place* (development in the current position) represents a middle ground between lateral transfer and upward mobility. It has become more common as opportunities for advancement have diminished in the wake of fierce global competition. Progress in place is based on the central premise that no job—no matter how broad or complex—fully taps individual potential. As a result, individuals can be developed for the future while remaining where they are, doing what they have always done, and gradually shouldering new duties or assignments. Stagnation is thus avoided by "loading" the job horizontally or vertically. (*Horizontal loading* means adding job responsibilities similar to what the individual has already done; *vertical loading* means offering new job responsibilities that challenge the individual to learn more.)

Related to progress in place is the notion of dual career ladders in which individuals may advance along two different career tracks: *a management track* (in which advancement is linked to increasing responsibility for people) and *a technical track* (in which advancement is linked to increasingly sophisticated responsibility within a given function or area of expertise). The organization may establish special rewards, incentives, and compensation programs to encourage advancement along dual career tracks.

Alternative Approaches

Experienced managers know that there is more than one way to fill a critical position.[37] Job movements, described in the previous section, represent a traditional approach, commonly associated with SP&M. Alternative approaches are probably being increasingly used as managers in cost-sensitive organizations struggle to meet SP&M challenges while finding themselves restricted in the external hiring and internal promoting that they may do.

One alternative approach might be called *organizational redesign*. When a vacancy occurs in a key position, decision-makers do not automatically "move someone into that place"; rather, they break up the work duties and reallocate them across the remaining key positions or people. The desired effect is to reduce headcount while holding results constant. It also develops the remaining key people by giving them exposure to a new function, activity, or responsibility. However, if rewards do not match the growing workload, exemplary performers who have been asked to do more may grow disenchanted. There is also a limit to how much can be loaded on people before they are incapable of performing effectively.

A second alternative approach is *process redesign*. Decision-makers do not automatically assume that a key position needs to be replaced when it becomes vacant; rather, they review that function from top to bottom, determining whether it is necessary at all—and if it can be done in new ways that require fewer people.

A third alternative approach is *outsourcing*. Rather than assume that all key positions need to be performed internally, decision-makers periodically reassess whether activities can be more cost-effectively handled externally. If headcount can be reduced through outsourcing, the organization can decrease succession demands.

A fourth alternative approach involves *trading personnel temporarily* with other organizations. This approach builds on the idea that organizations can temporarily trade resources for their mutual benefit. Excess capacity in one organization is thus tapped temporarily by others. An advantage of this approach is that high performers or high potentials who are not immediately needed by one organization can be pooled for use by others, who usually offset their salaries and benefits. A disadvantage is that lending organizations risk losing these talented workers completely if they are spirited away by those having greater need of their services and greater ability to reward and advance them.

A fifth alternative approach involves establishing *talent pools*. Instead of identifying one likely successor for each critical position, the organization sets out to develop many people for many positions. That is accomplished by mandated job rotations so that high potentials gain exposure to many organizational areas and are capable of making multifaceted contributions. While that sounds fine in theory, there are practical difficulties with using this approach. One is that productivity can decline as new leaders play musical chairs and learn the ropes in new organizational settings.

A sixth alternative approach is to establish *two-in-the-box arrangements*. Motorola has been known to use this approach. "Since most Motorola businesses are run by a general manager and an assistant general manager, the assistant slot is used to move executives from one business to another for a few years so they can gain a variety of experiences."[38] A form of overstaffing that would not be appealing to some organizations, this approach permits individual development through job rotations while preserving leadership continuity. It is akin to forming an executive team in which traditional functional senior executives are replaced by a cohesive team that collectively makes operating decisions, effectively functioning in the place of a chief operating officer.[39]

A seventh alternative approach is to establish *competitive skill inventories of high-potential workers outside the organization*. Rather than develop organizational talent over time, an organization identifies predictable sources of high-potential workers and recruits them on short notice as needed. A disadvantage of this approach is that it can engender counterattacks by organizations that have been "robbed" of talent.

Of course, there are other alternative ways by which to meet successor needs in key positions. Here is a quick review of a few of them:

▲ *Temping.* The organization makes it a practice to hire individuals from outside on a short-term basis to fill in during a search for a successor. The "temps" become candidates for consideration. If they do not work out, however, the arrangement can be severed on short notice.

▲ *Job Sharing.* An experienced employee in a key position temporarily shares the job with another as a means of on-the-job training—or assessing how well the candidate can perform.

▲ *Part-Time Employment.* Prospective candidates for key positions are brought in on a part-time basis. They are carefully assessed before employment offers are made.

▲ *Consulting.* Prospective candidates for key positions are brought in as consultants on projects related to the position duties. Their performance is carefully assessed before employment offers are made.

▲ *Overtime.* Prospective candidates from within the organization are asked to work in other capacities in addition to their current jobs. This represents overtime work. The employer then assesses how well the individuals can perform in the key positions, making allowances for the unusual pressure under which they are functioning.

▲ *Job Rotation.* Prospective candidates for key positions are developed from within by rotating, for an extended time span, into another job or series of jobs in preparation for the future.

▲ *Retirees.* The organization looks to individuals with proven track records to return to critical positions temporarily—or permanently. This is likely to be a key focus of interest in the future.[40]

The important point about SP&M is that numerous approaches may be used to satisfy immediate requirements. However, a continuing and systematic program is necessary to ensure that talent is being prepared inside the organization. As a starting point for describing what is needed to decision-makers in your organization, start with addressing the Frequently Asked Questions (FAQs) appearing in Appendix I at the end of this book.

Summary

This chapter opened with six dramatic vignettes to illustrate the importance of succession planning and management (SP&M), which was defined "as any effort designed to ensure the continued effective performance of an organization, division, department, or work group by making provision for the development, replacement, and strategic application of key people over time." A succession planning and management program was defined as a "deliberate and systematic effort by an organization to ensure leadership continuity in key positions, retain and develop intellectual and knowledge capital for the future, and encourage individual advancement." Succession planning and management is proactive and should not be confused with more limited-scope and reactive replacement planning, which is a form of risk management.

Succession planning and management is important for several reasons: (1) the continued survival of the organization depends on having the right people in the right places at the right times; (2) as a result of recent economic restructuring efforts in organizations, there are simply fewer people available to advance to the top ranks from within; (3) succession planning and management is needed to encourage diversity and multiculturalism in organizations and to avoid "homosocial reproduction" by managers; and (4) succession forms the basis for communicating career paths, establishing development and training plans, establishing career paths and individual job moves, communicating upward and laterally, and creating a more comprehensive human resources planning system.

Organizations sponsor systematic succession planning and management programs for various reasons. The three most important, based on my 2004 survey, are:

▲ To contribute to implementing the organization's strategic business plans

▲ To identify "replacement needs" as a means of targeting necessary training, employee education, and employee development

▲ To increase the talent pool of promotable employees

Approaches to succession planning and management may be distinguished by direction, timing, planning, scope, degree of dissemination, and amount of individual discretion. Succession needs may be met through traditional and alternative approaches. Succession planning and management should be linked to—and supportive of—strategic plans, human resource plans, human resource development plans, and other organizational planning activities.

CHAPTER 2

TRENDS INFLUENCING SUCCESSION PLANNING AND MANAGEMENT

Succession planning and management (SP&M) must be carried out against the backdrop of increasingly dynamic organizations.[1] Those organizations are responding, either proactively or reactively, to changes occurring in their external environments. As Leibman explains, "today's dynamic environment filled with global competition and business discontinuities defines the arena in which succession planning must flourish. To do so, a much more active orientation is required, one that is better characterized by succession management and its emphasis on ongoing and integrated processes."[2] For Leibman, succession management is more active than succession planning and must be carried out in a way that is tied to organizational strategy and is responsive enough to deal with rapidly changing organizational settings. That is an accurate view. To be effective, SP&M programs must anticipate—and not just react to—the changes wrought by an increasingly dynamic business environment.

Many trends drive the future workplace and workforce. Among them are the following[3]:

1. Changing Technology
2. Increasing Globalization
3. Continuing Cost Containment
4. Increasing Speed in Market Change
5. The Growing Importance of Knowledge Capital
6. An Increasing Rate and Magnitude of Change

These trends demand a new role for managers. They also call for a new, more strategic role for HR practitioners.[4] Trends such as these frame the future of SP&M efforts, and effective SP&M programs are built to help organizations manage and even capitalize on the effects of these trends.

This chapter examines key trends influencing SP&M. The chapter opens with an activity for you to consider on the drivers of change and trends. It then focuses on answering the question, "What trends are influencing SP&M?"

The chapter directs attention to ten key trends exerting special influence on SP&M:

1. The Need for Speed
2. A Seller's Market for Skills
3. Reduced Loyalty Among Employers and Workers
4. The Importance of Intellectual Capital and Knowledge Management
5. The Importance of Values and Competencies
6. More Software to Support Succession
7. The Growing Activism of the Board of Directors
8. Growing Awareness of Similarities and Differences in Succession Issues Globally
9. Growing Awareness of the Similarities and Differences of Succession Programs in Special Venues: Government, Nonprofit, Education, Small Business, and Family Business
10. Managing a Special Issue: CEO Succession

The chapter then offers conclusions about what these trends mean for SP&M. But first, take a moment to rate your organization on its handling of SP&M against the backdrop of the competitive environment. Complete the assessment questionnaire appearing in Exhibit 2-1. When you finish, score the results of your assessment. Then continue reading the chapter.

The Ten Key Trends

Trend 1: The Need for Speed

Time has emerged as a key strategic resource.[5] If you doubt that, then consider how often the phrase "reduction in cycle time" is used in companies today. Also consider how fast the speed of processing time in computers is advancing. Slashing the time it takes to get results is seen as a goal in its own right. This includes:

▲ Finding faster ways to transform basic research into applied research so as to create new products or services and thereby beat competitors to production or service delivery
▲ Entering new markets faster
▲ Reducing unnecessary or redundant steps in the production process through process improvement

Exhibit 2-1. An Assessment Questionnaire: How Well Is Your Organization Managing the Consequences of Trends Influencing Succession Planning and Management?

Directions: Use this questionnaire to structure your thinking about how well your organization is positioned to manage the *consequences* of key trends influencing SP&M. For each item listed in the left column below, rate how well you feel your organization is prepared to manage the consequences of the trends as they may influence SP&M.

Use the following scale to rate your opinions:

1 = *Not at all prepared* to manage the consequences of the trend as it influences SP&M.

2 = *Very unprepared* to manage the consequences of the trend as it influences SP&M.

3 = *Unprepared* to manage the consequences of the trend as it influences SP&M.

4 = *Somewhat prepared* to manage the consequences of the trend as it influences SP&M.

5 = *Prepared* to manage the consequences of the trend as it influences SP&M.

6 = *Well prepared* to manage the consequences of the trend as it influences SP&M.

7 = *Very well prepared* to manage the consequences of the trend as it influences SP&M.

If you wish, ask decision-makers in your organization to complete this assessment questionnaire individually. Then compile the results and feed the results back to the decision-makers so that they may see their collective views.

The Questionnaire

	How Well Is Your Organization Positioned to Manage the Consequences of the Trend as It Influences SP&M?						
	Not at All Prepared					Very Well Prepared	
Trend	*1*	*2*	*3*	*4*	*5*	*6*	*7*
1. The Need for Speed	1	2	3	4	5	6	7
2. A Seller's Market for Skills	1	2	3	4	5	6	7
3. Reduced Loyalty Among Employers and Workers	1	2	3	4	5	6	7

(continues)

Exhibit 2-1. (*continued*)

4. The Importance of Intellectual Capital and Knowledge Management	1	2	3	4	5	6	7
5. The Key Importance of Values and Competencies	1	2	3	4	5	6	7

Scoring

Add up the totals
of the columns above $\longrightarrow$
and place the sum in
the box at right

Interpreting the Score

If your score is lower than *19*, then your organization is not well prepared to manage the consequences of the trends as they may influence SP&M.

▲ Improving, through just-in-time inventory methods, the time match between the need for raw materials and their use in production so as to reduce inventory holding costs
▲ Reducing the time it takes to fill an order or ship a product from producer to consumer

Speed is only likely to become more important in the future. That sensitivity to speed is affecting human resources (HR) practices as well. Many companies keep statistics to see how long it takes to do the following[6]:

▲ Justify a position.
▲ Recruit for and fill a vacancy.
▲ Find talent to meet immediate needs or synchronize efforts.
▲ Train people.

In a more stable era, it might have been acceptable to permit a long lead time between the justification and filling of a position, or the selection of a qualified person and the realization of full productivity from that worker following training. But stable times are gone. Time is a resource easily wasted, and people must be found and oriented so that they can become productive as quickly as possible.

Trend 2: A Seller's Market for Skills

Employers in the United States, as in many other parts of the world, have traditionally taken workers for granted. Many managers still assume that, if their organizations will only pay enough, they can always find the people they need to fill any position. But that assumption is not always valid anymore. There are several reasons why.

First, the U.S. population is aging.[7] Fewer workers are entering at the bottom of organizational pyramids because there are fewer workers of traditional entry-level age. Those new workers have a work ethic and values different from those of previous generations. Many prize a balance of work and personal life that does not match the frenetic pace of many organizations today, where number of work hours for the average manager are on the rise.[8]

Second, more people are reaching traditional retirement ages. Some authorities contend that this will lead to a leadership shortage as senior managers, traditionally the oldest age group, take advantage of generous retirement plans.[9] Other authorities, however, caution against assuming that people will retire at traditional ages in the future, since retirement plans and other benefits are less secure than they once were.[10]

Third, until recently the U.S. economy sustained a broad expansion for the longest period in history. Many groups have benefited from this expansion. While there may be evidence that the rich are getting richer and the poor are getting poorer,[11] it is also true that (at least at the time this book goes to press) virtually anyone in America who wants a job can find one somewhere. This means that workers can afford to be more selective about where they work, which creates a seller's market for skills.

In response, many U.S. organizations have instituted retention programs to hold down turnover.[12] That is ironic, considering that many organizations in the 1990s implemented staff reduction plans through downsizings, layoffs, employee buyouts, and early retirement programs in order to slash payroll and benefit costs. But, while downsizings continue in the wake of rapid market changes and corporate mergers, acquisitions, and takeovers, many decision-makers in organizations are now looking for ways to attract and retain talent. That is particularly true in information technology jobs, where a much-publicized labor shortage is thought to be a driver for future mergers and acquisitions.

The change in attitude has spawned interest in ways to give people hope for the future. An SP&M program is one such way, of course. A reinvented career planning and development program is another, related way.

Trend 3: Reduced Loyalty Among Employers and Workers

There was a time when employees believed that they would get a job with one company and stay with that company until retirement. A stable employment record was considered an advantage during job interviews. Likewise, employers often assumed that, when they extended a job offer, they were establishing a long-term relationship with the worker. Even poor performers were tolerated, and sometimes moved out of the way and into harmless positions to preserve workers' feelings of trust and security with their employers.

This, of course, is no longer the case. One result of the downsizing of the 1990s was that employers changed the employment contract.[13] As competitive conditions became more fierce, organizational conditions became less stable. No longer were employers making a long-term commitment to their employees.

A legacy of this change is that employees have become more interested in short-term gains, especially in salaries, titles, development opportunities, and benefits. They want immediate rewards for good performance, since they distrust their employers' abilities to reward them in the future for hard work performed in the present.[14] They have changed from showing a tolerance for delayed gratification to demanding immediate gratification. This change in the employment contract has profound implications for traditional SP&M practices. Employees can no longer trust their employers to make good on promises of future advancement. And, given that attitude, employers can no longer count on high potentials or exemplary performers patiently performing for long periods before receiving rewards, advancement, or professional development.

Speed is now as important in managing succession issues as it is in managing other aspects of organizational practice. Managers must manage against a backdrop with the possibility of losing valuable talent if they do not identify it quickly and offer prompt rewards and development opportunities.[15]

Trend 4: The Importance of Intellectual Capital and Knowledge Management

Intellectual capital can be understood, at least in one sense, as the collective economic value of an organization's workforce.[16] The effective use of intellectual capital is *knowledge management.*[17] It is important to emphasize that, as the speed of decision making increases in organizational environments and operations, intellectual capital increases in value because it is essential for customers to deal with workers who know how to serve them quickly and effectively. This demands improved knowledge management of the workforce.

While land, capital, and information can be readily obtained from other sources—and, on occasion, leased, outsourced, or purchased—the organization's workforce represents a key asset. Without people who know what the organization does to serve its customers and how it does that, no organization could continue to function. In one example I like to use with my students, I ask them this question: What would a university be without its faculty, administrators, staff, and students? The answer is that it would be nothing more than assets ready for liquidation—land, buildings, equipment, and capital. Without the people, there would be no way to achieve the mission of the university by teaching, research, and service.

The same principle applies to business organizations. While traditional managers may view people as a cost of doing business, thought leaders realize that people represent the only asset that really matters in a competitive environment. People dream up new products and services. People make the leap from the results of basic research to the commercialization of applied research. People come up with technological advancements and use those advancements to achieve improved productivity and quality. People serve the customers, make the products, ship them to consumers, bill them, deposit the proceeds, and manage the organization's resources. Without people, the competitive game is lost. That is a lesson that is, unfortunately, too easy to forget at a time when many people are awed by rapid technological advancement. Of course, those impressive technological advancements are pointless unless people make use of them.

The implications of intellectual capital and knowledge management are important for SP&M. In a sense, succession planning and management is a means to an end. It is a tool of knowledge management, a means of ensuring that intellectual capital is properly serviced, retained, cultivated, and protected.

Trend 5: The Importance of Values and Competencies

People in organizations have high expectations of their leaders. These expectations are unlikely to diminish in the future. People want leaders who can get results and can, at the same time, model appropriate ethics. For these reasons, values and competencies have emerged as crucial to success in organizations.

As a later chapter will define them, values can be understood to mean deeply held beliefs. In the wake of high-profile scandals in the U.S. government, in other governments such as those of Japan and China, and in many businesses, values have emerged as a key issue of importance in organizational settings. Many multinational companies, for instance, have tried to address cultural differences by establishing core values honored internationally under one corporate umbrella.[18]

Competencies, while having different definitions,[19] have also emerged as key to management decision making, human resource practice,[20] and SP&M programs. Values represent a moral dimension to the way leadership is exercised and work is performed.[21] Competencies can represent the distinguishing features between high performers and average or below-average performers. More flexible than work activities or tasks, competency models are the glue that holds together a succession planning effort. The use of competency models is a distinguishing characteristic between traditional and cutting-edge SP&M programs. As work becomes more dynamic and divorced from the traditional "boxes" found on organization charts, there must still be a way to describe what performance is expected. Competency models have the advantage of providing that flexibility.

Trend 6: More Software to Support Succession

There is more software available to support SP&M, though it sometimes masquerades under such alternative names as *talent management*, *talent development*, or *human capital software*. That is both a blessing and a curse. It is a blessing because, when well formulated and implemented, software permits individuals and groups that are dispersed geographically to participate. Software can facilitate decision making on competency identification, values clarification, 360-degree assessment, individual development planning, identification of developmental resources to help build competencies (and thereby close developmental gaps), track individual progress (and thus encourage accountability), and even measure individuals' progress and the support provided by immediate supervisors.

But it can be a curse because some people believe that, when they buy a technology solution, they are also buying the solutions to their succession problems. They think that the software will give them ready-made, off-the-shelf, one-size-fits-all competency models, 360-degree assessments, individual development plans, tracking systems, and developmental methods. Of course, that is not true. Technology is like an empty glass. HR practitioners and senior managers cannot avoid the responsibility of filling the glass with corporate-culture-specific competencies, overseeing individual progress, providing real-time mentoring and coaching, and offering much more than is embedded in the technology. In short, technology can ease the work, but it will not remove it. (Chapter 12 of this book describes unique issues associated with the application of online technology to SP&M.)

Trend 7: The Growing Activism of the Board of Directors

Boards of directors are beginning to take a more active role in SP&M. The evidence clearly points in that direction. One reason has been the Sarbanes-Oxley Act of 2002. (See Exhibit 2-2.) A key effect of that act is to increase board accountability in business operations. And, of course, finding qualified successors for CEOs on down is an important issue that corporate boards must perennially address.[22]

Trend 8: Growing Awareness of Similarities and Differences in Succession Issues Globally

One size does not fit all—and that is as true of succession planning as it is of anything else. Unfortunately, it is a lesson that some multinational corporations (MNCs) have never learned. An all-too-common scenario is that the corporate headquarters in Europe, the United States, or Japan will establish succession planning guidelines and then roll them out worldwide, forgetting

Exhibit 2-2. The Sarbanes-Oxley Act of 2002

The Sarbanes-Oxley Act of 2002 has swept the corporate world, leading to widespread change.[1] Introduced in the wake of the spate of scandals that began with Enron, the Sarbanes-Oxley Act does have an impact on succession issues. It has prompted corporate boards of directors to take a more active role in succession issues. It has also prohibited practices that were previously regarded as retention strategies for key executives, such as permitting personal loans to executives or allowing CEOs to remain in the room as corporate boards deliberate financial packages.[2] Sarbanes-Oxley has also put real teeth in corporate codes of conduct and strengthened ethics programs in corporate settings. One indicator: "the ethics officer association, a Waltham, Mass.–based organization for managers of 'ethics, compliance and business conduct programs,' has seen membership jump more than 25 percent since last year."[3]

Notes

1. Steven C. Hall, "Sarbanes Oxley Act of 2002," *Journal of Financial Service Professionals* 57:5 (2003), 14.
2. Dale Buss, "Corporate Compasses," *HR Magazine* 49:6 (2004), 127–128, 130, 132; Robert J. Grossman, "HR on the Board," *HR Magazine* 49:6 (2004), 56–63.
3. Buss, "Corporate Compasses," p. 128.

---

that the world is a big place and national cultural differences do play a role in effective succession planning practices. The result is that, whatever the approach, it is only partly effective. An English-language-only literature search uncovered articles about SP&M in Europe,[23] the United States,[24] Asia,[25] the Middle East,[26] and New Zealand.[27] As Hickey notes in writing of SP&M in China, "a continued negligence of a systemic succession plan is seemingly retarding the growth and career development of domestic employees to localize the organization."[28] The same could, unfortunately, be said of many other locales around the world.

What are some of the problems that a global rollout may uncover? Here is a list of some typical problems and their causes:

▲ *U.S. firms will generally prize individualists who can claim credit for what they have done on their own.* That is not true in other cultures, where a willingness to "stick one's head above the crowd may mean it is cut off." In short, allowances may have to be made for cultural differences in which individual efforts are prized in those cultures where individualism is prized, while an individual's willingness and skill to influence groups may have to be identified and rewarded in more collectivistic cultures where team efforts are prized.

▲ *Some European firms—and some firms in developing nations—will prize "family heritage."* Ultimately, coming from the European tradition of aristocracy, this principle means that "not all people are created equal." Some people, as George Orwell once noted in *Animal Farm*, are "more equal than others" by virtue of birth family, socioeconomic status, schools attended, and social networks developed from school and family connections. In short, it means that one's family may mean that one is destined to be a senior executive no matter what corporate leaders in other nations may want because that is just the way things are done locally.

If a universal approach will not work globally, then what approach will work? The answer is that there is no simple answer. Goals may be established at corporate headquarters. But, if the approach is to be effective, corporate leaders should launch facilitated sessions that bring together regional leaders to have input on the goals, hear about best practices in Western nations (which may have the most advanced approaches), and (most importantly) discover what results are to be achieved by those practices. Then the regional leaders should engage in facilitated discussions where they can "invent" local approaches that will "work" in their home cultures, and will comply with the employment laws of each nation.

It is true that such an approach takes time, resources, patience, and hard work. But in the long run, that approach has the advantage of leading to "global goals" but using "local approaches to achieve those goals." It will work.

The alternative is to do as many companies do and just "roll out something" from corporate headquarters. Local people will shake their heads in wonderment, amazed that global corporate leaders know so little about the broad differences in local cultures, local realities, and even local labor laws. It just undermines the credibility of corporate leaders. As globalization exerts increasing influence, these "one size fits all" approaches will be increasingly out of step with good business practice. That is especially true when rapidly advancing technology makes it possible to have videoconferenced and real-time online discussions cross-culturally to facilitate ideas and approaches.

Trend 9: Growing Awareness of Similarities and Differences of Succession Programs in Special Venues: Government, Nonprofit, Education, and Small or Family Business

Just as one size of SP&M program may not fit all internationally, one approach to SP&M will not work in all venues. While there are many similarities in effective SP&M programs across business, government, and nonprofit sectors, there are some important differences as well. The same is true in settings such as educational institutions, small business, and family business.

Government

There are two key differences in succession planning programs between business and in governmental settings. (And it is worth pointing out that governmental entities may themselves differ across international, federal, state, municipal, county, and other governmental bodies.)

One difference is that some governmental entities have civil service systems that prohibit (by law) the naming of individuals to fill positions without competitive job searches. In some jurisdictions, all jobs must be posted. Individuals are then ranked according to their qualifications compared to the requirements listed on job descriptions. That approach means, in practical terms, that a government entity can commit to develop anyone who wishes to be developed—a method sometimes called a *talent-pool approach*. But identifying individual successors in advance may not be possible.

A second difference has to do with who may be regarded as the key customers of the effort. In business, the CEO plays the single most important role as customer. But in some governmental entities, the agency director is a political appointee who carries out the will of an elected official. In practical terms, that means that the most important owners of the SP&M process will be those government civil servants who do not change with the winds of every political election. They possess the collective institutional wisdom of the organization in their heads, and they must be appealed to on the grounds of a legacy if a government-agency SP&M program is to work. In many cases, government succession programs bear different titles and are called *workforce planning* or *human capital management initiatives.*[29]

Nonprofit

Nonprofit entities share characteristics with business and government. For that reason, an effective SP&M program in a nonprofit organization will most likely be a hybrid of what works in the private and public sectors. The senior-most leader must back the effort if it is to succeed, and (in that respect) the nonprofit SP&M program is like the private sector. But dedicated leaders who have made their careers in the organization, and are committed to its worthwhile mission, must also back the effort. And in that respect, the SP&M program in a nonprofit organization is akin to that of a governmental entity.

Education

Educational institutions vary widely in type, just as governmental entities do. One size SP&M program will not fit all. What works in a local school system may not work at a world-famous research university.[30] But it is clear that large universities are unique for the simple reason that many people must move to other higher educational institutions if they are to be promoted from department head to dean, dean to provost or chancellor, or chancellor or provost to president. That makes it difficult for one institution to justify expenditures on identifying and grooming talent for the future, since the beneficiaries of such efforts would most likely be other institutions. (In a school district, on the other hand, it may be possible to groom people to become principals because many such positions may be available.) Having said this, however, some higher-educational institutions have committed to leadership development programs to groom talent, and it is likely to be seen more in the future, for the simple reason that so many college professors and university administrators are at, or near, retirement age.

Small or Family Business

Succession planning in family businesses and succession planning in small businesses are specialized topics. Much has actually been written about them.[31] It should be noted that not all family businesses are small businesses and not all small businesses are family businesses. Some large, well-known companies like Ford were originally family businesses. In Europe or Asia, many large companies began—and some still are—essentially family dynasties. That is also true in some companies in the United States. And small businesses may be initiated by individuals without families or in partnerships of otherwise talented but unrelated entrepreneurs.

Family businesses exert an enormously powerful influence on the U.S. economy. Consider the following[32]:

> It has been estimated that family businesses generate approximately nine out of 10 new jobs. But despite the significant role they play in supporting the nation's economy, only about one in three survives to the second generation. The estimate of successful transfers to the third generation ranges from only 10 to 20%.

Family businesses represent a special succession challenge for the simple reason that many factors come into play. A founding entrepreneur, who is usually a parent and spouse, establishes a business. But what happens when he or she passes from the scene? Who carries on the legacy? In some cultures—and even in some parts of the United States—the principle of primogeniture is still very much apparent. Primogeniture is the view that the eldest son should be the primary inheritor. Based on the way that aristocratic titles have been passed down historically, it poses special problems in family succession, for the simple reason that the eldest son of a founding entrepreneur may (or may not) be the best equipped—by skills, vision, or motivation—to run the business.

Family succession has several issues associated with it. One issue centers on management. A second issue centers on tax and inheritance issues. A third issue centers on legal issues. A fourth issue centers on what might be called family psychology. So, the management issue has to do with answering this question: "Who is best equipped to run the business when the founder passes from the scene?" While founders may feel inclined to leave the business to a spouse or to an eldest son, that person may (in fact) not be the best choice.

The real issue has to do with a conflict between obligation to family and obligation to the business. Savvy founders will not necessarily let the obligation to the family prevail. If they do, they may destroy the business. What happens if, upon the founding entrepreneur's sudden death or disability, the spouse or eldest child is ill-equipped to manage the business? The answer is likely to be bankruptcy or a sell-off. That may not be best for the business, the employees, or the communities in which that business functions.

The second and third issues have to do with accounting and legal issues. Should the business be handed over before the founder's demise, in which case it is subject to gift tax, or should the handoff occur after the founder's demise, in which case it is subject to inheritance tax? Those questions are best addressed by competent financial and tax advisors. At the same time, if the business is handed over, it must be done legally. That requires competent legal advice to write a will that cannot be easily "broken" or a handoff agreement that makes the founder's relationship to the business clear.

The fourth and final issue has to do with family psychology. If the founder decides to hand over a controlling share of the business to one child in preference to others, for instance, then the reasons for that should be clear before his or her demise and the issue of financial fairness and equity addressed at that time. If the founder decides to hand over a controlling share of the business to a child and ignore the living spouse's claim on the assets, that is also a problem. The point to be made here is that conflicts should be worked through while all parties are alive. At times that may require the help of a skilled family psychologist. To ignore the problem is to beg trouble—and perhaps beg the dissolution of the business upon the founder's death or disability as family members squabble bitterly and ceaselessly over money.

Trend 10: Managing a Special Issue: CEO Succession

CEO succession has emerged as a special theme and research topic within the succession literature.[33] In that respect it is like other unique succession issues, such as the impact of cultural differences in making succession decisions, small business succession, and family business succession. The special interest in CEO succession should come as no big surprise. It has been a prominent topic for research, discussion, and investor interest. In fact, it has been a focus of attention in much the same way that succession to the throne has preoccupied citizens in those nations where a monarch is the titular head of state. That analogy between monarch in a nation and CEO of a company is particularly apt when thinking about the successors of founding entrepreneurs in small businesses, where a CEO's unexpected and sudden loss can have particularly devastating effects on the business.[34]

CEO succession has also become a particular center point for concern recently as CEO turnover globally has increased.[35] The findings of a study of CEO turnover,[36] reported in *The Financial Executive*, revealed that:

▲ Involuntary CEO successions increased by more than 70 percent from 2001 to 2002.

▲ Of all CEO departures globally in 2002, 39 percent were forced—and that compared to 35 percent in 2001.

▲ CEO turnover increased 192 percent in Europe and 140 percent in the Asia/Pacific region but only 2 percent in North America since 1995.

▲ The Asia/Pacific region accounted for the largest change (19 percent), nearly 1 in 5 CEO departures.

▲ North America accounted for only 48 percent of all successions worldwide in 2002 but accounted for a significantly higher 64 percent in 2001.

▲ Corporate boards have toughened their stance on CEO performance, since the board dismissed CEOs in 2002 when shareholder returns were only 6.2 percent below median regionally adjusted averages but at 11.9 percent below median regionally adjusted averages in 2001.

One important conclusion that can be drawn from these results is that organizations must pay more attention to ways to select CEOs and assimilate them.[37] Indeed, CEO succession is likely to continue to be a focus of attention. Most experts predict that the pace and magnitude of change in the world will continue to increase. As that happens, corporate boards are likely to be more demanding—and less forgiving—of CEO performance. That, in turn, will probably continue the trend of dropping job tenure for CEOs.

What Does All This Mean for Succession Planning and Management?

What will these trends mean for succession planning and management? The answer to that question is that, to be effective in the future, succession planning and management must be based on sensitivity to the need for speed,[38] must align organizational needs with individual needs in order to be responsive to a seller's market for skills, must emphasize a present orientation that will work in business settings where neither individuals nor organizations possess long-term loyalty, must recognize and cultivate the critical importance in competitive success of the organization's intellectual capital, must rely on (but not be led by) technology, and must be sensitive to unique needs by culture, industry or economic sector, and level on the chain of command.

Summary

As noted at the opening of this chapter, succession planning and management must be carried out against the backdrop of increasingly dynamic organizations. This chapter examined ten key trends exerting special influence on succession planning and management. The chapter then offered conclusions about what these trends mean for succession planning and management.

The next chapter makes the case for a newer approach to succession planning and management, one that is responsive to—and helps organizations be more proactive to—new competitive realities.

CHAPTER 3

MOVING TO A
STATE-OF-THE-ART APPROACH

What characteristics do state-of-the-art succession planning and management (SP&M) programs share in common? Read the cases appearing in Appendix II and then consider the summary of best-practice characteristics described below. While the cases do not necessarily describe every best practice, they are helpful in seeing how succession planning and management is handled among various organizations, in various industries.

Characteristics of Effective Programs

What characteristics of SP&M programs have most contributed to their effectiveness? Spend a moment to brainstorm the answer to that question. Then compare your answer to that question with the list of characteristics appearing below. (The list is not necessarily complete and is not meant to be arranged in order of importance.)

▲ *Characteristic 1: Top Management Participation and Support.* Top management participation and support must be strongly evident. Their personal involvement—and even that of the corporate board—should motivate participants and ensure that other members of the management team devote time and effort to the succession planning program. Without the CEO's personal attention, SP&M will probably receive far less attention than it presently does in these companies.

▲ *Characteristic 2: Needs-Driven with External Benchmarking.* Some effort should be made to compare best practices in other organizations to the organization where leaders feel the need to act on succession issues.

▲ *Characteristic 3: Focused Attention.* Organizational leaders should not allow succession planning to occur casually on its own. A systematic effort is focused on accelerating the development of individuals with verified advancement potential. It is worth emphasizing that it is not appropriate to assume that successful performance at one level guarantees, or is even an indicator of, success at higher levels of responsibility.

▲ *Characteristic 4: Dedicated Responsibility*. If a goal deserves attention, someone must be held responsible for achieving it and accountable for the consequences of it. That is as true of SP&M as it is of anything else.

▲ *Characteristic 5: Succession Planning and Management Extends to All Levels*. SP&M should extend to all organizational levels. Note that the greatest emphasis is placed in some organizations at the lowest management levels, where the most positions and people exist. In the other cases, attention is devoted to levels where business needs (or risks of loss due to retirement) are greatest.

▲ *Characteristic 6: A Systematic Approach*. In most organizations, continuing processes should be put in place to focus attention on succession planning.

▲ *Characteristic 7: A Comparison of Present Performance and Future Potential*. Management succession should not be a function of personal favoritism, seniority, or even demonstrated track record. Instead, the organization should possess some means by which to compare present job performance and future potential. The organization should identify individual developmental needs for top-level talent.

▲ *Characteristic 8: Clarification of High-Level Replacement Needs*. Organizational leaders should make the effort to determine the retirement plans of key officers. (In this book the term *key job incumbent* refers to an individual presently occupying a key position.) In that way, the organization is better able to identify developmental time spans for specific key positions.

▲ *Characteristic 9: An Obligation to Identify and Prepare Successors*. Each executive should take responsibility, and be held accountable, for identifying and preparing successors.

▲ *Characteristic 10: Specific Developmental Programs Established and Conducted*. Individuals thought to have high potential should participate in planned developmental programs to prepare them for the future, without necessarily being promised anything. Programs of this kind are often used in large corporations and may extend over many years.[1] Such programs may be viewed in three stages, which are based on the level of participants' experience with the organization. In stage 1, there is a relatively large pool of prospective high potentials. They range from little experience through eight years with the organization. They are taught general management skills. Only 6 percent of those in stage 1 make it to stage 2, where they participate in tailor-made developmental experiences, intensive on-the-job development, and specialized courses, and they occupy important positions. A smaller percentage of those in stage 2 progress to stage 3, where they occupy important positions while they are carefully groomed for more senior positions.

▲ *Characteristic 11: High Potentials Work While Developing*. The organization should not emphasize classroom or online training or off-the-job development to the exclusion of action learning or learning from experience.[2] For this reason, high-potential employees are expected to produce while participating in the developmental program.

▲ *Characteristic 12: Developmental Programs Establish Familiarity with Who, What, When, Where, Why, and How.* Large companies are so large that developmental experiences are, in part, established to familiarize future leaders with the organization's environment. That is a key emphasis of some developmental programs. As a result, participants become much more knowledgeable about the corporate culture—who does what, when they do it, where business-related activities are performed, why they are worth doing, and how they are accomplished. In this way, the internal development program emphasizes knowledge, skills, and abilities unique to the organization and essential to success in performing at higher organizational levels.

▲ *Characteristic 13: Developmental Experiences Encourage Critical Questioning.* Top managers who address high-potential employees find that they are occasionally confronted with critical questions about "the way we have always done it." Critical questioning encourages creative thinking by top managers, as well as by high-potential employees.

▲ *Characteristic 14: Succession Planning Emphasizes Qualities Necessary to Surpass Movement to the Next Higher-Level Job.* Exemplary SP&M programs emphasize more than merely preparing individuals to move from one "box" on the organization chart to the next higher-level "box." Instead, they emphasize the building of competencies leading to advancement beyond the next job. They are, thus, long term and strategic in scope and tend to build competencies in line with company business objectives and values.

▲ *Characteristic 15: Formal Mentoring Emphasized.* Mentoring and coaching have been the subject of growing attention in recent years as management writers have recognized that individual development is more heavily influenced by the on-the-job work environment than by off-the-job training, education, or development experiences.[3] (Indeed, as much as 90 percent of an individual's development occurs on the job.[4]) A mentor or coach provides advice about dealing with challenges presented by the work environment, including interpersonal problems and political issues. "Mentoring occurs when a talented junior person forms an attachment to a sensitive and intuitive senior person who understands and has the ability to communicate with the individual."[5] Mentors are teachers. They are not in positions of authority over their protégés or mentees. Nor do they necessarily serve as special advocates and cheerleaders for their protégés, as sponsors do. Mentors are typically chosen by the protégé or mentee; hence, most mentoring occurs informally. However, some organizations sponsor formal mentoring programs in which an effort is made to match promising junior employees with more experienced, high-performing senior employees.

Other Characteristics

On your list, you may have identified other characteristics of an effective SP&M program. In reality, of course, there are no "right" or "wrong" characteristics. Indeed, there isn't a foolproof formula for success. But there are certain essentials to a good succession process[6]:

▲ A Systematic (rather than anecdotal) Way of Identifying Candidates

▲ Cross-Divisional Sharing of People and Information

▲ Leadership That Rewards Managers for Promoting (rather than holding on to) Their Best Employees

▲ Career Paths That Move Not Just Up a Specialized Ladder but Across the Company

▲ Frequent Opportunities for Employees to Accept New Challenges

▲ Recognition That Employees Have a Stake in the Company and Share Its Successes

In my survey of succession planning practices, I asked about the characteristics of effective SP&M programs. The survey results are presented in Exhibit 3-1. I have used those results to create a questionnaire, shown in Exhibit 3-2, which you can use to assess issues for inclusion in the SP&M program in your organization.

The Life Cycle of Succession Planning and Management Programs: Five Generations

In my consulting practice, I have discovered that many decision-makers in organizations that possess no SP&M program would like to leap in a single bound from no program to a state-of-the-art program. That is rarely possible or realistic. It makes about as much sense as trying to accelerate an automobile from a standing stop to 100 miles per hour in one second.

It makes much more sense to think in terms of a phased-in roll-out. The basis for this roll-out approach is my view that organizations go through a life cycle of development as they implement SP&M programs. At each generation, they gain sophistication about what to do, how to do it, and why it is worth doing.

The first generation of SP&M is a simple replacement plan for the CEO. This is easiest to sell if the organization does not have such a plan, since most CEOs realize what might happen to their organizations if they are suddenly incapacitated. (See Exhibit 3-3.) The target of the SP&M program in the first generation is the CEO only, and involving the CEO ensures that he or she

(text continues on page 66)

Exhibit 3-1. Characteristics of Effective Succession Planning and Management Programs

Characteristics of Effective Succession Planning Programs	Does Your Organization's Succession Planning Program Have This Characteristic?		How Important Do You Believe This Characteristic to Be for an Effective Succession Planning Program?	
How Your Organization:	Yes	No	Not at All Important	Very Important
			1 2 3 4 5 6 (Mean Response)	
A Tied the succession planning program to the organizational strategic plans?	89%	11%	4.89	
B Tied the succession planning program to individual career plans?	56%	44%	4.00	
C Tied the succession planning program to training programs?	67%	33%	3.67	
D Established measurable objectives for program operation (such as number of positions replaced per year)?	67%	33%	3.67	
E Identified what groups are to be served by the program, in priority order?	33%	67%	3.44	

F	Established a written policy statement to guide the program?	78%	22%	3.78
G	Articulated a written philosophy about the program?	78%	22%	3.67
H	Established a program action plan?	100%	0%	4.56
I	Established a schedule of program events based on the action plan?	67%	33%	4.22
J	Fixed responsibility for organizational oversight of the program?	89%	11%	4.00
K	Fixed responsibility of each participant in the program?	78%	22%	3.78
L	Established incentives/rewards for identified successors in the succession planning program?	11%	89%	3.22

(continues)

Exhibit 3-1. (continued)

	Characteristics of Effective Succession Planning Programs How Your Organization:	Does Your Organization's Succession Planning Program Have This Characteristic?		How Important Do You Believe This Characteristic to Be for an Effective Succession Planning Program?	
		Yes	No	Not at All Important	Very Important
				1 2 3 4 5 6 (Mean Response)	
M	Established incentives/rewards for managers with identified successors?	11%	89%	3.00	
N	Developed a means to budget for a succession planning program?	56%	44%	4.00	
O	Devised means to keep records for individuals who are designated as successors?	56%	44%	3.78	
P	Created workshops to train management employees about the succession planning program?	33%	67%	4.00	
Q	Created workshops to train individuals about career planning?	56%	44%	4.11	
R	Established a means to clarify present position responsibilities?	100%	0%	4.00	

S	Established a means to clarify future position responsibilities?	67%	33%	3.89
T	Established a means to appraise individual performance?	67%	33%	4.00
U	Established a means to compare individual skills to the requirements of a future position?	44%	56%	3.89
V	Established a way to review organizational talent at least annually?	67%	33%	4.00
W	Established a way to forecast future talent needs?	67%	33%	3.89
X	Established a way to plan for meeting succession planning needs through individual development plans?	56%	44%	3.89
Y	Established a means to track development activities and prepare successors for eventual advancement?	44%	56%	3.89
Z	Established a means to evaluate the results of the succession planning program?	44%	56%	3.89

Source: William J. Rothwell, *Results of a 2004 Survey on Succession Planning and Management Practices. Unpublished survey results* (University Park, Penn.: The Pennsylvania State University, 2004).

Exhibit 3-2. Assessment Questionnaire for Effective Succession Planning and Management

Directions: Complete the following Assessment Questionnaire to determine how well your organization is presently conducting SP&M. Read each item in the Questionnaire below. Circle *(Y)* for *Yes, (N/A)* for *Not Applicable,* or an *(N)* for *No* in the left column opposite each item. Spend about 15 minutes on the questionnaire. When you finish, score and interpret the results using the instructions appearing at the end of the Assessment Questionnaire. Then share your completed Questionnaire with others in your organization. Use the Questionnaire as a starting point to determine the need for a more systematic approach to SP&M in your organization.

The Assessment Questionnaire

Circle your response below:

In your organization, would you say that SP&M:

Y	N/A	N	1.	Enjoys top management participation, involvement and support?
Y	N/A	N	2.	Is geared to meeting the unique needs of the organization?
Y	N/A	N	3.	Has been benchmarked with best-in-class organizations?
Y	N/A	N	4.	Is a major focus of top management attention?
Y	N/A	N	5.	Is the dedicated responsibility of at least one high-level management employee?
Y	N/A	N	6.	Extends to all levels rather than being restricted to top positions only?
Y	N/A	N	7.	Is carried out systematically?
Y	N/A	N	8.	Is heavily influenced by a comparison of present performance and future potential?
Y	N/A	N	9.	Is influenced by identification of high-level replacement needs?
Y	N/A	N	10.	Has sensitized each executive to an obligation to identify and prepare successors?
Y	N/A	N	11.	Has prompted the organization to establish and conduct specific developmental programs that are designed to accelerate the development of high-potential employees?
Y	N/A	N	12.	Is guided by a philosophy that high-potential employees should be developed while working rather than by being developed primarily through off-the-job experiences?

Y   N/A   N   13. Has prompted the organization to focus developmental programs on increasing the familiarity of high-potential employees with who does what, when they do it, where they do it, why they do it, and how they do it?

Y   N/A   N   14. Has prompted the organization to focus developmental programs on the critical questioning of "the way things have always been done"?

Y   N/A   N   15. Emphasizes the qualities or competencies necessary to surpass movement to the next higher-level job?

Y   N/A   N   16. Has prompted your organization to examine, and perhaps use, formal mentoring?

Y   N/A   N   17. Is conducted in a systematic way?

Y   N/A   N   18. Encourages the cross-divisional sharing of people and information?

Y   N/A   N   19. Is reinforced by a leadership that actively rewards managers for promoting (rather than holding on to) their best employees?

Y   N/A   N   20. Is supported by career paths that move not just up a specialized ladder but across a continuum of professional competence?

Y   N/A   N   21. Is supported by frequent opportunities for employees to accept new challenges?

Y   N/A   N   22. Is driven, in part, by recognition that employees have a stake in the organization and share its successes?

Y   N/A   N   23. Has prompted an explicit policy favoring promotion from within?

Total _____

Scoring and Interpreting the Assessment Questionnaire

Give your organization *1 point for each Y* and a *0 for each N or N/A* listed above. Total the points from the Y column and place the sum in the line opposite to the word *TOTAL* above. Then interpret your score in the following way:

(continues)

Exhibit 3-2. (continued)

Score

Above 20 points	Succession planning and management appears to be handled in an exemplary manner in your organization.
18–20 points	The SP&M efforts of your organization could stand improvement. However, SP&M is being handled effectively, for the most part.
14–17 points	Succession planning and management is a problem in your organization. It deserves more attention.
Below 14 points	Your organization is handling SP&M in a crisis mode. It is very likely that successors for critically important positions have not been identified and are not systematically developed. Immediate corrective action is desirable.

properly assumes an important leadership role for the program and does not try to delegate it prematurely to Human Resources or to other groups.

As I tell my clients, the CEO is the real customer for most SP&M efforts—and my view is supported by the opinions of members of many boards of directors. When the SP&M effort begins with the CEO, he or she understands what is involved in establishing a state-of-the-art SP&M program and is able to tailor it to suit his or her vision and strategy. Furthermore, he or she sets the example and sends a powerful message of personal commitment and support that is needed to make subsequent generations of such an effort successful.

It is worth noting that HR plays an important role. But it is essential to emphasize that HR does not "own" this effort. The "owner" is the CEO, and it is a position that (on this topic) he or she cannot delegate. HR leaders can certainly help: They can coordinate the effort, once leadership by the CEO has been exercised. They can provide advice and counsel about what to do, why it should be done, and how it should be done. But the CEO must lead the effort and be personally committed to it. Lacking the CEO's personal support, commitment, and participation, SP&M efforts will fail.

The second generation is a simple replacement plan for the CEO and his or her immediate reports—that is, the senior leaders of the organization, the senior executive team. By extending the SP&M effort to the management tier below CEO and by identifying the successors of that group, senior managers are involved firsthand in designing and implementing a succession effort. Since they are the targets of that effort, they understand it, have a chance to refine it, and develop ownership in it. By actively participating in the effort, they gain a thorough understanding of it so that they can communicate to others in the third generation.

A key advantage of using the senior executive team as guinea pigs, so to speak, is that they are usually already well developed in their positions and are highly knowledgeable about what it takes to succeed in the business, industry,

Exhibit 3-3. A Simple Exercise to Dramatize the Need for Succession Planning and Management

For a dramatic and compelling exercise to emphasize the need for an SP&M program, ask your CEO or the managers in your organization what the following people share in common:

△ Donald Terner, President, Bridge Housing Corp., San Francisco, Calif.

△ Robert E. Donovan, President and Chief Executive Officer, Abb Inc., Norwalk, Conn.

△ Claudio Elia, Chairman and Chief Executive Officer, Air & Water Technologies Corp., Somerville, N.J.

△ Stuart Tholan, President, Bechtel-Europe/Africa/Middle East/Southwest Asia, San Francisco, Calif.

△ John A. Scoville, Chairman, Harza Engineering Co., Chicago, Ill.

△ Leonard Pieroni, Chairman and Chief Executive Officer, Parsons Corp., Pasadena, Calif.

△ Barry L. Conrad, Chairman and Chief Executive Officer, Barrington Group, Miami, Fla.

△ Paul Cushman III, Chairman and Chief Executive Officer, Riggs International Banking Corp., Washington, D.C.

△ Walter Murphy, Senior Vice President, AT&T Submarine Systems Inc., Morristown, N.J.

△ Robert A. Whittaker, Chairman and Chief Executive Officer, Foster Wheeler Energy International, Clifton, N.J.

△ Frank Maier, President, Ensearch International Ltd., Dallas, Tex.

△ David Ford, President and Chief Executive Officer, Interguard Corp. of Guardian International, Auburn Hills, Mich.

Answer: These were the people on board the plane with Commerce Secretary Ron Brown when it crashed in 1996. Don't you wonder if they had replacements ready in their organizations?

Used with permission from *Nursing Management,* 25:6 (June 1994), pp. 50–56, © Springhouse Corporation (www.Springnet .com).

and corporate culture. By participating in the development of the SP&M effort, they ensure that it fits the corporate culture and aligns with organizational strategy. What is more, they set an example and, by doing that, send a powerful message to others in the organization that the SP&M effort is important and worthy of action, interest, and participation.

The third generation is an SP&M program for middle managers, who are usually the direct reports of the senior executive team, and perhaps (if the organization's leaders support it) for others on the organization chart as well. It is at this point that the model of SP&M, described later in this chapter (see Exhibit 3-5), is first widely used. Policies and procedures for SP&M are drafted if they were not already prepared formally in earlier generations; competency models by department or hierarchical level are first developed if they were not already prepared formally in earlier generations; value statements are crafted; and other key components of a modern SP&M program are designed, developed, and refined. By extending to this third tier and by identifying the successors of that group, middle managers are involved firsthand in designing and implementing an effort. Since they are the targets of the succession effort, they come to understand it and develop ownership in it. They also help refine it for their level and for those below them on the organization chart. The third generation is the most risky, since more people are involved and many new policies, procedures, and practices are first established, tested, and implemented.

The fourth generation moves beyond simple replacement plans to focus on the development of internal talent pools. Internal talent pools are groups of people inside the organization who are being developed for the future. Everyone is considered a possible successor for key positions and given such tools as career maps to help them prepare themselves for the future. In this generation, succession issues are divorced from the organization chart. Instead of targeting specific individuals to be successors, the organization's decision-makers use the many tools put in place in the third generation. It is possible in this generation to use competency models, performance appraisals, individual development plans, full-circle multirater assessments, and other sophisticated methods to help all workers develop to realize their potential.

The fifth generation focuses on the development of external as well as internal talent pools. External talent pools are groups of people outside the organization who are possible sources of talent for the future. Instead of waiting until key positions come open to source talent, the organization's decision-makers include in their talent pools temporary and contingent workers, retired workers, outsourcing agents, vendors, consultants, and even (perhaps) members of their organization's supply and distribution channels. In short, decision-makers look around the organization's external environment to see what talent exists outside as well as inside their organizations that could be tapped. In that way, they lead the target and slash the time needed to fill critical positions.

The fifth generation of SP&M is the most sophisticated. It is not easy—and usually not even possible—for an organization to make a single leap from no SP&M effort to a fifth-generation approach. Too much infrastructure and management support, not to mention the learning that occurs in generations one through four, are needed to make it work. The risks of failure are far too high. A better approach is to think in terms of a gradual phase-in, moving to a generation that meets the needs of the organization. (Not all organizations need a fifth-generation approach.) That phase-in can occur fastest in organizations that are small, face a stable market, and possess low turnover in the management ranks. That phase-in occurs more slowly in organizations that are larger, face dynamic or fiercely competitive markets, and possess high turnover in the management (or high potential) ranks.

Another way to think about generations of succession planning programs is, of course, possible. Indeed, the Dow Chemical Company Case (described in Exhibit 3-4) presents such an alternative view of the life cycle of succession planning and management programs.

Identifying and Solving Problems with Various Approaches

The cases appearing in the Appendix summarize several exemplary approaches to SP&M in organizations of varying sizes and industry categories. However, not all organizations handle SP&M as effectively or efficiently. Indeed, two experts speaking at an American Management Association Human Resources Conference indicated that succession planning is being woefully "ignored by a majority of American companies."[7]

Many problems bedevil current approaches to SP&M. Exhibit 3-5 summarizes the chief difficulties in using succession planning that were described by the respondents to my 2004 survey on succession planning practices. Additionally, I review seven common problems affecting SP&M programs below.

Problem 1: Lack of Support

"One of the major drawbacks HR managers face in establishing a company succession plan is the lack of support from top company executives."[8] Indeed, "the attitude of too many corporation executives is 'why bother?' "[9] If top managers lack a sense of urgency, no SP&M program can be effective.

If top managers are unwilling to support a systematic approach to succession planning, it cannot succeed. If that is the case, the best strategy is to try to win over one or more credible idea champions. Especially promising for those roles are well-respected top managers who have recently—and, if possible, personally—experienced the work-related problems that stem from having no successor prepared to assume a critically important position when a vacancy occurs.

Problem 2: Corporate Politics

A second problem with succession planning is that it can be affected by corporate politics. Instead of promoting employees with the most potential or the best track record, top managers—or, indeed, any level of management employee—may "use the corporate ladder to promote friends and allies, while punishing enemies, regardless of talent or qualifications."[10] If allowed to operate unchecked, corporate politics can supplant performance and potential as an advancement criterion.

(text continues on page 72)

Exhibit 3-4. The Dow Chemical Company's Formula for Succession

Ben & Jerry's, in its challenge to Haagen-Dazs in the great American ice cream wars, actually considered the issue of the succession of a chief executive through an essay contest dubbed "Yo, I wanna be your CEO." Cooler heads prevailed, and Ben & Jerry's is now headed by an experienced executive.

Nevertheless, today's business headlines are too full of corporate embarrassments in the form of chief executives staying on too long and stifling potential successors or rivals, divided boards which are often out of touch with shareholders' interests, internal power struggles which lead to a mass exodus of talent when a new chief executive is finally selected, and damage to the company as an all-too-public search erodes confidence and impedes the smooth running of the business.

Helping to select the right successor is the ultimate obligation of a chief executive. While this is done in concert with the board of directors, the responsibility for the quality of candidates and the attractiveness of the job rests with current management. Among the key tasks addressed by boards, succession is often the most neglected. This is because the issue arises relatively infrequently.

Succession strategy in most companies must make six transitions:

1. *From an Annual Event to a Continuous Process.* Companies need to create an environment of continuous succession "thinking" rather than annual succession "planning." There should be more frequent senior-management meetings, more time devoted to follow-up at regular staff meetings, more emphasis on succession issues in business planning and greater incorporation of succession issues into performance evaluation and management. For example, managers should be developing at least one person as their potential replacement.

2. *From a Short-Term Replacement Strategy to a Long-Term Development and Retention Strategy.* A balance must be struck between the need for immediate replacements and the need for a steady supply of ready talent. Employees will obviously appreciate the attention paid to their development and continuous improvement.

3. *From an Emphasis on Whom a Company Has to an Emphasis on What a Firm Needs.* Companies must create an atmosphere in which external talent can be hired to fill critical skill gaps, independent of job openings. Dow mainly promotes from within, but, says Popoff, "the benefit and vigor that accrue to us in matching an outside hire with a clear internal need is not lost on employees, managers or shareholders."

4. *From Position Blockage to Appropriate Turnover in Key Positions.* Companies must promote and reward capable managers of people, rather than emphasizing technical over managerial skills. If all of a company's managers are good at managing

people, they can routinely assess the potential of incumbents in key positions, develop appropriate action plans, avoid positions becoming blocked and generate appropriate turnover.

5. *From Insufficient Bench Strength to a Pool of Ready Talent.* Dow has created a Genesis award to recognize people development. In a company with many highly competent technical and professional people, the award program provides insight on who is actually practicing good people management. The Genesis award is Dow's most-sought-after award. Winners of the award are introduced at the annual shareholders' meeting.

6. *From Subjective Evaluation to an Emphasis on Results.* Dow has established specific measurements to evaluate succession results. The measurements include: the percentage of key jobs which have at least two ready successors; the percentage of key posts filled externally; the percentage of developmental action plans implemented; and the extent to which the process contributes positively to business results.

At Dow, all management directors must relinquish their management positions at the age of 60, or five years after their last significant promotion, whichever is later. But they remain on the board of directors until they reach the age of 65. During their final five years on the board, they have no line-management responsibilities and their pay is stepped down annually to their retirement salary at age 65.

Says Popoff: "These former members of management are some of the best, toughest, most knowledgeable, best intentioned and hardest working directors I have come to know." After years of service with the company, people such as the former chief executive, the director of research and head of international operations know where the bodies are buried. They are familiar with all the facts and myths of the company. Along with the outside directors and the chairman, they play a key role in ensuring an appropriate selection from the talent pool for all key executive posts.

Board members who are former Dow managers have a special ability to test the internal heirs apparent and work with them to ensure a smooth transition, or to look outside objectively if the internal pool of talent is lacking.

Succession planning plays a key role in the company's ability to pursue its long-term strategies and achieve lasting results. Clearly, good management does not happen by itself, and succession planning is critical to its continuation. The good news is that most firms now give succession planning a lot of attention. The bad news is that too many companies still fail to get it right.

Time was when companies had different people dealing with career and succession planning. But succession planning is increasingly being viewed in broader and integrated terms, not least because firms are now less predictable and it is therefore relatively pointless to identify specific successors for specific jobs for the future. Con-

(continues)

Exhibit 3-4. (*continued*)

tinual restructuring and reallocation of executive responsibilities to meet changing priorities are now the normal practice. Within this context, companies need to pay attention to the strategic process of succession management. The Dow Chemical Company model would appear to have many virtues.

Note: This is a précis of an article entitled "Reflections on succession," which was originally published in Arthur D. Little's *Prism*, third quarter, 1996, pp. 109–116. The article is based on a presentation that Frank Popoff made to the Chief Executives' Club of Boston.

Source: "The Dow Chemical Company's Formula for Succession," *Human Resource Management International Digest* 5:1 (1997), 9–10. Used with permission of *Human Resource Management International Digest*.

Exhibit 3-5. Chief Difficulties with Succession Planning and Management Programs

Question: What are the chief difficulties that your organization has experienced with a succession planning program? *Please describe them briefly below.*

△ Identifying the high potentials

△ Preparing individual development plans

△ Making succession plans a real workable process that people (managers) actually use when making decisions, not just a file that is put on a shelf

△ Pushing succession down in the organization

△ Senior management positions filled usually by political appointment

△ The quality of the candidate is not good enough

△ Getting succession management to flow downward from the executive level to middle management

△ Monitoring and evaluating successors

Source: William J. Rothwell, *Results of a 2004 Survey on Succession Planning and Management Practices.* Unpublished survey results (University Park, Penn.: The Pennsylvania State University, 2004).

To solve this problem, decision-makers must insist on formal ways to identify work requirements and assess performance and potential rather than permit subjective judgments to prevail. (Methods of conducting formal assessments will be described in later chapters of this book.) Informal judgments are notoriously prone to numerous problems. Among them are recency bias (performance or potential is assessed with a heavier-than-desirable emphasis on recent and singular successes or failures); pigeonholing or stereotyping (supervisors develop impressions of individuals that are difficult to change); the halo or horn effect (supervisors are overly influenced in their judgments of individuals by singular events); the Pygmalion effect (supervisors see what they expect to see); and discrimination (treating people differently solely as a function of sex, race, age, or other factors unrelated to job performance). Left unchecked, informal judgments may also lead supervisors to pick successors like themselves (the "like me" bias).

Problem 3: Quick-Fix Attitudes

A third problem with the traditional approach to succession planning is that it can encourage quick-fix attitudes. Effectiveness is sacrificed to expediency. That can have far-ranging consequences because ill-chosen leaders can prompt higher-than-normal turnover among their followers, create employee morale problems, and even bankrupt an otherwise sound business. Leadership does matter, and leaders cannot be cultivated quickly or easily.[11] Excellent leaders can only be cultivated over time.

Problem 4: Low Visibility

Top-level executives do not always see the fast, direct benefits of SP&M. The further they are removed from daily operations—and numerous direct reports—the less valuable SP&M can seem to be to them. HR managers will propose and install various SP&M efforts, but they will often be replaced when top-level executives see no immediate benefits stemming from them.[12]

To solve this problem, succession must be made a high-visibility issue. Further, it must enjoy the active support—and direct participation—of workers at all levels. Without showing active support and participating directly, top managers will have no ownership stake in succession efforts.

Problem 5: The Rapid Pace of Organizational Change

Traditional replacement planning once worked well enough in stable environments and organizations. In those settings, vacancies could be predicted, candidates could be trained for targeted jobs, and a homogeneous workforce led to easy transitions and assured continuity.

But the rapid pace of organizational change has raised serious questions about the value of the traditional, fill-in-the-box-on-the-organization-chart approach to replacement-oriented succession planning. Indeed, one management consultant has asked, "Is succession planning worth the effort?"[13] And he arrived at this conclusion: "The simple answer is no. Predicting succession (over, say, a three-to-five-year time frame) in an era of constant change is fast becoming an impossibility."[14]

To solve this problem, decision-makers need to look beyond a simple technological solution, such as the use of succession planning software for personal computers designed to accelerate the organization's ability to keep pace with staffing needs and changes. That can help, but more dramatic solutions are also needed. Possible examples are to focus on work requirements, competencies, and success factors so as to maximize the value of developmental activities; use full-circle, multirater assessments; increase the use of job rotations to prompt management employees to become more flexible; use action learning and real-time education to equip management employees with the flexibility they need to cope with rapid change; establish team-based management so that key work requirements develop, and are spread across, different individuals; and move beyond a focus on "filling boxes on an organization chart" to "meeting work requirements through innovative means."[15]

Problem 6: Too Much Paperwork

Top managers in most organizations have a low tolerance for paperwork. A colleague of mine jokes that "top managers in my organization won't respond to a one-page survey or read beyond the first page of a memo." One reason for this is that top managers are often overburdened with paperwork, since they receive it from so many quarters. Technology, which was once seen as a blessed solution to information overload, now appears to be a major cause of it—as stressed-out managers cope with burgeoning messages by electronic mail, cell phones, faxes, and other sources.

Hence, one problem with the traditional approach to succession planning is that it may require substantial paperwork to:

▲ Assess present work requirements or competencies.

▲ Appraise current individual performance.

▲ Assess future work requirements or competencies.

▲ Assess individual potential for advancement.

▲ Prepare replacement charts.

▲ Identify future career paths or career maps.

▲ Identify key positions requiring replacements.

▲ Establish individual development plans (IDPs) to help individuals narrow the gap between their present work requirements/performance and future work requirements/potential.

▲ Follow up on IDPs.

While full-time specialists or part-time HR generalists can provide assistance in recordkeeping, they can seldom supply the details for every person, position, and requirement in the organization. Perhaps the best approach is to minimize the amount of paperwork, but that is difficult to do. Whenever possible, however, succession planning coordinators, management development professionals, or human resource professionals should supply information that is readily available from sources other than the immediate organizational superiors of employees participating in succession planning efforts. That way, the superiors can focus their attention on identifying the talent to implement business strategy, identifying critical positions and high-potential talent, and formulating and following through on developmental planning.

Problem 7: Too Many Meetings

Just as the traditional approach to succession planning can create resistance owing to the massive paperwork it can generate, so too can it lead to resistance because it can require numerous and time-consuming meetings. For instance, to carry out SP&M, management employees may need to participate in the following:

▲ *Kickoff Meetings*. If an annual SP&M procedure is in place, management employees may be required to attend kickoff meetings, conducted by the CEO, that are intended to reinforce the importance of the effort.

▲ *Organizational, Divisional, Functional, or Other Meetings*. These meetings may focus on SP&M for each job category, organizational level, function, or location.

▲ *Work Requirements Meetings*. If the organization makes it a policy to base succession on identifiable work requirements, competencies, success factors, or other "objective criteria," then management employees will usually be involved in meetings to identify these criteria.

▲ *Employee Performance Appraisal Meetings*. In most organizations, management employees appraise the performance of their immediate subordinates as a part of the SP&M program.

▲ *Career Path Meetings*. If the organization attempts to identify predictable, desirable, or historical relationships between jobs, then management employees may be asked to participate in that effort by attending meetings or training.

▲ *Career Planning Meetings*. If the organization makes an effort to discover individual career goals and interests as a means to do a "reality check" on possible successors, then management employees may have to take time to meet with each employee covered in the succession plan.

▲ *Potential Assessment Meetings*. Assessing individual potential is future-oriented and may require meetings different from those required for performance appraisal.

▲ *Development Meetings*. Planning for individual development, as a means of narrowing the gap between what individuals know or do presently and what they must know or do to qualify for advancement, may require time-consuming individual meetings.

▲ *Training, Education, and Developmental Meetings*. As one means by which succession plans may be realized, meetings centered on training, education, and development may demand considerable time.

While meetings can be consolidated to save some time, each meeting listed above serves an important purpose. Attending meetings can require a significant time commitment from employees at all levels.

Integrating Whole Systems Transformational Change and Appreciative Inquiry into Succession: What Are These Topics, and What Added Value Do They Bring?

Since the publication of the second edition of this book, much excitement has been centered on two (relatively new) developments in change management. One is called *whole systems transformational change* (WSTC), the other is called *appreciative inquiry*. Both can have a bearing on SP&M programs and are therefore deserving of attention.

What Is Whole Systems Transformational Change, and How Can It Have a Bearing on SP&M?

Whole systems transformational change (WSTC) is "an adaptable and custom-tailored wisdom-creating learning experience that often results in a paradigm shift."[16] It usually involves bringing together the key decision-makers of an organization for an intense event, usually lasting several days but planned for in advance. It is an approach that involves everyone and leads to change at the speed needed in modern business. Think of a problem-solving session that may involve hundreds or even thousands of people, all focused on solving the same or related problems, and you have the idea.

How can WSTC have a bearing on SP&M? The answer is that, quite often, the installation of an SP&M program requires many people to be involved. Additionally, the human resources system may be missing many key elements to support an intervention as robust as the introduction of an SP&M intervention. For example, there may be no competency models, no 360-degree capability, no individual learning plans, and no technology to support the SP&M program. Creating these takes time and can lead to a loss of faith in the SP&M program from executives or others. Worst yet, executives and other senior leaders in the organization may not share the same goals or vision for the SP&M program. Under normal circumstances, there are no easy ways to solve these problems. But a WSTC brings the key stakeholders together, facilitating a process whereby they "thrash out" the key decisions, build key support systems, and communicate among themselves to achieve some comparability in goals.

The WSTC is, in short, a possible tool—though it is also a philosophy—for bringing about the rapid but large-scale change needed to support a SP&M intervention.

What Is Appreciative Inquiry, and How Can It Have a Bearing on SP&M?

Is a glass half empty, or is it half full? That simple question actually has profound implications. It speaks to the difference between a problem-centered orientation to the world and a strength-leveraging orientation. Most managers are problem-oriented. They do not believe in fixing what is not broken. Hence, they tend to focus on the negative—what is wrong, what the problems are, and (with people) what their deficiencies or gaps are. But the problem with always focusing on the negative is that it shuts people down and depresses or demotivates them.

Appreciative inquiry (AI), however, requires a paradigm shift. It takes its name quite literally from asking about (that is, inquiring) what is going well (that is, appreciation).

Hence, the phrase *appreciative inquiry* literally means "asking questions about things worth appreciating." Appreciative inquiry thus focuses on what is going right, what the strengths are, and (with people) what their unique talents or abilities are.[17]

How can this idea be applied to SP&M? There are many answers to that simple question, and the space here is insufficient to treat them all. Suffice it to say that, instead of focusing on what deficiencies or gaps people possess, AI indicates that a better approach is to identify individuals' strengths and talents, and then capitalize or build on those strengths. One goal is to energize people with positive feelings about what they can achieve, what they do well, and what is good about them. Another goal is to encourage people to discover and capitalize on their strengths and talents.

While there are many potential applications of AI to SP&M, I will point to just one. In conducting a 360-degree assessment, an organization will typically collect scores on individuals and then schedule a session to discuss in what competencies that individual is deficient. A goal is to pinpoint developmental gaps and then discuss ways to fill them by using developmental experiences, such as training or coaching.

But when AI is used, the tenor of the feedback session for 360-degree assessment shifts from what is wrong with the person to what is uniquely right about the person. Attention is devoted to discussing what others perceive to be that person's unique strengths, talents, and abilities. The individual is encouraged to mentor others in areas where he or she is strong. The individual is also encouraged to think about how he or she could better leverage the strengths that he or she possesses. The difference in results can be profound. Instead of walking out of the room depressed, an individual may walk out energized and excited.

AI has many potential applications to SP&M.[18] We have only scratched the surface. But it is worth thinking about how AI may mean new, fresh, and positive approaches to developing people. Think about that as you read the rest of this book.

Requirements for a Fifth-Generation Approach

Minimum requirements for a fifth-generation approach to SP&M include the following:

▲ A Policy and Procedure Statement, in Writing, to Govern SP&M

▲ A Statement of Values Governing the Effort (which may be included in the policy and procedure statement)

▲ Competency Models for the Groups Targeted

▲ Full-Circle, Multirater Assessment Efforts (or other ways to assess individual potential)

▲ Individual Development Plans

▲ Skill Inventories for Talent Pools Inside and Outside the Organization

Of course, it goes without saying that senior management involvement and support are essential requirements—as are, particularly, the personal commitment and participation of the CEO.

Key Steps in a Fifth-Generation Approach

How should systematic SP&M be carried out in organizational settings? While the answer to this question may vary by national culture, organizational culture, and top management values, one way is to follow a "seven-pointed star model for systematic succession planning and management." That model is illustrated in Exhibit 3-6. The steps in the model, summarized below, provide the foundation for this book—and the foundation for many best-practice SP&M programs in many organizations.

Step 1: Make the Commitment

As a first step, the organization's decision-makers should commit to systematic SP&M and establish an SP&M program. To some extent, this represents a "leap of faith" in the value of planned over unplanned approaches to SP&M. In this step the organization's decision-makers should:

▲ Assess current problems and practices.

▲ Assess and demonstrate the need for the program.

▲ Determine the organization's exact SP&M program requirements.

▲ Link the SP&M program directly to organizational and human resource strategic plans.

▲ Benchmark SP&M practices in other organizations.

▲ Clarify the roles of different groups in the program.

▲ Formulate a program mission statement.

Exhibit 3-6. The Seven-Pointed Star Model for Systematic Succession Planning and Management

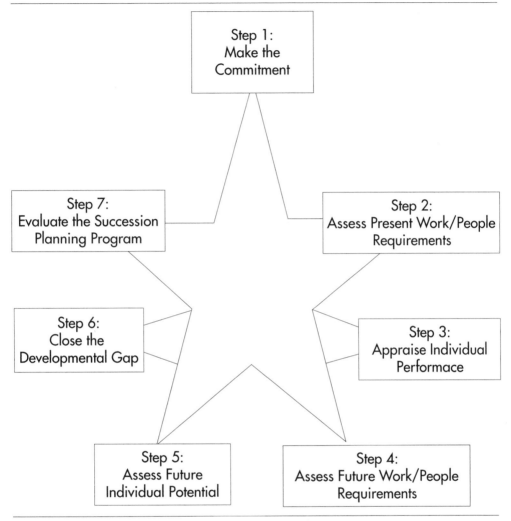

▲ Write a policy and procedures to guide the program.

▲ Identify target groups to be served by the program.

▲ Establish program priorities.

▲ Prepare an action plan to guide the program.

▲ Communicate the action plan.

▲ Conduct SP&M meetings as necessary to unveil the program and review progress continually.

▲ Train those involved in the program as necessary.

▲ Counsel managers about SP&M problems in their areas of responsibility.

Step 2: Assess Present Work/People Requirements

As a second step, decision-makers should assess the present work require-ments in key positions. Only in that way can individuals be prepared for ad-vancement in a way that is solidly grounded on work requirements. In this step, decision-makers should clarify where key leadership positions exist in the organization and should apply one or more approaches to determining work or competency requirements.

Step 3: Appraise Individual Performance

How well are individuals presently performing their jobs? The answer to this question is critical because most SP&M programs assume that individuals must be performing well in their present jobs in order to qualify for advancement. As part of this step, the organization should also begin establishing an inven-tory of talent so that it is clear what human assets are already available.

Step 4: Assess Future Work/People Requirements

What will be the work or competency requirements in key leadership positions in the future? To answer this question, decision-makers should make an effort to assess future work requirements and competencies. In that way, future lead-ers may be prepared to cope with changing requirements and organizational strategic objectives.

Step 5: Assess Future Individual Potential

How well are individuals prepared for advancement? What talents do they pos-sess, and how well do those talents match up to future work requirements? To answer these questions, the organization should establish a process to assess future individual potential. That future-oriented process should not be con-fused with past- or present-oriented employee performance appraisal.

Step 6: Close the Developmental Gap

How can the organization meet SP&M needs by developing people internally or using other means to meet succession needs? To answer this question, the organization should establish a continuing program for leadership develop-ment to cultivate future leaders internally. Decision-makers should also ex-plore alternatives to traditional promotion-from-within methods of meeting succession needs.

Step 7: Evaluate the Succession Planning Program

To improve, the SP&M program must be subjected to continual evaluation to assess how well it is working. That is the seventh and final step of the model. The results of evaluation should, in turn, be used to make continuous program improvements and to maintain a commitment to systematic SP&M.

Summary

This chapter listed the characteristics that are found in exemplary succession planning and management programs. It then summarized typical problems afflicting succession planning and management programs, and suggested possible solutions to them. It also presented a seven-pointed star model for systematic succession planning and management.

COMPETENCY IDENTIFICATION AND VALUES CLARIFICATION: KEYS TO SUCCESSION PLANNING AND MANAGEMENT

Competency identification and values clarification are increasingly important foundations for an effective succession planning and management (SP&M) program. But what are competencies? How are competencies used in SP&M? How are competencies identified and used to guide SP&M efforts? What are values, and what is values clarification? How are values used in SP&M? How are values clarification studies conducted and used for SP&M? This chapter answers these questions.

What Are Competencies?

The word *competence* was first linked to a human trait in 1959.[1] Using that work as a starting point, David McClelland focused attention on competencies in 1973.[2] McClelland noticed that standardized intelligence tests were not good predictors of job success, and he wondered why. Competencies as understood today stemmed from his initial questioning about why standardized intelligence tests did not predict job success. Other authors and researchers, of course, contributed to the development of competency identification, modeling, and assessment as known and practiced today.[3]

Although the term *job competency* has different meanings, it can be understood to mean "an underlying characteristic of an employee (i.e., motive, trait, skill, aspects of one's self-image, social role, or a body of knowledge) that results in effective and/or superior performance in a job."[4] *Competency identification* is the process of discovering job competencies.[5] A *competency model* is the result of competency identification.[6] *Competency assessment* is the process of comparing an individual to an existing competency model,[7] and that can be done by many means—including full-circle, multirater assessment.

Organizations have made extensive use of competency models in recent years, which have been widely accepted.[8] One reason is that competency models can help to clarify differences between outstanding (exemplary) and average performers—an increasingly important issue in a fiercely competitive global business environment. A second reason is that competency models are superior to work-based approaches, which rely on descriptions of work activities only, in pinpointing what people need to be successful. Increasingly, knowledge is only part of what is needed to be a successful performer. Also needed are appropriate attitudes and motivation, which are not well examined in traditional job descriptions or traditional performance appraisals.

How Are Competencies Used in Succession Planning and Management?

Competency models are essential building blocks on which to base an SP&M effort. Without them, it is difficult to:

▲ Link and align the organization's core competencies (strategic strengths) to job competencies.

▲ Define high-potentials or other broad categories of employees.

▲ Clarify exactly what present and future competencies are essential to success in the organization and in its various departments, jobs, or occupations.

▲ Provide a basis for performance management by creating a work environment that encourages high performance among all workers.

▲ Establish clear work expectations for the present and future.

▲ Create full-circle, multirater assessments that are tailor-made to the unique requirements of one corporate culture.

▲ Devise competency menus that describe how individuals might be developed for the future.

▲ Formulate individual development plans (IDPs) to help individuals narrow the developmental gap between what competencies they need to be successful (as described by the competency model) and what competencies they presently possess (as identified by a full-circle, multirater assessment or other approaches to examining current performance or future potential).

Conducting Competency Identification Studies

Competency studies may have different goals. The goals must be clear before the resulting studies will be useful. Those who set out to conduct competency studies should be clear what they are trying to do, why they are doing it, and what their stakeholders (such as the CEO) are seeking. Elaborate studies do little good if nobody knows what they are for, nobody really wanted them, or nobody knows how to use them.

A *present competency study*, to define the term, focuses on one department, job category, or occupational group. In conducting a competency study of this kind, it is usually important to create two distinct groups—exemplary performers and average performers—for the department or other unit studied. The goal is usually to discover the difference between the highest performers in the group and the average performers in that same group. When completed, the present competency study clarifies what are the essential competencies for success at present.

A *future competency study* also focuses on one department, job category, or occupational group. But in conducting a competency study of this kind, it is usually important to start by describing the organization's strategic goals and objectives. What results will the organization seek in the future? Why will those results be sought? What competencies are necessary to realize those results? A different approach is needed from that in a present competency study. Often, there may be nobody in the organization who is an exemplary performer when compared to future requirements. It may thus be necessary to do scenario planning to discover the competencies needed in a future business environment. That also requires a level of sophistication that few internal practitioners possess—or have time to use if they do.

A *derailment competency study*, to define the term, focuses on the characteristics linked to failure—or to falling off the fast track—for those in one department, job category, or occupational group. In conducting a derailment study, it is usually important to identify individuals who have failed assignments, dropped off the high-potential list, experienced career plateauing, or otherwise become ineligible for a list of successors or high potentials. The goal is to determine why people who were once considered high potentials fell off the track or reached a career plateau. Once that is known, of course, strategies can be formulated to help them develop and surmount their failures—and help others avoid similar problems. Causes of derailment might include, among others, problems with morals (such as sexual indiscretions) or problems with health-related issues (such as alcoholism or drug-related ailments).

Different approaches to competency identification have been devised.[8] While space is not available here to review each approach to competency identification, those who are serious about SP&M will search out information about available approaches. They will select an approach that is compatible with the organization's corporate culture, since introducing competency modeling to an organization that has not used it before is really a change effort in its own right.

Competency modeling offers a newer way to identify characteristics linked to exemplary job performance than traditional job analysis. An advantage of competency modeling is its rigor. Another is its ability to capture the (otherwise ineffable) characteristics of successful job performers and job performance. It can provide valuable information on key positions and high-potential employees on which to base SP&M practices.

Unfortunately, competency modeling does have disadvantages. One is that the term's meaning can be confusing. Another, more serious, disadvantage is that rigorous approaches to competency modeling usually require considerable time, money, and expertise to carry out successfully. Rarely can they be done internally except by the largest organizations. These can be genuine drawbacks when the pressure is on to take action—and achieve results—quickly.

Using Competency Models

Competency models have emerged as a foundation for state-of-the-art SP&M programs. Lacking them, organizations will rarely be able to proceed beyond a simple replacement approach to SP&M. They provide a blueprint for building competence needed at present or in the future, and they provide a norm or criterion against which to measure individual development requirements. They are especially important when an organization commits to developing talent pools, since they provide a standard against which all individuals may be assessed.

New Developments in Competency Identification, Modeling, and Assessment

What's new in competency identification, modeling, and assessment? One new development is that competency modeling seems to have caught on. Businesses in the United States are estimated to be spending about $100 million per year in identifying competency models for their organizations.[9] And yet much work remains to be done. Not all competency modeling efforts are effective. One reason is that HR professionals and operating managers alike are not properly trained in, or do not understand, what competency models are for and how they relate to organizational requirements.

Another new development is that differences in thinking, and philosophical views, about competency modeling are becoming more pronounced. A key question to consider is, "What does the competency model focus on?" It is, of course, possible to study *derailers*—that is, what leads to failure. It is also possible (and many organizations do this) to focus on what is required to qualify for each level of the corporate hierarchy. But perhaps most important, it is possible to focus on what measurable productivity differences may exist between the most productive performers in a job category and those who are fully trained but are not the most productive (called *fully successful performers*). The real value added is in discovering what differences exist between exemplary and fully successful performers and then integrating hiring, succession planning and management, and career-development efforts to create more exemplary performers in the organization.[10] The goal is to leverage up the competitive advantage of the organization by gaining the productivity advantages yielded by more high performers, pound for pound, than other organizations in the same industry may have. Another issue is what to focus on. Should the goal be to meet deficiencies or to leverage individual strengths?

A third new development is that many technology packages are now available to support competency identification and modeling efforts. They often come packaged as part of larger HR information systems (HRISs) or human capital management (HCM) suites and should be sought using those keywords. They may also appear in learning management systems (LMSs).

Unfortunately, some practitioners think that the competency software will do their thinking for them, which is (of course) not the case. Effective competency identification, assessment, and modeling are hard work.[11] Technology is no shortcut—and sometimes has the tendency to cause a short circuit—to effective practice.

Identifying and Using Generic and Culture-Specific Competency Development Strategies to Build Bench Strength

How is it possible to "build" competencies? The answer is to use competency development strategies. *Competency development strategies* are methods by which individuals can improve their competencies. Competency development strategies close gaps between what should be (as described in a competency model) and what is (as measured by approaches such as 360-degree assessments and assessment centers). Examples of competency development strategies may include the following:

- ▲ Attending a Classroom Training Course
- ▲ Participating in Online Training
- ▲ Reading a Book
- ▲ Reading an Article
- ▲ Listening to an Audiotape
- ▲ Watching a Videotape

These are just examples, and many other approaches are possible. Of course, to be successful, the developmental strategy must be focused on the competency. Hence, if the competency to be developed is "budgeting skill," then the developmental strategy should be focused on that topic.

Competency development strategies may be divided into two categories: (1) generic and (2) corporate culture-specific. A *generic competency development strategy* is necessarily general. To build budgeting skill, then, any book on the topic will do. Any training program on budgeting will do. No effort is made to tie the development strategy to the unique conditions prevailing in the corporate culture.

A *corporate culture-specific development strategy*, on the other hand, is specific to the organization. To build budgeting skill, an individual might do the following:

▲ Watch (shadow) someone in the organization who is especially good at budgeting.

▲ Perform budgeting with someone in the company.

▲ Interview someone experienced in the company about what is necessary for an acceptable or even exemplary budget.

Many resources exist to identify generic development strategies.[12] Those can be purchased from outside vendors, found in books, or uncovered on the Web. All that is needed is to identify appropriate but general material linked to every competency in a competency model. Corporate culture-specific development strategies require investigation. One way to identify them is to identify exemplary performers—individuals who are particularly good at demonstrating a competency. Then interview them. For example, ask them:

▲ Who in this organization would you advise people to talk to if they want to build this competency?

▲ What kind of work activities or assignments should individuals be given if they are to build this competency in this organization?

▲ Where should people go to find centers of excellence for this competency in this organization?

▲ How would you advise someone in this company who wants to build this competency to go about learning how it is done here?

Use the interview guide provided in Exhibit 4-1 for this purpose. Then feed back the interview results to exemplary performers, verify that the assignments would actually build the targeted competencies in the company, and put them online so that individuals may access them as they prepare their individual development plans.

What Are Values, and What Is Values Clarification?

Simply stated, *values* are beliefs about what is good or bad. *Values clarification* is the process of making clear what values take priority over others, what is more important than other things. While competencies clarify differences between individual performers, values add an ethical dimension. They de-

Exhibit 4-1. An Interview Guide to Collect Corporate-Culture-Specific Competency Development Strategies

Directions: Use this interview guide to collect information about how to build competencies in the context of your organization's unique corporate culture. Select several exemplary performers who have been identified as especially good (exemplary) at demonstrating a given competency. Indicate that competency next to the label "competency" below. Then spend about 15 minutes to interview each exemplary performer using the questions appearing below. When you are finished, analyze the results by identifying common themes or patterns across all the interview results.

Competency:

Name _____   Title _____

Years of Experience in Job _____   Date _____

Interviewed by: _____

1. Think of a time when you were asked to demonstrate this competency.

    What was the situation?

    When did this situation occur?

    What did you do?

    How do you believe the experience helped you demonstrate this competency?

    If your mentee participated in an experience like this, would it help to build the competency?

2. Who are some people in the organization who are exceptionally good at demonstrating this competency to whom you could refer your mentee?

3. What are some work experiences in the organization that you believe your mentee should be given to build or demonstrate the competency?

4. How might the pressure to produce by specific deadlines help to build or demonstrate the competency?

5. Where would you send people—that is, what geographical locations—to build and /or demonstrate this competency? (Where are the centers of excellence for this competency in the organization, and why do you think so?)

6. List special and specific work assignments that would be particularly useful in building or demonstrating this competency.

7. If someone asked you for advice on how to build this competency in this organization, what advice would you give them?

8. Could you think of some upcoming or pending company projects that might be especially useful to build this competency? What would they be, and why do you think they could help to build the competency?

---

scribe ethical expectations for those who live and work in one corporate culture.

Values have commanded increasing interest in organizational settings. Consider the following: At a recent annual meeting of Eli Lilly and Company, Chairman and CEO Randall Tobias extended the meeting by over two hours to discuss the core values of the company and their importance to the future of the organization.[13] Similarly, in a recent interview in *Organizational Dynamics,* Herb Kelleher, Chairman and CEO of Southwest Airlines, discussed the central role that values play in that organization.[14] *Fortune* magazine reported that over 50 percent of U.S. corporations have a values statement—more than double that of a decade ago.[15]

How Are Values Used in Succession Planning and Management?

Values statements and values clarification, like competency models, are essential building blocks on which to base a succession planning and management effort. Without them, it is difficult to add an ethical dimension to the development of people in various departments, job categories, or occupations. Much like competency models, they help to do the following:

▲ Link and align the organization's core values to group and individual values.

▲ Define high potentials or other broad categories of employees.

▲ Clarify exactly what present and future values are essential to success in the organization and in its various departments, jobs, or occupations.

▲ Provide a basis for performance management by creating a work environment that encourages value-based performance.

▲ Establish the values underlying work expectations for the present and future.

▲ Create full-circle, multirater assessments that are tailor-made to the unique requirements of one corporate culture.

▲ Provide another basis to formulate individual development plans (IDPs) to help individuals develop themselves to meet present and future challenges.

Conducting Values Clarification Studies

Many tools and techniques are available to help organizations clarify their values. Some organizations undertake values clarification through small group activities.[16] Others use unique approaches, such as teaching championship automobile racing.[17] At least two other approaches may be used. One is simple; the other is more complicated—but may be more meaningful.

A Simple Approach: Top Management Values Clarification

A simple way to clarify the values of the organization is to ask top managers what values are most important. To use this approach, provide a brief introduction to what values are, why they are important, and how they are used. Then ask senior executives—either in a meeting or online—to describe what they believe to be the most important values for the organization at present and in the future. When that list has been gathered from individuals, feed it back to them, allow them to discuss the list, and ask them to vote on the most important. When they finish this activity, ask them to define each value and state its importance to the organization and to individuals.

A More Complicated Approach: Values Clarification from Top Performers

A more complicated approach to carrying out values clarification is to ask top performers or high potentials in the organization to describe their values. That can be done through *behavioral event interviewing*—a rigorous method used in competency modeling in which individuals are asked to describe the most difficult ethical situation they have ever faced in their jobs and describe what they were thinking, feeling, and doing at each step as they faced that situation. The values statements should appear as part of their discussion. (If they do not, then the interviewer should be sure to ask probing questions to elicit comments about the values in which the high potentials believe.) The values identified by individual high potentials can then be summarized. What is important is not what one person says but rather what similar thematic patterns surface from many respondents.

Once the values have been identified, they can be fed back to high potentials in focus groups for further discussion and refinement. When that process is completed, the value statements can be given to top managers for approval or modification. In this way, the values clarified for the organization match the work-related beliefs of the best performers and are validated by top managers.

Using Values Clarification

Values clarification provides an additional, and increasingly important, dimension to SP&M. Without it, individuals may be equipped with sound competencies but may lack the ethical dimension that is so important to leadership in the future. Values can also be integrated with competency models so that it is possible to create a success profile or description of leadership requirements essential at all organizational levels, departments, job categories, or occupations in the future. Alternatively, it is possible to prepare values lists and assessment instruments against which to compare individuals.[18] In other words, it is possible to use values as a driving force for building high potentials and competence in organizations. Like competencies, then, values can be the glue that holds together all key aspects of a SP&M program.

Bringing It All Together: Competencies and Values

Organizations today need both competencies and values. It is just not enough to make people good performers. They must be ethical as well and possess a moral dimension that is consistent with the image the organization wishes to purvey. Lacking values, high potentials cannot be successful in the long term and cannot bring credit to the organization.

Summary

As this chapter emphasized, competencies and values are increasingly important foundations for an effective succession planning and management program. The chapter defined competencies and explained how they are used in succession planning and management, then defined values and explained how values can be used in succession planning and management. A major point of the chapter was that, without competencies and values, creating a state-of-the-art succession planning and management program will be difficult because they provide the blueprints for the talent to be created.

The next chapter describes how to lay the foundation for a succession planning and management program by taking subsequent steps in planning and implementing a program that will be successful in one organizational setting or corporate culture.

PART II

LAYING THE FOUNDATION FOR A SUCCESSION PLANNING AND MANAGEMENT PROGRAM

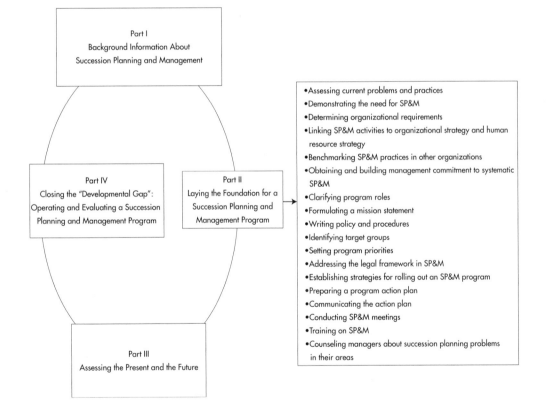

Part I
Background Information About
Succession Planning and Management

Part IV
Closing the "Developmental Gap":
Operating and Evaluating a Succession
Planning and Management Program

Part II
Laying the Foundation for a
Succession Planning and
Management Program

Part III
Assessing the Present and the Future

- Assessing current problems and practices
- Demonstrating the need for SP&M
- Determining organizational requirements
- Linking SP&M activities to organizational strategy and human resource strategy
- Benchmarking SP&M practices in other organizations
- Obtaining and building management commitment to systematic SP&M
- Clarifying program roles
- Formulating a mission statement
- Writing policy and procedures
- Identifying target groups
- Setting program priorities
- Addressing the legal framework in SP&M
- Establishing strategies for rolling out an SP&M program
- Preparing a program action plan
- Communicating the action plan
- Conducting SP&M meetings
- Training on SP&M
- Counseling managers about succession planning problems in their areas

MAKING THE CASE FOR MAJOR CHANGE

For many years, introducing and consolidating change has been a centerpiece of debate among managers and writers about management. Many believe that the essence of management's job is to be instruments for progressive change—or, at least, to create an environment suitable for change.

Establishing a systematic succession planning and management (SP&M) program in an organization that never had one is a major change effort. It requires a quantum leap from the status quo, what some call a "transformational change." Success depends on demonstrating, at the outset, a need for change. The only exception is the rare case in which decision-makers have already reached a consensus to depart radically from past practice.

To make the case for change in SP&M it will usually be necessary to:

▲ Assess current problems and practices.

▲ Demonstrate the need.

▲ Determine organizational requirements.

▲ Link SP&M to the strategic plan and human resource plan.

▲ Benchmark SP&M processes in other organizations.

▲ Obtain and build management commitment to systematic SP&M.

These issues are the focus of this chapter. They may seem to be monumental issues—and sometimes they are—but addressing them is essential to lay a solid foundation on which to build a systematic SP&M program.

Assessing Current Problems and Practices

Information about current problems and practices is needed before it is possible to build a convincing case for change. Planning for the future requires information about the past and present.

Assessing Current Problems

Crisis is a common impetus for change. As problems arise and are noticed, people naturally search for solutions. As the magnitude and severity of the problems increase, the search for a solution intensifies.

The same principles apply to SP&M. If the organization has experienced no crises in finding qualified successors, retaining talented people, maintaining leadership continuity, or facilitating individual advancement, then few decision-makers will feel an urgent need to direct attention to these issues. On the other hand, SP&M is likely to attract increasing attention when problems like these surface:

▲ Key positions are filled only after long delays.

▲ Key positions can be filled only by hiring from outside.

▲ Key positions have few people "ready now" to assume them (that is called *weak bench strength*).

▲ Vacancies in key positions cannot be filled with confidence.

▲ Key positions are subject to frequent or unexpected turnover.

▲ Replacements for key positions are frequently unsuccessful in performing their new duties.

▲ High performers or high-potential employees are leaving the organization in droves.

▲ Individuals routinely leave the organization to advance professionally or to achieve their career goals.

▲ Decision-makers complain about weak bench strength.

▲ Employees complain that decisions about whom to advance are not based on who is best qualified but rather on caprice, nepotism, and personal favoritism.

▲ Employees and decision-makers complain that decisions about whom to promote into key positions are adversely affected by discrimination or by expediency.

To build a case for a systematic approach to SP&M, ask decision-makers if they face the problems listed above. Additionally, focus attention on identifying the most important problems the organization is facing and review how those problems are influenced by existing SP&M practices. If possible, document actual succession problems that have been experienced in the past—including "horror stories" (anecdotes about major problem situations) or "war stories" (anecdotes about negative experiences), if possible. Although anecdotes do not necessarily provide an accurate indication of existing conditions, they can be powerfully persuasive and can help convince skeptical decision-makers that a problem warrants investigation. Use them to focus attention on the organization's present SP&M practices—and, when appropriate, the need to change them from informal to systematic. Also, consider using approaches to identify and overcome objections to a SP&M program. (See Exhibit 5-1.)

In my 2004 survey, I asked the respondents to indicate whether SP&M had become more important to their organizations over the last few years. Their answers are revealing, indicating that many current problems have emerged that necessitate increased attention to SP&M. (See Exhibit 5-2.)

Exhibit 5-1. Strategies for Handling Resistance to Implementing Succession Planning and Management

Possible Cause of Resistance	Possible Strategies for Handling the Cause
Managers or employees resist a SP&M program because they believe it will:	
Mean that they have to give up something (such as a say in who is promoted).	△ Consider establishing a council to advise on matters related to the program. △ Emphasize that organizational superiors of all individuals can and will be involved in making decisions.
Require work for no reason (they see no need for it).	△ Start by describing how and why other organizations have used succession planning. △ Show reasons for the program that go beyond mere replacement planning and include individual development.
Do more harm than good.	△ Try to find out why managers and employees feel this way and ask for their advice about how to prevent abuses of the program.
Be managed by people who are not trustworthy or managed in a way that is not ethical.	△ Hire an external consultant to establish the framework for the program and isolate the nature of the possible concerns.
Require too much time, effort, or resources.	△ Explain what information is required to make SP&M useful and then seek the advice of those who resist the program on this basis by asking for their suggestions about the best ways to get that information. △ Double-check to determine whether you are recommending that the program be installed too quickly rather than gradually implemented.

Exhibit 5-2. The Importance of Succession Planning and Management

Question: Has succession planning become *more important* to your organization over the last few years? If yes, briefly tell why; if no, briefly tell why.

All respondents answered yes, and provided the following reasons:

△ Leadership is the key to a healthy business in a "down" business environment.

△ It has been added to the President's Management Agenda.

△ Board of directors requirements. It is now a corporate governance issue. Investors look for it.

△ Because up to $^1/_3$ of our employees will be eligible to retire within the next few years.

△ The marketplace has changed and succession planning allows us to continue to grow.

△ Turnover among execs participating in succession plans due to minimal executive openings.

△ A large number of organizational employees are ready for retirement in five years.

Source: William J. Rothwell, *Results of a 2004 Survey on Succession Planning and Management Practices.* Unpublished survey results (University Park, Penn.: The Pennsylvania State University, 2004).

Assessing Current Practices

In large organizations using an informal approach to SP&M, nobody is aware of the methods being used within the organization. Nor should they be. After all, in those settings SP&M is handled idiosyncratically—or not at all—by each manager. As a consequence, nobody is aware of the organization's existing practices.

A good place to start, then, is to find out what practices are currently being used in the organization. Exemplary, albeit isolated, approaches may already be in use, and they may serve as excellent starting points on which to begin a systematic approach. They enjoy the advantage of a track record because they have already been tried out in the organization and probably have one or more managers who support them.

To emphasize this point, I am aware of one Fortune 500 corporation that uses an informal approach: Managers establish their own SP&M approaches as they feel they are warranted, and those activities vary dramatically. Most managers make no effort to conduct SP&M. As vacancies occur, replacements are frantically sought. Filling key positions is a crisis-oriented activity. (That is often true in organizations without systematic SP&M programs, as my 2004 survey revealed; see Exhibit 5-3.)

But even in this organization, one major operating division has established

Exhibit 5-3. Making Decisions About Successors (in Organizations Without Systematic Succession Planning and Management)

Question: How are decisions made about successors for positions in your organization? *Circle all appropriate response codes below.*

	Percentage Response
We usually wait until positions are vacant and then scurry around madly to find successors.	21%
We "secretly" prepare successors.	32%
Whenever a position opens up, we rely on expediency to identify someone to fill it, hoping for the best.	37%
Other Methods	11%
Total	100%

Source: William J. Rothwell, *Results of a 2004 Survey on Succession Planning and Management Practices.* Unpublished survey results (University Park, Penn.: The Pennsylvania State University, 2004).

a practice of circulating a confidential memo each year to department managers to request their nominations for their own replacements. No attempt is made to verify that the candidates possess the requisite knowledge and skills suitable for advancement; no attempt is made to verify that the candidates are willing to accept new assignments; and no attempt is made to ensure their availability, if needed, or to prepare them for advancement. However, the practice of circulating a memo is an excellent place to start a systematic approach to SP&M. It can be a focal point to direct attention to the issue—and to the need to adopt a systematic approach.

Use three approaches to assess the current status of SP&M in the organization: (1) talk to others informally; (2) send out an electronic mail question; or (3) conduct a written survey.

Talk to Others Informally

Ask key decision-makers how they are handling SP&M practices. Begin by talking to the chairman or chief executive officer, if possible, because that person is likely to be more aware of the processes than others. Then discuss the matter with other top managers. Pose questions such as the following:

▲ How is the organization presently handling SP&M? What is being done at the highest levels? At the lower levels? In different divisions? In different locales?

▲ In your opinion, what *should* the organization be doing about SP&M—and why do you believe so?

▲ What predictable losses of key personnel are anticipated in your area of responsibility? For example, how many pending retirements are you aware of? Will pending promotions lead to a domino effect in which a vacancy in one key position, filled by promotion from within, will set off a chain reaction that leads to a series of vacancies in many other positions?

▲ What people or positions are absolutely critical to the continued successful operation of your division, function, department, or location? How would you handle the sudden and unexpected loss of a key person? Several key people?

▲ Have you experienced the loss of a key person in the last year or two? How did you handle it? If you had to do it again, would you handle it the same way? If so, why? If not, why not?

▲ What regular efforts, if any, do you make to identify possible replacements for key people or positions in your part of the organization? (For example, do you discuss this issue as part of management performance appraisals, during business planning activities, or in other ways?)

▲ What efforts, if any, do you make to identify individuals with the potential to advance beyond their current positions?

▲ How do you prepare individuals to advance when you perceive they have potential? What systematic efforts are made to train, educate, or develop them for future positions?

▲ What strongly held beliefs do you have about SP&M? For instance, do you believe the organization should inform possible successors of their status (and thereby risk creating a crown prince problem) or conceal that information (and risk losing high-potential employees who are tapped for better advancement prospects elsewhere, perhaps by other organizations or even by competitors)? How do you believe the organization should handle plateaued workers, who will advance no further, and blocked workers, who are unable to advance beyond their current positions because they are blocked by plateaued workers above them?

When you finish interviewing decision-makers, prepare a summary of the results about SP&M practices in the organization. Cite individual names only if given explicit permission to do so. Include a summary of current information on effective SP&M practices obtained externally—from sources such as this book—and then ask if more attention can be devoted to the topic. The reactions you receive should provide valuable clues to how much interest and support exists among key decision-makers to explore a systematic approach to SP&M.

Send Out an Electronic Mail Question

A top manager in a large corporation focused attention on systematic SP&M merely by sending out an e-mail message to his peers. He posed this question: "Assume that you lost a key department manager on short notice through death or disability. (You can choose any department you wish.) Who is "ready" to assume that position? Name anyone."

That question provoked a flurry of responses. By merely posing this question, he served an important role as a change champion—and drew attention to weak bench strength in the organization's supervisory ranks. Try the same approach in your organization—or find just one top manager who will pose a similar question to colleagues by e-mail. That will certainly draw attention to the issue. It may also open debate or create an impetus for change.

Conduct a Written Survey

A written survey may be used as an alternative to informal discussions. Unlike informal discussions, however, a written survey is a high-profile effort. Many people will probably see it. For that reason, be sure to follow the organization's protocol for authorizing a written survey. That may mean discussing it, prior to distribution, with the CEO, the vice president of human resources, or others they suggest. Ask for their approval to conduct the survey—and solicit their input for questions of interest to them. In some organizations they may also wish to attach their own cover letters to the survey, which is desirable because it demonstrates their awareness and support—and may even increase the response rate.

Use the survey appearing in Exhibit 5-4 as a starting point, if you wish. It may save you time in developing your own survey, tailor-made to your organization's needs.

Once the survey has been completed, feed the results back to the decision-makers. In that way they can read for themselves what their peers have to say about the organization's current approach to SP&M. That can help them focus on specific problems to be solved and on achieving a consensus for action among themselves. However, conducting surveys is not without risk. They may, for instance, bring to the surface influential opposition to a systematic SP&M program. That will make it more difficult to make the case for that approach in the future.

Demonstrating the Need

Few decision-makers are willing to invest time, money, or effort in any activity from which they believe few benefits will be derived. It is thus essential to tie SP&M issues directly to pressing organizational problems and to the organization's core mission. But exactly how is that done?

(text continues on page 104)

Exhibit 5-4. A Questionnaire for Assessing the Status of Succession Planning and Management in an Organization

Cover Memo

To: Top Managers of _____ Corporation

From: _____

Subject: Survey on Succession Planning and Management Practices

Date: _____

Succession planning and management may be understood as *"any effort designed to ensure the continued effective performance of an organization, division, department, or work group by making provision for the development, replacement, and strategic application of key people over time."* It may be *systematic* or *informal*. In systematic SP&M, an organization's managers attempt to prepare successors for key positions; in informal succession planning, no effort is made to prepare successors—and, as vacancies occur in key positions, managers respond to the crises at that time.

Please take a few minutes to respond to the questions appearing below. When you are finished, return the completed survey to *(name)* by *(date)* at *(location)*. Should you have questions, feel free to call me at *(phone number)*.

Thank you for your cooperation!

The Survey

Directions: Please take a few minutes to write down your responses to each question appearing below. This questionnaire is intended to be anonymous, though you are free to sign your name if you wish. You will receive a confidential report that summarizes the key responses of all respondents and recommends action steps.

1. In your opinion, how well is this organization presently conducting SP&M? (*Circle your response in the left column*)

Very Well   *Briefly explain why you feel as you do:*
Adequately
Inadequately
Very Poorly

2. Should this organization establish/improve its approaches to SP&M?

   Yes   *Briefly explain why you feel as you do:*

   No

3. In your area of responsibility, have you established:
   (*Circle your response in the center column below*)

		Response		
Question		*Yes*	*No*	*Your Comments*
A.	A systematic means to identify possible replacement needs stemming from retirement or other predictable losses of people?	Yes	No	
B.	A systematic approach to performance appraisal so as to clarify each individual's *current performance*?	Yes	No	
C.	A systematic approach to identifying individuals who have the potential to advance one or more levels beyond their current positions?	Yes	No	
D.	A systematic approach by which to accelerate the development of individuals who have the potential to advance one or more levels beyond their current positions?	Yes	No	
E.	A means by which to keep track of possible replacements by key position?	Yes	No	

4. What special issues, if any, do you believe that a systematic SP&M program designed and introduced in this organization should be careful to address?

(continues)

Exhibit 5-4. *(continued)*

5. What other comments do you have to make about a systematic SP&M program?

    Please return the completed survey to *(name)* by *(date)* at *(location)*. Should you have questions, feel free to call me at *(phone number)*. You will receive a summary of the anonymous survey results by *(date)*.

Thank You for Your Cooperation!

The answer to that question may vary across organizations. Each organization is unique; each organization has its own culture, history, and leadership group. But there are several possible ways by which to demonstrate the need for a systematic SP&M program. They are described below.

Hitchhiking on Crises

The first way to demonstrate need is to hitchhike on crises. As key positions become vacant or key people depart unexpectedly, seize that opportunity to poll decision-makers informally. Begin by summarizing the recent crisis. Contrast what happened with what could have happened if a systematic approach to SP&M had been used. Describe the impact of poorly planned SP&M on customers and employees, if possible. Then describe possible future conditions—especially future staffing needs that may result from recent downsizing, early retirement offers, or employee buyouts. Ask decision-makers whether they believe it is time to explore a systematic approach to meeting succession needs. Then be ready to offer a concrete proposal for the next steps to take.

Seizing Opportunities

A second way to demonstrate need is to seize opportunities. In one organization, for example, the human resources department studied top managers' ages and projected retirement dates. The results were astonishing: all the top managers were due to retire within five years and no replacements had been identified or developed. In that case, the HR department detected a brewing crisis and helped avert it. The organization subsequently established a systematic SP&M program that enjoyed strong support—and great success.

Any major strategic change will normally create opportunities. For instance, as electrical utilities are deregulated, decision-makers realize that the future success (and even survival) of these organizations often depends on identifying and developing new leaders who can thrive in a highly competitive, market-driven environment. That raises questions about the developmental needs of successors who had been nurtured during a period of regulation. It also prompts developmental activities to increase the market-oriented skills of future leaders.

Use the worksheet appearing in Exhibit 5-5 to focus attention on ways to hitchhike on crises and to seize opportunities.

Showing the Bottom-Line Value

A third way to demonstrate the need for a systematic SP&M program might be called *showing the bottom-line value*. However, making that case for SP&M can be tough to do. As Jac Fitz-enz writes:

> One of the difficulties in trying to measure the work of planners is that their output is primarily a plan of the future. By definition, we will not know for 1, 3 or perhaps 5 years how accurate their predictions were. In addition no one is capable of predicting future events, and therefore it is not fair to blame the planner for unforeseeable events. It is impossible to measure the value of a long-term plan in the short term. Planners thus often feel frustrated because they cannot prove their worth with concrete evidence.[1]

Those involved in succession planning and management may feel that they face exactly the same frustrations to which Fitz-enz alludes. However, he has suggested ways to measure each of the following:

▲ Workload (How many positions need to be filled?)

▲ Speed of Filling Positions (How long does it take to fill positions?)

▲ Results (How many positions were filled over a given time span?)

Succession planning and management may thus be measured by the number of key positions to be filled, the length of time required to fill them, and the number of key positions filled over a given time span. Of course, these measures are not directly tied to such bottom-line results for an organization as return on equity, return on investment, or cost-benefit analysis. But they are good places to start.

As Fitz-enz rightly points out, the central questions to consider when quantifying program results are these[2]:

Exhibit 5-5. A Worksheet for Demonstrating the Need for Succession Planning and Management

Directions: How can the need for a systematic SP&M program be demonstrated in an organization? Use the questions below to help you organize your thinking. Answer each question in the space appearing below it. Then compare your responses to those of others in the organization. Add paper if necessary.

1. What *crises*, if any, have occurred in placing high-potential individuals or filling key positions in recent years? Describe the situations and how the organization coped with them. Then describe what happened (the outcomes of those strategies).

   Make a list of the crises, if any, and briefly describe:

2. What *opportunities*, if any, have you noticed that may affect the knowledge, skills, and abilities that will be needed by workers in the organization in the future? (In particular, list strategic changes and then draw conclusions about their implications for knowledge, skills, and abilities.)

Make a list of strategic changes:	*Describe how those strategic changes are likely to affect the knowledge, skills, and abilities needed by workers in the organization in the future:*

▲ What variables are really important to the organization?
▲ What results can be influenced by action?

Meaningful, quantifiable results can be obtained only by focusing attention directly on answering these questions. Decision-makers must be asked what they believe to be the most important variables and actions that can be taken by the organization. This information, then, becomes the basis for establishing the financial benefits of an SP&M program.

When measuring SP&M results, decision-makers may choose to focus on such issues as these:

▲ How long does it take to fill key positions? (Measure the average elapsed days per position vacancy.)

▲ What percentage of key positions are actually filled from within? (Divide the number of key positions filled from within by the total number of key positions.)

▲ What percentage of key positions are capable of being filled from within? (Divide the number of high-potential workers available by the number of expected key position vacancies annually.)

▲ What is the percentage of successful replacements out of all replacements? (Divide the number of retained replacements in key positions by all replacements made to key positions.)

Of course, issues of importance to top managers, and appropriate measures of bottom-line results, will vary across organizations. The point is that these issues must be identified before appropriate criteria and bottom-line measures can be assigned. Indeed, the best ways to measure SP&M results come from the goals and objectives established for the SP&M program.

Another way to view the bottom-line measure of a SP&M program is to compare the expenses of operating the program to the benefits accruing from it. That may be difficult, but it is not impossible to do. As a first step, identify direct and indirect program expenses. Direct expenses result solely from operating an SP&M program. An example might be the salary of a full- or part-time SP&M coordinator. Indirect expenses result only partially from program operations. They may include partial salary expenses for managers involved in developing future leaders or the cost of materials to develop high potentials.

As a second step, identify direct and indirect program benefits. (This can be tricky, but the key to success is involving decision-makers so that they accept and have ownership in the program benefits that are claimed.) Direct benefits are quantifiable and financially oriented. They might include savings in the fees of search firms. Indirect benefits might include the goodwill of having immediate successors prepared to step in, temporarily or permanently, whenever vacancies occur in key positions.

As a third step, compare the costs and benefits. Will the organization gain financially if a systematic approach to SP&M is adopted? In what ways? How can the relative effectiveness of the program be related directly to the organization's pressing business issues and core mission?

For additional information on cost-benefit analysis, review the numerous approaches that have been suggested for evaluating the bottom-line value of training programs.[3] Use those approaches to clarify costs and benefits of a systematic SP&M program.

Of course, other ways—apart from hitchhiking on crises, seizing opportunities, and showing the cost-benefit ratio for program operations—might be used to demonstrate the need for a systematic approach to SP&M. Consider: How has the need been successfully demonstrated for other new programs in the organization? Can similar approaches be used to demonstrate a need for a systematic SP&M program?

Determining Organizational Requirements

All organizations do not share identical requirements for SP&M programs. Differences exist owing to the organization's industry, size, stage of maturity, management values, internally available expertise, cost, time, and other considerations. Past surveys confirm that these issues—and others—can affect the appropriate design of SP&M programs.[4]

However, top management goals are always key considerations. What do top managers believe to be essential for a SP&M program? The most important questions on which to focus attention might include the following:

▲ How eager are top managers and other decision-makers to systematize the organization's SP&M process(es)?

▲ How much time and attention are decision-makers willing to devote to assessing key position requirements? Identifying leadership competencies? Identifying success factors for advancement in the organization? Conducting multirater assessments? Appraising individual performance? Preparing and implementing individual development plans (IDPs) to ensure the efficient preparation of individuals for advancement into key positions?

▲ How stable is the current organizational structure? Work processes? Can either—or both—be reliably used to plan for leadership continuity or replacements?

▲ How willing are decision-makers to devote resources to cultivating talent from within?

▲ How much do decision-makers prefer to fill key position vacancies from inside rather than from outside the organization?

▲ How willing are decision-makers to use innovative alternatives to simple replacements from within?

Begin determining the essential requirements of an SP&M program by interviewing top managers. Pose the questions appearing above. Add others as pertinent to the organization. (As a starting point, use the interview guide appearing in Exhibit 5-6 for this purpose.) Then prepare and circulate a written proposal for an SP&M program that conforms to the consensus opinion of key decision-makers.

Linking Succession Planning and Management Activities to Organizational and Human Resource Strategy

Succession planning and management should be linked to organizational and human resource strategy. However, achieving those linkages can be difficult.

Exhibit 5-6. An Interview Guide for Determining the Requirements for a Succession Planning and Management Program

Directions: Use this interview guide to help you formulate the requirements for a systematic SP&M program for an organization. Arrange to meet with top managers in your organization. Pose the questions appearing in the left column below. Record notes in the right column below. Then use the results of the interview as the basis for preparing a proposal for a systematic SP&M program for the organization. (You may add questions to the left column, if you wish.)

Questions	*Notes on Responses*
1. What are your thoughts about approaching succession planning and management in this organization *in a planned way?*	
2. How should we define *key positions* in this organization?	
3. How should we clarify the requirements to qualify for key positions? (Some people call these competencies—characteristics of successful performers.)	
4. How should we assess current individual job performance?	
5. How stable do you believe the current organizational structure to be? Will it be adequate to use as the basis for identifying key positions requiring successors in the future?	

(continues)

Exhibit 5-6. (continued)

Questions	Notes on Responses
6. How do we determine the qualifications or requirements (competencies) for each key position in the future?	
7. How do you feel that we can identify individuals who have the potential to meet the qualifications for key positions in the future?	
8. What do you believe are the essential resources that must be provided by the organization in order to accelerate the development of high-potential employees?	
9. How should we keep track of high-potential employees?	
10. What other thoughts do you have about the essential requirements for an effective succession planning and management program in this organization? Why do you believe they are essential?	

Linking Organizational Strategy and Succession Planning and Management

Organizational strategy refers to the way in which a business chooses to compete. Important steps in the process include: (1) determining the organization's purpose, goals, and objectives; (2) scanning the external environment to identify future threats and opportunities; (3) appraising the organization's present strengths and weaknesses; (4) examining the range of strategies; (5) choosing a strategy that is likely to seize maximum advantage from future opportunities by building on organizational strengths; (6) implementing strategy, particularly through changes in structure, policy, leadership, and rewards; and (7) evaluating strategy periodically to assess how well it is helping the organization to achieve its strategic goals and objectives.

Achieving effective linkage between organizational strategy and SP&M is difficult for three major reasons. First, while effective strategy implementation depends on having the right people in the right places at the right times, it is not always clear who the right people are, where the right places are, and when those people will be needed. Second, strategy is frequently expressed in a way that does not lend itself easily to developing action plans for SP&M. For instance, decision-makers may focus attention on "increasing market share" or "increasing return-on-investment"—without describing what kind of leadership will be needed to achieve those ambitious goals. Third, organizational strategy as practiced may differ from organizational strategy as theorized,[5] which complicates the process of matching leadership to strategy. That can happen when the daily decisions do not match written organizational strategy.

To overcome these problems, decision-makers must take active steps to build consideration of SP&M issues into the formulation of strategic plans. During the review of organizational strengths and weaknesses, for instance, decision-makers should consider the organization's leadership talent. What kind of expertise is presently available? During strategic choice and implementation, decision-makers should also consider whether the organization has the right talent to "make it happen." Who possesses the knowledge and skills that will contribute most effectively to making the strategy a reality? How can individuals be developed to help them acquire that knowledge and those skills? How can the organization establish an action plan to manage its human assets as effectively as its financial assets? Only by answering these questions—and taking active steps to narrow the gap between available and necessary talent—can the organization link its strategy and its succession planning and management.

Linking Human Resource Strategy and Succession Planning and Management

Human resource strategy is the means that the organization chooses to make the most effective use of its HR programs and activities to satisfy organizational needs. Important steps in this process parallel those in organizational strategy making: (1) determining the purpose, goals, and objectives of the HR function; (2) scanning the external environment to identify future threats and opportunities affecting HR inside and outside the organization; (3) appraising the organization's present HR strengths and weaknesses; (4) examining the range of HR strategies available; (5) choosing an HR strategy that is likely to support the organizational strategy; (6) implementing HR strategy through changes in such programs as training, selection, compensation, benefits, and labor relations; and (7) evaluating HR strategy periodically for how well it supports organizational strategy.

Unfortunately, efforts to integrate HR strategy and organizational strategy have met with only mixed success. As Golden and Ramanujam write, "the lack of integration between human resource management (HRM) and strategic business planning (SBP) processes is increasingly acknowledged as a major source of implementation failures. It is often alleged that companies develop strategic plans based on extensive marketing and financial data but neglect the human resource requirements necessary to successfully implement them."[6] Numerous theories have been developed over the years to identify ways to link organizational and HR strategy.[7] However, little evidence exists to show that great strides have been made in this area.[8]

To link HR planning and SP&M, decision-makers should examine how well HR policies and practices help—or hinder—leadership continuity, individual advancement, and the cultivation of internal talent. More specifically:

▲ How does the organization conduct recruitment, selection, and placement? How much consideration is given during this process to long-term retention and development of prospective or new employees?

▲ How does the organization conduct training, education, and development? How much (relative) attention is given to the long-term cultivation of employee talent—as opposed to focusing attention on training individuals to meet immediate requirements?

▲ How well do existing compensation and benefit practices support internal placement? Transfers? Promotions? Are actual disincentives established to dissuade employees from wanting to accept promotions or assume leadership roles?

▲ How do existing labor relations agreements affect the organization's promotion, rotation, transfer, and other employment practices?

To integrate HR strategy and SP&M, examine existing HR program efforts—such as selection, training, compensation, and benefits—against succession planning and management needs. Identify HR practices that could encourage or that presently discourage effective SP&M. Then take active steps to ensure that HR practices facilitate, and do not impede, long-term efforts to groom talent from within.

Benchmarking Best Practices and Common Business Practices in Other Organizations

Discussions with top managers and other key decision-makers in an organization should yield valuable information about the needs that an SP&M program should meet. But that information can be supplemented by benchmarking SP&M practices in other organizations. Moreover, the results of benchmarking may intensify the interests of key decision-makers in SP&M because they may demonstrate that other organizations are using better, or more effective, methods. As Robert C. Camp explains, "Only the approach of establishing operating targets and productivity programs based on industry best practices leads to superior performance. That process, being used increasingly in U.S. business, is known as benchmarking."[9]

Benchmarking has also surfaced in recent years as a powerful tool for improving organizational work processes and is frequently associated with Total Quality Management (TQM). Its primary value is to provide fresh perspectives, and points for comparison, from other organizations. It can thereby accelerate the process of introducing a state-of-the-art program by comparing existing practices in one organization to the best practices already in use elsewhere.

Although there are various means by which to conduct benchmarking, Camp suggests that it should be carried out in the following way[10]:

1. Identify what is to be benchmarked.
2. Identify comparative companies.
3. Determine a data collection method and collect data.
4. Determine the current performance "gap."
5. Project future performance levels.
6. Communicate benchmark findings and gain acceptance.
7. Establish functional goals (based on the results of the benchmarking study).
8. Develop action plans (based on the results of the benchmarking study).
9. Implement specific actions and monitor progress.
10. Recalibrate benchmarks.

Typically, then, benchmarking begins when decision-makers make a commitment. They clarify their objectives and draft questions to which they seek answers. Comparable organizations, often but not always in the same industry, are chosen. A suitable data collection method is selected, and written questionnaires and interview guides are frequently used for data collection. Site visits (field trips) are arranged to one or more organizations identified as being "best-in-class."

Benchmarking should not be pursued as a "fishing expedition"; rather, it should be guided by specific objectives and questions. Participants should start out with some familiarity with the process, such as succession planning and management practices. (That may mean that they have to be briefed before participating in a site visit.) Several key decision-makers should go on the site visits so they can compare practices in other organizations with their own. That is an excellent way, too, to win over skeptics and demonstrate that "the way we have always done it here" may not be the best approach.

Most Fortune 500 companies are well known for their effective succession planning and management practices. Blue-chip firms such as Motorola, Xerox, IBM, AT&T, General Electric, Coca-Cola, and General Motors—among others—are recognized for conducting effective succession planning and management. They may rightly be considered "best-in-class" companies. Appropriate contacts at these organizations should be located through such professional societies as the Human Resource Planning Society (P.O. Box 2553, Grand Central Station, New York, NY 10163), the American Management Association (1601 Broadway, New York, NY 10019), the American Society for Training and Development (1640 King Street, Alexandria, VA 22313), or the Society for Human Resource Management (606 N. Washington Street, Alexandria, VA 22314).

Always develop questions before making a site visit. (See the list of possible benchmarking questions in Exhibit 5-7.) Then contact representatives from two or three of those organizations and ask if benchmarking visits to their locations are possible. If so, send them the questions in advance of the visit so that they have time to prepare their responses. Sometimes they may wish to see the questions in advance before they commit to a visit.

It may be difficult to arrange benchmarking visits on SP&M. Many organizations consider the process sensitive to their operations—and revealing of their corporate strategies. Consequently, one approach is to seek access to organizations where you or others in your company have personal contacts. If necessary, begin with local organizations that have successfully established SP&M programs. Identify them by talking to your peers in local chapters of the American Society for Training and Development (ASTD), the Society for Human Resource Management (SHRM), or other professional societies.

Obtaining and Building Management Commitment

Securing management commitment to systematic SP&M may not occur rapidly. Skeptics are difficult to convince in short order. It will take time and proof of tangible evidence of success to win them over.

Opinions About Succession Planning and Management

My 2004 survey of SP&M practices revealed sharp disparities in opinions about systematic SP&M programs. Examine Exhibit 5-8. Then consider how you

(text continues on page 118)

Exhibit 5-7. An Interview Guide for Benchmarking Succession Planning and Management Practices

Directions: Use this interview guide to help you prepare questions in advance of a benchmarking visit to another organization. Share these questions before your visit to an organization known for its effective SP&M practices. (Add questions as appropriate for your organization.) Pose the questions appearing in the left column below. Then record notes in the right column. Use the results in formulating a proposal for improving SP&M practices in your organization.

Questions	*Notes on Responses*
1. What mission statement has been established for succession planning and management in your organization?	
2. What goals and objectives have been established for succession planning and management in your organization?	
3. What policy and philosophy statement has been written to guide succession planning and management in your organization? *(Would it be possible to obtain a copy?)*	
4. How does your organization define *key positions?* What positions, if any, are given special attention in your succession planning program? Why are they given that attention?	

(continues)

Exhibit 5-7. (*continued*)

5. How does your organization identify, describe, or clarify the requirements of key positions? (*For example, has your organization made an effort to identify job responsibilities, competencies, or success factors by level?*)

6. How does your organization assess *current job performance* for succession planning and management purposes? (*Do you use the organization's existing performance appraisal system—or something else?*)

7. Does your organization use replacement charts based on the current organization chart? (*If not, why?*)

8. How does your organization determine the qualifications, requirements, or competencies for each key position in the future?

9. How does your organization attempt to integrate succession planning and management with organizational strategy? With human resource strategy?

Questions	Notes on Responses
10. How does your organization identify successors for key positions?	
11. How does your organization identify *high-potential employees (who are capable of advancing two or more levels beyond their current placement)*?	
12. How does your organization establish Individual Development Plans (IDPs) to plan, guide, and accelerate the development of high-potential employees?	
13. What special programs, if any, has your organization established to accelerate the development of high-potentials?	
14. What special computer software, if any, does your organization use in its succession planning and management activities? Why was it chosen?	
15. How does your organization evaluate the results of succession planning and management activities?	

(continues)

Exhibit 5-7. (continued)

16. What special problems has your organization encountered with succession planning and management? How have those been solved?

Exhibit 5-8. Opinions of Top Managers About Succession Planning and Management

Question: How would you summarize the opinions of top managers in your organization about a succession planning program? *Circle all response codes below that apply.*

Opinions of Top Management	Percentage Response
They don't believe succession planning is worth the time required for it.	9%
They have no clue why such a program might be worthwhile.	9%
They believe that a succession planning program is worthwhile but are not aware of how to manage it efficiently and effectively.	55%
They believe a succession planning program is worthwhile and that a formal program is better than an informal program.	27%
I don't know what they think about a succession planning program.	- 0 -
Other Comments	*None*
Total	100%

Source: William J. Rothwell, *Results of a 2004 Survey on Succession Planning and Management Practices.* Unpublished survey results (University Park, Penn.: The Pennsylvania State University, 2004).

would answer those questions about top management opinions in your organization. Turn then to Exhibit 5-9 and consider how you would characterize your own opinions about systematic SP&M.

Understanding How to Secure Management Commitment

To understand how to secure management commitment, Diane Dormant's classic ABCD model remains a helpful tool.[11] ABCD is an acronym based on

Exhibit 5-9. Opinions of Human Resource Professionals About Succession Planning and Management

Question: How would you summarize *your* opinions about a succession planning program? *Circle all response codes below that apply.*

Your Opinions	Percentage Response
I don't believe such a program is important.	- 0 -
I believe that other methods work better in identifying and preparing possible successors.	- 0 -
I believe a succession planning program is worthwhile but other programs are more important for this organization right now.	- 0 -
I believe a succession planning program is important.	36%
Succession planning is critically important to this organization at this time.	64%
Other Opinions	*None*
Total	*100%*

Source: William J. Rothwell, *Results of a 2004 Survey on Succession Planning and Management Practices.* Unpublished survey results (University Park, Penn.: The Pennsylvania State University, 2004).

the first letter of several key words. Dormant's model suggests that large-scale organizational change—such as the introduction of a systematic SP&M program—can be understood by examining **a**dopters (who is affected by the change?), **b**lackbox (what is the change process?), **c**hange agent (who is making the change?), and **d**omain (the change context).[12]

The most valuable feature of Dormant's model is her view that different strategies are appropriate at different stages in the introduction of a change. The change agent should thus, to facilitate change, take actions that are keyed to the adopter's stage in accepting an innovation.

Dormant believes that adopters progress through five identifiable stages in accepting an innovation.[13] During the first stage—awareness—adopters have little information about the innovation. They are passive and are generally unwilling to seek information. In that stage, change agents should advertise the innovation, making efforts to attract attention and provide positive information.

In the second stage—self-concern—adopters are more active. They express concern about how they will be individually affected by a change and pose questions about the consequences of an innovation. Change agents in this stage should enact the role of counselor, answering questions and providing relevant information.

In mental tryout—the third stage—adopters remain active and ask pointed questions related to their own applications of an innovation. Change agents should enact the role of demonstrators, providing relevant examples and demonstrating to adopters how they may apply an innovation to their unique situations.

In hands-on trial—the fourth stage—adopters are interested in learning how to apply an innovation to their own situations. Their opinions about the innovation are being formed from personal experience. Change agents should provide them with training and detailed feedback about how well they are applying the innovation. Testimonials of success will be persuasive during this stage, helping to shape the conclusions reached by the adopters about an innovation.

Adoption is the fifth and final stage. By this point adopters have integrated the innovation into their work and are interested in specific problem solving that is related to their own applications. Change agents should provide personal support, help adopters find the resources they need to perform effectively, and provide rewards for successful implementation.

Applying these stages to the process of obtaining and building management support for systematic SP&M should be apparent. The appropriate strategies that change agents should use depend on the stage of acceptance. (See Exhibit 5-10.)

An important point to bear in mind is that a succession planning program will be effective only when it enjoys support from its stakeholders. Indeed, the stakeholders must perform SP&M for it to work. In short, they must own the process. Hence, obtaining and building management commitment to SP&M is essential for a systematic program to work.

The Key Role of the CEO in the Succession Effort

The CEO's role in the SP&M process is the key to success—or failure—in private-sector organizations. Let me state it clearly: It is a make-or-break role. While it may seem that CEOs are asked to be "involved" in everything, which is sometimes interpreted to mean "give lip service to it and then delegate it," SP&M does not fall in that category. To put it in blunt terms, if the CEO is not hands-on involved in leading the succession effort, it will fail. SP&M cannot be just delegated to the HR department, for the simple reason that HR cannot hold senior executives accountable for talent development in the same way that the CEO can. Well-known CEOs like former G.E. Chairman Jack Welch devote much of their time to thinking about, and acting on, succession issues.[14]

Fortunately, several factors have come together to put SP&M on the CEO's personal radar screen. One factor is that boards of directors are becoming more involved with succession. Consider:

Exhibit 5-10. Actions to Build Management Commitment to Succession Planning and Management

Stage of Acceptance	Appropriate Actions
Awareness	△ Advertise SP&M to management employees. △ Provide general information about SP&M.
Self-Concern	△ Answer questions. △ Provide relevant information.
Mental Tryout	△ Provide relevant examples of applications of SP&M policy/practices to specific functions or activities within the organization. △ Demonstrate how SP&M may be used in each organizational area.
Hands-on Trial	△ Offer training on SP&M. △ Meet with top managers individually to discuss SP&M in their areas. △ Collect and disseminate testimonials of success.
Adoption	△ Provide personal support to top managers on applications of systematic SP&M. △ Help program users perform effectively through individualized feedback and counseling. △ Identify appropriate rewards for SP&M.

Succession planning has become the second most important topic discussed by boards. (Top of the list is making sure that the right chief executive is in place to begin with.) The frequency with which chief executives come and go adds to the pressure. The average chief executive's tenure has dwindled in the past decade from eight years to less than five. That leaves little time to groom the next generation. Big companies rarely pick from outside. To do so is usually a sign that they are in trouble. For the board, drawing up a succession plan is a good way to spot future problems. But there are advantages for the boss, too. After all, one way to secure a sort of immortality is to pick one's own successor. In most companies, the succession process is controlled mainly by the chief executive.

> However, many CEOs are uncooperative, partly because they hate the idea of retirement.
>
> Even Disney now listens. Sarah Teslik, executive director of the Council of Institutional Investors, a lobbying group, says that she has demanded for years that Disney draw up a succession plan, but Michael Eisner, the company's domineering CEO, has refused to allow it. When she talked to senior Disney executives two months ago, they assured her that a plan now existed—although they refused to say what it is. Ms. Teslik thinks that behavior has been changed by the insistence in the Sarbanes-Oxley Act that boards meet in "executive session"—that is, without the executives present. "I personally asked Mr. Sarbanes for this provision for that purpose," she recalls. "How can directors talk about your succession while you are in the room?"[15]

A new survey of boardroom practice by Korn/Ferry International, another search consultancy, finds that only 33 percent of boards had a management succession committee or process in 2001. By this year, that had leapt to 77 percent.

A second factor is that aging senior executives have placed personal pressure on CEOs to pay attention to succession, lest they find themselves saddled with the workload of a retiring senior executive while harried HR staff try to source a qualified replacement. A third factor is that terrorism has made succession a prudent risk-management issue—one sure to be brought up by increasingly cautious auditors.

But what exactly should CEOs do? Here are some practical suggestions:

1. Discuss the issue with the board, his or her key reports, and the VP of HR to decide what succession program would be most desirable for the organization. Of course, that information can be gathered by an external consultant—often a good idea—and then handed to the CEO in a report that recommends actions and next steps.

2. Become familiar enough with issues associated with succession to be able to discuss the topic intelligently. That includes otherwise arcane topics—to CEOs at least—such as competency modeling.

3. Insist on an action plan that senior executives can buy into.

4. Hold senior executives accountable for grooming talent in their divisions and departments, perhaps by changing the executive bonus plan

to put a portion of the bonus at risk for making or not making measurable goals for talent development.

5. Chair periodic meetings of senior executives to discuss how they are grooming talent—and especially HiPos—in their areas.

Of course, there is much more that CEOs can do. But they must be convinced of the importance of SP&M to do anything. Just to provide a basis for reflection, rate your CEO on his or her role in SP&M, using the simple rating sheet in Exhibit 5-11.

Summary

When preparing to introduce a systematic succession planning program, begin by assessing the organization's current succession planning and management problems and practices, demonstrating the business need for succession planning and management, determining the organization's unique succession planning and management requirements, linking the succession planning and management program to the organization's strategic plans and human resource plans, benchmarking succession planning and management processes in other organizations, and obtaining and building management commitment.

This chapter has reviewed these steps and thereby demonstrated ways by which to make the case for change. The next chapter emphasizes the importance of clarifying the roles of each level of management in the succession planning and management program; developing a program mission statement, policy, and philosophy; identifying target groups; and setting program priorities.

Exhibit 5-11. Rating Your CEO for His/Her Role in Succession Planning and Management

Directions: For each item listed in the left column below, check a box in the right column to indicate whether your organization's CEO is actively performing successfully. Be honest.

The CEO of My Organization:	*Yes*	*No*
Takes a hands-on approach to succession issues.	☐	☐
Sets a positive example by choosing his or her own successor.	☐	☐
Sets a positive example by developing his or her own successor.	☐	☐
Considers succession issues whenever he or she makes business decisions of strategic import.	☐	☐
Discusses his or her thinking about succession issues with others.	☐	☐
Holds managers accountable for succession issues.	☐	☐
Holds managers accountable for developing talent.	☐	☐
Rewards managers for developing talent.	☐	☐
Chairs "talent shows" of the organization in which the developmental needs of promising people are discussed and by which senior managers are held accountable for developing the people they have.	☐	☐
Total Score (*Add up the yes and no boxes and then insert the sums where indicated at right. Obviously, the more yes boxes your CEO has, the closer his/her role is to being successfully engaged in the succession planning and management efforts of your organization.*)	*Number of Yes Boxes* _____	*Number of No Boxes* _____

CHAPTER 6

STARTING A SYSTEMATIC PROGRAM

An organization should be ready to start a systematic succession planning and management (SP&M) program once the case has been persuasively made that one is needed. Starting a systematic SP&M program usually involves taking such actions as conducting a risk analysis and building a commitment to change; determining roles in the SP&M program; formulating a mission statement; writing a program policy; clarifying the procedures; identifying groups targeted for action; defining the roles in the SP&M program of the CEO, senior managers, and others; and setting program priorities. This chapter focuses on these issues.

Conducting a Risk Analysis and Building a Commitment to Change

Where do an organization's leaders begin in conducting a risk analysis? In building a commitment to change? Those are, of course, related questions.

A *risk analysis* is simply an assessment of what level of risk an organization faces owing to the loss of key people. (Key people exist at all levels and not just at the top.) The risk analysis is conducted in one of several ways. For example, one way has been mentioned earlier in this book. First, the organization's payroll system is used to project the estimated dates of retirement eligibility for the entire workforce. Second, the percentage of the whole organization eligible for retirement over rolling three-year periods is assessed. Third, the same analysis is done by job code, geographical location, functional area or department, and hierarchical level. The aim is to cast a wide net, looking for trouble spots where high percentages of a whole group, such as the entire accounting department or the St. Louis office, for example, would be eligible for retirement during a given three-year period. Use three-year periods because problems may not be apparent in a single year. But if the cumulative percentage of the retirement-eligible workforce over a rolling three-year period is high—say, over 50 percent—then you can mark it as a trouble spot and move on.

The goal of this exercise is to find parts of the organization where the risks are the highest of losing people. While skeptical managers may not see a need for a succession program for an entire organization, they can be convinced to do something if they see a high percentage of the entire workforce or those in one area are affected.

There are other ways to do risk analysis. Sometimes they can be just as effective and persuasive to decision-makers. For instance:

▲ *Do "what if" scenarios.* Pose questions to decision-makers: How long would it take to replace a key person owing to sudden death, disability, or resignation? And what would the organization do in the meantime to ensure that the work gets done? Ask decision-makers to estimate the economic or other impacts that would result from the sudden loss of a key person at any level.

▲ *Do historical studies.* Look to the past. Ask what key people losses have been experienced by the organization in the past and how they were handled. (I have found that the sudden loss of a handpicked successor for the CEO's job is sometimes a most persuasive way to launch an SP&M program, for the simple reason that the CEO feels the pain personally and will not suffer in silence for long.)

▲ *Build awareness.* Prepare a simple visual aid with the organization chart showing, in red, the percentage of people at risk of loss owing to retirement; prepare another visual aid that shows the years of experience at risk of loss in key departments.

Other approaches to building persuasive cases for action are possible. Data and measurements can help. Just think—what data are most likely to convince decision-makers of the need to establish a succession program, and how can that data be gathered? Then set out to collect that information, analyze it, and present it to decision-makers. Do not forget, however, that decision-makers, once convinced of the need for action, will expect you to have in hand an action plan or series of recommendations about how to establish the SP&M program.

Clarifying Program Roles

What are roles? How can roles in an SP&M program be clarified so that organizational members know what they should do to support the effort? This section answers these questions.

Understanding Roles

A *role* is an expected pattern of behaviors and is usually linked to a job in the organization. Although most organizations outline responsibilities in job descriptions, few job descriptions are sufficiently detailed to clarify how job incumbents should carry out their duties or interact with others. However, roles do permit such clarification. Indeed, "a role may include attitudes and values as well as specific kinds of behavior. It is what an individual must do in order to validate his or her occupancy of a particular position."[1]

Role theory occupies a central place in writings about management and organizations. Internalizing a role has often been compared to the communication process. (See Exhibit 6-1.) *Role senders* (role incumbents) bring to their roles expectations about what they should do, how they should do it, and how they should interact with others. Their expectations are influenced by their previous education, experience, values, and background. They are also influenced by what they are told about the role during the recruitment, training, and selection process. *Role receivers*—others in the organization with whom role senders interact—observe these behaviors and draw conclusions from them based on their own expectations. They provide feedback to indicate whether the behavior matches what they expect. That feedback, in turn, may affect the role senders' expectations and behaviors.

To complicate matters, individuals enact more than one role in organizations. For instance, they may serve as superiors, colleagues, and subordinates. They may also enact roles outside the organization, such as spouse, parent, child, citizen, churchgoer, or professional. Each role may carry its own culturally bound expectations for behavior.

Enacting multiple roles can lead to role conflict. For example, supervisors may be expected by their employers to act in the best interests of the organization. That means they must occasionally make hard-eyed business decisions. On the other hand, supervisors may also be expected to represent the interests and concerns of their subordinates to the employer. To cite another example, human resource managers may perceive their role to be facilitative and feel that they should provide advice to operating managers when they decide HR issues. But operating managers may expect them to act forcefully and proac-

Exhibit 6-1. A Model for Conceptualizing Role Theory

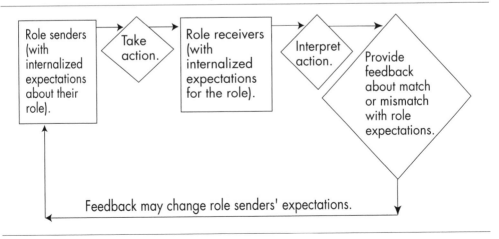

tively on their own, spearheading new initiatives and taking steps to avert future HR problems. In both examples, conflicting expectations may lead role incumbents to experience pressure and frustration. Effective performance is influenced by congruence in role expectations. Role senders can achieve desired results only when they know what they are expected to do and when role receivers make their expectations clear.

Applying Role Theory to Succession Planning and Management

As role theory indicates, performance is influenced by shared role expectations. As one step in establishing systematic SP&M, clarify program roles so that individuals throughout the organization are aware of what they are expected to do and how they are expected to behave.

At the outset, direct attention to the roles to be enacted by three important groups: (1) management employees, (2) program facilitators, and (3) program participants. These roles may overlap. In each case, however, it is important to bring to the surface what group members already believe about their roles in SP&M, feed that information back to them, provide information about alternative roles, and seek consensus on desirable roles.

Think of the roles of *management employees* as ranging along one continuum from active to passive and along another continuum from supporter to opponent. (See the grid in Exhibit 6-2 to help conceptualize those roles.) Management employees who take an active role believe that SP&M should occupy much of their time. They should be defining present work requirements, planning for future work requirements, appraising individual performance, assessing individual potential, planning for individual development, and participating in developmental activities. On the other hand, management employees who take a passive role believe that issues other than SP&M should occupy their time. A supporter sees systematic SP&M as a valuable activity; an opponent has reservations about it.

Think of *facilitators' roles* as ranging along a continuum from directive to nondirective. Facilitators who take a directive role indicate what they expect from those participating in a systematic SP&M program. They then attempt to enforce these expectations, providing briefings, training, or written directions to help others understand what they are supposed to do. Operating managers and top managers who are assigned responsibilities as SP&M coordinators may adopt that role, particularly during the start-up phase when many may be confused about what they are supposed to do.

On the other hand, facilitators who take a nondirective role attempt to identify what various stakeholders want from the program and what behaviors the stakeholders believe to be associated with those desired program results. They collect information from stakeholders, feed it back to them, and help them establish their own roles and action plans. Much time may be spent

Exhibit 6-2. Management Roles in Succession Planning and Management: A Grid

	Active	△ Champions succession planning efforts vigorously. △ Views management's role as one geared to developing and motivating people.	△ Opposes succession planning vigorously. △ Views management's role as one geared to making profits—even when that means demotivating people.
Level of Effort			
	Passive	△ Expresses general support for succession planning, with reservations about some approaches. △ Wishes more "study" and "analysis" to be conducted.	△ Prefers to devote time to other activities.
		Supporter	Opponent
		Level of Support	

individually, helping managers and employees at different levels understand what their roles should be.

Participant roles range along one continuum from aware to unaware and along another continuum from organizationally focused to personally/individually focused. Participants are defined as those tapped by the organization to be involved in the SP&M process. They are usually designated to be developed for one or more future positions. They may be aware or unaware that they have been thus designated by the organization as possible successors. They may be focused on satisfying their personal needs in the future (an individual focus) or on satisfying the organization's needs (an organizational focus).

To clarify roles, ask managers, facilitators, and participants to answer the following questions:

▲ What are you presently doing to help the organization meet its succession needs in the future?

▲ What should you do to help the organization establish a systematic SP&M program to meet succession needs in the future?

▲ What do you believe should be the role(s) of managers and employees in supporting an effective SP&M program in the organization?

Pose these questions in group or staff meetings or circulate written surveys as appropriate. (If neither approach will work owing to a desire to keep an

SP&M program "secret," then ask top managers these questions and ask how roles to support SP&M may be clarified at other levels in the organization.)

Formulating a Mission Statement

Why is an organization undertaking a systematic succession planning program? What outcomes do stakeholder groups desire from it? These questions should be answered during the program start-up phase in order to achieve agreement among stakeholders about the program's purpose and desired results.

The lack of a mission statement has been called the Achilles' heel of SP&M programs. As Walter R. Mahler and Stephen J. Drotter have pointed out years ago, these programs have too often been established without careful thought given to purpose or desired outcomes. "Company after company," they write, "rushed into program mechanics. Time went by and disillusionment set in. The programs did not live up to their promises."[2] The reason for this, they believe, is that the program mission was never adequately clarified at the outset.

What Is a Mission Statement?

A mission statement describes the purpose of a program or the reason for its existence. Sometimes it is called a *purpose statement*. *Mission* and *purpose* may be regarded as synonymous.

Formulating a mission statement is a first step in organizational planning. Writers on organizational strategy suggest that formulating an organizational mission should precede formulating strategy. An organizational mission statement answers such questions as these: Why is the organization in business? What results is it trying to achieve? What market does it serve? What products or services does it offer?

Mission statements may also be formulated for organizational functions (such as operations, finance, marketing, or personnel), divisions, locations, or activities. At levels below the organization, mission statements for functions, divisions, locations, or activities should answer such questions as these:

▲ Why does the function, division, location, or activity exist?

▲ How does it contribute to achieving the organization's mission? Its strategic plans?

▲ What outcomes or results are expected from it?

Mission statements may also provide philosophical statements (What do we believe?), product or service descriptions (What is to be made or sold?), customer descriptions (Whose needs are to be served?), and rationale (Why is the mission worth performing?).

What Questions Should Be Answered by a Mission Statement?

Like any organizational effort, an SP&M program should have a mission statement to explain why it exists, what outcomes are desired from it, why those outcomes are valuable, what products or services will be offered, who will be served by the program, and other issues of importance. However, mission statements for SP&M programs will vary across organizations. After all, not all programs are designed to serve the same purpose, achieve the same results, or offer the same products or services. So what specific issues should be addressed in a mission statement for an SP&M program?

One way to begin to answer that question is to focus on issues of particular importance to the organization. In that way, decision-makers will formulate the program's mission. Such issues may include:

1. What is a key position?
2. What is the definition of a high potential (HiPo)?
3. What is the organization's responsibility in identifying HiPos, and what should it be?
4. What is the definition of an exemplary performer?
5. What is the organization's responsibility in identifying and rewarding exemplary performers? What should it be?
6. How should the organization fill key positions?
7. What percentage of vacancies in key positions should be filled from within? From outside? Handled through other means?
8. What percentage of key positions should have at least one identifiable backup (successor)?
9. In what percentage of key positions should there be *holes* (that is, no designated successors)?
10. What is the maximum time that exemplary performers should remain in their positions?
11. What should be the maximum allowable percentage of avoidable turnover among high potentials? Exemplary performers? What should be done to reduce it?
12. What should be the maximum allowable percentage of failures in key positions after individual advancement?
13. What percentage of key positions should be filled with employees from legally protected labor groups—such as women, minorities, and the disabled?
14. How desirable are international assignments for designated successors?
15. How should HiPos be prepared for advancement?
16. What should be the role and responsibility of each employee and the HR department in the process of developing HiPos?

17. How much should individual career goals be exposed, considered, and tracked in succession planning?

18. How openly should the organization communicate with individuals who are identified to be HiPos about their status?

Of course, additional questions may also be posed to help clarify program purpose. Use the Worksheet appearing in Exhibit 6-3 to help clarify the mission of SP&M in an organization.

How Is a Mission Statement Prepared?

Prepare a mission statement by using any one of at least three possible approaches: "Ask, formulate, and establish"; "Recommend and listen"; or "Facilitate an interactive debate." In the "Ask, formulate, and establish" approach, someone takes an initial step by "asking" questions about succession planning in the organization. That launches a dialog to establish the program mission. Often that duty falls to human resource generalists, human resource development specialists, or management development specialists, although others—such as the CEO, a vice president of human resources, or a specially appointed SP&M coordinator—could function as change champions to focus attention on the need for change. As a second step, change champions should compile the answers received from different decision-makers. They should then "formulate" and circulate a proposal based on those answers. As a third and final step, decision-makers hammer out their own responses, using the proposal as a starting point. In so doing, they establish a mission statement for an SP&M program.

A key advantage of this approach is that it requires little initial effort from busy top managers. Others undertake the groundbreaking work to collect information about SP&M, compile it, and base recommendations on it. (That is what officers in the armed services call "staff work.") On the other hand, a key disadvantage of this approach is that executives do not participate in the information-gathering process, so they will have no collective ownership in the results. A subsequent step is thus required to capture their support and thereby achieve consensus on the necessary actions to take.

The "Recommend and listen" approach is different. It relies on considerable expertise by the HR generalists, HRD specialists, or management and leadership development specialists. To use this approach, they must start out with a thorough grasp of the organization's culture, top management desires and values, and state-of-the-art SP&M practices. From that perspective, they "recommend" a starting point for the program, providing their own initial answers to the key questions about the program mission listed in Exhibit 6-3. They prepare and circulate their recommendations for a systematic SP&M program, usually in proposal form. They then "listen" to reactions from key decision-

Exhibit 6-3. A Worksheet to Formulate a Mission Statement for Succession Planning and Management

Directions: Use this worksheet to help you formulate the mission of the succession planning and management (SP&M) program in your organization. For each question posed in the left column, write an answer in the right column. When you finish, circulate the worksheet among decision-makers. Compile their responses and then feed them back as a catalyst for subsequent decision making about the mission statement of the succession planning and management program in the organization. Add paper or questions appropriate to your organization as necessary.

Questions	Answers
1. What is a key position?	
2. What is the definition of a high-potential (HiPo)?	
3. What is the organization's responsibility in identifying HiPos, and what should it be?	
4. What is the definition of an exemplary performer?	
5. What is the organization's responsibility in identifying and rewarding exemplary performers? What should it be?	
6. How should the organization fill key positions?	
7. What percentage of vacancies in key positions should be filled from within? From without? Handled through other means?	
8. What percentage of key positions should have at least one identifiable *backup* (successor)?	
9. In what percentage of key positions should there be *holes* (that is, no designated successors)?	

(continues)

Exhibit 6-3. (*continued*)

Questions	Answers
10. What is the maximum time that exemplary performers should remain in their positions?	
11. What should be the maximum allowable percentage of avoidable turnover among high-potentials? Exemplary performers? What should be done to reduce it?	
12. What should be the maximum allowable percentage of *failures* in key positions after individual advancement?	
13. What percentage of key positions should be filled with employees from legally protected labor groups—such as women, minorities, and the disabled?	
14. How desirable are international assignments for designated successors?	
15. How should HiPos be prepared for advancement?	
16. What should be the role and responsibility of each employee and the HR Department in the process of developing HiPos?	
17. How much should individual career goals be surfaced, considered, and tracked in succession planning?	
18. How openly should the organization communicate with individuals who are identified to be HiPos about their status?	

19. Write a draft mission statement for the succession planning and management program of the organization in this space. Be sure to answer these questions: (1) Why does the program exist? (2) How does it contribute to achieving the organization's mission and strategic plans? and (3) What measurable outcomes or results should be expected from it?

makers, using the initial proposal as a catalyst to stimulate debate and discussion.

The advantage of this approach is that it usually has a shorter cycle time than "Ask, formulate, and establish." It also relies more heavily on expert information about state-of-the-art SP&M practices outside the organization, thereby avoiding a tendency to reinvent the wheel. But these advantages exist only when those using the approach have a thorough grasp of the organization's current SP&M problems and practices, culture, decision-maker preferences, and state-of-the-art practices. Otherwise, it can provoke time-consuming conflicts among decision-makers that will only prolong efforts to achieve top-level consensus.

The most complex approach is to "Facilitate an interactive debate." HR generalists, HRD specialists, management and leadership development specialists, or others function as group facilitators rather than as expert-consultants. The first step is to prepare a forum for key decision-makers to carry out an "interactive debate" about the SP&M program's mission. While the forum's content may be dictated by the CEO—or even by members of the board of directors—HR professionals set up the process for the debate. (*Content* refers to the issues on which the forum will focus; *process* refers to the means by which those issues will be examined.) That usually means that the CEO and the HR professional (or the CEO and an external facilitator) must work closely together to plot the best means by which to explore the most important succession planning and management issues. Such a debate may take the form of an off-site retreat lasting several days or several meetings spread across several months. During the debate, top-level decision-makers work through numerous small-group activities to clarify the mission, philosophy, and procedures governing the SP&M program.

The second step is to summarize the results. Someone must prepare a written statement that contains key points of agreement after the retreat or after each meeting. That task usually falls to an HR professional or to an external facilitator, who prepares a presentation or handout. However, the CEO or other top-level decision-makers feed these key points back to the retreat participants.

The third and final step is to conduct follow-up activities to ensure agreement. Follow-up activities may be conducted in several ways. One way is to hold a follow-up meeting with the participants to surface any points of confusion or disagreement. This can be done in small groups (at the end of a retreat) or individually with participants (after the retreat). Another way is to establish a top-level committee to govern SP&M in the organization and/or at various levels or locations of the organization.

An interactive debate does focus initial attention on key issues that should be addressed to formulate a clear program mission statement. That is an advantage of the approach. But it also requires much time and strong personal involvement from the CEO and others. That is its chief disadvantage.

Writing Policy and Procedures

Why is the organization undertaking an SP&M program? What results are desired from it? How can consistent program operations be ensured? Decision-makers may answer these questions by preparing written program policy and procedures.

What Is a Succession Planning and Management Policy, and What Are Succession Planning and Management Procedures?

Policy is a natural outgrowth of mission. Typically stated in writing, it places the organization on record as supporting or opposing an approach to action. Procedures flow from policy and provide guidelines for applying it. Writing a policy on SP&M clarifies what the organization seeks to do; writing procedures clarifies how the policy will be applied. Typical components of an SP&M policy include a mission statement, philosophical statements, and procedures. A sample SP&M policy appears in Exhibit 6-4.

How Are Policies and Procedures Written?

Succession planning and management policy and procedures should usually be written only after decision-makers agree on program mission and goals. Crises, problems, or issues of importance should provide clues about what to include in the policy and procedures, and they will usually be implicit in the mission. As decision-makers prepare a mission statement they will typically consider what may be rightfully included in a written program policy and procedure.

In many cases, the appropriate approach to use in writing policies and procedures stems from the approach used in preparing the mission statement. For instance, if an "Ask and formulate" approach was used in formulating the mission statement, then prepare a draft SP&M policy and procedures to

Exhibit 6-4. A Sample Succession Planning and Management Policy

Mission Statement

The purpose of the succession planning and management program in [*company or organization name*] is to ensure a ready supply of internal talent for key positions at all times. This organization is fully committed to equal employment opportunity for all employees, regardless of race, creed, sex, national origin, sexual orientation, or disability.

Policy and Philosophy

It is the policy of the [*company or organization name*] to help employees develop to the full extent of their potential and, to the extent possible for the organization, to help them achieve realistic career goals that satisfy both individual and organizational requirements.

This organization is firmly committed to promotion from within, whenever qualified talent is available, for key positions. This organization is also firmly committed to helping employees develop their potential so that they are prepared and qualified to assume positions in line with individual career goals and organizational requirements.

Procedures

At least once each year, the organization will sponsor:

△ *A replacement planning activity* that will assess how well the organization is positioned to meet replacement requirements by promotions or other personnel movements from within.

△ *Individual performance appraisal* to assess how well individuals are meeting their current job requirements.

△ *Individual potential assessment* to assess how well individuals are presently equipped for future advancement. Unlike performance appraisal—which is typically focused on past or present performance—the focus of individual potential assessment will be on the future.

△ *Individual development planning* to provide the means for action plans to help individuals narrow the developmental gap between what they already know or can do and what they must know or do to qualify for advancement.

The succession planning and management program will rely heavily on the processes listed above to identify individuals suitable for advancement. The program will work closely in tandem with an in-house career planning program, which is designed to help individuals identify their career goals and take proactive steps to achieve them.

accompany the proposal submitted to executives. If a "Recommend and listen" approach was chosen, then draft an SP&M policy and procedures to accompany the mission statement in the initial proposal to management. If the approach chosen was to "Facilitate an interactive debate," then committees in the organization will usually be the means by which to draft policy and procedures, oversee refinements, and issue updates or modifications to policy and procedures.

Identifying Target Groups

Who should be the focus of the SP&M program? Should the program be geared to top-level executive ranks only? Should it encompass other groups, levels, or parts of the organization? Answering these questions requires decision-makers to identify target groups.

Most of what has been written about SP&M programs has directed attention to replacing top-level executive positions. Substantial research has been conducted on SP&M for the CEO[3]; other writings have focused on the CEO's immediate reports. Relatively little has been written about SP&M for other groups, though many experts on the subject concede that the need has never been greater for effective SP&M efforts at lower levels. Indeed, interest in multiskilled, team-based management and cross-training stems from the recognition that more time, resources, and attention must be focused on systematically developing human capabilities at all levels and across all groups.

The results of my 2004 survey on SP&M practices revealed that the respondents' organizations are not consistently identifying and developing successors. (See Exhibit 6-5.)

Establishing Initial Targets

Where exactly is the organization weakest in bench strength? The answer to that question should provide a clue about where to establish initial targets for the SP&M program. (See the activity in Exhibit 6-6. If necessary, circulate it to top managers or ask them to complete it in an initial program kickoff meeting or mission statement retreat.)

Direct attention to three specific areas first, since they are a common source of problems: successors for top management positions; successors for first-line supervisory positions; and successors for unique, tough-to-fill technical or professional positions.

Top management positions are fewest in absolute numbers, but they are often critically important for formulating and implementing organizational strategy. They may grow weak in bench strength in organizations that experience significant employee reductions in the middle management ranks as a result of forced layoffs, employee buyouts, or early retirement offers.

Exhibit 6-5. Targeted Groups for Succession Planning and Management

Succession planning may not be carried out with all groups in an organization. For each group listed below, indicate whether *your* organization makes a deliberate effort to identify and develop successors.

	Group	Does Your Organization Make a Deliberate Effort to *Identify* Successors in This Group? *(Percentage Response)*		Does Your Organization Make a Deliberate Effort to *Develop* Successors in This Group? *(Percentage Response)*	
		Yes	No	Yes	No
A	Executives	89%	11%	100%	0%
B	Middle Managers	67%	33%	56%	44%
C	Supervisors	44%	56%	56%	44%
D	Professionals	33%	67%	22%	78%
E	Technical Workers (Engineers, Computer Specialists)	11%	89%	11%	89%
F	Sales Workers	22%	78%	22%	78%
G	Clerical and Secretarial Workers	11%	89%	22%	78%
H	Hourly Production or Service Workers	22%	78%	33%	67%

Source: William J. Rothwell, *Results of a 2004 Survey on Succession Planning and Management Practices.* Unpublished survey results (University Park, Penn.: The Pennsylvania State University, 2004).

Supervisory positions are largest in absolute numbers, so continuing turnover and other personnel movements leave these ranks subject to the greatest need for replacements. As a port of entry to the management ranks, supervision is also critically important because many middle managers and executives start out in the supervisory ranks. Supervisors are often promoted from the hourly ranks, lacking management experience, or are hired from outside the organization. They are areas of weakness in organizations that have not planned management-development programs or that provide little or no incentive for movement into supervision—such as organizations in which unionized hourly workers earn substantially more than supervisors, who are ineligible for overtime pay but must work overtime anyway.

Exhibit 6-6. An Activity for Identifying Initial Targets for Succession Planning and Management Activities

Directions: Use this activity to identify initial target groups for the SP&M program in an organization. For each job category listed in the left column below, list the priority (1 = highest priority) order in the center column. Then, in the right column, briefly explain why the job category was assigned that level of priority. Circulate this activity to decision-makers and ask them to complete it. Compile the results and feed them back to decision-makers to emphasize what job categories were generally perceived to be the rightful target for the SP&M program. Add paper as necessary. (If appropriate, modify the list of job categories so they coincide precisely with any special labels/titles associated with them in the organization.)

Job Category	List by Priority Order (1 = Highest)	What Is Your Reasoning?
1. Executives	_____	
2. Individuals Preparing for Executive Positions	_____	
3. Middle Managers	_____	
4. Individuals Preparing for Middle Management	_____	
5. Supervisors	_____	
6. Individuals Preparing for Supervision	_____	
7. Professional Workers	_____	
8. Individuals Preparing to Be Professional Workers	_____	
9. Technical Workers	_____	
10. Individuals Preparing to Become Technical Workers	_____	
11. Sales Workers	_____	
12. Individuals Preparing to Become Sales Workers	_____	
13. Clerical Workers	_____	

14. Individuals Preparing to Become Clerical Workers   _____

15. Hourly Production or Service Workers   _____

16. Individuals Preparing to Become Hourly Production or Service Workers   _____

17. Other Job Categories   _____

Tough-to-fill *technical or professional positions* are often limited in number. Managers may be kept awake at night, tossing and turning, at the mere thought of losing a member of this group because recruiting or training a successor on short notice is difficult or nearly impossible. Choose one group—or all three—as initial targets for the SP&M program if the results of the activity in Exhibit 6-6 demonstrate the need. Otherwise, use the results of the activity in Exhibit 6-6 to identify the initial targets for the program. Verify the groups chosen with decision-makers.

Expanding Succession Planning and Management to Other Groups

Although the organization may have neither the time nor the resources to establish a systematic SP&M program that encompasses all people and positions, decision-makers may agree that such a goal is worth achieving eventually. For that reason, periodically administer Exhibit 6-6 to decision-makers to assess which groups should be targeted for inclusion and in what priority order.

Of course, decision-makers may wish to prioritize groups in ways other than by job category. For instance, they may feel that bench strength is weakest in any of the following areas:

▲ Geographical Locations
▲ Product or Service Lines
▲ Functions of Organizational Operation
▲ Experience with Specific Industry-Related or Product/Service-Related Problems
▲ Experience with International Markets

Ask decision-makers about where they perceive the organization to be weak in bench strength. Then target the SP&M program initially to improve bench strength at that level. While continuing efforts at that level, gradually extend the effort to include other groups.

Clarifying the Roles of the CEO, Senior Managers, and Others

What roles should be played in the SP&M program by the CEO, senior managers, the HR program, individuals, and other groups?

The Roles of the CEO and Other Senior Managers

As noted in Chapter 5, the CEO's role in the success of an effective SP&M program is a make-or-break proposition. If he or she is willing to provide hands-on involvement, the program begins with an excellent chance of success. On the other hand, if he or she classifies SP&M as something that everyone else should do, then the program begins with the hallmarks of a disaster in the making. This is because only the CEO can hold other senior executives accountable for grooming talent, and only he or she can reward or punish them for their results. The VP of HR cannot do that.

An excellent starting point is to sit down with the CEO and ask, "What role do you want to play in SP&M, and why do you want to play that role?" It also helps to ask, "What results do you want to see from the SP&M program, and what role do you think you should play in helping to achieve those results?" From the answers to that, HR staff or others may prepare a role description of what part the CEO wants to play. The same approach may be used with other senior managers. By clarifying expected roles—and the actions associated with them—accountability is being established.

The Role of the HR Department

What should be the role of the HR department in the SP&M effort? The reality is that many roles are possible. And if the role of HR is not clarified, it can wreak havoc on the effort as expectations clash with realities.

In most organizations, including best-practice firms, HR's role is a coordinative one. While that term *coordinative* may be a mouthful, it basically means that: (1) someone within HR is given responsibility for collecting information and following up to gather information for the SP&M effort; (2) the HR function must supply the technology to support data gathering about individuals, organizational needs, present and future competencies, present performance and future potential, individual development plans, competency development strategies, and so on.

A common problem in starting SP&M programs is that HR has no staff available, or at least staff with sufficient credibility, to assign. Another problem is that the HR function is lacking in what might be called the infrastructure to support a succession program. *Infrastructure* means that nothing exists to support the succession effort—no technology, no competency models, no working performance management systems, no 360-degree assessment tools (or other methods of assessing potential), no individual development plans (IDPs), or anything else that will be needed for a good effort.

There is no simple solution to this problem. Someone must be assigned the responsibility—someone who is an exemplary performer in HR, perhaps even a HiPo, since that person must have credibility with the CEO, senior managers, and even board of director members. That HR person must then receive training on succession. While many HR people end up self-taught on this topic, it is still helpful to send the assigned person to whatever training might be available on succession.

The Role of Individuals

Of course, other useful questions to ask—and ones that are too often lost in the shuffle of thinking about getting the SP&M program up and rolling—are these: "What role(s) should individuals play in developing themselves for the future?" and "How do we discover what career goals people have set for themselves for the future?" It should not be assumed, of course, that everyone wants to be promoted. Some people look at what their bosses go through and say "No, thanks." Decision-makers must learn sensitivity to the desire for work-life balance, a topic of growing interest. Career planning programs can, of course, be most helpfully integrated with SP&M programs in this respect.

The Roles of Other Stakeholders

The board of directors may want to play a role in the organization's succession effort. If so, board members must be asked what role they want to play. Perhaps even a board committee will be established to oversee succession. That is a recommended approach because it focuses the attention of the CEO and other senior leaders on the issue, ensuring accountability. And it also helps to protect shareholder interests, at least in companies where stocks are traded, against the devastating impact on the company that can result from the sudden loss of key people such as the CEO or other senior leaders.[4]

Setting Program Priorities

Much work needs to be done to establish a systematic SP&M program. But rarely, if ever, can it be accomplished all at once. Someone has to set program priorities, both short term and long term. That may be done by top-level decision-makers, a full-time or part-time SP&M coordinator, or a committee representing different groups or functions within the organization.

Initial priorities should be set to address the organization's most pressing problems—and to rectify the most serious weaknesses in bench strength. Subsequent priorities should be set to reflect a long-term plan for systematic SP&M in the organization.

In addition to the activities already described in this chapter—such as clarifying roles, formulating a mission statement, writing a program policy, clarifying program procedures, and identifying the program's targeted groups—other actions will have to be undertaken. Priorities should be established on what actions to take—and when—depending on the organization's needs. These activities include:

▲ Preparing an action plan to guide program start-up

▲ Communicating the action plan

▲ Training managers and employees for their roles in the systematic SP&M program

▲ Organizing kickoff meetings and periodic briefing meetings to discuss the program

▲ Counseling managers on handling unique succession planning problems, such as dealing with poor performers, managing high performers, grooming and coaching high-potentials, addressing the special problems of plateaued workers, and managing workplace diversity

▲ Defining present and future work requirements, processes, activities, responsibilities, success factors, and competence

▲ Appraising present individual performance

▲ Assessing future individual potential

▲ Providing individuals with the means by which to carry out career planning within the organization

▲ Tracking performance and potential

▲ Preparing and following through on individual development plans (IDPs) to help close gaps between what people know or do and what they must know or do in the future to qualify for advancement and ensure leadership continuity

▲ Tracking innovative efforts to meet replacement needs

▲ Establishing effective approaches to evaluating the benefits of systematic SP&M

▲ Designing and implementing programs geared to special groups (such as high-potentials, plateaued workers, high performers, or low performers) or to meet special needs (such as reducing voluntary turnover of key employees after downsizing, handling cultural diversity, using succession planning in autonomous work teams, and integrating SP&M with such other organizational initiatives as quality or customer service)

Depending on an organization's unique needs, however, some issues may demand immediate attention—and action.

Take this opportunity to consider program priorities in the organization. Use the activity that appears in Exhibit 6-7 to establish initial program priorities in the organization. (If you are the coordinator of the SP&M program, you may choose to circulate the activity to key decision-makers for their reactions, feed back the results to them, and use their reactions as a starting point for setting program priorities. Alternatively, share the activity with a standing committee on SP&M established in the organization, if one exists. Ask committee members to complete the activity and then use the results as a basis for setting initial program priorities.) Revisit the priorities at least annually. Gear action plans according to the program priorities that are established.

Addressing the Legal Framework

Legal issues should not be forgotten in SP&M. That is especially true because employee complaints filed with the Equal Employment Opportunity Commission have been on the increase in recent years. Those responsible for formulating and implementing an SP&M program should familiarize themselves with government laws, rules, regulations, and other provisions—both in the United States and, if they do business internationally, in other nations as appropriate. Competent legal advice should be sought when the organization's decision-makers have reached agreement on the goals and objectives of the SP&M program. Additionally, employers should take special care to avoid real or perceived employment discrimination of all kinds. Private-sector employers should also take care to ensure that SP&M programs are consistent with company human resource policies and procedures as described in company documents (such as employee handbooks or policy and procedure manuals). Public-sector employers falling under state or federal civil service rules should double-check their program descriptions to ensure that SP&M programs are consistent with policies and procedures governing hiring, promotion, training, and other policies.

A complex web of employment law exists at the federal government level in the United States. Key national employment laws are summarized in Exhibit 6-8. Under the supremacy clause of the U.S. Constitution, federal laws take precedence over local laws unless no federal law exists or federal law specifically stipulates that local laws may be substituted for federal law. In addition to national labor laws, each state, county, and municipality may enact and enforce special laws, rules, regulations, or ordinances affecting employment in a local jurisdiction. The latter may influence succession planning and management practices.

Exhibit 6-7. An Activity for Establishing Program Priorities in Succession Planning and Management

Directions: Use this activity to help establish priorities for the succession planning program in an organization. For each activity listed in the left column below, set a priority by circling a number for it in the right column. Use the following scale:

1 = A top priority that should be acted on *now*

2 = A secondary priority that is important but that can wait awhile for action

3 = A tertiary priority that should only be acted on after items prioritized as 1 or 2 have received attention

Circulate this activity among decision-makers as appropriate. If you do so, compile their responses and then feed them back as a catalyst for subsequent decision making. Add paper as necessary. (You may also wish to add other activities of interest.)

		Priority	
Activity	Top 1	Secondary 2	Tertiary 3
1. Preparing an Action Plan to Guide Program Start-Up	1	2	3
2. Communicating the Action Plan	1	2	3
3. Training Managers and Employees for Their Roles in the Systematic Succession Planning Program	1	2	3
4. Organizing Kickoff Meetings and Periodic Briefing Meetings to Discuss the Program	1	2	3
5. Counseling Managers on Handling Unique Succession Planning Problems	1	2	3
6. Defining Present and Future Work Requirements, Processes, Activities, Responsibilities, Success Factors, and Competencies	1	2	3
7. Appraising Present Individual Performance	1	2	3
8. Assessing Future Individual Potential	1	2	3
9. Providing Individuals with the Means by Which to Carry Out Career Planning Within the Organization	1	2	3

10.	Tracking Performance and Potential	1	2	3
11.	Preparing, and Following Through on, Individual Development Plans (IDPs)	1	2	3
12.	Using, and Tracking, Innovative Efforts to meet Replacement Needs	1	2	3
13.	Establishing Effective Approaches to Evaluating the Benefits of Systematic Succession Planning	1	2	3
14.	Designing and Implementing Programs Geared to Meeting Special Needs	1	2	3
15.	Other (specify)	1	2	3

Of special importance to SP&M programs is the Uniform Guidelines on Employee Selection Procedures. Private-sector employers must ensure that all employment decisions are in compliance with these procedures. If they do not do so, they may risk a grievance under the Equal Employment Opportunity Commission or a "right to sue" letter when mediation efforts with the EEOC fail. Public-sector employers may find themselves falling under different standards established by the applicable branch of government.

Establishing Strategies for Rolling Out the Program

As an increasing number of employers begin to implement SP&M programs, they face dilemmas in how to roll them out. That is a frequent issue for consultants specializing in this area. I advise my clients to start at the top, with the CEO. The CEO is the real "customer" who must be satisfied, and it is wise to "follow the generations" in a roll-out strategy. That means it is best to begin with the CEO and select his or her immediate successors first—a simple replacement strategy. The CEO and his immediate reports—that is, the senior executive team—should be next. That, too, is a simple replacement plan. However, as internal consultants from human resources or external consultants work with the senior executive team, they begin to understand what issues are important in such a program and experience it firsthand. Their involvement and participation ensures their ownership and understanding. Next, middle managers are included. That is a third-generation plan. As middle managers are included, the program formulated by the senior executives is fire-tested with middle managers. That sets the stage for the talent pools and skill inventories that characterize generation-four and generation-five plans.

Of particular importance is the communication strategy. That is often an issue that should be addressed separately from the action plan. The CEO and senior executives should pay careful attention to how the SP&M programs are

(text continues on page 154

Exhibit 6-8. U.S. Labor Laws

Name of Law and Date of Enactment	Legal Citation	Brief Description of Key Provisions
Davis-Bacon Act (1931)	40 U.S.C. and sect; 276 et seq.	The Davis-Bacon Act applies to federal construction and repair contracts over $2,000. The Act requires contractors to pay their employees a specified minimum wage determined by the Secretary of Labor to be prevailing for similar work in that geographic area. Over 60 other federal laws make compliance with Davis-Bacon provisions a precondition for state and local contracts when a portion of the funding for those contracts comes from the federal government. The Act is enforced by the Wage and Hour division of the Department of Labor.
The National Labor Relations Act (Wagner Act and Taft-Hartley Act) (1947)	29 U.S.C. and sect; 151	The National Labor Relations Act protects the right of employees to choose whether to be represented by a union. The Act protects against coercion by employers or unions in making this choice and establishes the ground rules for union representation elections. The Act establishes collective bargaining between employers and unions. The Act is enforced by the National Labor Relations Board.
Fair Labor Standards Act (1938)	29 U.S.C. and sect; 201 et seq	The Fair Labor Standards Act provides minimum wage and overtime requirements. Under the FLSA all nonexempt employees are entitled to cash overtime for all hours worked over 40 in a workweek. The Act is enforced by the Wage and Hour Division of the Department of Labor and private lawsuits.
Labor-Management Reporting and Disclosure Act (Landrum-Griffin Act) (1959)	29 U.S.C. and sect; 401 et seq	The Labor-Management Reporting and Disclosure Act, or the Landrum-Griffin Act, establishes a set of rights for employees who are members of unions. They include the right to vote, attend meetings, meet and assemble with other members, and freely express views and opinions. The Act also requires all labor unions to adopt a constitution and bylaws, and

		contains certain reporting requirements for labor organizations, their officers, and employees. This Act is enforced by the Office of Labor Management Standards of the Department of Labor.
Contract Work Hours Safety Standards Act (1962)	40 U.S.C. and sect; 327 et seq	This Act sets a standard 40-hour workweek for employees of federal contractors and regulates work in excess of the standard week including the requirement to pay overtime. The Act is enforced by the Wage and Hour Division of the Department of Labor.
Equal Pay Act (1963)	29 U.S.C. and sect; 201 et seq	The Equal Pay Act prohibits discrimination in pay and benefits on the basis of sex for jobs in the same establishment that require equal skill, effort, and responsibility and which are performed under similar working conditions. The Act is enforced by the Equal Employment Opportunity Commission.
Title VII of the Civil Rights Act (1964)	42 U.S.C. and sect; 2000 et seq.	Title VII makes it unlawful for an employer with 15 or more employees to discriminate against individuals with respect to hiring, compensation, terms, conditions, and privileges of employment on the basis of race, color, religion, national origin, or sex. Title VII is enforced by the Equal Employment Opportunity Commission.
Executive Order 11246 (1965)	42 U.S.C.A. and sect; 2000e	Executive Order 11246 prohibits job discrimination by employers holding Federal contracts or subcontracts on the basis of race, color, sex, national origin, or religion and requires affirmative action to ensure equality of opportunity in all aspects of employment. The Order is enforced by the Office of Federal Compliance Contract Programs of the Department of Labor.
Service Contract Act (1965)	41 U.S.C. and sect; 351 et seq.	This Act is analogous to the Davis-Bacon Act in the area of service contracts performed by private companies doing work for the federal government. The Act requires contractors that provide services to the federal government to provide their employees a specified minimum

(continues)

Exhibit 6-8. (*continued*)

Name of Law and Date of Enactment	Legal Citation	Brief Description of Key Provisions
		wage and fringe benefits plan determined by the Secretary of Labor to be prevailing in the locality. The Act is enforced by the Wage and Hour Division of the Department of Labor.
Age Discrimination in Employment Act (1967)	29 U.S.C. and sect; 621 et seq.	The Age Discrimination in Employment Act, or ADEA, makes it unlawful for an employer with 20 or more employees to discriminate against individuals that are 40 years or older, with respect to hiring, compensation, terms, conditions, and privileges of employment on the basis of age. The Act is enforced by the Equal Employment Opportunity Commission.
Federal Coal Mine Health and Safety Act (1969)	30 U.S.C. and sect; 801 et seq.	This Act empowers the Secretaries of Labor and Health and Human Services to promulgate health and safety standards for the mining industry. The Act is enforced by the Mine Safety and Health Administration of the Department of Labor.
Occupational Safety and Health Act (1970)	29 U.S.C. and sect; 553, 651 et seq.	The Occupational Safety and Health Act, or OSHA, requires all employers to provide a workplace that is free from recognized hazards that cause, or are likely to cause, death or serious physical harm to employees. The Act also establishes the Occupational Safety and Health Administration, which is responsible for promulgating workplace safety standards and regulations for various industries. The Act is enforced by the Occupational Safety and Health Administration.
Rehabilitation Act (1973)	29 U.S.C. and sect; 701 et seq.	The Rehabilitation Act prohibits employers that receive federal grants, loans, or contracts from discriminating in their employment practices against individuals with disabilities. The Act is enforced by the Department of Labor.

Employee Retirement Income Security Act (1974)	29 U.S.C. and sect; 301, 1001 et seq.	The Employment Retirement Income Security Act, or ERISA, governs the operation of pensions and retirement benefits provided by private-sector employers to their employees. The Act does not require that employers provide such benefits, but regulates the conduct of employers that do provide such plans. The Act is enforced by the Pension and Welfare Benefits Administration of the Department of Labor.
Vietnam Era Veterans' Readjustment Assistance Act (1974)	38 U.S.C. and sect; 4301	VEVRAA makes it unlawful for employers to discriminate against veterans of the Armed Forces in their employment practices. It also provides veterans with certain reemployment, seniority, health benefits, and pension rights with respect to prior employment. The Act is enforced by the Office of Veterans Employment and Training of the Department of Labor.
Black Lung Benefits Reform Act (1977)	30 U.S.C. and sect; 901 et seq.	This Act provides benefits to coal miners who are totally disabled due to pneumoconiosis and to the surviving dependents of miners whose death was a result of this disease. The Act is enforced by the Office of Workers' Compensation Programs of the Department of Labor.
Labor-Management Cooperation Act (1978)	29 U.S.C.A. and sect; 141 note, 173, 175a.	The Labor-Management Cooperation Act encourages the establishment and operation of joint labor-management activities designed to improve labor relations, job security, and organizational effectiveness. The Act authorizes the Federal Mediation and Conciliation Service to provide assistance, contracts, and grants to joint labor-management committees that promote these purposes.
Pregnancy Discrimination Act (1978)	42 U.S.C. and sect; 2000 et seq.	The PDA, a 1978 amendment to Title VII of the 1964 Civil Rights Act, makes it unlawful for an employer to discriminate on the basis of pregnancy or childbirth. The Act is enforced by the Equal Employment Opportunity Commission.

(continues)

Exhibit 6-8. *(continued)*

Name of Law and Date of Enactment	Legal Citation	Brief Description of Key Provisions
Multi-Employer Pension Plan Amendments Act (1980)	29 U.S.C. and sect; 1001a et seq.	This Act regulates the operation of multi-employer pension plans and provides protection and guarantees for the participants and beneficiaries of distressed plans. The Act is enforced by the Pension and Welfare Benefits Administration of the Department of Labor.
Job Training Partnership Act (1982)	29 U.S.C. and sect; 1501 et seq.	This Act creates Private Industry Councils composed of business owners and executives as well as representatives of organized labor to assist state and local governments in the development and oversight of job training programs. The Act is enforced by the Employment and Training Administration of the Department of Labor.
Migrant and Seasonal Agricultural Protection Act (1983)	29 U.S.C. and sect; 1801 et seq.	This Act governs the terms and conditions of employment for migrant and seasonal agricultural workers and regulates the employment practices of agricultural employers, agricultural associations, and farm labor contractors. The Act is enforced by the Wage and Hour Division of the Department of Labor and by private lawsuits.
Immigration Reform and Control Act (1986)	29 U.S.C. and sect; 1802 et seq.	The Immigration Reform and Control Act, or IRCA, requires employers to verify that applicants for employment are authorized to work in the United States. The Act provides civil and criminal penalties for knowingly employing unauthorized aliens and also prohibits discrimination based on national origin or citizenship if the alien is authorized to work. The Act is enforced by the Department of Justice and the Immigration and Naturalization Service.

Economic Dislocation and Worker Adjustment Assistance Act (1988)	29 U.S.C. and sect; 1651–53	This Act provides federal funds to the states for basic readjustment and retraining of workers who have been terminated because of layoffs or plant closures and who are unlikely to return to their previous occupations. The Act is managed by the Employment Standards Administration of the Department of Labor.
Employee Polygraph Protection Act (1988)	29 U.S.C. and sect; 2001 et seq.	This Act makes it unlawful for an employer to require, request, suggest, or cause an employee or applicant to submit to a lie detector test. In addition, it prohibits the employer from threatening or taking any adverse employment action against an employee or applicant who refuses to take a lie detector test. The Act is enforced by a private right of action in the federal district courts.
Worker Adjustment and Retraining Notification Act (1988)	29 U.S.C. and sect; 2101et seq.	The Worker Adjustment and Retraining Notification Act, or WARN, requires employers with 100 or more employees to give 60 days advance notice to employees of impending plant closings or layoffs involving 50 or more employees. The Act is enforced by private lawsuits.
Whistleblower Protection Statutes (1989)	10 U.S.C. and sect; 2409; 12 U.S.C.; 1831j; 31 U.S.C. and 5328; 41 U.S.C. 265.	The Whistleblower Protection statutes protect employees of financial institutions and government contractors from discriminatory and retaliatory employment actions as a result of reporting violations of the law to federal authorities. The Act is enforced by the Wage and Hour Division of the Department of Labor.
Americans with Disabilities Act (1990)	42 U.S.C. and sect; 12101 et seq.	The Americans with Disabilities Act, or ADA, makes it unlawful for an employer with 15 or more employees to discriminate against qualified individuals with disabilities with respect to hiring, compensation, terms, conditions, and privileges of employment. The Act is enforced by the Equal Employment Opportunity Commission.

(continues)

Exhibit 6-8. (continued)

Name of Law and Date of Enactment	Legal Citation	Brief Description of Key Provisions
Older Workers Benefit Protection Act (1990)	29 U.S.C. and sect; 623 et seq.	This amendment to the Age Discrimination in Employment Act makes it unlawful for an employer to discriminate with respect to employee benefits on the basis of age. It also regulates early retirement incentive programs. The Act is enforced by the Equal Employment Opportunity Commission.
Civil Rights Act (1991)	42 U.S.C. and sect; 1981 et seq.	The Civil Rights Act of 1991 amended the 1964 act, and the Americans with Disabilities Act (ADA), to allow compensatory and punitive damages, but places caps on the amounts that can be awarded. The Act also provides for jury trials in suits brought under these laws.
Family and Medical Leave Act (1991)	29 U.S.C. and sect; 2601 et seq.	The Family and Medical Leave Act, or FMLA, requires that employers with 50 or more employees provide up to 12 weeks of unpaid leave, within any 12-month period, to employees for the care of a newborn or adopted child, for the care of a seriously ill family member, or for treatment and care of the employee's own serious medical condition. The Act is enforced by the Wage and Hour Division of the Department of Labor.
Congressional Accountability Act (1995)	2 U.S.C. and sect; 1301 et seq.	When many of the above laws were enacted, Congress was expressly exempted from compliance. The Congressional Accountability Act extends coverage of eleven laws to Congress in its capacity as an employer.

Source: Originally downloaded from Labor Policy Association. (1997). U.S. Employment Laws. Website: http/www.lpa.org/lpa/ laws.html. Washington, D.C.: Labor Policy Association. See also http://www.dol.gov/asp/programs/guide.htm.

described to middle managers and other stakeholders. If they do not give special attention to the communication strategy, so as to make the business goals and the policies and procedures clear, they risk broad-scale failure of the plan. Human resource practitioners cannot do it all. They need to work with the CEO and senior executive team—and sometimes with external consultants as well—to craft a communication strategy that explains how the SP&M program works and why it exists.

Summary

Starting up a systematic SP&M program usually requires an organization's decision-makers to:

- ▲ Conduct a risk analysis and build a commitment to change.
- ▲ Clarify the desired program roles of management, employees, facilitators, and participants.
- ▲ Prepare a program mission statement.
- ▲ Write a program policy and procedures.
- ▲ Identify groups targeted for program action, both initially and subsequently.
- ▲ Clarify the roles of the CEO, senior managers, and others.
- ▲ Establish program priorities.
- ▲ Address the legal framework in succession planning and management.
- ▲ Plan strategies for rolling out a succession planning and management program.

The next steps in starting the program are covered in the following chapter. They include preparing a program action plan, communicating it, training management and employees for enacting their roles in the program, and conducting program kickoff meetings, program briefing sessions, and counseling periods.

CHAPTER 7

REFINING THE PROGRAM

Beyond startup, some additional steps will usually need to be taken before a systematic succession planning and management (SP&M) program becomes operational. These steps include:

▲ Preparing a program action plan
▲ Communicating the action plan
▲ Conducting SP&M meetings
▲ Training on SP&M
▲ Counseling managers to deal with SP&M issues uniquely affecting them and their work areas

This chapter briefly reviews each topic listed above, providing tips for effectively refining an SP&M program in its early stages.

Preparing a Program Action Plan

Setting initial program priorities is only a beginning. Turning priorities into realities requires dedication, hard work, and effective strategy. Preparing a program action plan helps conceptualize the strategy for implementing systematic SP&M in the organization.

An action plan activates and energizes an SP&M program. It is a natural next step after setting program priorities because it indicates how they will be met.

Components of an Effective Action Plan

An action plan is akin to a project plan. It answers all the journalistic questions:

▲ Who should take action?
▲ What action should they take?
▲ When should the action be taken?

▲ Where should the action be taken?

▲ Why should the action be taken?

▲ How should action be taken?

In this way, an action plan provides a basis for program accountability.

How to Establish the Action Plan

Take several steps when establishing an action plan. First, list priorities. Second, indicate what actions must be taken to achieve each priority. Third, assign responsibility for each action. Fourth, indicate where the actions must be performed. Fifth and finally, assign deadlines or time indicators to indicate when the actions should be completed—or when each stage of completion should be reached. The result of these steps should be a concrete action plan to guide the SP&M program. (Fill in the worksheet appearing in Exhibit 7-1 to clarify the program action plan.)

Communicating the Action Plan

Few results will be achieved if an action plan is established and then kept secret. Some effort must be made to communicate the action plan to those affected by it and to those expected to take responsibility for participating in its implementation.

Problems in Communicating

Communicating about an SP&M program presents unique problems that are rarely encountered in other areas of organizational operations. The reason: many top managers are hesitant to share information about their programs widely inside or outside their organizations. They are reluctant to share information outside the organization for fear that succession plans will reveal too much about the organization's strategy. If an SP&M program is closely linked to, and supportive of, strategic plans—and that is desirable—then revealing information about it may tip off canny competitors to what the organization intends to do.

They are reluctant to share information inside the organization for fear that it will lead to negative consequences. High-performing or high-potential employees who are aware that they are designated successors for key positions may:

▲ Become complacent because they think advancement is guaranteed. This is called the crown prince phenomenon.

Exhibit 7-1. A Worksheet for Preparing an Action Plan to Establish the Succession Planning and Management Program

Directions: Use this worksheet to help you formulate an action plan to guide the start-up of an SP&M program in your organization. In column 1, list program priorities (*what* must be done first, second, third, and so on?) and provide a rationale (*why* are these priorities?). In column 2, list what tasks must be carried out to transform priorities into realities (*how* will priorities be achieved?). In column 3, assign responsibility for each task. In column 4, indicate (if applicable) special locations (*where* must the tasks be accomplished or the priorities achieved?). In column 5, assign deadlines or time indicators.

Circulate this worksheet among decision-makers—especially top-level managers who are participating on an SP&M committee. Ask each decision-maker to complete the worksheet individually. Then compile their responses, feed them back, and meet to achieve consensus on this detailed action plan. Add paper and/or priorities as necessary.

Column 1	Column 2	Column 3	Column 4	Column 5
Program Priorities and Rationale	Tasks	Responsibility	Location(s)	Deadlines/ Time Indicators
(By when should each task be completed? What must be done in order of importance, and why are these priorities?)	(How will priorities be achieved?)	(Who is responsible for each task?)	(Where must tasks be accomplished, if that is applicable?)	(Assign deadlines or time indicators.)

▲ Grow disenchanted if organizational conditions change and their status as successors is no longer assured.

▲ "Hold themselves for ransom" by threatening to leave unless they receive escalating raises or advancement opportunities.

Of course, the opposite can also happen. If high potentials are kept unaware of their status, they may seek advancement opportunities elsewhere. Equally bad, good performers who are not presently identified as successors for key positions may grow disenchanted and demotivated, even though they may already be demonstrating that they have that potential. A poorly handled communication strategy can lead to increases in avoidable or critical turnover, thereby costing the organization precious talent and driving up training costs.

Choosing Effective Approaches

As part of the SP&M program, decision-makers should review how the organization has historically communicated about succession issues—and consider how it should communicate about them. Establishing a consistent communication strategy is vital.

Valuable clues about the organization's historical communication strategy may be found in how key job incumbents were treated previously and how wage and salary matters are handled. If key job incumbents did not know that they were designated successors before they were eligible for advancement or if the organization's practice is not to publish salary schedules, then it is likely that a "closed" communication strategy is preferred. That means information is kept secret, and successors are not alerted to their status. On the other hand, if key job incumbents did know that they were designated successors before they were promoted or if salary schedules are published, then an "open" communication strategy is preferred. That means people are treated with candor.

Choose an approach to communication based on the preferences of decision-makers. If their preferences seem unclear, ask questions to discover what they are:

▲ How, if at all, should employees be informed about the SP&M program? (For instance, should the mission statement and/or policy and procedures on SP&M be circulated?)

▲ How should the organization characterize the roles of employee performance appraisal, individual potential assessment, and individual development planning in SP&M?

▲ How should decisions about individual selection, promotion, demotion, transfer, or development in place be explained to those who ask?

▲ What problems will result from informing individuals about their status in succession plans? From *not* informing them?

▲ What problems will result from informing employees about the SP&M program? What problems will result from *not* informing them?

Ultimately, the organization should choose a communication policy that is consistent with the answers to the questions above. Often the best approach is to communicate openly about the SP&M program in general, but conceal the basis for individual personnel actions in line with good business practice and individual privacy laws. Individuals should be encouraged to develop themselves for the future, but should understand, at the same time, that nothing is being "promised"; rather, qualifying is a first step but does not, in itself, guarantee advancement.

Conducting Succession Planning and Management Meetings

It is a rare organization that does not need at least one meeting to lay the foundation for a systematic SP&M program. Often, four meetings are necessary during startup: one of top decision-makers to verify the need for the program; a second, larger meeting to seek input from major stakeholders; a third, smaller committee meeting of change champions to hammer out a proposal to guide program startup; and a fourth meeting to introduce the program and reinforce its importance to management employees who will play critical roles in cultivating, nurturing, coaching, and preparing the leaders of the future at all levels. Later, periodic meetings are necessary to review program progress and ensure continuous improvement.

Meeting 1: Verifying the Need

In the first meeting, a handpicked group—usually limited to the "top of the house"—meets to verify that a genuine need exists to make SP&M a more systematic process. In this meeting it is common to review current practices and problems that stem from an informal approach to SP&M. This meeting usually stems directly from a crisis or from the request of one who wants to introduce a new way to carry out SP&M.

Meeting 2: Seeking Input

In the second meeting, a larger group of key decision-makers is usually assembled to surface SP&M problems and to galvanize action. This meeting may take the form of an executive retreat. Executives should properly be involved in the program formulation process, since—regardless of the initial targeted group for the SP&M program and its initial priorities—such a program has important strategic implications for the organization. Despite recent moves to involve employees in organizational decision making, it has long been held that executives have the chief responsibility for organizational strategy formulation. That is borne out by numerous research studies of executive roles.[1] It is also consistent with the commonsense view that someone must assume leadership when beginning new initiatives.[2]

Planning an executive retreat focused on SP&M should usually be a joint undertaking of the CEO and a designated coordinator for the SP&M program.

(The coordinator may be the vice president of personnel or human resources, a high-level staff generalist from the HR function, the training director, an OD director, or a management development director.) A designated coordinator is needed because busy CEOs, while they should maintain active personal involvement in the SP&M program if it is to work, will seldom have the necessary time to oversee daily program operations. That responsibility should be assigned to someone or it will be lost in the shuffle of daily work responsibilities. Hence, naming a program coordinator is usually an advisable choice.

While a designated coordinator may be selected from a high level of the line (operating) management ranks—and that will be a necessity in small organizations not having an HR function—the individual chosen for this responsibility should have a strong commitment to SP&M, considerable knowledge about the organization's HR policies and procedures as well as applicable HR laws, expertise in state-of-the-art management and leadership development and human resource development practices, in-depth knowledge about the organization's culture, and credibility with all levels of the organization's management. (It doesn't hurt, either, if the individual chosen for this role is perceived to be a high-potential in his or her own right.)

The CEO and the SP&M coordinator should meet to hammer out an action plan for the executive retreat focused on collecting input. The retreat should be held soon after the CEO announces the need for a systematic SP&M program and names a program coordinator. Invitations should be extended to the CEO's immediate reports. The retreat should usually be held off-site, at a quiet and secluded location, to minimize interruptions. The focus of the retreat should usually be on:

▲ Explaining the need for a more systematic approach to SP&M
▲ Formulating a (draft) program mission statement
▲ Identifying initial target groups to be served by the program
▲ Setting initial program priorities

An executive retreat is worthwhile because it engages the attention—and involvement—of key players in the organization's strategic planning activities, thereby creating a natural bridge between SP&M and strategic planning. The retreat's agenda should reflect the desired outcomes. Presentations may be made by the CEO, the SP&M coordinator, and the vice president of HR. Outsiders may be invited to share information about SP&M—including testimonials about succession programs in other organizations, war stories about the problems that can result when SP&M is ignored, and descriptions of state-of-the-art SP&M practices. An important component of any retreat should be small-group activities geared to surfacing problems and achieving consensus. (Many of the activities and worksheets provided in this book can be adapted for that purpose, and the CD-ROM accompanying this book contains a briefing on succession suitable for such a meeting.) In many cases, a retreat will end when the CEO appoints a standing committee to work with the succession planning coordinator to report back with a detailed program proposal.

In some organizations, the CEO or the SP&M coordinator may prefer that the retreat be facilitated by third-party consultants. That is desirable if the consultants can be located and if they possess considerable expertise in SP&M and in group facilitation. It is also desirable if the CEO feels that third-party consultants will increase the credibility and emphasize the importance of the program.

Meeting 3: Hammering Out a Proposal

A standing SP&M committee should be established to continue the program formulation process begun in the executive retreat. A committee format is really the best approach to (1) maintain high-level commitment and support, (2) conserve the time required to review the fruits of the committee's investigations, and (3) provide a means for senior-level involvement in SP&M. The SP&M coordinator should be automatically named a committee member, though not necessarily committee chair. If the CEO can be personally involved—and that is highly desirable—he or she should be the chair. Committee members should be chosen for their interest in SP&M, their track records of exemplary performance, their proven ability to develop people, and their keen insight into organizational culture.

In most organizations, a committee of this kind should meet frequently and regularly during program startup. Initial meetings should focus on investigating organizational SP&M needs, benchmarking practices in other organizations, and drafting a detailed proposal to guide the SP&M program.

Meeting 4: The Kickoff Meeting

In the fourth meeting, the program is introduced to those previously involved in the second meeting and any others, as appropriate. This is typically called a kickoff meeting.

In most cases, this meeting should focus on program details—and the part that the meeting participants should play to ensure program success. In short, a kickoff meeting should seek answers to two questions: (1) What is the SP&M program in the organization? and (2) What do the participants need to do to make the program successful?

When organizing a kickoff meeting, pay attention to the following questions:

1. Who will be invited?
2. What exactly should participants know or be able to do upon leaving the meeting?

3. When should the kickoff meeting be held? For instance, would timing it to follow a strategic planning retreat be desirable?

4. Where should the kickoff meeting be held? If maximum secrecy is desired, an off-site location is wise.

5. Why is the meeting being held? If the aim is to reinforce the importance of this new effort, then the CEO should usually be the keynote presenter.

6. How will the meeting be conducted?

Specific training on program details can then be offered later on establishing work requirements, appraising present individual performance, assessing future individual potential, establishing career goals, establishing individual development plans (IDPs), and using training, education, and development to help meet succession needs.

Meeting 5: Periodic Review Meetings

Conduct periodic review meetings after the succession planning program has been established. These meetings should focus on such issues as:

▲ The linkage between SP&M and organizational strategic plans (that may be handled during strategic planning retreats)

▲ The progress made in the SP&M program

▲ Any need for revisions to the program's mission statement, governing policy and procedures, target groups, priorities, action plans, communication strategies, and training relevant to the succession planning program

▲ The status of succession issues in each organizational component, including periodic meetings between the CEO and senior executives

The last of these should be familiar to executives in most major corporations. Once a quarter, senior executives from each part of the corporation meet with the CEO and a top-level committee to review the status of SP&M in that part of the corporation. Common topics in such meetings include: (1) reviewing employee performance; (2) identifying and discussing high potentials; (3) discussing progress made on individual development plans; and (4) addressing critical strengths and weaknesses having to do with individual development. Such meetings serve to keep the SP&M program on target and to emphasize its importance to senior executives, who should be held accountable for "people development" as much as for "market development" or "financial development."

Training on Succession Planning and Management

Implementing a systematic approach to SP&M requires new knowledge and skills from those expected to cultivate the organization's internal talent. Some means must be found to train them so that they are the most efficient and effective in their new role.

Matching Training to Program Planning

Training to support SP&M should be designed to match program priorities. Indeed, to plan training on SP&M, examine program priorities first, and use them as clues for designing initial training efforts.

In most cases, when organizations establish systematic SP&M, training should be undertaken to answer the following questions:

▲ What is the organization's SP&M program? What are its mission, policy, procedures, and activities?

▲ What are the desirable roles of management employees, succession planning and management facilitators, and individual employees in the SP&M program?

▲ What is the organization's preferred approach to clarifying present and future work requirements? How should it relate to SP&M as a source of information about activities, duties, responsibilities, competencies, and success factors in key positions?

▲ What is the organization's performance appraisal system, and how should it relate to succession as a source of information about individual job performance?

▲ What is the organization's formally planned individual career planning program (if one exists), and how does it relate to succession as a source of information about individual career goals and aspirations?

▲ What is the organization's potential assessment program (if one exists, as it should), and how does it relate to succession as a source of information about individual potential for future advancement?

▲ How do the organization's training, education, and development programs relate to preparing individuals for succession and advancement?

▲ What is an individual development plan? Why is planning for individual development important? How should programs for individual development be designed? Implemented? Tracked?

▲ How does the organization keep track of its human talent?

▲ How should the organization evaluate and continuously improve its SP&M program?

▲ How should the organization handle special issues in SP&M—such as high performers, high potentials, and plateaued workers?

▲ How should the SP&M program be linked to the organization's strategy? To HR strategy? To other plans (as appropriate)?

Refer to the draft training outlines appearing in Exhibit 7-2 and to the training material provided on the CD-ROM accompanying this book as starting points for developing in-house training sessions on SP&M. Note that such training should be tailor-made to meet organizational needs.

As an alternative, decision-makers may prefer to contract with qualified external consultants to design and deliver training on SP&M for the organization. Such consultants may be located through word-of-mouth referrals from practitioners in other organizations, those who have written extensively on SP&M, or organizations listed on the Web. They are especially appropriate to use when in-house expertise is limited, external consultants will lend initial credibility to the program, the pressure is on to obtain quick results, or in-house staff members are unavailable. If decision-makers decide to use external assistance, then the consultants should be invited in for a day or two to discuss what assistance they can provide. They should be asked for references from previous organizations with which they have worked. Before their arrival, they should also be given detailed background information about the organization and its existing SP&M programs and challenges.

Many external consultants will begin by meeting individually with key decision-makers and will then provide a brief group presentation about SP&M issues. Both can serve a valuable purpose. Individual meetings will emphasize the importance of the issue. Group meetings will help to informally educate participants about state-of-the-art practices outside the organization, which can create an impetus for change.

Ensuring Attendance at Training: A Key Issue

Perhaps the single most challenging aspect of offering training on SP&M is securing the critical mass necessary to ensure consistent approaches throughout the organization. It is particularly difficult to ensure that key managers will attend group training—and they are precisely the most important to reach because they exert the greatest influence on SP&M issues. But no matter what is done, some key managers will claim that they have too much work to do and cannot spare valuable time away from work to attend. Others will not attend and will offer no explanation. But it may prove to be impossible to fit them into any group training schedule that is established. No magic elixir will solve these problems. It amounts to a matter of commitment. If members of the board of directors and the CEO are genuinely committed to ensuring effective succession planning, then they will become personally involved to ensure

(text continues on page 170)

Exhibit 7-2. Sample Outlines for In-House Training on Succession Planning and Management

Purpose

To provide an opportunity for skill-building on employee performance appraisal, potential assessment, and individual development planning

Targeted Participants

Individuals, such as key position incumbents and immediate organizational superiors of high-potentials, who have important roles to play in implementing the action plan governing the succession planning program

Objectives

Upon completion of this training, participants should be able to:
1. Explain the organization's business reasons for establishing an SP&M program and the relationship between SP&M and strategic planning and human resources planning.
2. Describe the mission, policy, procedures, and activities of the SP&M program.
3. Review the roles and responsibilities of managers in preparing their employees to assume key positions in the organization.
4. Explain how the organization clarifies work requirements and identifies key positions.
5. Explain the role of employee performance appraisal in SP&M and describe the organization's performance appraisal procedures.
6. Conduct effective employee performance appraisal interviews.
7. Explain the role of employee potential assessment in SP&M and describe the organization's procedures for potential assessment.
8. Conduct effective employee potential assessments.
9. Explain the role of individual development planning in SP&M and describe the organization's procedures for individual development planning.
10. Select and oversee appropriate internal development approaches.
11. Explain when promotion from within is—and is not—appropriate for filling key vacancies.
12. Review the organization's approach to inventorying human talent.

Outline—Session 1
"Introducing Succession Planning and Management"

I. Introduction
   A. Purpose of the session
   B. Objectives of the session
   C. Organization (structure) of the session
II. Defining Succession Planning and Management (SP&M)
   A. What is it?
   B. Why is it important generally?
III. Relating SP&M to the Organization
   A. What are present organizational conditions?
   B. What are the organization's strategic plans/goals?
   C. What are the organization's human resources plans and goals?
   D. What is the need for SP&M, given organizational strategy and human resource plans?
IV. The Purpose of the SP&M Program
   A. Mission
   B. Policy
   C. Procedures
   D. Activities
V. Roles in SP&M
   A. What should be the role of the immediate organizational superior?
   B. What should be the individual's role in SP&M?
VI. Defining Work Requirements
   A. Job Analysis/Competency Models
   B. Job Descriptions and Specifications/Competency Models
   C. Other Approaches
VII. Identifying Key Positions
   A. How are they defined?
   B. Where are they located?
   C. How will key positions change in the future—and why?
VIII. Conclusion
   A. Summary
   B. Action planning for on-the-job action
   C. Session evaluations

(continues)

Exhibit 7-2. (continued)

Outline—Session 2
"Conducting Effective Employee Performance Appraisals for
Succession Planning and Management"

   I. Introduction
      A. Purpose of the session
      B. Objectives of the session
      C. Organization (structure) of the session
  II. Defining Employee Performance Appraisal
      A. What is it?
      B. Why is it important generally?
 III. Relating Employee Performance Appraisal to SP&M
      A. Approaches
      B. Current method
      C. Relationship between appraisal and SP&M
 IV. Reviewing the Organization's Performance Appraisal Procedures
      A. Overview
      B. Step-by-step description of procedures
  V. Conducting Effective Performance Appraisal Interviews
      A. Overview
      B. Using the form to structure the interview
 VI. Role Plays (practice appraisal interviews)
VII. Conclusion
      A. Summary
      B. Action planning for on-the-job action
      C. Session evaluations

Outline—Session 3
"Conducting Effective Employee Potential Assessment for
Succession Planning and Management"

   I. Introduction
      A. Purpose of the session
      B. Objectives of the session
      C. Organization (structure) of the session
  II. Defining Employee Potential Assessment
      A. What is it?
      B. Why is it important generally?
 III. Relating Employee Potential Assessment to SP&M
      A. Approaches
      B. Current method
      C. Relationship between potential assessment and SP&M

  IV. Reviewing the Organization's Potential Assessment Procedures
     A. Overview
     B. Step-by-step description of procedures
   V. Conducting Effective Potential Assessment
     A. Overview
     B. Using existing forms and procedures
     C. Gathering individual career planning information for use with potential assessment
  VI. (*Optional*) Role Plays (practice potential assessment interviews)
 VII. Conclusion
     A. Summary
     B. Action planning for on-the-job action
     C. Session evaluations

Outline—Session 4
"Conducting Effective Individual Development Planning"

    I. Introduction
     A. Purpose of the session
     B. Objectives of the session
     C. Organization (structure) of the session
   II. Defining Individual Development Planning
     A. What is it?
     B. Why is it important generally?
  III. Relating Individual Development Planning to SP&M
     A. Approaches
     B. Current method
     C. Relationship between individual development planning and SP&M
  IV. Reviewing Approaches to Individual Development Planning
     A. Overview
     B. Step-by-step description of approach
   V. Facilitating Effective Individual Development Planning
     A. Overview
     B. Approaches to individual development planning
     C. Relating individual career planning to individual development planning
  VI. Conclusion
     A. Summary
     B. Action planning for on-the-job action
     C. Session evaluations

the attendance of the targeted training participants. They will also attend themselves—and perhaps help deliver the training—and thereby demonstrate hands-on interest and support. Their participation and involvement will exert a powerful, but subtle, inducement for others to attend. But if they are unwilling to be involved, no amount of cajoling or threatening is an effective substitute. Moreover, they must set the example and follow the policies established for the organization.

Here are a few tips for securing attendance at group training on SP&M, assuming that adequate top management commitment exists:

▲ Draft a memo for the chairman or CEO to initial to go out with training invitations. Stress who will be in attendance, what issues will be discussed, and why the training is important.

▲ Pick an opportune time. Check dates to make sure that the dates chosen for training do not conflict with other, predictable dates.

▲ If possible, tie the training on succession planning to other events— such as strategic planning retreats—in which the targeted participants are already scheduled to attend.

▲ Field-test the training materials on a small, handpicked group of supportive managers. Be sure that all time is effectively used and that every training activity relates directly to SP&M practices in the organization.

▲ If possible, videotape a well-rehearsed practice session and share it before the session with the chairman, CEO, or other key management personnel. Ask for their suggestions about revision before the session.

Other Approaches to Training Management Employees

There will always be some management employees who will be unable to attend group training on SP&M, even when vigorous steps are taken to ensure attendance. They will have legitimate reasons for not attending. But that will not alter the fact that they missed the training. They are the group most likely to operate in a way inconsistent with organizational policy because they missed the opportunity to learn about it firsthand.

Deal with this audience through a form of "guerrilla warfare." Make sure that it is clear who they are. Then use any of the following tactics to train them:

▲ Meet with them individually, if their numbers are small enough to make that practical and if they are not so geographically dispersed that traveling to their locations is prohibitively expensive. Deliver training personally.

▲ Videotape a practice session of the training and send it to those unable to attend. Then follow up with them later for their questions and reactions.

▲ Ask another manager who did attend—such as the CEO—to describe to them the key lessons of the training in his or her own words. (That should reinforce the importance of the message.)

Training Participants in Succession Planning and Management

Training for participants in SP&M will be greatly affected by the organization's communication strategy. If decision-makers do not wish to inform individuals of the organization's SP&M practices, then no training will typically be given; on the other hand, if the organization adopts a policy of openness, then training on SP&M may be offered.

There are three general ways of offering such training: (1) direct training; (2) training integrated with other issues; and (3) training tied to career planning.

Direct Training

In direct training, employees are informed of the organization's SP&M policy and procedures. They are briefed in general terms, usually without specific descriptions of how the program is linked to existing organizational strategy. They learn how the SP&M program is linked to defining work requirements and job competencies, appraising present employee performance, assessing future individual potential, and establishing individual development plans.

Training Integrated with Other Issues

When training on SP&M is integrated with other issues, employees are told how their training, education, and development efforts factor into qualifying for advancement. No promises are made; rather, the value of planned learning activities is stressed as one means by which the individual can take proactive steps to qualify for leadership positions.

Training Tied to Career Planning

Organizational succession planning and individual career planning represent mirror images of the same issue. Succession planning and management helps the organization meet its HR needs to ensure that it is equipped with the talent needed to survive and succeed. On the other hand, individual career planning helps the individual establish career goals and prepare for meeting those goals—either inside or outside the organization.

When training on SP&M is tied to training on career planning, individuals are furnished with information about work requirements at different levels and in different functions or locations. They also learn about performance requirements in different job categories and about future success factors. With this information, they can establish their own career goals and take active steps to prepare themselves for advancement by seeking appropriate training, education, and development experiences.

Counseling Managers About Succession Planning Problems in Their Areas

Succession planning and management coordinators should make a point of meeting periodically with managers to discuss SP&M issues in their work areas and to offer individualized counseling about how to deal with those problems. If that counseling is requested, it indicates that executives have accepted SP&M, they value advice about people management issues, and they are making honest efforts to meet the SP&M needs of their organization.

The Need for Individual Counseling Sessions

Executives sometimes have need of third-party advice. In some cases they will be reluctant to share those problems with anyone—including the CEO—for fear that they will be perceived as unable to manage tough-to-handle management situations. Individual counseling with these executives by the SP&M coordinator can serve an invaluable purpose for improving SP&M practices. For this reason, the CEO and other decision-makers in the organization should actively encourage such sessions.

Who Should Conduct the Sessions?

The SP&M coordinator should arrange to meet with senior executives to conduct individual counseling sessions on a regular basis. However, the coordinator must first seize the initiative to arrange the meetings until the coordinator has gained sufficient credibility to be sought out for help by executives.

The SP&M coordinator should call each senior executive periodically and ask when they can meet. Although these individual meetings can be time-consuming, they are the best way to demonstrate commitment to the effort—and get real payoffs from it. Individual meetings are usually best timed sometime ahead of periodic SP&M meetings, such as those held quarterly in many corporations. By meeting ahead of time, the SP&M coordinator and the executive in charge of that work area can discuss sensitive personnel issues that executives may be reluctant to bring up in group meetings—or share over the phone or by mail.

Essential Requirements for Effective Counseling Sessions

To conduct effective counseling sessions, follow these general guidelines:

1. Send questions in advance, making the purpose of the session clear.
2. Tailor the questions to issues that will be treated in regularly scheduled group meetings with the CEO so that their relevance is immediately apparent.

3. Keep the meeting short and on target unless asked to offer advice on specific issues.

4. Always assume that everything is said in strictest confidence. (This point deserves strong emphasis.)

5. Be alert to casual remarks or questions that may indicate problems, probing with additional questions to learn more as appropriate.

Common Succession Planning and Management Problems—and Possible Solutions

Succession planning and management coordinators who meet to counsel managers on "people problems" unique to their areas should be prepared to deal with complex problems. Many events may derail the progress of otherwise high-potential employees, and an SP&M coordinator should be prepared to offer advice on what to do about those problems. Reclaiming high-potential employees on the verge of derailing their careers is an important role, and one that is often informally loaded on the SP&M coordinator.

Over the years I have been asked to offer executives advice on how to counsel high potentials experiencing the following problems that threatened to derail their futures:

▲ An executive engaged in a high-profile extramarital affair with a subordinate

▲ An executive accused of blatant sexual harassment—but where the accusation could not be substantiated

▲ An executive, slated for the CEO spot, who was recognized as an alcoholic by everyone except himself

▲ A male executive who was grossly insubordinate to his female superior

▲ An executive renowned for her technical knowledge who was notorious for her inability to work harmoniously with her peers

▲ An executive who experienced a major personality conflict with his immediate superior

These are merely samples of the problems about which the SP&M coordinator may be asked to offer advice.

Although few SP&M coordinators are trained psychologists or psychiatrists, they should be able to apply the following steps, which I have found helpful when advising executives about "people problems."

Step 1: *Ask for information about the present situation.* What is happening now? Where is the executive obtaining information? When and how was this information revealed? Was the information obtained firsthand, or is the executive relying on intermediaries, rumors, or speculation? What steps have been taken to separate fact from fancy?

Step 2: *Ask for information about corrective actions already attempted.* What efforts, if any, have already been made to correct the problem? What were the results of those actions? What efforts have been made to alert the affected individual to the problem or to clarify desired behavior or performance?

Step 3: *Determine the problem's cause, if possible, and assess whether it can be solved.* What does the executive believe is the cause of the problem? Does the person who is experiencing the problem know what to do? (If not, it may indicate a training need.) Is the person engaging in undesirable behavior deliberately and maliciously? (If so, it may indicate a disciplinary problem.) Has anyone asked the person experiencing the problem to identify its cause and possible solution(s)? Can the individual avoid derailing his or her career, or have matters already gone so far that others have lost all confidence for improvement?

Step 4: *Establish an action plan.* Emphasize the importance of properly managing the organization's human resources to the executive who is receiving the counseling. Express strong confidence in the executive's ability to deal with the problem. Offer to help in any way possible. Suggest such steps as these: (1) Put the problem in writing and meet with the person having the problem so as to make it as clear as possible; (2) encourage the executive to clarify, in writing, what needs to be done, how it should be done, and what will happen if it is not done.

Step 5: *Follow up.* After meeting with the executive who has had a problem, the SP&M coordinator should make a point of following up later to see how the problem was resolved or is being managed.

By following the five steps outlined above, SP&M coordinators should be able to identify and resolve most "people problems." That is a valuable service in its own right to an organization, and it can help people who are in danger of derailing get "back on track."

Summary

This chapter focused on refining the succession planning and management program. It summarized what was needed to prepare a program action plan, communicate the action plan, and counsel managers on succession planning and management problems—particularly those having to do with "people problems"—unique to their areas of responsibility.

To be successful, however, any succession planning and management program should be based on systematic analyses of present job requirements or competencies, future job requirements or competencies, present individual performance, and future individual potential. Conducting such analyses is not for the faint-hearted, the ill-prepared, or the uncommitted. These processes require hard work and diligence, as the next section of this book will show.

PART III

ASSESSING THE PRESENT AND THE FUTURE

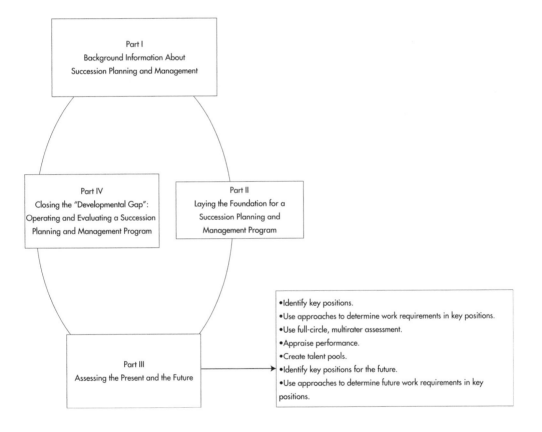

Part I
Background Information About
Succession Planning and Management

Part IV
Closing the "Developmental Gap":
Operating and Evaluating a Succession
Planning and Management Program

Part II
Laying the Foundation for a
Succession Planning and
Management Program

Part III
Assessing the Present and the Future

• Identify key positions.
• Use approaches to determine work requirements in key positions.
• Use full-circle, multirater assessment.
• Appraise performance.
• Create talent pools.
• Identify key positions for the future.
• Use approaches to determine future work requirements in key positions.

CHAPTER 8

ASSESSING PRESENT WORK REQUIREMENTS AND INDIVIDUAL JOB PERFORMANCE

Leaders must know the present before they can plan the future.[1] They must realistically view the organization's strengths and weaknesses before they can navigate around future external threats and seize opportunities as they arise. That can be a daunting task because leaders are biased observers: they are, after all, accountable in large measure for an organization's strengths and weaknesses. It is thus easy for them to overlook weaknesses, since the causes of those weaknesses may be rooted in their own past decisions; it is easy for them to overlook strengths, which they may take for granted. Managers, it has been shown,[2] will persist in an ill-fated course of action because they fall prey to the *gambler's fallacy*, that "more effort will lead to a big payoff." But some efforts never pay off; rather, they lead to mounting losses. That is why organizations replace leaders after a repeated string of failures.

Many of the same basic principles apply to succession planning and management (SP&M). Before leaders can effectively plan for succession, they must be aware of the organization's work requirements and the strengths and weaknesses of its leadership. Indeed, having the right person for the right job at the right time is a strategic issue of key importance that has long been a major challenge to top managers. But to know who those people are and what they must do, the organization must first be able to furnish answers to such questions as these:

▲ What are the organization's key positions?
▲ What are the work requirements or competencies required in key positions?
▲ How should individual performance be appraised?

This chapter focuses on answering these questions. It thus emphasizes examining present conditions. The next chapter focuses on anticipating future conditions. Taken together, they are a starting point for long-term and systematic SP&M.

Identifying Key Positions

To achieve maximum benefits from a systematic succession planning program, begin by identifying the key positions. The reason for doing this is that key positions underscore and dramatize important work processes that must be carried out and results that must be continuously accomplished. Key positions warrant attention because they represent strategically vital leverage points affecting organizational success. When they are left vacant—or when the work is left undone, for whatever reason—the organization will not be able to meet or exceed customer expectations, confront competition successfully, or follow through on efforts of crucial long-term significance.

Identifying Key Positions

A *key position* exerts critical influence on organizational activities—operationally, strategically, or both. Key positions have traditionally been viewed as those at the pinnacle of the organization's chain of command. The most obvious reason is that important decision making has been done at the top of most organizations and imposed downward. But, as decision making has become more decentralized, as a result of increasing employee involvement and the application of principles linked to high-involvement work organizations, key positions have become diffused throughout organizations. Hence, they may reside at many points on the organization chart.

Key positions are not identical across organizations. There are several reasons why. One reason is that all organizations do not allocate work in exactly the same way. Positions sharing job titles in different organizations do not necessarily perform identical duties. A second reason is that top managers in different organizations do not share the same values. As a result, they may vest job incumbents with more or less responsibility, which is influenced by their own perceptions (and values) about which activities are most important. A third reason is that organizations do not share identical strengths and weaknesses or face identical environmental threats and opportunities. Hence, a key position in one organization may not be a key position in another. Key positions are thus unique to a single organization.

Let's focus on six ways to identify key positions:

By the Consequences/Uproar Resulting from a Pending or Existing Vacancy

When the organization lacks a key position incumbent—defined as someone occupying a key position at any level, in any function, or at any location—it is apparent because important decisions cannot be reached, orders cannot be shipped, production cannot proceed, customers' needs cannot be satisfied, or bills are left unpaid. In short, a vacancy in a key position creates an uproar because an important activity is placed "on hold" until the right talent is secured to make an informed decision, complete a process, or achieve results. This delay can prove costly, placing an organization at risk to competitors who do not face such a handicap. Possible results include loss of customers, market share, and (in the worst cases) bankruptcy.

One way, then, to recognize a key position is by the consequences of—or uproar caused by—not filling a vacancy when it exists or is expected. I call this the *uproar method* of identifying key positions. Generally, the greater the uproar created by an existing or a pending vacancy, the greater the importance of that key position and the work process(es) over which it exerts influence.

By Organization Charting

Prepare a current organization chart. Show all functions. List the leader's name in each function, if the organization is sufficiently small to make that possible. Then list the number of people assigned to carry out the function. Pose these questions: (1) "What does this function uniquely contribute to the organization's mission?" and (2) "Could this function operate effectively if the leader were gone?"

The answer to the first question provides valuable clues about organizational processes. It should be expressed in terms of the inputs, transformational processes, and outputs of that function relative to the organization's work. That tells why the function is important—and what it does to accomplish the results desired from it.

The answer to the second question yields clues about key positions. If the answer is no, then the next question to ask is, "Why is that leader so valuable? What is it that makes him or her important—and potentially tough to replace? Does he or she possess specialized expertise or carry out specialized work duties?" (If so, then it is a key position.) "Do the staff members collectively assigned to that function lack the ability to achieve results in the absence of a leader?" (If so, then a potential replacement need has been identified that should be shored up.)

If the answer is yes, then ask, "Why is the function able to operate without the leader? Are others particularly key to its operation?" If that is the case, then the leader does not occupy a key position, but one or more workers do.

If this activity is carried to its natural conclusion, key positions should be easily identified on the organization chart. Each key position is tied to a critically important organizational function, result, or work process. A vacancy in any key position will represent a *hole*, a gap between an organizational requirement and the human talent needed to meet that requirement.

By Questioning

Most senior executives have a keen grasp of their areas of responsibility. Ask them what they regard as key positions within their own areas by posing a question like, "What positions in your area of responsibility are so important that, if they suddenly became vacant, your part of the organization would face major problems in achieving results?" Ask for the titles of the positions to be listed, not the names of job incumbents. Then ask, "Why are these positions so important?" Don't provide clues; rather, allow executives to furnish their own rationales. (That tactic is likely to lead to the best information.)

By Historical Evidence

Has the organization experienced crises or uproars in the past resulting from unexpected departures by key job incumbents? Use evidence of past uproars as indicators of where key positions are located. Scan personnel records to obtain the names and job titles of people who departed in the last few years. Then contact their former supervisors in the organization to find out which departures posed the greatest problems for the organization and why they posed problems. Were they in tough-to-fill positions? Did they possess unique, difficult-to-replace knowledge and skills? What was it exactly that made these losses so important? How was the uproar handled? If a vacancy occurred in the same position again, would it still cause an uproar? Why? Compile the answers to these questions as evidence of key positions.

By Network Charting

Network charting is a technique of communication analysis that has been used in identifying employment discrimination.[3] But its applications are potentially much more powerful in charting the decision-making process in organizations. The idea is a simple one: trace the path of communication flows during one or more decisions to answer such questions as "Who is included?" "Who is excluded?" and "Why are some individuals included or excluded?"

A key assumption of network charting is that decision-makers will seek information only from individuals who occupy important positions and/or who are viewed as credible, trustworthy, and knowledgeable about the issues. Significantly, it has also been shown that decision-makers prefer to include people like themselves—and exclude people unlike themselves—from decision-making processes. Hence, communication flows in the same way that succession decisions are often made—that is, through homosocial reproduction,[4] the tendency of leaders to perpetuate themselves by sponsoring people who are in some way like themselves. As Rosabeth Moss Kanter describes the process, "Because of the situation in which managers function, because of the position of managers in the corporate structure, social similarity tends to become extremely important to them. The structure sets in motion forces leading to the replication of managers as the same kind of social individuals. And the men who manage reproduce themselves in kind."[5]

Network charting can be carried out by interviewing people or by retracing communication flows. But another way, though time-consuming, is to shadow a key decision-maker to determine firsthand what positions and what individuals are included in making a decision and why they are included. In this application of network charting, the aim is not to uncover employment discrimination; rather, it is to determine which positions are considered key to decision making in each part of the organization. The results should yield valuable information about key positions in—and the route of work processes through—the organization.

By Combination

A sixth and final approach is to combine two or more other approaches listed above. Academic researchers call this *triangulation*,[6] since it involves verifying information by double-checking it from multiple sources. Radar and sonar operators originated the approach, I believe, as a way to obtain a definite fix on an object. Practically speaking, however, many organizations have neither time nor resources to double-check key positions. Often, only one approach is used.

What Information Should the Organization Maintain About Key Positions?

Once key positions have been identified, additional questions will present themselves. For example:

▲ Who occupies those key positions now? What are their qualifications? What background, education, experience, or other specialized knowledge did they bring to their positions?

▲ What are the work requirements in key positions? (See the next section below.)

▲ When are those key positions likely to become vacant? Can some key vacancies be predicted based on the announced retirement or career plans of key position incumbents?

▲ Where are key positions located in the organization? (Answer that question based on the organization's structure, job categories, and geographical locations.)

▲ How is performance appraised in the organization? How well do performance appraisal practices match up to information about work requirements or competencies by position?

▲ How well are the key position incumbents presently performing? Did their backgrounds, education, and experience properly equip them to perform? If not, what are they lacking?

▲ How did key job incumbents secure their positions? Were they groomed to assume their positions, recruited from outside, transferred from within, or did they reach their positions through other means?

By answering these questions, the organization can begin to establish an information system to track key positions, key position incumbents, and individual performance.

Three Approaches to Determining Work Requirements in Key Positions

Once key positions have been identified, direct attention to determining the work requirements in those positions. After all, the only way that individuals can be prepared as replacements for key positions is to clarify first what the key position incumbents do and what kind of characteristics they possess. At least three ways may be used to do that, and they are described below.

1. Conducting Job and Task Analysis

Job analysis summarizes or outlines the activities, responsibilities, duties, or essential functions of a job. *Task analysis* goes a step beyond job analysis to determine what must be done to carry out each activity or meet each responsibility, duty, or essential function. The result of a job analysis is called a *job description*; the result of a task analysis is called a *task inventory*. Some authorities distinguish between the terms *job* and *position*:

> A job consists of a group of related activities and duties. Ideally, the duties of a job should consist of natural units of work that are similar and related. They should be clear and distinct from those of other jobs to minimize misunderstanding and conflict among employees and to enable employees to recognize what is expected of them. For some jobs, several employees may be required, each of whom will occupy a separate position. A position consists of different duties and responsibilities performed by only one employee.[7]

It is thus important to distinguish between a *job description*, which provides information about an entire job category (such as supervisors, managers, or executives), and a *position description*, which provides information unique to one employee. In most cases, the focus of determining work requirements for SP&M is on positions, since the aim is to identify work requirements unique to key positions.

What Is a Position Description?

A *position description* summarizes the duties, activities, or responsibilities of a position. Hence, it literally describes a position in one organizational setting. It answers this question: "What are incumbents in the position expected to do in the organization?"

No universal standards exist either for job descriptions or for position descriptions.[8] In most organizations, however, position descriptions list at least the title, salary or wage level, location in the organization, and essential job functions. An *essential job function*, a legal term used in the Americans with Disabilities Act, is an activity that must be conducted by a position incumbent. More specifically, it "is [a job activity] that's fundamental to successful performance of the job, as opposed to marginal job functions, which may be performed by particular incumbents at particular times, but are incidental to the main purpose of the job. If the performance of a job function is only a matter of convenience, and not necessary, it's a marginal function."[9]

Some organizations add other features to job descriptions, and the same features may be added to position descriptions as well. These additions may include, for instance, the approximate time devoted to each essential job function, the percentage of a position's total time devoted to each essential job function, the relative importance of each essential job function to successful performance, and a job specification listing the minimum qualifications required for selection.

How Is Position Analysis Conducted?

Position analysis is conducted in the same way as job and task analysis. As Carlisle notes, "the process of analyzing jobs and tasks involves at least three key steps. First, the job or task is broken down into its component parts. Second, the relationships between the parts are examined and compared with correct principles of performance. Third, the parts are restructured to form an improved job or task, and learning requirements are specified."[10]

Use the worksheet appearing in Exhibit 8-1 as a guide for preparing a current key position description. For ideas about what essential job functions to list, see *The Dictionary of Occupational Titles* (published by the U.S. Department of Labor), works on the Americans with Disabilities Act,[11] and references about management job descriptions.[12]

Advantages and Disadvantages of Position Descriptions

Position descriptions are advantageous for identifying work requirements for three reasons. First, most organizations have at least job descriptions, which can be an important starting point on which to base more individualized position descriptions. Second, position descriptions can be the basis for making and justifying many personnel decisions—including selection, appraisal, and

Exhibit 8-1. A Worksheet for Writing a Key Position Description

Directions: Give careful thought to the process of writing this position description, since it can be critically important in recruiting, selecting, orienting, training, appraising, and developing a job incumbent for a key position. The best approach is to ask the key position incumbent to write the description and then to review it several levels up, down, and across the organization. (In that way, it should be possible to obtain valuable information about the desired results necessary for this position at present—some of which even the current position incumbent may be unaware of.) For now, focus on what the position incumbent is *presently doing* and what others in the organization *want the key position incumbent to be doing in the future*. Add paper if necessary.

Title: (*Fill in the position title*) _____

_____

Salary Level: (*Note the present pay grade*) _____

Organizational Unit/Department: (*Note the present placement of the position in the organizational structure*) _____

_____

Immediate Supervisor: (*Note to whom the position incumbent presently reports on the organization chart by title*)

_____

_____

Position Summary: (*In one or two sentences, summarize the purpose—or mission statement—for this position. Answer this question: why does it exist?*)

_____

_____

_____

Position Duties/Responsibilities/Activities/Key Results/Competencies/Essential Functions: (*Make a list in the left column below of the most important position duties, responsibilities, activities, key results, competencies, or essential functions. If necessary, use a separate sheet to draft the list and then record the results of your deliberations in priority order in the space below. Be sure to list the most important duty, responsibility, activity, key result, or essential function first. Begin each statement with an action verb. Then, in the right column, indicate the approximate percentage of time devoted to that activity.*)

List of Position Duties/
Responsibilities/Activities/
Key Results/Essential Functions:

Approximate % of
Time Devoted to
Each:

training—and not just decisions linked to succession planning and management. Third and finally, legislation—particularly the Americans with Disabilities Act—has made written expressions of work requirements important as legal evidence of what is necessary to perform the work.[13]

However, position descriptions are by no means foolproof. First, they tend to focus on activities, not so much on results. Second, they may leave out important personal characteristics that are crucial to successful job performance. Third, they date quickly. Keeping them updated can be a time-consuming chore.

2. Identifying Competencies and Developing a Competency Model

Competency identification is a possible step beyond job and task analysis as a means of clarifying key position requirements. In this context, *competency* refers to "an underlying characteristic of an employee (that is, motive, trait, skill, aspects of one's self-image, social role, or a body of knowledge) which results in effective and/or superior performance in a job"[14]; *competency identification* pinpoints competencies; and a *competency model* "includes those competencies that are required for satisfactory or exemplary job performance within the context of a person's job roles, responsibilities and relationships in an organization and its internal and external environments."[15]

Competency models have emerged as the mainstream approach used in many organizations to integrate all facets of human resource management. Competency identification was described at greater length in Chapter 4. Most well-known companies have based their succession programs on competency models, which become blueprints of the talent to be developed.

3. Rapid Results Assessment

A new approach to competency modeling is needed to maximize the strengths and minimize the weaknesses of traditional approaches. Such a new approach may involve the marriage of a traditional approach to competency assessment, such as McLagan's Flexible Approach,[16] with the so-called DACUM method. DACUM is short for Developing A Curriculum.[17] It has been widely used in job and task analysis for technical positions and in establishing occupational curricula at community colleges. Seldom, however, has it been described as a means by which to determine work requirements in management or professional positions.

To use DACUM in its traditional sense, select a facilitator who is trained in the approach. Convene a panel consisting of eight to twelve people who are expert in the job. Then take the following steps[18]:

1. Orient the committee to DACUM.
2. Review the job or occupational area of concern.
3. Identify the general areas of responsibility of the job.
4. Identify the specific tasks performed in each area of responsibility.
5. Review and refine task and duty statements.
6. Sequence task and duty statements.
7. Identify entry-level tasks.

The result of a typical DACUM panel is a detailed matrix illustrating work activities. They are arranged in order of difficulty, from the simplest to the most complex activities. In DACUM's traditional application, panel members approach descriptions of "personality characteristics" as an additional activity. For instance, at the conclusion of the DACUM session panel members may be asked a question such as, "What personal characteristics describe an effective job incumbent?" That question should elicit responses from panel members such as "Punctuality," "Good attendance," "Ability to work harmoniously with coworkers," or "Dresses appropriately." Rarely are such characteristics linked to specific, measurable behaviors, though they may be critical to successful job performance.

In practice, a DACUM panel usually meets in a quiet room for one or more days. The facilitator asks panelists to list work activities, in round-robin fashion, in no particular order. Each activity is written with Magic Marker on a sheet of paper and posted on a blank wall at the front of the room. Because panelists can list activities quickly, most DACUM facilitators need one or two confederates to assist them by writing the activities and posting them on the wall. Panelists who are unable to think of an activity are skipped. The process continues until all the panelists exhaust activities to list.

At that point, the facilitator calls a break. With the help of confederates—and perhaps one or more panelists or other job experts—the facilitator devises descriptive categories for the activities and groups related activities. When finished, the facilitator reconvenes the panel. Panelists add, subtract, or modify categories and verify activities. Finally, they sequence categories and activities from most simple to most complex. These steps closely resemble classic brainstorming, which consists of two steps: idea generation and idea evaluation.[19]

To use DACUM as a tool for competency assessment, facilitators should take additional steps. Once a DACUM job matrix has been completed and verified, facilitators should adjourn the panel and plan to convene at another time. Once the panel is reconvened, facilitators should present panelists with the DACUM job matrix, either as an individualized handout or as a large wall chart. Facilitators should then progress around the room, focusing panelists' attention on each cell of the job matrix, and asking panelists to (1) list underlying motives, traits, aspects of self-image, social roles, or body of knowledge that effective job incumbents should exhibit to carry out that activity; and (2) work outputs or results stemming from each activity. The answers should be written inside each cell.

Once again, the panel should be adjourned briefly. As in the first panel meeting, facilitators should make an effort to eliminate duplication and economically list personal characteristics and work outputs for each activity. When facilitators are finished, they should again reconvene the panel and seek verification and consensus on the results. If the meeting runs too long, facilitators may adjourn and follow up by written survey, thereby turning traditional brainstorming into a modified delphi process.[20]

The value of this approach should be apparent. First, it is much faster than traditional competency modeling. (That is a major advantage, and it is worth emphasizing.) Second, this approach—like traditional DACUM—has high face validity because it uses experienced job incumbents (or other knowledgeable people). It should gain ready acceptance in the organization. Third, it permits the personal involvement of key decision-makers, thereby building the ownership that stems from participation. Fourth and finally, it enjoys the key advantage of a competency-based approach in that the modified DACUM moves beyond the traditional focus on work activities or tasks to include descriptions of underlying characteristics and/or outputs.

Of course, this new approach—which I have chosen to call *rapid results assessment*—does have its disadvantages. The results do not have the research rigor of other competency-assessment approaches. Hence, rigor is sacrificed for speed. Second, the results of the approach will depend heavily on the credibility of the individual panelists. If inexperienced people or poor performers participate, the results will be viewed with suspicion.

Rapid results assessment can provide valuable information for succession planning and management. If the assessment process is focused on key positions—and DACUM panels include immediate superiors, peers, incumbents, and even subordinates—it can yield powerful information about role expectations for incumbents in these positions. It can also provide the basis, as DACUM does, to select, appraise, train, reward, and develop people who are being groomed for key positions.

Using Full-Circle, Multirater Assessments

Since the publication of the first edition of this book in 1994, many organizations have begun to use full-circle, multirater assessments as a means to appraise an individual's present performance or future potential.[21] (And it is worth emphasizing that those are two different things. Remember: *Successful performance in a current position is no guarantee of success at a higher-level position, for the simple reason that requirements differ by level.*) Such assessments—sometimes called 360-degree assessments because they examine an individual from a full circle around him or her—are useful ways to collect much data from organizational superiors, subordinates, peers or colleagues, and even customers, suppliers, distributors, and family members. They usually indicate how well an individual is performing (or has the potential to perform) when compared to competency models or work requirements. Many full-circle, multirater assessment questionnaires can be purchased from commercial vendors or accessed online, though off-the-shelf solutions should be used cautiously because they are not corporate-culture specific.

Questions to Consider

But many questions arise when decision-makers contemplate using full-circle, multirater assessments. Among them are the following:

1. Who will be assessed, and by whom will they be assessed?
2. What will be assessed? Will it be present performance, future potential, or both?
3. When will the assessment occur?
4. Why is the assessment being conducted? Since full-circle, multirater assessment is expensive, will the benefits in improved accuracy and credibility of results outweigh the costs?
5. How will the assessment be conducted? Will it be conducted online, on paper, or by a combination? What will be done with the results, how will the results be interpreted and fed back to the individuals, and how will they be used?

These questions should be answered before the organization undertakes the use of full-circle, multirater assessments. (Use the worksheet appearing in Exhibit 8-2 to consider these questions.)

Advantages and Disadvantages of Full-Circle, Multirater Assessments

There are many advantages to full-circle, multirater assessments. They consolidate feedback from many people surrounding an individual about his or her present performance or future potential. The feedback alone is powerful in creating an impetus for change and individual development. Moreover, the ratings have much power in tapping into multiple perspectives, since (as the old saying goes) "what you think depends on where you sit in the organization."

But there are disadvantages to full-circle, multirater assessments, and they should be considered before the organization incurs the expense of using them. First, these assessments can be expensive and are thus worthwhile only when decision-makers know what they want and why they want it. Second, if individuals are rated against criteria such as competencies or work require-

Exhibit 8-2. A Worksheet for Considering Key Issues in Full-Circle, Multirater Assessments

Directions: When decision-makers begin thinking about using full-circle, multirater assessment, there are many issues they should clarify at the outset.

Use this worksheet to help guide their thinking. For each question appearing in the left column below, take notes about their answers in the right column. There are no "right" or "wrong" answers in any absolute sense, of course. But it is important to clarify the answers to these questions.

Questions	Answers
1. Who will be assessed, and by whom will they be assessed?	
2. What will be assessed? Will it be present performance, future potential, or both?	
3. When will the assessment occur?	
4. Why is the assessment being conducted?	
5. How will the assessment be conducted? (Will it be conducted online, on paper, or by a combination?)	
6. What will be done with the results, how will the results be interpreted and fed back to the individuals, and how will they be used?	

ments that are not unique to the corporate culture (as is true if off-the-shelf or online instruments are used without modification), the results may not be too useful or meaningful. In fact, the results may be misleading. After all, performance and potential are influenced by the corporate cultural context in which individuals perform. Third, when large numbers of people are subjected to these assessments, the task of data analysis can be daunting. (Consider: one person may have as many as twelve raters. If 100 people are subjected to assessment, that means 1,200 ratings must be compiled and fed back individually.)

Feeding Back the Results of Full-Circle, Multirater Assessments

Since the last edition of this book was published, I have had ample opportunity to conduct full-circle, multirater assessments during consulting engagements. And one insight I have gained from those experiences is that it is not so much the initial design of the assessment that is so important as it is the feedback session that occurs after the assessment. When the full-circle, multi-rater assessment of an individual is finished, what is done with that? That is the key question, and it is worthy of some consideration.

The results of a full-circle, multirater assessments can be helpful in pin-pointing present performance gaps or future developmental gaps. The feedback session—which can occur in a meeting conducted by an immediate supervisor, HR professional, external consultant, or some combination of all of these—must be well planned. The goal should be to establish a plan for improvement (if the meeting focuses on present performance), an individual learning plan (if the meeting focuses on future potential), or both.

Begin the meeting by presenting the results of the assessment. Start with small talk to set the person at ease. (If you wish, provide the assessment to the person before the meeting so that he or she has had time to study it.) Then provide the feedback, hitting the high points. Walk the person through the results and then offer interpretations. Be sure to mention strengths as well as weaknesses. If you wish, you may ask the person what he or she believes the results might mean, what could be done about them, and what actions should be taken.

It is worth noting that individuals cannot necessarily identify the best strategies for developing themselves for the future. That is input that the immediate supervisor should provide and that is why it is worth having the immediate supervisor in the room if the feedback session on the full-circle, multirater assessment is provided by an HR professional or external consultant. The immediate supervisor is best positioned to provide input about the corporate-culture-specific developmental assignments that could build essential competencies, and the immediate supervisor is also best positioned to describe specific situations that may explain an individual's ratings. When the meeting is over, a development plan should have been agreed to. It can then be filed or placed on an online system for later review.

The Future of Full-Circle, Multirater Assessments

It is likely that full-circle, multirater assessment will only be used more frequently in the future. For that reason, those managing SP&M programs should become familiar with sources that describe how to establish and use them.[22]

Appraising Performance and Applying Performance Management

For an SP&M program to be effective, it must be based on information about work requirements in key positions and about the performance of incumbents and prospective successors. Hence, employee performance appraisal should be an important source of information for SP&M. But what is performance appraisal, and how should it be linked to SP&M?

Defining Performance Appraisal

Performance appraisal is the process of determining how well individuals are meeting the work requirements of their jobs. Just as most organizations prepare job descriptions to answer the question "What do people do?" most organizations also prepare performance appraisals to answer the question "How well are people performing?" It is important to emphasize that performance appraisals are properly viewed within the context of *performance management*,[23] which is the process of creating a work environment in which people want to perform to their peak abilities and are encouraged to develop themselves for the future. (See Exhibit 8-3.) Like so many terms in the HR field, *performance management* can be a term in search of meaning and can refer (variously) to after-the-fact performance appraisal, before-the-fact performance planning, during-performance feedback, and the whole cycle of planning for performance, identifying and knocking down performance barriers, providing feedback during performance, and giving feedback upon the completion of performance.

Performance appraisals are commonly used to justify pay raises, promotions, and other employment decisions. They are also critically important for SP&M, since few organizations will advance individuals into key positions when they are not performing their present jobs adequately.

While a fixture of organizational life, employee performance appraisal has not been immune to criticism. Indeed, it is rare to find managers who will enthusiastically champion the performance appraisal practices of their organizations. In recent years, appraisals have been increasingly prone to litigation.[24] Moreover, appraisals have been attacked by no less than the late curmudgeonly guru of Total Quality Management, W. Edwards Deming. Deming faulted employee performance appraisal for two primary reasons. First, Deming believed that performance appraisal leads to management by fear. Second, appraisal "encourages short-term performance at the expense of long-term planning."[25] It prompts people to look good in the short run, with potentially devastating long-term organizational effects.

The central point of Deming's argument is that people live up to the expectations that their superiors have for them. That is the *Pygmalion effect*, which takes its name from the ancient artist who fell in love with his own sculpted creation of the woman Galatea. The Pygmalion effect asserts that managers who believe that their employees are performing effectively will create a self-fulfilling prophecy. The underlying assumption, then, is that the world is influenced by viewers' beliefs about it.

When performance appraisal is conducted in a highly critical manner, it

Exhibit 8-3. The Relationship Between Performance Management and
Performance Appraisal

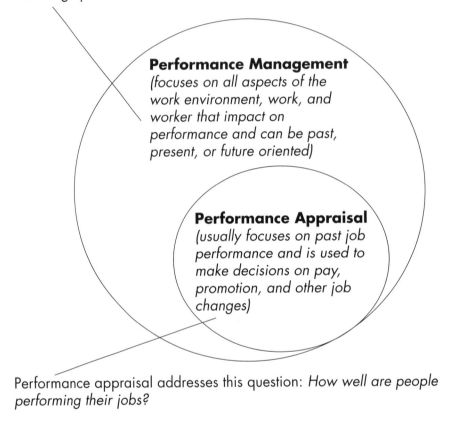

Performance management addresses this question: *What is necessary to encourage performance now and in the future?*

Performance Management
(focuses on all aspects of the work environment, work, and worker that impact on performance and can be past, present, or future oriented)

Performance Appraisal
(usually focuses on past job performance and is used to make decisions on pay, promotion, and other job changes)

Performance appraisal addresses this question: *How well are people performing their jobs?*

has the potential to demotivate and demoralize people. Indeed, research evidence indicates that performance appraisal interviews focusing on "what people are doing wrong" can actually lead to worse performance.

How Should Performance Appraisal Be Linked to Succession Planning and Management?

Despite harsh attacks from critics, performance appraisal is likely to remain a fixture of organizational life. One reason is that, despite their flaws, written appraisals based on job-related performance criteria are superior to informal, highly subjective appraisals at a time when employees are increasingly prone to litigate. In the absence of written forms and formal procedures, managers do not cease appraising employees; rather, they simply do it in a less structured fashion. Worse yet, they may face no requirement to provide employees with feedback—with the result that they can never improve. Indeed, few can dispute that employees will not improve their performance—or develop in line with succession plans—if they have received no timely, concrete, and specific feedback on how they are doing or what they should do to improve. While annual performance appraisals are no substitute for daily feedback, they should be used together to help employees develop.[26] Otherwise, the organization will have no records of employee performance, other than the faulty memories and unarticulated impressions of supervisors and other employees, on which to base pay, promotion, transfer, or other decisions.

There are many approaches to performance appraisal, and much has been written on the subject.[27] (Different types of appraisals are summarized in Exhibit 8-4.) To be effective, however, performance appraisal should be based as closely as possible on the work that employees do. Used in conjunction with individual potential assessments—which compare individuals to future job assignment possibilities or future competencies—they can be a powerful tool for employee improvement and development. For that reason, the best appraisal is one that examines employee performance point-by-point to present responsibilities of the present competencies.

One way to do that is to begin with a position description. Employees should then be appraised against each activity. In this way, the organization can maintain precise and detailed records of employee performance in each facet of the individual's job; and the individual will receive specific feedback about how well he or she is performing. The problem is that such appraisals can be time-consuming to write and conduct. And, in the case of individuals who are performing poorly, their immediate superiors must take the time to explain what needs to be improved and how it should be improved. To save time, some organizations attempt to develop simple, easy-to-fill-out appraisals to ease the paperwork burden on supervisors. Unfortunately, the easier an appraisal is to fill out, the less useful it is in providing feedback to employees.

To solve that problem, try developing free-form appraisals that use job descriptions themselves—or competencies—as the basis for appraisal. (See Exhibit 8-5 for a worksheet to help prepare such an appraisal.) Another approach is to develop appraisals so that they are geared to future improvement rather than past performance. In that way, they are focused less on what employees are doing wrong and more on what they can do right. If that approach is followed consistently, it can provide useful information to employees about what they should do to prepare themselves for the future—and qualify for succession.

Creating Talent Pools: Techniques and Approaches

A *talent pool* is a group of workers who are being prepared for vertical or horizontal advancement. *Vertical advancement* usually means promotion up

(text continues on page 199)

Exhibit 8-4. Approaches to Conducting Employee Performance Appraisal

Approach	Focus	Brief Description
Global Rating	Focuses on the individual's overall job performance.	The appraiser is asked to characterize an individual's overall job performance on a single scale or in a single essay response. *Chief Advantage:* Appraisers can make responses quickly. *Chief Disadvantage:* Performance is more complex than a single rating can indicate.
Trait Rating	Focuses on traits related to the individual's performance. Examples of traits might include "initiative" or "timeliness."	Appraisers are asked to characterize an individual's job performance over a specific time span using a series of traits. Often, trait ratings are scaled from "excellent" through "unacceptable." The appraiser is asked to check an appropriate point on the scale. However, traits can also be assessed by an essay response in which the appraiser is asked to write a narrative about the individual's performance relative to the trait. *Chief Advantage:* Appraisers can make responses quickly. *Chief Disadvantage:* Traits can have different meanings, so consistency of rating and job-relatedness of traits may be critical issues to deal with.

Dimensions/ Activity Rating	Focuses on each job activity, duty, responsibility, or essential function.	Think of a dimensional rating as a "job description that has been given scales to assess performance." Appraisers are asked to rate individual performance on *each* job activity, duty, responsibility, or essential job function. Responses may be provided by checking a mark on a scale or by writing an essay.

Chief Advantage:
 This approach to appraisal makes a deliberate effort to tie performance appraisal to job duties, thereby ensuring job-relatedness.

Chief Disadvantage:
 To work effectively, both appraiser and performer must agree in advance on the duties. That means job descriptions must be updated regularly, and that can become time-consuming.

Behaviorally Anchored Rating Scales (BARS)	Focuses on job behaviors—observable activities—distinguishing exemplary from average performers.	A BARS performance appraisal typically consists of 5 to 10 vertical scales that are developed through a critical incident process to distinguish effective from ineffective performance. Each scale represents actual performance. A BARS rating system is often compatible with a competency-based approach.

Chief Advantage:
 Since each BARS is tied directly to job activities, this approach to performance

(continues)

Exhibit 8-4. (continued)

Approach	Focus	Brief Description
		appraisal enjoys high face validity. It can also lead to improved job performance by clarifying for performers exactly what behavior is desirable and undesirable.
		Chief Disadvantage: To work effectively, BARS requires considerable time and effort to devise. That can exceed the resources—or commitment—of many organizations.
Management by Objectives (MBO)	Focuses on the results of job performance rather than processes to achieve results.	Before the appraisal period begins, the appraiser and performer jointly agree upon job results desired. At the end of the appraisal period, the results are compared to the objectives established at the outset of the appraisal period.
		Chief Advantages: The focus is on results rather than on methods of achieving them. Both appraiser and performer are involved in establishing performance objectives.
		Chief Disadvantages: For the appraiser and performer to reach agreement, much time may be required. Writing performance objectives can turn the process into a "paper mill."

Exhibit 8-5. A Worksheet for Developing an Employee Performance Appraisal Linked to a Position Description

Directions: Use this worksheet to develop a "free-form" employee performance appraisal that is based specifically on the position description. In the left column below, indicate what the position description indicates are the duties, activities, responsibilities, key result areas, competencies, or essential job functions. Then, in the right column, indicate how performance in the position may be measured.

What are the position's activities, duties, responsibilities? (List them from an up-to-date position description.)	*How should performance be measured for each activity, duty, or responsibility? (Indicate appropriate ways to measure successful performance.)*

the organization's chain of command. Of course, in recent years, promotions have been diminishing in number. *Horizontal advancement* usually means that the individual's competencies are enhanced so that he or she has a broader scope of knowledge, skills, and abilities in keeping with the organization's direction or his or her occupation.

The use of talent pools is one reason that SP&M is different from replacement planning. Instead of identifying only one or several backups for key positions, as is common in replacement planning, the idea of talent pools is to create as many backups as possible among people who are willing to develop themselves. (Of course, there are cost-benefit implications to committing to talent pools. Organizational leaders should not promise them if they are not willing to pay for them.)

To create talent pools, organizations should possess competency models by departments, job categories, hierarchical levels, or occupations. The competency models may describe present competencies or desired future competencies. Also important, as described in Chapter 4, are value statements that indicate desired corporate values or desired ethical conduct.

Begin the process of creating a talent pool by clarifying targeted groups. Answer such questions as these:

▲ Who is included?

▲ What is a talent pool? How many talent pools should exist in the organization?

▲ When is each talent pool to be formed?

▲ Where is each talent pool to be located? (What is its geographical scope?)

▲ Why is each talent pool desirable?

▲ How will the talent pool be analyzed for current bench strength and desired future bench strength, and how will the status of each talent pool be tracked and assessed?

▲ How will individuals in the talent pool be developed for the future?

There are as many ways to define talent pools as there are to define competency models. In other words, it is possible to have talent pools by department, by hierarchical level on the organization's chain of command, by job category, by region, by occupation, and by other means.

It is worth emphasizing that, if talent pools are formed, no one person should be designated as a successor for a key position. Instead, the logic is that all people in the talent pool will be developed in line with present and future organizational and individual needs. To be effective, a talent pool should be paired with competency models, appropriate performance management practices to encourage individual development and performance, appropriate potential assessment strategies, and appropriate developmental efforts. When a vacancy occurs, the individuals compete. Instead of giving the job to those with the longest time in position or those who are personal favorites of immediate supervisors, individuals are then prepared to compete on the basis of demonstrated track records in performing their work and developing themselves.

Thinking Beyond Talent Pools

It is an intriguing question to ask "What is beyond talent pools?" After all, some organizational leaders have not even committed to develop everyone who is willing to be developed, which is the fundamental philosophy that underlies talent pooling. But for those organizations that have committed to talent pooling and have had some experience with it, opportunities may exist to push the concept further.

One way to do that is to move away from thinking about developing people to meet the minimum requirements for positions.[28] Instead, a goal may be to leverage the talent base of the organization by developing people to the level of exemplary performers. (Of course, that assumes that organizational leaders know who the exemplary performers are, based on objective performance measures rather than perceptions that may be biased.) To clarify the point by example, suppose the organization commits to develop supervisors to department managers. Any supervisor who wishes to join a program for that purpose is participating in a talent pooling effort. But suppose the organization's leaders decide that they do not want to "set the bar" at the lowest level needed to qualify for consideration but rather at the highest level. To that end, they will need to know what distinguishes the best-in-class (exemplary) department managers from those who are merely fully successful.

Why would an organization's leaders commit to do this? The answer seems clear. Exemplary performers may be as much as twenty times more productive than their fully successful counterparts. If the organization could get more exemplary performers, then the organization would be more competitive, efficient, and effective.

There is yet another possible way to move beyond talent pooling. Many talent pooling efforts focus only on building job competencies. But if that notion is expanded to include psychological assessments, individual career planning, and value modeling efforts, the notion of "development" can move beyond mere preparation for work to betterment of the person as a person.

Psychological assessment, in particular, seems to be the focus of much attention. "Psychologist Robert Hogan has administered personality tests to well over a million people in the past three decades and claims that at least 55 percent of managers in American corporations are unfit for their jobs," writes Kaihla. "That may explain why his company, Hogan Assessment Systems, and many major test vendors are reporting double-digit growth this year over last. Business is booming for the headshrinkers."[29]

Growing awareness exists, and is bolstered by thinking from the competency movement, that it is as much the person in the job as it is the work he or she is to do that is so important. That has prompted organizations to rely on a growing number of psychological assessments to help make or support employment decisions, including succession decisions.[30] The danger, of course, is that psychological assessments, or assessments like the Myers Briggs Type Indicator (MBTI), will be improperly used by poorly trained people—or will be used as the only reason to "rule people out" for promotions for which they may otherwise be well qualified. A good strategy is to look for instruments, like the Hogan (see www.hoganassessments.com/HPI.aspx) or the Neo (see www.rpp.on.ca/neopir.htm), that are based on the Big Five personality characteristics. Those assessments should be administered and interpreted only by people who know what they are doing. And HR practitioners should train managers how to use personality assessments in combination with other methods of assessment to examine an individual's likelihood of success in a future position. For more information on personality assessment, check out such Web sites as www.acsu.buffalo.edu/~stmeier/c6.html and www.erin.utoronto.ca/~w3psyuli/PSY230/PSY230Notes07.htm.

This section was meant to stimulate some thought. What could be done to move beyond talent pooling to achieve quantum leaps in improvement? I have offered several ideas. Perhaps you have some as well.

Summary

This chapter has emphasized present conditions. More specifically, it addressed the following questions:

▲ What are the organization's key positions?

▲ What are the work requirements or competencies required in key positions?

▲ How should individual performance be appraised?

▲ What methods should be used to keep track of the organization's work requirements and individual performance?

The next chapter focuses on anticipating future conditions as essential in succession planning and management. It thus discusses how to identify future work requirements in key positions and how to assess individual potential.

CHAPTER 9

ASSESSING FUTURE WORK REQUIREMENTS AND INDIVIDUAL POTENTIAL

Having information about present work requirements or competencies and individual job performance provides only a one-dimensional picture. To make the picture complete—and thus provide the basis for systematic succession planning and management (SP&M)—information is also needed about future work requirements and individual potential.[1] Hence, this chapter focuses on assessing future work requirements and individual potential. More specifically, the chapter addresses these questions:

- ▲ What key positions and talent requirements are likely to emerge in the organization's future?
- ▲ What will be the work requirements in those positions?
- ▲ What is individual potential, and how should it be assessed?

Identifying Key Positions and Talent Requirements for the Future

Neither key positions nor their work requirements will remain forever static. The reason, of course, is that organizations are constantly in flux in response to pressures exerted internally and externally. As a result, SP&M coordinators need to identify future key positions and determine future work requirements if they are to be successful in preparing individuals to assume key positions. They must, in a sense, cope with a moving-target effect in which work requirements, key positions, and even high-potential employees are changing.[2]

But how can they be certain what positions will be key to the organization in the future? Unfortunately, the unsettling fact is that no foolproof way exists to predict key positions. About the best that can be done is to conduct careful reviews of changes in work and people, and draw some conclusions about the likely consequences of change.

Applying Environmental Scanning

As a first step in predicting key positions in the future, begin by applying environmental scanning. This can be understood as a systematic process of examining external trends.[3] Focus attention on economic, governmental/legal, technological, social, geographical, and other issues and trends affecting the organization's external environment. (Use the worksheet in Exhibit 9-1 for this purpose.) For best results, involve decision-makers in this process, since key positions in the future should reflect the organization's strategic plans and changing work processes.

Applying Organizational Analysis

As a second step in predicting key positions in the future, turn next to organizational analysis. This is the systematic process of examining how an organization is positioning itself to address future challenges.[4] It can also be understood as any effort made to assess an organization's strengths and weaknesses. Consider the following questions:

▲ How well positioned is the organization presently to respond to the effects of future trends?

▲ What action steps can the organization take to meet the threats and opportunities posed by future trends?

▲ How can the organization maximize its strengths and minimize its weaknesses as the future unfolds in the present?

As these questions are answered, pay particular attention to likely changes in (1) *organizational structure* (What will be the reporting relationships? How will divisions, departments, work units, and jobs be designed?), and (2) *work processes* (How will work flow into each part of the organization? What will be done with it? Where will the work flow to?).

Structure and processes are important issues because key positions result from decisions made about how to structure responsibility and organize the work process.[5] To direct attention to likely key positions in the future, then, decision-makers should examine how the organization will respond to external pressures by structuring responsibility and organizing work processes. Key positions will emerge—and old ones will fade—based on the way the organization chooses to respond to environmental demands. Use the activity appearing in Exhibit 9-2 to help decision-makers address these issues.

Preparing Realistic Future Scenarios

As a third and final step in predicting key positions in the future, compare the results obtained from environmental scanning and organizational analysis.

Exhibit 9-1. A Worksheet for Environmental Scanning

Directions: What trends evident in the external environment will affect the organization in the future? Answering that question should prove valuable in strategic business planning, human resource planning, and succession planning. Environmental scanning attempts to identify those trends—and, more important, to predict their effects.

Use this simple worksheet to structure your thinking about trends that will affect your organization in the future and what their effects are likely to be. Answer each question appearing in the worksheet below. Then compare your responses to what other decision-makers in the organization have written.

1. What trends outside the organization are most likely to affect it in the next 1–5 years? Consider economic conditions, market conditions, financial conditions, regulatory/legal conditions, technological conditions, social conditions, and other trends that might uniquely affect the organization.

   List of trends likely to affect the organization:

2. For *each* trend you listed in response to question 1 above, indicate *how* you think that trend will affect the organization. Describe the trend's possible consequence(s), outcome(s), or result(s). (*While you may not be able to do that with complete certainty, try to gaze into the crystal ball and predict what will happen as a result of a trend.*)

   List effects/consequences:

Exhibit 9-2. An Activity on Organizational Analysis

Directions: How will your organization respond to the trends evident in the external environment that will likely affect it in the future? Use this worksheet to help you structure your thinking about how external environmental trends will affect work in the organization.

Obtain answers to the activity appearing in Exhibit 9-1. Then answer each question appearing in the worksheet below. Finally, compare your responses to what other decision-makers write. Use the responses to consider future work requirements in the organization.

1. For each consequence, outcome, or result you listed in response to question 2 in Exhibit 9-1, indicate *what functions/positions in the organization are most likely to be affected* and *how* you think those functions/positions will be—or should be—affected.

   List each consequence, out-come, or result.

   Describe what functions/positions are most likely to be affected and how you think they will be—or should be—affected.

2. How should the organization respond to future trends? Should workflow change? Should work methods change? Should the organization's structure change? Are any changes likely as a response to increasing external competitive pressure? How does the organization's strategic plan indicate that those challenges will be met? Will new key positions emerge as a result of changes to organizational strategy? Will old key positions fade in importance while new ones become more important? Will new competencies be required, and (if so) what are they and where will they need to be demonstrated?

   Provide your thoughts:

Draw an organization chart as decision-makers believe it should appear in the future. Write the expected future mission of each organizational function on the chart. (Make several versions of that chart at different future time intervals—at, say, one year, three years, five years, and ten years into the future.) Then add the names of possible leaders and their successors.

This process is called *preparing realistic future scenarios*. It is based on the process of scenario analysis, which has been widely applied to futures research and strategic planning.[6] Use the activity appearing in Exhibit 9-3 to help decision-makers structure their thinking in preparing realistic scenarios to identify future key positions. While not foolproof or failsafe, this approach is one way to move beyond traditional thinking about SP&M to "lead" the target—what hunters do when they shoot ahead of a moving target.

Three Approaches to Determining Future Work Requirements in Key Positions

Determining future work requirements means predicting possible or probable work activities, duties, and responsibilities in future key positions. Once likely future key positions have been identified, direct attention to predicting work or competency requirements for those positions. Move beyond present- or past-oriented descriptions to assess future work or competency requirements in key positions. To that end, apply one or more of the three approaches described below.

1. Future-Oriented Job and Task Analysis

To conduct future-oriented job and task analysis for key positions, focus attention on summarizing expected future activities, responsibilities, duties, or essential functions.[7] Extend the analysis by examining future tasks linked to those activities, responsibilities, duties, or essential job functions. Write position descriptions as they should exist at a future time if the organization is to be successful in meeting the competitive challenges it faces. In this way, the effects of organizational strategic plans on key positions can be mirrored, and thereby aligned, in position descriptions and task inventories. By comparing present and future position descriptions, decision-makers should be able to uncover important disparities—and, accordingly, information about desirable developmental opportunities to groom individuals for advancement. Use the activity appearing in Exhibit 9-4 to prepare future-oriented key position descriptions.

However, future-oriented position descriptions are no panacea. They are prone to the same disadvantages as traditional (present-oriented) position descriptions: (1) a focus on activities, not results; (2) a lack of details about all elements essential to job success, including personal characteristics and attitudes; and (3) a requirement for continual, and time-consuming, revision because they date so rapidly. Additionally, they may be based on inaccurate (or

Exhibit 9-3. An Activity for Preparing Realistic Scenarios to Identify Future Key Positions

Directions: The future can seem difficult to envision if predictions about it are left vague. Use this activity to make predictions more tangible. Using responses to questions appearing in Exhibits 9-1 and 9-2, create a detailed description of the likely future situation of your organization at the end of 5 years from the present. Do that by answering the questions appearing below. When you finish answering the questions, compare what you wrote to what other key decision-makers/strategists have written. Develop an overall scenario that describes the "best-guess situation" of the way the future will appear for the organization.

1. What is your "best guess" of how the organization will be functioning in 1 to 5 years, based on environmental scanning or organizational diagnosis? Describe the organization's situation, competition, profitability, and structure:

2. What positions do you believe will be key (that is, critically important) in 1 to 5 years? List their job titles below. What competencies will incumbents in those positions need to possess/demonstrate to be successful?

simply wrongheaded) assumptions about the future. However, such disadvantages may be outweighed by their specificity and by helping individuals to envision the future into which they—and their organizations—are headed.

2. Future Competency Models

Competency modeling lends itself to a future orientation better than any other approach.[8] To give a future orientation to competency models, simply direct attention to the future rather than to the present or past. Ask the organization's strategists to review each key position for underlying employee characteristics (including motives, traits, skills, self-image, social roles, or bodies of knowledge), which should, if assumptions about the future prove correct, simultaneously result in superior performance and actions consistent with orga-

Exhibit 9-4. An Activity for Preparing Future-Oriented Key Position Descriptions

Directions: An organization's strategic plans can seem vague to employees—and even to strategists—until they are made job-specific. Use this activity to help clarify how key positions should change to help the organization realize strategic goals and implement strategic business plans.

In the left column below, list current job activities for each key position. Then, using the results of Exhibits 9-1, 9-2, and 9-3, list how those job activities should change between the present and 1 to 5 years in the future for the job incumbent to function in line with expected environmental trends and organizational changes made to cope with them.

Ask each key job incumbent to complete this activity for his/her position. Then ask strategists to review the results of the activity for each key position in the organization and identify the competencies needed. Use the results as a basis for future-oriented succession planning.

Current Job Activities for Each Key Position	*How Should These Activities Be Carried Out in 1–5 Years, and What Competencies Should Job Incumbents Possess/Demonstrate?*

nizational strategy. Apply competency modeling approaches with an emphasis on future, rather than past or present, competencies. Then use the resulting competency models as a guide to prepare individuals for advancement into key positions.

Alas, however, future competencies may not be identical to present or past competencies. Indeed, they may even conflict with them. For instance, think about such examples as IBM after downsizing or AT&T after deregulation. In each case, what was required for future success was not what had been historically required—or even desired—by the organization. That created a dilemma.

Managers who succeeded under the old conditions were suddenly outmoded and were even unfit to counsel a new generation about what it would take for them to succeed. In these settings, managers had to identify—and cultivate—talent that was quite different from their own if their organizations were to survive. Exemplary future competence, then, represents a moving target, an ideal, a description of what people will probably have to know, do, or feel to perform successfully amid the vague uncertainties of the future.[9]

Future-oriented competency models, like future-oriented position descriptions, suffer from the same strengths and weaknesses as their traditional counterparts. While more rigorous than job analysis, a competency model can be confusing to those who do not clearly understand what it is. Additionally, future-oriented competency models usually require considerable time and expertise to carry out successfully. That may require strategists to devote significant time and resources to it, which they may be reluctant to do.

3. Future-Oriented Rapid Results Assessment

This approach to competency identification has very real potential to help decision-makers plan for future work requirements in key positions. Nor does it require substantial expertise, time, or resources to carry out. To use it, simply focus attention on desirable future competencies. Apply the steps depicted in Exhibit 9-5. Then use those steps to examine competencies in each key position in the organization. Use the results as the basis to plan for individual development and organizational SP&M generally.[10]

Rapid results assessment enjoys important advantages: It can be conducted quickly; it enjoys high face validity because it uses experienced and exemplary job incumbents (or other knowledgeable people) on which to base position-specific information; it permits the personal involvement of key decision-makers, thereby building their ownership in the results; and it can be used to move beyond a focus on mere work activities or tasks to include descriptions of underlying characteristics or work outputs. However, it shares the disadvantages of its traditional counterpart: The results are not as rigorous nor as complete as other competency modeling methods, and the results are heavily dependent on the credibility of the individual panelists. Additionally, as in other future-oriented approaches, it is only as good as the assumptions about the future on which it is based.

Assessing Individual Potential: The Traditional Approach

The centerpiece of most SP&M programs is some means by which to assess individual potential. This effort seeks to determine how to make best use of the organization's existing human resource assets. However, assessing future potential should not be confused with appraising present job performance. Performance appraisal is linked to present job performance; potential assessment is linked to future advancement possibilities. Potential assessment is a critically important activity, if only because as many as one-third of all leader-

Exhibit 9-5. Steps in Conducting Future-Oriented "Rapid Results Assessment"

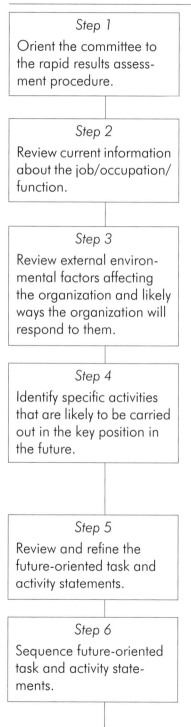

Step 1
Orient the committee to the rapid results assessment procedure.

△ Assemble a group of 5–13 knowledgeable individuals—including exemplary job incumbents and their immediate exemplary superiors.
△ Brief group members on the need to predict changing work requirements.

Step 2
Review current information about the job/occupation/function.

△ Assemble information about one or more specific key jobs/positions in the organization.
△ Focus attention in this step on "what job incumbents do now."

Step 3
Review external environmental factors affecting the organization and likely ways the organization will respond to them.

△ Brief group members on trends in the external environment and the organization that may change—or require change—in job duties, activities, responsibilities, tasks, competencies, or essential job functions.

Step 4
Identify specific activities that are likely to be carried out in the key position in the future.

△ Ask group members to identify how they believe key positions will be affected by changing external environmental conditions.
△ Go around the meeting room and ask each group member to list an activity that he or she envisions will be carried out in the future—and continue this process until group members exhaust ideas.

Step 5
Review and refine the future-oriented task and activity statements.

△ Ask group members to review the activities they defined in the previous step, eliminating redundancy and identifying names for general categories.

Step 6
Sequence future-oriented task and activity statements.

△ Ask group members to sequence the future-oriented task and activity statements they identified in the previous step so that they are arranged from easiest to most difficult to learn.

(continues)

Exhibit 9-5. (continued)

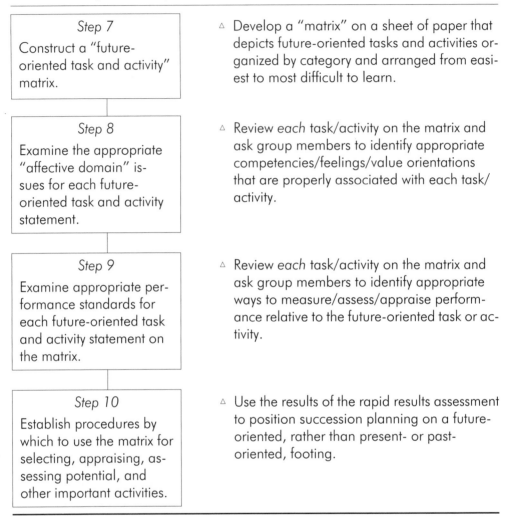

Step 7 Construct a "future-oriented task and activity" matrix.	△ Develop a "matrix" on a sheet of paper that depicts future-oriented tasks and activities organized by category and arranged from easiest to most difficult to learn.
Step 8 Examine the appropriate "affective domain" issues for each future-oriented task and activity statement.	△ Review *each* task/activity on the matrix and ask group members to identify appropriate competencies/feelings/value orientations that are properly associated with each task/activity.
Step 9 Examine appropriate performance standards for each future-oriented task and activity statement on the matrix.	△ Review *each* task/activity on the matrix and ask group members to identify appropriate ways to measure/assess/appraise performance relative to the future-oriented task or activity.
Step 10 Establish procedures by which to use the matrix for selecting, appraising, assessing potential, and other important activities.	△ Use the results of the rapid results assessment to position succession planning on a future-oriented, rather than present- or past-oriented, footing.

ship positions (it has been estimated) would not be filled by present incumbents if decision-makers had it to do over again.[11]

What Is Individual Potential Assessment?

Individual potential assessment is a systematic process of examining individuals' possibilities for job change or movement. It is usually associated with determining whether individuals "have what it takes" to advance to positions of greater management responsibility or positions demanding greater technical knowledge. It should be linked to—and serve as one basis for determining—employee training, education, and development activities, which (collectively) represent a vehicle to help an individual qualify for advancement.[12] It should also be linked to individual career planning activities, which have (unfortunately) been deemphasized in recent years owing to widespread downsizing and economic restructuring.

What Is a High Potential?

The term *high potential* has more than one possible meaning. High potentials, who should be identified through the individual potential assessment process, represent the organization's inventory of future leaders. They are usually individuals who are capable of advancing two or more levels beyond their present placement, individuals who are slated for key positions, or those who have not reached a career plateau. (Other definitions are also possible.[13]) It is important to define the term in a way unique to each organization. In fact, each organization may have several definitions.

Distinguishing Between Exemplary Performers and High Potentials

Individuals who are high potentials are almost always exemplary performers who are identified through the performance appraisal process and who exceed minimum job expectations. Exceptional performance in the current job is usually a necessary prerequisite to advancement.[14] However, not all exemplary performers are high potentials because advancement potential is based on different criteria from present performance.

In any organization or organizational unit, individuals may be classified into four distinct groups based on their performance and their potential. To that end, think of a grid with two axes.[15] (See Exhibit 9-6.) One axis represents present performance and is divided between high and low performance; the second axis represents future potential and is divided between high and low potential. The result is a performance/potential grid that closely resembles the Boston Consulting Group's widely used portfolio analysis technique for use in strategic planning. It is also a method for making investments decisions.

As shown in Exhibit 9-6, *stars* (see the upper left cell of the performance/potential grid) are exemplary individual performers in their present positions. They are also perceived to have high potential for future advancement.[16] A major corporate asset, they are properly regarded as high potentials and are a source of replacements for key positions. An effective HR strategy for stars involves a twofold effort to make the most of their current performance while systematically preparing them for advancement—and even accelerating their development, if possible. Above all, the organization should make every effort to seek to recruit and retain them, keeping their turnover minimal.

Workhorses (see the upper right cell of the performance/potential grid) are exemplary performers in their current jobs who are perceived to have poor

Exhibit 9-6. How to Classify Individuals by Performance and Potential

The Performance/Potential Grid

Future Potential

		High	Low
Present Performance	High	**Stars** *HR strategy:* △ Keep turnover low. △ Take steps to accelerate their development.	**Workhorses** △ Keep turnover low. △ Keep them motivated and productive where they are.
	Low	**Question Marks** *HR strategy:* △ Convert them to stars. △ Counsel them to accelerate their development.	**Deadwood** △ Convert them to workhorses. △ Terminate them if they cannot be salvaged.

Source: George S. Odiorne, *Strategic Management of Human Resources: A Portfolio Approach* (San Francisco: Jossey-Bass, 1984), p. 305. Adapted with permission of the publisher.

future potential.[17] Since they are highly productive where they are, they should remain there. An effective strategy for workhorses is to harness their skills while keeping them motivated and productive. Turnover in their ranks, as with stars, should be kept minimal.

Question marks (see the lower left cell of the performance/potential grid) are poor performers in their present positions who are perceived to have high future potential.[18] The best HR strategy for dealing with them is to focus on improving their present performance, thereby turning them into stars. Their immediate supervisors should be trained to apply appropriate techniques—such as coaching, mentoring, and (when warranted) corrective action steps—to make them more productive.

Finally, *deadwood* (see the lower right cell of the performance/potential grid) consists of individuals who are neither good performers in their present jobs nor perceived to have future advancement potential.[19] While their ranks may have been dramatically reduced in the 1990s owing to downsizing and other reductions in force, their ranks may be swollen in some international subsidiaries where the national culture emphasizes good relationships between bosses and subordinates rather than performance (results).

A twofold HR strategy is most effective with deadwood. First, their immediate organizational superiors should make every effort to help them improve their present performance. If successful, that strategy will convert deadwood to workhorses. If unsuccessful, that strategy should be followed up by fair and even-handed efforts, consistent with the organization's disciplinary policies and practices, to move them out of the job—or even out of the organization.

Identifying High Potentials

How can the organization identify high potentials? There are several ways to answer that question because approaches to assessing individual potential are as diverse as employee performance appraisal, and sometimes resemble each other.

Global Assessment

One way to assess potential is to ask senior executives to furnish the names of individuals in their areas of responsibility who they feel have high potential according to the definition established in the organization. This is called *global assessment*. (See Exhibit 9-7 for a sample worksheet to be used in making global assessments.)

It is a simple approach, but it is not very effective, for several reasons. First, few senior executives (except those in very small organizations) will know everyone in their areas of responsibility. Second, unless the definition of "high potential" is made quite clear, senior executives are likely to respond to a request for names based on their perceptions. Those perceptions about individuals can be colored too much by recent events (*recency bias*), extremely bad incidents (*the horn effect*), or extremely good incidents (*the halo effect*). Indeed, perceptions can lead to personal favoritism, discrimination, or pigeonholing in which individual potential is difficult to change once assessed.

Success Factor Analysis

A second approach to individual potential assessment is based on success factor analysis, the process of examining traits or other characteristics perceived to lead to organizational success or advancement. One research study, for instance, revealed that successful women share such characteristics as exemplary educational credentials, a track record of hard work and good performance, supportive mentoring relationships, effective interpersonal skills, and a willingness to take career and work risks.[20]

Success factors may be identified through various means. One way is to ask executives what traits they think will lead to success in the organization. These traits may then be collected in the way depicted in Exhibit 9-8. Executives can be asked to check off what they believe those traits are. Lists completed by numerous executives may be compiled and used as the basis for developing

Exhibit 9-7. A Worksheet for Making Global Assessments

Directions: Use this worksheet to list individuals whom you consider to be "high-potentials" in your organizational area of responsibility. A "high-potential" is an individual who has the capacity to be promoted two or more levels. List the names below, provide their present titles, and the time they have spent in the present positions. Be prepared to discuss, in the future, *why* you believe these individuals have the capacity to be promoted two or more levels. If possible, rank them by their potential—with 1 = highest potential. (Do *not* use current position as a basis for ranking; rather, use your judgment about individual ability to perform at a higher level.)

Names	Titles	Time in Present Positions

an individual potential assessment form, perhaps like the one shown in Exhibit 9-9.

An alternative is to conduct critical incident interviews with organizational strategists. This approach is based on critical incident analysis, which has been used in training needs assessment. Critical incidents were first identified for pilots during World War II. They were asked what situations (incidents), if ignored, might lead to serious (critical) consequences.

If this approach is used, individual interviews should be conducted with strategists with a structured interview guide like the one shown in Exhibit 9-8. The results should then be analyzed and become the basis for establishing success factors. These, in turn, can be used in assessing individual potential and, when appropriate, identifying developmental opportunities.

Three Approaches to Individual Potential Assessment

There are three basic approaches to assessing individual potential. Each is based on a different philosophy. They are worth reviewing.

Exhibit 9-8. A Worksheet to Identify Success Factors

Directions: Use this worksheet to identify success factors. A "success factor" is a past experience or personal characteristic linked to, and correlated with, successful advancement in the organization. Identify success factors by asking individuals who have already achieved success—such as key position incumbents—about their most important developmental experiences and about what they did (or skills they demonstrated) in the midst of those experiences.

Pose the following questions to key position incumbents. Then compile and compare the results. Ask other key position incumbents in the organization to review the results.

1. What is the single most difficult experience you encountered in your career? (*Describe the situation below.*)

2. What did you *do* in the experience you described in response to question 1? (*Describe, as precisely as you can, what actions you took—and what results you achieved as a result.*)

3. Reflect on your answer to question 2. What *personal characteristics* do you feel you exhibited or demonstrated in the action(s) you took? How do you feel they contributed to your present success?

Leader-Driven Individual Potential Assessment

The first approach might be called leader-driven. It is the traditional approach that was probably first used in business. Individual potential is assessed by the organization's strategists—and often solely by key position incumbents for their own subordinates in their immediate areas of responsibility.

The process may be a formal one, in which the organization has established forms for this purpose that are completed periodically on all employees or on a select group of employees (such as those designated as high potentials). Alternatively, the process may be informal: Each function or organiza-

Exhibit 9-9. An Individual Potential Assessment Form

Directions: Individual potential may be assessed through many different approaches. One approach is to ask their immediate organizational superiors to rate employees—particularly those felt to be high-potentials—against various success factors, skills, competencies, values, or abilities that are felt to be correlated with future success at a higher level of responsibility.

Ask key job incumbents to rate their subordinates on each of the following generic success factors. (It is better to use success factors specific to the unique organizational culture.) A separate form should be completed on each high-potential. The completed forms may then be used as one source of information about individual strengths/weaknesses.

Ask the raters to place an x in the appropriate spot in the right column below the scale and opposite the success factor listed in the left column. Then ask raters to send their completed forms to the HR Department or to the organization's Succession Planning Coordinator. There are no "right" or "wrong" answers in any absolute sense. However, raters may vary in their potential assessments, depending on how they interpret the success factors and the rating scale.

Success Factors (or competencies needed at a targeted level)	Scale								
	Needs Improvement			Adequate			Exceeds Requirements		
	1	2	3	4	5	6	7	8	9
Appraising									
Budgeting									
Communicating									
Controlling									
Dealing with Change									
Developing Employees									
Influencing Others									
Making Changes									
Making Decisions									
Managing Projects Effectively									
Organizing									
Planning									
Representing the Organization Effectively									
Staffing the Unit/ Department									

tional unit is asked to submit names of individuals who have advancement potential.

This approach is characterized by secrecy. Employees have little or no say in the process; indeed, they are not always aware that it is being carried out. No effort is made to double-check individual potential assessment results with individual career aspirations or plans to ensure that an appropriate match exists. An advantage of this approach is that it can be done quickly. Leaders simply fill out forms and return them to the human resources department, the SP&M coordinator, or a designated executive. Employees do not challenge the results because they are unaware of what they are. The organization thus retains strong control over SP&M and its results.

A disadvantage of this approach, however, is that employees have no stake in outcomes they did not help to shape. If the results are ever used in making succession decisions, employees may refuse promotions or transfers that conflict with their perceptions of their own desired work-life balance or their own career goals.

Participative Individual Potential Assessment

A second approach might be called participative assessment. Both individuals and their immediate organizational superiors enact important roles in the assessment process. Hence, it is participative. Periodically—such as once a year—employees undergo an individual potential assessment. It may be timed at the halfway point of the annual performance appraisal cycle so that potential assessment is not confused with performance appraisal.

Although there are many ways to carry out the process, one approach involves distributing individual assessment appraisal forms to employees and their immediate organizational superiors. Employees and superiors complete the forms, exchange them, and later meet to discuss the individual's advancement capabilities. As with performance appraisals, the forms for individual potential assessment are usually prepared by the human resources department, distributed from that department, and the results returned to that department for filing in personnel records. (Alternatives to that approach are possible. For instance, completed individual assessment appraisal forms may be retained by the leader of each organizational unit.)

An advantage of this approach is that it allows "reality testing." Individuals learn of possibilities for the future, which may interest them and motivate them; organizational representatives learn more about individual career goals and aspirations, thereby improving the quality of their succession plans. In this way, the assessment process provides an opportunity for mutual candor and information-sharing.

Key to this process is the individual potential assessment interview. It should be carried out in a quiet, supportive setting that is free of interruptions. The employee's immediate organizational superior should set the pace, discussing his or her perceptions about the individual's strengths and weaknesses for advancement—and the realistic possibilities for that advancement. Having an agenda can make an interview of this kind run smoothly. Another advantage is that employees have a stake in the assessment process. If the organization should have a need to make a succession decision, the likelihood is greater that employees will accept offers of promotions or transfers that match their career goals and organizational needs.

A disadvantage of this approach is that it can rarely be done quickly. Leaders and employees must devote time to it if it is to be valuable. Indeed, to gain the full benefits from it, leaders must be trained on effective interviewing skills. Another disadvantage is that the value of participative assessment is a function of the interpersonal trust existing between leaders and their employees. However, trust is not always present, nor is complete candor.

Several factors affect trust. Among them are past dealings between the organization and individual; the perceived candor of the organization's representative; and the match between individual career goals and organizational opportunities. To cite two examples, suppose that an employee has personal aspirations that may eventually lead to her departure from the organization. She may be unwilling to share that information for fear of how it might affect her prospects for promotion. Likewise, leaders may be unable to share information about pending changes affecting the organization—such as the sale of a division or the dissolution of a product line—that may also impact career goals or succession plans.

Empowered Individual Potential Assessment

In this third approach, leaders provide guidance and direction but do not determine the outcomes or make final decisions affecting individual potential. Instead, they just share information and offer coaching suggestions. Individuals remain chiefly responsible for their own self-assessment and their own self-development.

Once a year, employees are encouraged to complete individual potential assessment forms, share them with their immediate organizational superiors, and then schedule meetings to discuss them with their superiors. (Some may even decide to discuss their forms with their mentors.) The form is usually created and supplied by the human resources department. However, it may—or may not—be called an individual potential assessment form. Alternative names might include career planning assessment form or individual development planning form (see Exhibit 9-9). In this approach, the initiative rests entirely with employees. They conduct their own individual assessments; they schedule assessment meetings with their immediate organizational superiors or with mentors in other parts of the organization; they are not required to participate in the assessment process, which remains voluntary. As with other approaches, however, it is usually kept separate from performance appraisals so as not to confuse present performance and future potential. Individual potential assessment becomes a tool to help individuals understand how to qualify for advancement within the framework of the organization's needs and their own career goals.

An advantage of this approach is that, like other empowerment efforts, it can be quite motivating to employees. Further, it discourages a philosophy of entitlement in which employees with a long service record feel that promotions are "owed" to them. Instead, the responsibility for advancement rests squarely on their shoulders, and they are expected to take an active role in setting their own career directions and finding the necessary resources to develop in line with those directions.

Another advantage of this approach is that employees are not given the impression, which is possible with other approaches, that they are guaranteed advancement. Management should state the message, loud and clear, that "we can't guarantee promotions, but we can guarantee that those who have taken the steps to obtain the necessary qualifications for a higher-level position will be given due consideration."

However, the chief disadvantage of this approach is that the organization sacrifices control over employees. Indeed, it may not always be apparent whether replacements exist for each key position. It thus creates a talent pool rather than a position-oriented succession plan. In practical terms, this means that nobody may know at any time if even one person is "ready" to assume important positions in the organization.

Empowered individual potential assessment is likely to remain important, a mainstream approach. One reason is that it matches current thinking about the need to decentralize decision making and give the control to those who deal with customers or consumers daily. A second reason is that this approach can unleash individual initiative rather than stifle it, thereby motivating people to want to qualify for advancement.

The Growing Use of Assessment Centers and Portfolios

Since the previous editions of this book appeared in print, the world has changed. Organizations are now using assessment centers and portfolios to assess individual potential. But what are they?

Assessment Centers

Assessment centers are back as a tool for potential assessment in succession management.[21] Of course, an *assessment center* is a process and should not be confused with a place. The idea is simple enough: create a realistic simulation of the work performed by those at targeted levels—for example, top management work—and then run individuals through the process to determine how well they perform in a higher-level (or targeted) position.

Assessment centers went out of fashion for a time owing to the hard work and expense involved in setting them up. After all, they must be based on the actual work performed (rather than subjective impressions) or the competencies linked to successful performance. The individual's progress in the assessment center is rated by trained assessors who must judge the performance of the individuals. There is still concern in some circles about the time and cost involved in establishing and maintaining assessment centers and concern about the possibility of not being able to defend against discrimination complaints. An alternative is to send individuals through outsourced assessment centers, established by universities or by consulting companies. Unfortunately, the latter approach means that individuals may be rated against some other organization's competency models, which could be a formula for misidentifying the abilities of individuals.

Ten classic errors have been identified in the use of assessment centers, and organizations that set out to use them should do their best to avoid these[22]:

1. Poor Planning
2. Inadequate Job Analysis
3. Weakly Defined Dimensions
4. Poor Exercises
5. No Pretest Evaluations
6. Unqualified Assessors
7. Inadequate Assessor Training
8. Inadequate Candidate Preparation
9. Sloppy Behavior Documentation and Scoring
10. Misuse of Results

Of course, the value of this approach is that it is thus possible to see individuals in action before they are promoted. That is a significant advantage. Assessment centers also do a good job of identifying actual behaviors—that is, observable actions—that are far more valid and reliable than notoriously weak job interviews.

Work Portfolios

How does an employer assess an individual's relative readiness for a higher-level job? One way is to focus on behaviors, which are essentially observable demonstrations. Competencies can be manifested as behaviors. And, of course, full-circle, multirater (that is, 360-degree) assessment is one way to measure behaviors because raters are usually asked how often or how well they have seen an individual demonstrate behaviors linked to competencies.

Of course, an alternative to measuring behaviors is to focus on the outputs or outcomes of competencies. For instance, if examining the typing behavior of a secretary, a rater can focus on what he or she does while typing. But since that may be pointless, another way to measure the demonstration of competencies is through work samples. A work sample is literally an example of the work output. For a secretary, a work sample may be a typed letter or report. The rater can judge the quality of what the secretary produces.

How does measuring outputs or outcomes relate to succession planning and management? The answer to that question should be apparent. If, for example, a supervisor being groomed for the job of manager would be expected to produce budgets as part of the manager's job, then he or she could prepare a budget and present it as an example of his or her work. If the supervisor does not do budgeting in his or her present job, then that can become the focus of developmental activities on a competency like "budgeting skill." Carrying out that skill may be essential to qualify for promotion to manager, for instance.

A *work portfolio*, sometimes called a *dossier*, began in the art world. Artists must convince gallery owners to show their work. Since gallery space and time are limited, gallery owners want to know what quality of work the artist produces. To address that concern, artists compile examples of their best works—such as watercolors, charcoal drawings, oil paintings, or photos of sculptures—to show the gallery owner. These are assembled in a portfolio that the artist can carry with him or her. The gallery owner then judges the quality of the work—presumably the best work that the artist has done—and decides whether the artist's talents warrant an art show.

The same idea can be applied to rating individuals' abilities. They can be asked to assemble a portfolio that represents their best work—or, alternatively, represents the best work that they could prepare to show what they could do in a job they do not yet hold. For instance, a management consultant who is interviewing for an entry-level job might present examples of marketing materials he or she has prepared, proposals written, deliverables produced, and letters of testimony from satisfied clients. Similarly, a supervisor who is interviewing to become a department manager could provide examples of work outputs that are linked to essential requirements of the department manager's job.

To create a work portfolio, start with the competency model or with a job description and ask: what are the outcomes, tangible or intangible, of that competency or work activity? The portfolio can then be prepared with the resume at the front, a targeted job description or competency model, and then work samples representing the supervisor's efforts to demonstrate the real work performed by department managers. Work portfolios may then be compared for quality and the person whose work portfolio is best may be invited to participate in additional steps of the selection process.

The value of work portfolios is that they go to work results. It is not a matter of impressing interviewers alone, though participating in interviews may still be essential to be selected. But work portfolios have the advantage of focusing attention on desired results. Of course, a disadvantage is that raters may not assess the same work in the same ways without training and/or agreed-upon guidelines for rating that work. Additionally, job applicants must understand clearly what they are being asked to provide by way of work samples. If they are not, then what can happen may not be good. For example, "when Optum, Inc., a White Plains, N.Y., software company, asked applicants to submit work samples, 'we got in personal poetry and song lyrics,' says Kelly Vizzini, director of corporate marketing."[23] One time when I asked for a writing sample from a job applicant, he used a dolly to wheel in eleven large three-ring binders full of material he had written. Unfortunately, when that happened, I was away from my desk, and he left before I could return. When I did return, I was amazed to see an enormous stack of material sitting on my desk, which I had no room to store.

But the approach can also work well. Another time I conducted some supervisory training for a large organization. The Operations Manager wanted her thirty-five supervisors to take paper-and-pencil examinations. I dissuaded her of that and, instead, convinced her to have each supervisor assemble a notebook—a work portfolio—of his or her best work. That way, the Operations Manager could see for herself what level of work they performed, and that prompted much discussion as she reviewed what they regarded as good work samples. She was then able to use those work samples as a focal point for developing the supervisory group—and assess individuals for their potential for future advancement.

Summary

As this chapter has shown, information about future work requirements and individual potential is essential to an effective succession planning and management program. When paired with information about present work requirements and individual job performance, it becomes the basis for preparing individual development plans to narrow the gaps between what individuals already know and do and what they must know and do to qualify for advancement.

PART IV

CLOSING THE "DEVELOPMENTAL GAP": OPERATING AND EVALUATING A SUCCESSION PLANNING AND MANAGEMENT PROGRAM

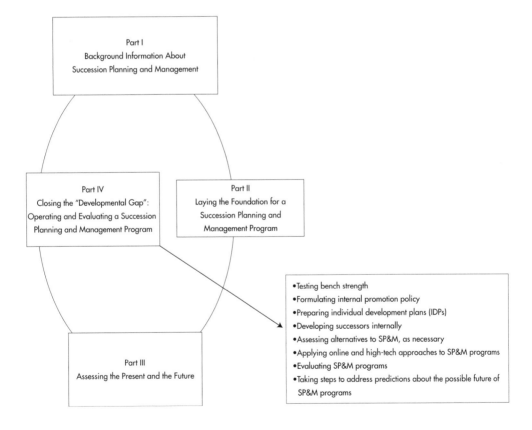

Part I
Background Information About
Succession Planning and Management

Part IV
Closing the "Developmental Gap":
Operating and Evaluating a Succession
Planning and Management Program

Part II
Laying the Foundation for a
Succession Planning and
Management Program

Part III
Assessing the Present and the Future

- Testing bench strength
- Formulating internal promotion policy
- Preparing individual development plans (IDPs)
- Developing successors internally
- Assessing alternatives to SP&M, as necessary
- Applying online and high-tech approaches to SP&M programs
- Evaluating SP&M programs
- Taking steps to address predictions about the possible future of SP&M programs

DEVELOPING INTERNAL SUCCESSORS

For a succession planning and management (SP&M) program to be effective, the organization must have some means by which to replace key job incumbents as vacancies occur in their positions. Promotion from within is a time-honored and crucially important, albeit traditional, way to do that.

But, to prepare individuals for promotion, the organization has an obligation to do more than merely identify present and future work requirements and performance. Some way must also be found to clarify—and systematically close—the developmental gap between what possible successors can already do and what they must do to qualify for advancement. *Individual development planning* is the process of clarifying that developmental gap; internal development uses planned training, education, development, and other means to close the gap and thereby meet succession needs.

This chapter focuses on determining the organization's collective succession needs, using promotion from within to meet those needs, clarifying individual developmental gaps, and closing those gaps systematically through planned training, education, and development. More specifically, then, this chapter addresses the following questions:

▲ What is bench strength, and how can the leaders of an organization test bench strength?

▲ Why is internal promotion so important for succession, and when is it—and when is it not—appropriate for meeting SP&M needs?

▲ What is an individual development plan (IDP)? How should one be prepared, followed up, and evaluated?

▲ What are some important methods of internal development, and when should they be used?

Testing Bench Strength

Once key positions and work requirements have been identified, the organization should test bench strength. That is important because it provides information about the organization's collective succession needs. That information can, in turn, dramatize the importance of taking action to meet SP&M needs.

What Is Bench Strength?

Bench strength is the organization's ability to fill vacancies from within. Testing bench strength means determining how well the organization is able to fill vacancies in key positions from within.

Turnover saps bench strength. There are two kinds of turnover. *Unavoidable turnover* is outside the immediate control of the organization. It is the loss of personnel through death, disability, and retirement. It may also include turnover resulting from organizational action, such as layoff, early retirement, buyout, or other means. Although many line managers would like to include promotions and transfers from their areas in the definition of unavoidable turnover, most HR departments do not include internal movements in the definition of unavoidable turnover.

On the other hand, *avoidable turnover* is initiated by employees. It is a loss resulting from resignation as individuals leave the organization, typically moving to positions in other organizations. Although turnover of any kind is costly because the organization must find and train replacements, avoidable turnover is worse because it could be avoided if the organization could find some way to retain the employees.

Avoidable turnover from key positions—or the less of high potentials—can be particularly distressing because it creates unnecessary crises. (This is sometimes called *critical turnover*.[1]) One aim of any SP&M program should thus be to find ways to reduce avoidable turnover among high potentials or key position incumbents—or at least find the means to keep it stable.

Approaches to Testing Bench Strength

To test an organization for bench strength, ask decision-makers how they would replace key positions in their areas of responsibility or ensure that work requirements will be met through other, more innovative, means. Use any of the means described below.

By Replacement Charting

Prepare an organization chart to show the range of possible replacements for each key position in a work area. (See Exhibits 10-1 and 10-2.) Note how many holes can be identified. A *hole* is a position in which no internal replacement can be identified. The lower the percentage of holes relative to key positions, the greater is the organization's bench strength.

Exhibit 10-1. A Sample Replacement Chart Format: Typical Succession Planning and Management Inventory for the Organization

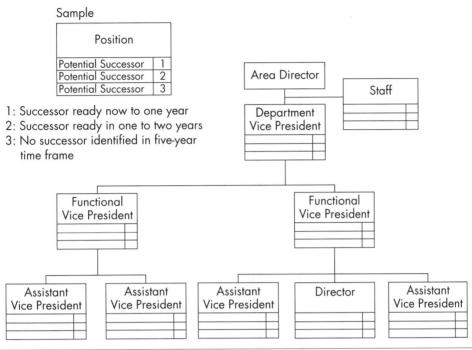

Sample

Position	
Potential Successor	1
Potential Successor	2
Potential Successor	3

1: Successor ready now to one year
2: Successor ready in one to two years
3: No successor identified in five-year time frame

Source: Norman H. Carter, "Guaranteeing Management's Future through Succession Planning," *Journal of Information Systems Management* (Summer 1986), 19. Used by permission of the *Journal of Information Systems Management.*

By Questioning

Ask senior executives who will replace key-position incumbents in their areas in the event of a vacancy. Note how many holes by function can be identified. Track the holes. The lower the percentage of holes to key positions, the greater is the organization's bench strength.

By Evidence

Using the results of an analysis of personnel records over the last few years, find out which departures created the worst problems for the organization. Note the number of such problems relative to total departures (turnover). The higher the percentage, the weaker the bench strength.

By Combination

Use a combination of the methods identified above to assess bench strength. Note the percentage of holes. Feed that information back to decision-makers to dramatize the value and importance of the SP&M program.

Exhibit 10-2. Succession Planning and Management Inventory by Position

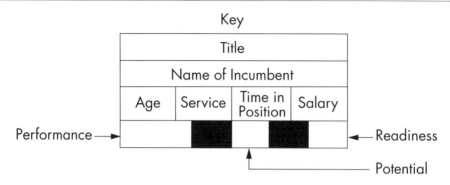

Key

Performance Rating	Definition
X	New—in position less than three months. Not evaluated.
1	Unsatisfactory results and performance.
2	Marginal—does not meet requirements of position (with learning discounted). Attitude and/or initiative not acceptable. Remedial action indicated.
3	Satisfactory—generally meets job requirements but room for improvement. If in a major learning phase, considerable room for improvement.
4	Above average—surpasses overall job requirements but lacks strength in some areas.
5	Superior—some elements of performance may rate as exceptional, but overall performance falls below an exceptional rating.
6	Exceptional—general all-around excellence in quality/quantity of work, initiative, self-development, new ideas, and attitude. Rapid learner.

Potential

A	Outstanding—can advance two levels above present position.
B	Considerable—can advance at least one level above present position and/or assume substantial added responsibility at present level.
C	Some—can assume added responsibilities at present level.
D	Limited—at or near capacity in present position.
E	Key capacity in current position—vital technical knowledge precludes movement.
X	New—in position less than three months. Not evaluated.

Readiness

R/O	Qualified to move now.
R1	Within one to two years.
R2	Within two to four years.
N/A	Current level appropriate.

Source: Norman H. Carter, "Guaranteeing Management's Future through Succession Planning," *Journal of Information Systems Management* (Summer 1986), 20. Used by permission of the *Journal of Information Systems Management.*

Managing Talent Shows

Talent shows go by many names. Sometimes they are called monthly, quarterly, or annual succession planning and management meetings that focus on identifying available talent in the organization eligible for promotion, discussing special developmental assignments that should be given to individuals from various divisions, evaluating the size of the organization's talent pool relative to expected needs, or discussing how well senior managers have been grooming talent in their divisions or departments. One outcome of a talent show—sometimes called a *development meeting* or even (jokingly) a "beauty pageant"—is a verified list of high potentials and developmental assignments for them. Another, more subtle outcome of a talent show is that it provides a means by which to hold senior managers accountable for developing talent by encouraging them to discuss, either in public with their peers or in private with the CEO and the VP of HR, how well they are handling the development of talent in their divisions or departments.

It is worth mentioning that talent shows are the typical culmination of an annual succession process. There are three phases.

Phase I: Preparation

Senior managers must prepare for their meeting. A major value-added that can be provided by the HR department is to hold meetings with each senior manager before the meeting with the CEO or their peers to discuss what they will say and how they will say it. The reason to do that is that managers have a tendency to focus on "what is wrong." That management-by-exception philosophy, while possibly desirable in other areas of management by economizing the time spent, can be devastating to the reputations of successors. The point is that public meetings to discuss development with the CEO or with peers should focus on "what we are going to do and what we want the outcomes to be" rather than "what is wrong" with someone. HR professionals can work through the problems that lead up to various developmental actions. In that way, public meetings can focus on actions to be taken and the desired results—and not on what is "wrong" with someone.

Phase II: The Meeting

The meeting itself must be planned. An agenda needs to be assembled. Someone in HR is usually assigned that task. It may be the vice president of HR, or it may be a key report of the VP of HR. But the agenda should ensure that time is economically used.

One key issue to work out in advance is what the purpose of the meeting is to be. Several purposes are possible. One type of meeting focuses on rating possible successors and verifying a talent pool. That may require time for open-air discussions. Another type of meeting focuses on discussing the progress made in developing talent by division. A third type of meeting focuses on high potentials and what developmental assignments should be recommended to leverage their talents, challenge them, and build their competencies for the future.

It is particularly important to pay attention to the group process of any talent show. One reason is that the relative willingness of people to speak their minds honestly is quite important to making good decisions. It is not desirable to have one or a few people dominating these meetings. At the end of each meeting, a discussion should focus on such group process questions as "How well did we work together?" and "How could we work together more effectively in the future?"

Phase III: The Follow-Up

One thing that is often forgotten—but that must not be forgotten—is follow-up to ensure that actions are taken as they have been agreed upon. Often it falls to HR professionals to follow up. That may require e-mails, phone calls, personal visits, and other contacts to ensure that agreed-upon actions are taken. One reason that is important is that lack of follow-through is a common problem in succession. A second reason is that decisions are pointless if they are not acted on. Someone must pay attention to that. It will not just take care of itself. (See Exhibit 10-3 for more information about talent shows.)

Formulating Internal Promotion Policy

The centerpiece of a systematic SP&M program is a written policy favoring internal promotion. Lacking such a policy, organizations may have difficulty keeping ambitious high potentials and exemplary performers who seek advancement. If they grow discouraged, they can contribute to a devastating increase in avoidable, and critical, turnover. It is thus essential for the organization to make all reasonable efforts to retain them. One way to do that is to place the organization "on the record" as favoring promotion from within. Not only does a promotion-from-within policy motivate employees by showing that their efforts can pay off through promotion, but promotion from within also saves the organization money in recruiting, selecting, and training newcomers.[2]

Essential Components of an Internal Promotion Policy

To be effective, an internal promotion policy should do the following:

▲ Unequivocally state the organization's commitment to promoting employees from within whenever possible and whenever they are qualified to meet the work requirements of new positions. (But it is best to cap promotions at 80 percent to avoid too much inbreeding.)

Exhibit 10-3. Talent Shows: What Happens?

At Eli Lilly, the direct managers of high-potential individuals participate in intensive assessment discussions with other executives concerning the individual's strengths, development needs, and career potential. The individual's manager then provides her with the key points of feedback from the assessment discussion. Afterward, the individual works with the manager to develop a personal career plan that reflects her perceived career potential and also factors in her career interests and goals. The career plan is reviewed by the manager and individual and is updated when needed or, at a minimum, on an annual basis.

The amount of time that executives in many companies are devoting to succession planning is a clear reflection of the increased priority placed on developing top talent. At Dow Chemical, the Human Resource Council—a small group that includes the CEO and a handful of his key staff members—spends five days each year off-site on succession planning: talking about candidates, reviewing development plans, and directing development assignments. At Corning, executives in each major unit spend one to four days per year in people reviews that extend down well below the managerial level. The involvement of senior executives is often expressed in very personal ways. In a number of companies, CEOs, such as former General Electric's Jack Welch, review job assignments and compensation recommendations for several hundred managers.

Source: John Beeson, "Succession Planning," *Across the Board* 37:2 (2000), 39. Used by permission.

▲ Define internal promotion.
▲ Explain the business reasons for that policy.
▲ Explain the legitimate conditions under which that policy can be waived and an external candidate can be selected.

Since an internal promotion policy will (naturally) build employee expectations that most promotions will be made from within, decision-makers should anticipate challenges—legal and otherwise—to every promotion decision that is made. For that reason, the policy should be reviewed by HR professionals, operating managers, and legal professionals before it is implemented or widely communicated. In any case, reviewing the policy before adoption is more likely to build consistent understanding and ownership of it.

When Are Internal Promotions Appropriate or Inappropriate?

Internal promotion is appropriate to meet a vacancy in a key position when a qualified replacement from the organization is:

▲ *Ready* to assume the duties of the key position by demonstrated mastery of at least 80 percent of the position requirements and progress toward meeting or exceeding the remaining 20 percent of the position requirements.

▲ *Willing* to accept the position, expressing a desire to do the work.

▲ *Able* to accept the position by having his or her own replacement prepared in a reasonably short time span and by being ready to assume the duties of a key position.

But promotion from within is not appropriate for meeting SP&M needs when any of these conditions cannot be met. Alternatives to internal promotions are thus appropriate when a qualified internal candidate cannot be found after a reasonable search, when possible candidates refuse to accept a position, or when possible candidates cannot be freed up from their present duties in a reasonable time.

The Importance of Job Posting

Job posting is an internal method of notifying and recruiting employees for new positions in the organization. To begin such a program, the organization should establish a policy that position opening notices will be posted in prominent locations, such as next to building entrances and exits, near cafeteria entrances, on bulletin boards, near restrooms, or online. A typical job posting notice contains information about the position that is open, such as its title, pay grade, organizational location, and desirable starting date. Employees from all areas of the organization are encouraged to apply, and selection decisions are typically made on the basis of the applicant who brings the best qualifications to the job. (In some organizations, however, seniority may be an overriding factor in making a selection decision. Additionally, posting may be restricted to include only some, but not all, job categories or functions in the organization.)

In many cases, positions are posted internally while also advertised externally. In that way, both internal and external applicants are attracted. The organization can thus seek the most qualified applicant, whether or not that person is presently employed by the organization.

The major benefit of job posting is that it gives individuals a say in their career directions. Further, it permits the organization to consider applicants from outside the immediate work area, from which successors for key positions may frequently be selected.[3] It also reduces the chance of *employee hoarding*, in which an employee's manager blocks promotions or transfers of high-potential or exemplary performers so they will remain forever trapped, though very productive, in the manager's work area.[4]

The major drawback to job posting has more to do with the management of such programs than with the posting concept itself. If employees are allowed to jump to new jobs merely to realize small wage increases, posting can be costly and demoralizing, especially to those responsible for training "mercenary job hoppers." Hence, to be used effectively as a tool in SP&M, job posting should be done for all jobs. However, careful restrictions should be placed on the process to ensure that employees remain in their positions for a period sufficient to recoup training costs.

Preparing Individual Development Plans

Testing bench strength should clarify the organization's collective SP&M needs. However, it does not indicate what individuals should do to qualify for advancement to key positions. That is the reason for preparing individual development plans.

What Is an Individual Development Plan?

An *individual development plan* (IDP) results from a comparison of individual strengths and weaknesses on the current job and individual potential for advancement to possible key positions in the future. Preparing an IDP is a process of planning activities that will narrow the gap between what individuals can already do and what they should do to meet future work or competency requirements in one or more key positions.

An IDP is a hybrid of a learning contract, a performance contract, and a career-planning form. A *learning contract* is an agreement to learn. Contract learning has enjoyed a long and venerable history.[5] It is particularly well suited to participative, learning organizations that seek to balance individual career needs and interests with organizational strategy and work requirements. A *performance contract* is an agreement to achieve an identifiable, measurable level of performance.[6] Sometimes tied to performance appraisal, it is directed toward future performance improvement rather than past performance. Finally, a *career-planning form* is a tool for helping individuals identify their career goals and establish effective strategies for realizing them in the future. A career-planning form is typically linked to an organizational career planning program, which can reinforce and support SP&M.

An IDP goes a step beyond performance appraisal for the individual's present job and potential assessment of the individual's capability for future advancement to other, often key, positions in the organization. It results in a detailed plan to furnish individuals with the necessary development they need to qualify for advancement into their next positions.

Developing an IDP usually requires a systematic comparison of the individual's present abilities (as indicated by competency requirements, work activities appearing on job descriptions, and current performance as measured by performance appraisals) and future capabilities (as revealed through individual potential assessment). The IDP should narrow the gap between them, providing a clear-cut plan by which to prepare the individual for future advancement.

How Are Individual Development Plans Prepared?

Preparing an IDP shares strong similarities to preparing a learning contract. Take ten key steps when preparing individual development plans. (Exhibit 10-4 depicts these steps in a simple model.)

Step 1: Select Possible Key Positions for Which to Prepare the Individual

Begin by targeting a family of key positions in the organization for the individual. In most cases, this should be done only after a significant dialog has taken place between the individual and an organizational representative. As Deegan notes, "it is important that the individual understand the illustrative nature of the position you select as the targeted one and focus not on that specific job but on the family of jobs represented by it. Otherwise there may be disappointment if that job is not offered even though a future offer might actually meet the person's needs better as well as those of the firm."[7] Of course, if it is anticipated that the individual will be prepared for a specific key position that will soon become vacant, then planning should be focused on that position after discussion with the individual.

Step 2: Consider the Likely Time During Which the Individual Must Be Prepared

Time affects what kind of—and how many—developmental activities can be carried out. When individuals are slated for rapid advancement, there is little or no time for preparation. Hence, those developmental activities that are selected should be absolutely critical to effective job performance. There is thus a need to prioritize developmental activities. That should be done, of course, even when time is ample. The key issue in this step, then, amounts to this: How much time is available for development?

Step 3: Diagnose Learning Needs

Exactly what is the difference between the individual's present knowledge and skills and the work requirements of the key position for which the individual is to be prepared? The answer to that question clarifies the developmental gap.

One way to determine this difference is to compare the individual's present work requirements and performance to those required in a targeted key position. (You might think of that as akin to conducting a performance appraisal on a position to which the individual aspires or for which he or she is being groomed.) As a simple example, it may involve comparing how well an employee could perform his or her immediate supervisor's job.

Another way to determine this difference is to ask the key position incum-

Exhibit 10-4. A Simplified Model of Steps in Preparing Individual Development Plans (IDPs)

Step One:
Selecting Possible Key Positions for
Which to Prepare the Individual or Competencies
Needing Development

Step Two:
Considering the Likely Time during Which
the Individual Must Be Prepared

Step Three:
Diagnosing Learning Needs/Competency-Building Needs

Step Four:
Specifying Learning Objectives
Based on the Results of Step Three

Step Five:
Specifying Learning Resources and Strategies
Needed to Achieve Learning Objectives

Step Six:
Specifying Evidence of Accomplishment

Step Seven:
Specifying How the Evidence
Will Be Validated

Step Eight:
Reviewing the Contract
with Consultants

Step Nine:
Carrying Out the Contract

Step Ten:
Evaluating Learning and Outcomes

bent to review the individual's present work requirements and performance against the requirements of the incumbent's position and to recommend planned developmental activities to narrow the gap between what the employee already knows and can do and what he or she should know or do to perform in the place of the key position incumbent.

When diagnosing learning needs, be aware that the quality of the results depends on the quality of the diagnosis. Shortcuts are not conducive to useful outcomes. While busy executives might prefer to short-circuit this process, that will usually prove to be counterproductive.

Step 4: Specify Learning Objectives Based on the Results of Step 3

Learning objectives are the outcomes or results that are sought from planned developmental activities. Needs represent deficiencies or problems to be solved; objectives, on the other hand, represent desired solutions. Each need should be linked to one—or more—learning objectives to ensure that each "problem" will be solved.

Learning objectives should always be stated in measurable terms. As Robert F. Mager has noted, learning objectives should usually have three components[8]:

▲ *Resources*. What equipment, tools, information, or other resources must be provided for the learner to demonstrate the necessary knowledge, skills, or abilities?

▲ *Criteria*. How will achievement of learning objectives be measured? What minimum performance standards must be achieved for the individual to demonstrate competence?

▲ *Conditions*. Under what conditions must the learner perform?

Use the worksheet appearing in Exhibit 10-5 to prepare learning objectives based on individual developmental needs.

Step 5: Specify Learning Resources and Strategies Needed to Achieve the Learning Objectives

Learning strategies are the means by which learning objectives are to be achieved. There are many strategies by which to achieve learning objectives. Appropriate learning strategies depend on the learning objectives that are to be met. They answer this question: What planned learning activities will help narrow the gap between what individuals already know and what they must know to meet key position requirements in the future?

Learning resources are what must be provided to achieve the learning objectives. Resources might include people, money, time, expertise, equipment, or information. *People resources* could include trainers, coaches, mentors, or sponsors. *Money resources* could include funding for participation in on-the-job or off-the-job developmental experiences. *Time resources* could include

Exhibit 10-5. A Worksheet for Preparing Learning Objectives Based on Individual Development Needs

Directions: Use this worksheet to help you prepare specific, measurable learning objectives to guide the process of meeting individual development needs.

In the left column below, indicate activities, responsibilities, duties, tasks, or essential job functions to which the individual needs exposure in order to qualify for advancement. Then, in the right column below, draft specific and measurable learning objectives to describe what individuals should be able to know, do, or feel upon completion of a planned development/learning experience tied to those activities, responsibilities, duties, tasks, or essential job functions. When you finish drafting the objectives, double-check them to ensure that you have listed (1) resources, such as information, equipment, or tools that are necessary for demonstrating the objective; (2) measurable criteria by which to assess how well the learning objective was achieved.

Indicate Activities, Responsibilities, Duties, Tasks, or Essential Job Functions to Which the Individual Needs Exposure in Order to Qualify for Advancement	*Specific and Measurable Learning Objectives*

released time from work to participate in planned training, education, or developmental activities. Expertise could include access to knowledgeable people or information sources. Equipment could include access, for developmental purposes, to specialized machines or tools. (Use the worksheet in Exhibit 10-6 to identify the resources necessary to develop individuals for key positions for which they have been targeted.)

Step 6: Specify Evidence of Accomplishment

How can the organization track accomplishment of learning objectives? Answer that question by providing clear, measurable learning objectives and regular feedback about the learner's progress to the learner and those interested in the learner's development. If possible, use short, informal project appraisals or more formalized, written developmental appraisals to document individual progress, provide evidence of accomplishment, and give the individual specific feedback that can lead to future performance improvement.

Step 7: Specify How the Evidence Will Be Validated

Be clear about the means by which achievement of learning objectives will be validated. Will a knowledgeable expert, such as a key position incumbent, review the results? Will the learner be asked to complete an oral interview to demonstrate results? Will learners' performance on developmental projects be reviewed by those with whom they work? These questions must be answered separately for each learning objective and for each learning project or assignment on which the learners are to work to qualify for advancement.

Step 8: Review the Contract with Consultants

Before the individual development plan is approved, it should be reviewed by knowledgeable experts. In this context, experts and consultants are meant to have broad meanings. For instance, experts and consultants might include any—or all—of the following:

▲ Members of SP&M Committees
▲ Friends
▲ Spouses
▲ Immediate Organizational Superiors
▲ The Learners' Peers
▲ The Learners' Subordinates
▲ Academic Experts
▲ Recognized Authorities in Other Organizations

Depending on the organization, the individual, and the key position for which the individual is being prepared, other experts or consultants might prove

Exhibit 10-6. A Worksheet for Identifying the Resources Necessary to Support Developmental Experiences

Directions: Use this worksheet to help you identify the resources necessary to support planned learning/developmental experiences.

In the left column below, indicate learning objectives and the planned learning/developmental experiences that will be used in helping an individual qualify for promotion. Then, in the right column below, indicate specifically what resources—such as information, money, trainers, equipment, time, and so forth—will be needed to allow the individual to meet each learning objective and participate in each planned learning/developmental experience.

Learning Objectives and Planned Learning/Developmental Experiences Intended to Help an Individual Qualify for Advancement	*What Specific Resources Will Be Needed to Achieve Each Objective and Participate in Each Planned Learning/Developmental Experiences?*

useful. For instance, individuals may wish to identify their own mentors and ask for their advice while negotiating an IDP. In unionized settings, union members may also wish to include union representatives.

Ask the experts to provide information on which they are qualified to comment. For instance, from their perspective, does an IDP appear to have identified the right learning needs, established the right learning objectives, identified the most appropriate learning strategies and resources, and established the best means by which to evaluate results? Is it practical and capable of being completed in the time allowed? What suggested changes, if any, do the "experts" recommend—and why?

Step 9: Carry Out the Contract

I have found that the implementation of IDPs is the Achilles' heel of many otherwise exemplary SP&M programs. While well conceived, many IDPs are not well executed. Hence, some means must be established to ensure account-ability—and monitor results during the IDP's time span. That can be done by planning quarterly IDP review meetings with representatives from each major area of the organization so they can report on the progress made in their areas. Alternatively, an SP&M coordinator can pay visits to individual managers to review the progress made on IDPs in their areas of responsibility. The effect of these actions is to draw attention to the plans—and to maintain an impetus for action.

Step 10: Evaluate Learning and Outcomes

Be sure that results (learning outcomes) are measured against intentions (learning objectives and needs). There are several ways to do that. One way is to establish periodic developmental assessments, much like project-oriented performance appraisals. If this approach is used, develop a simple feedback form to provide documentation of learners' progress on each developmental experience. They can then be reviewed upon completion of learning objec-tives or at agreed-upon intervals during the developmental experiences.

A second way is to provide a checklist on the IDP form to indicate whether learning objectives have been achieved. That is a simpler, albeit less ambitious and rigorous, approach than periodic developmental assessments. However, it does have the advantage of being a time-efficient approach that makes it more likely to be used by busy decision-makers. A sample individual develop-ment plan (IDP) is shown in Exhibit 10-7.

Developing Successors Internally

Internal development is a general term that refers to those developmental activities sponsored by the organization that are intended to help an individual

Exhibit 10-7. A Sample Individual Development Plan

Directions: Use this individual development plan to help an individual qualify for advancement. The individual's immediate organizational superior should complete the form and then discuss it with the individual. If the individual feels that modifications to it should be made, then the reasons for that should be discussed.

Employee's Name _____ Job Title _____

Department _____ Time in Position _____

Appraiser's Name _____ Job Title _____

Department _____ Time in Position _____

Today's Date _____ Plan Covering _____ to _____
            mo./day/yr.   mo./day/yr.   mo./day/yr.

1. For what key position(s) should this individual be prepared? Alternatively, what kind of competencies should be developed? Over what time span?

2. What are the individual's career plans/objectives?

3. What learning objectives should guide the individual's development? (*Note to appraiser: Be sure to systematically compare the individual's current job description to a current job description for the targeted position[s] and list the identifiable gap below. Alternatively, compare the individual's present competencies to those needed in a future position/level.*)

(continues)

Exhibit 10-7. (continued)

4. By what methods/strategies may the objectives be met? (*Indicate a specific learning plan below, indicating learning objectives, strategies by which to achieve the objectives, deadlines for achieving each result, and a checklist indicating whether the learning objective was achieved.*) Add paper if necessary.

			Verified?	
Learning		Deadlines/	Yes	No
Objectives	Strategies	Benchmark Dates	( )	( )

5. How can the relative success of each learning objective be measured?

| Learning | |
| Objectives | Evaluation Approach |

qualify for advancement by closing the gap between present work requirements/performance and future work requirements/potential. Indeed, it is the means by which individual potential is realized as the future unfolds in the present.

There are several approaches to internal development. Many ways have been devised to develop individuals in their present positions,[9] and as many as 300 ways have been devised to develop individuals.[10] My 2004 survey identified common approaches to internal development. The survey results are summarized in Exhibit 10-8, and each strategy is briefly summarized in Exhibit 10-9.

Other strategies may also be used. These include:

1. *Who-Based Strategies.* These learning strategies focus on pairing up high potentials with individuals who have special talents—or management styles—worthy of emulation. For example, matching up a high potential with a participative manager or those possessing special abilities in startups, turnarounds, or shutdown efforts.

2. *What-Based Strategies.* These learning strategies focus on giving high potentials exposure to specific types of experiences, such as projects, task forces, committees, jobs, or assignments that require analytical skills, leadership skills, or skills in starting up an operation, shutting down an operation, converting a manual to an automated process, or another project of a specific kind. Additionally, service on interteam, interdepartmental, or interdivisional

(text continues on page 250)

Exhibit 10-8. Methods of Grooming Individuals for Advancement

There are many ways by which to implement succession plans, since individuals may be groomed in different ways. Review the list of possible methods by which to groom individuals in column 1 below. Then, in column 2, check (√) yes or no to indicate whether your organization is using it and, in column 3, circle the code indicating how effective you feel that method is in developing people to assume future responsibilities. In column 3, use the following scale: **1** = Not at All Effective; **2** = Not Very Effective; **3** = Somewhat Effective; **4** = Effective; **5** = Very Effective.

	Column 1	Column 2		Column 3	
	Possible Methods by Which to Groom Individuals	Is Your Organization Using This Method to Develop People?		How Effective Do You Feel This Method Is for Developing People to Assume Future Job Responsibilities?	
		Yes	No	Not at All Effective	Very Effective
				1 2 3 4 5 (Mean Response)	
A	Off-the-Job Degree Programs Sponsored by Colleges/Universities	56%	44%	3.8	
B	On-Site Degree Programs Sponsored by Colleges/Universities	11%	89%	2.78	

(continues)

Exhibit 10-8. (continued)

C	Off-the-Job Public Seminars Sponsored by Vendors	56%	44%	3.11
D	Off-the-Job Public Seminars Sponsored by Universities	100%	0%	3.44
E	In-House Classroom Courses Tailor-Made for Management-Level Employees	89%	11%	3.67
F	In-House Classroom Courses Purchased from Outside Sources and Modified for In-House Use	56%	44%	3.22
G	Unplanned On-the-Job Training	78%	22%	3.33
H	Planned On-the-Job Training	100%	0%	4.11
I	Unplanned Mentoring Programs	44%	56%	3.33
J	Planned Mentoring Programs	89%	11%	4.33
K	Unplanned Job Rotation Programs	11%	89%	3.11
L	Planned Job Rotation Programs	56%	44%	4.22

Source: William J. Rothwell, *Results of a 2004 Survey on Succession Planning and Management Practices.* Unpublished survey results (University Park, Penn.: The Pennsylvania State University, 2004).

Exhibit 10-9. Key Strategies for Internal Development

Strategy	How to Use It	Appropriate and Inappropriate Uses
1. Off-the-Job Degree Programs Sponsored by Colleges/Universities	△ Clarify job-related courses tied to work requirements of key positions. △ Compare individual skills to work requirements. △ Identify courses related to individual needs. △ Tie job requirements to degree/course requirements, if possible.	△ *Appropriate:* —For meeting specialized individual needs that are not widely enough shared to warrant on-site training △ *Inappropriate:* —For meeting highly specialized needs unique to one employer
2. On-Site Degree Programs Sponsored by Colleges/Universities	△ Same basic procedure as listed in #1 above.	△ *Appropriate:* —When funding and time are available —When several people share similar needs —When in-house expertise is not available △ *Inappropriate:* —When conditions listed above cannot be met —For meeting highly specialized needs
3. Off-the-Job Public Seminars Sponsored by Vendors	△ Compare work requirements to the instructional objectives indicated by information about the off-the-job seminar.	△ *Appropriate:* —When needs are limited to a few people —When in-house expertise does not match the vendor's △ *Inappropriate:* —For meeting needs unique to one employer

(continues)

Exhibit 10-9. (continued)

Strategy	How to Use It	Appropriate and Inappropriate Uses
4. Off-the-Job Public Seminars Sponsored by Universities	△ Same as #3 above.	△ Appropriate: —Same as #3 above △ Inappropriate: —Same as #3 above
5. In-House Classroom Courses Tailor-Made for Employees	△ Define specific instructional objectives that are directly related to work requirements in key positions. △ Use the courses to achieve instructional objectives for many individuals.	△ Appropriate: —When adequate resources exist —When in-house expertise is unavailable —When needs can be met in time △ Inappropriate: —For meeting requirements unique to one organization —For meeting objectives requiring lengthy and experiential learning
6. In-House Classroom Courses Purchased from Outside Sources and Modified for In-House Use	△ Identify a learning need shared by more than one person. △ Find published training material from commercial publishers and modify for in-house use. △ Deliver to groups.	△ Appropriate: —When several people share a common learning need —When expertise exists to modify materials developed outside the organization —When appropriate training materials can be located
7. Unplanned On-the-Job Training	△ Match up a high-potential employee with an exemplary performer in a key position. △ Permit long-term observation of the exemplar by the high-potential.	△ Appropriate: —When time, money, and staffing are not of primary importance △ Inappropriate: —For efficiently and effectively preparing high-potentials to be successors for key job incumbents

8. Planned On-the-Job Training	△ Develop a detailed training plan allowing a "tell, show, do, follow-up approach" to instruction.	△ *Appropriate:* —When key job incumbent is an exemplar —When time and safety considerations permit one-on-one instruction △ *Inappropriate:* —When the conditions listed above cannot be met
9. Unplanned Mentoring Programs	△ Make people aware of what mentoring is. △ Help individuals understand how they can establish mentoring relationships and realize the chief benefits from them. △ Encourage key job incumbents and exemplars to serve as mentors.	△ *Appropriate:* —For establishing the basis for mentoring without obligating the organization to oversee it —For encouraging individual autonomy △ *Inappropriate:* —For encouraging diversity and building relationships across "unlike" individual —For transferring specific skills
10. Planned Mentoring Programs	△ Match up individuals who may establish useful mentor-protégé relationships. △ Provide training to mentors on effective mentoring skills and to protégés on the best ways to take advantage of mentoring relationships.	△ *Appropriate:* —For building top-level ownership and familiarity with high-potentials —For pairing up "unlike individuals" on occasion △ *Inappropriate:* —For building specific skills

(continues)

Exhibit 10-9. (continued)

Strategy	How to Use It	Appropriate and Inappropriate Uses
11. Unplanned Job Rotation Programs	△ Arrange to move individuals into positions that will give them knowledge, skills, or abilities they will need in the future, preferably (but not necessarily) geared to advancement. △ Track individual progress.	△ Appropriate: —When sufficient staffing exists —When individual movement will not create a significant productivity loss to the organization △ Inappropriate: —When the conditions listed above cannot be met
12. Planned Job Rotation Programs	△ Develop a specific Learning Contract (or IDP) that clarifies the learning objectives to be achieved by the rotation. △ Ensure that the work activities in which the individual gains experience are directly related to future work requirements. △ Monitor work progress through periodic feedback to the individual and through performance appraisal geared to the rotation and related to future potential.	△ Appropriate: —When there is sufficient time and staffing to permit the rotation to be effective △ Inappropriate: —When time and staffing will not permit planned learning

committees can give the individual visibility and exposure to new people and new functions.

3. *When-Based Strategies.* These learning strategies focus on giving high potentials exposure to time pressure. For example, meeting a nearly impossible deadline or beating a wily competitor to market.

4. *Where-Based Strategies.* These learning strategies focus on giving high potentials exposure to special locations or cultures. For example, sending high

potentials on international job rotations or assignments to give them exposure to the business in another culture or else send them to another domestic site for a special project. Like any job rotation or temporary assignment, international assignments should be preceded by a well-prepared plan that clarifies what the individual is to do and learn—and why that is worth doing or learning. This approach will shape expectations and thereby exert a powerful influence on what people learn as well as on how they perform.

5. *Why-Based Strategies.* These learning strategies focus on giving high potentials exposure to mission-driven change efforts that are, in turn, learning experiences. For example, asking high potentials to pioneer startup efforts or to visit competitors or "best-in-class" organizations to find out "why they do what they do."

6. *How-Based Strategies.* These learning strategies focus on furnishing high potentials with in-depth, "how-to" knowledge of different aspects of the business in which they are otherwise weak. Examples might include lengthy job assignments, task force assignments, or job rotations that expose a high potential to another area of the business with which he or she is unfamiliar.

The Role of Leadership Development Programs

Leadership development programs are quite important to succession planning. Indeed, in some cases, a leadership development program is the banner under which potential successors are developed in a systematic, and even visible, way. Leadership programs may also develop groups of people so as to create talent pools.

Much has been written about leadership development[11] and leadership development programs.[12] Their value is that they can provide groups of people with structure—that is, an organizational scheme—by which to build competencies systematically. There are two basic philosophies that can drive leadership programs. (And they may be summarized with the age-old question: Are leaders born, or are they made?) One philosophy is to make it easy for anyone to get into the program but tough to stay in, or to "graduate." That philosophy goes well with a talent pool approach to SP&M. A second philosophy is to make it very difficult to qualify for the program but easy to stay in. That philosophy goes well with an approach that integrates employee selection with development.

Some decision-makers prefer to use a leadership development program as a means to fire-test prospective successors. They are tested at every turn while in the program. That tough-love philosophy suggests that qualifying for promotion means "earning one's stripes." Those who prefer not to do that do not have to. (But they will not be promoted, either.) Those who do have the tenacity to stick with it end up by earning credibility with followers.

The Role of Coaching

Coaching is a means to the end of building talent. While much has been written about it,[13] and it is true that coaching can be applied for many purposes to correct deficiencies in performance or to build skills, it is important to SP&M because it can be an important tool in grooming prospective successors for the future. Generally speaking, training is planned and focused, while coaching tends to be more spur-of-the-moment and driven by moment-by-moment efforts to help others perform.[14] In an age where speed equals advantage, real-time grooming has appeal to many managers as a means of competency-building at the speed of change.

James Hunt and Joseph Weintraub provide specific advice about how managers should coach. They should do the following:[15]

▲ Make the effort to identify their best people. Coaching is not just a "fix-it strategy" for poor performers; rather, it is also to be used to prepare promising people for the future.

▲ Encourage their people to seek out coaching, whether planned or spontaneous.

▲ Watch how they react to what their people do. In other words, good managers avoid strong emotions and criticism of their best people.

▲ Make time to provide coaching and let people know that.

▲ Ask questions and avoid dogmatic statements about what people should do. By asking questions, managers force employees to think things through. That has a development purpose. In time, employees will begin to think like the manager. But dogmatic orders will discourage questions and will not prompt people to think for themselves or even model how their immediate supervisor thinks.

▲ Listen carefully to what people say—and how they say it. Listening also demonstrates that the manager actually cares about their people, and the importance of emotional bonding should not be minimized.

▲ Model the behaviors of those who need coaching. Let employees see the manager ask for help and use it.

▲ Provide useful feedback. Make sure it is timely and specific. If people do not ask for feedback on what they did, give it to them anyway if it will help their development for the future.

▲ Be sure to recognize positive performance and comment on it as well as the not-so-good work that people do.

Various organizations now offer certification in coaching,[16] and information about the competencies of effective coaches may be found through a simple Web search.[17]

The Role of Executive Coaching

Executive coaching has grown in popularity.[18] Some people have even hung out their shingles as full-time executive coaches. Professional societies have been formed of executive coaches[19]; people can be certified as executive coaches[20]; and in some quarters executive coaches rank right up there with personal trainers as an executive perk. Executive coaching competencies have been identified, and they are distinct from more general coaching competencies.[21]

But the importance of executive coaching in succession cannot be understated.

One strategy is to go ahead and promote people who are clearly not ready for more demanding managerial (or technical) responsibility and then give those people executive coaches as a way to offer them real-time, on-the-job training. While that is not a strategy that the author of this book advocates, it is one that is being used in organizations where the leaders fell asleep on succession matters until it was too late.

There are two kinds of executive coaches. They should be clearly distinguished.

A *job content coach* provides guidance to individuals who are not up to snuff on the job content. An example would be to assign the organization's retired CEO to the current CEO as a coach. The former CEO clearly understands what the job entails and can provide guidance accordingly.

A *process coach* is different. Akin to a process consultant, a process executive coach focuses on the image that the executive projects, the impact that he or she has on a group, and how he or she works with a group to achieve results. No knowledge of the job content is needed. But what is needed is awareness of the specialized competencies associated with process consultation, an organization development intervention invented by Edgar Schein.[22]

The executive coaching process should be clearly focused and implemented. It begins with establishing a contract between the coach and the coachee that sets forth the goals of the effort and describes the schedule. Nondisclosure agreements are typical, especially when the coach is made privy to sensitive, even proprietary, information during the course of the consulting engagement. The work plan for the consulting effort is clearly stated. Not all work has to be carried out face-to-face, and it is possible to arrange phone conversations, Web conversations, instant chats, and other real-time, virtually enabled approaches to the executive coaching process. Executive coaches may also administer psychological assessments to the executive, ranging from those that are available off-the-shelf to those that require a license or degree to administer.

The Role of Mentoring

A mentor is simply a teacher. Mentoring is thus the process of teaching others. In common language, a mentor is a helper who assists people in learning. The person receiving help is called a *mentee* or a *protégé*. Mentors should not be confused with sponsors. A *sponsor* is someone who actually opens doors and provides access to visibility, people, and assignments or experiences; a *mentor* is someone who provides advice. Of course, it is possible that mentors can become sponsors or that sponsors can engage in mentoring.

Mentoring has fired the imagination of managers and others, and much has been written about it in recent years.[23] One reason is that mentors can help build bench strength and talent in organizations by providing support to others to build their competencies in line with company needs. Mentoring, like coaching and executive coaching, can thus provide a means to the end of building bench strength. But mentoring implies something different from coaching. While a coach provides support and direction just as a mentor does, a mentor is interested in helping someone succeed. By definition, mentors are usually not the immediate organizational supervisors of those they mentor, since a reporting relationship may interfere with the objectivity essential to a true helping relationship. (In short, a mentor cannot stand to gain or lose by his or her mentee, but a coach can. In fact, just as athletic coaches are self-interested in how well their players perform, so are immediate supervisors.)

Mentoring programs may be established by organizations. They may be formal (planned) or informal (unplanned). A typical approach to a formal program is that the organization's HR department will play matchmaker, pairing up a promising person who wants a mentor to someone who is at least one or more levels above that person on the organization chart but outside the immediate chain of command. The HR department may even pay for breakfast, lunch, or dinner for the two people to meet and determine if their relationship might have promise. If so, then they continue it on their own without further HR department involvement. Also, typically, a formal mentoring program may involve training for aspiring mentors and/or mentees, since people do not just naturally know how to play these parts. (The CD-ROM included with this book provides a short program on mentoring.)

In an informal mentoring program—which is an oxymoron, since something unplanned cannot really be a "program"—individuals are merely encouraged to seek out and approach others who may be helpful to them and to their development. Successful people have almost always had mentors. Consequently, mentoring requires mentees to take initiative to seek out those who might help them and then ask for help. That help could be situation-specific, such as "How do I deal with this situation?" or comprehensive, such as "How do I systematically prepare myself for the future and then follow through on my plan for individual development?"

Mentors are helpful because they may be in the job that the mentees aspire to, and hence they are well positioned to offer advice. After all, one key assumption of succession planning and management is that individuals cannot direct their own development for the simple reason that they have no experience base to draw on. And it is in exactly this respect that a mentor can help.

How can mentoring play a role in succession planning and management? The relationship should be obvious. In closing developmental gaps between the competencies that individuals possess now and what they need to possess to qualify for advancement, they must seek out people, work assignments, and other experiences that will prepare them for the future and will equip them with the competencies they need. Mentors can provide advice about what people to seek, what work assignments to seek, and (perhaps most important though sometimes overlooked) mentors can provide advice on handling company politics that may help or hinder progress. To gain the most from a mentoring effort, start with a plan. That plan can be prepared by the mentee to "ask for help," but should be very clear about what help is needed.

A unique problem to consider in mentoring is the so-called *developmental dilemma*. The development dilemma takes its name from a special problem that may come up in the mentoring process. In the years following the Clarence Thomas and Anita Hill scandal that rocked the nation, cross-gender mentoring has been complicated by concerns over appearances. The point is that older male executives who mentor younger female executives, or older female executives who mentor younger male executives, may be misperceived in those relationships. Typically a mentoring relationship requires interactions such as meetings behind closed doors, breakfast, lunch or dinner meetings, or other meetings in otherwise less than formal settings. Since tongue wagging is a popular pastime, it is common for others to talk about what they think they see. The situation is so bad in some quarters that older executives will have mentoring meetings only if they can bring a third person along as chaperone or else meet in open air areas where everything can be seen.

How can this problem be handled? Some ways that the organization can help is to:

1. Provide advice about how to deal with the problems of perceptions and how to manage them.
2. Take steps to clarify for others who may see two people meeting to clarify, casually but in advance, what the meeting is about and why it is being conducted to give those who wag their tongues less to talk about.
3. Ignore the problem all together and only deal with rumors as they spring up.
4. Provide training to mentors and mentees, covering cross-gender issues as part of the discussion.

The Role of Action Learning

Action learning is yet another way—like coaching, executive coaching, mentoring, and leadership development programs—to build competencies. Action learning, while invented in 1971 by Reg Revans,[24] literally means *learning through action.* While various approaches to it exist,[25] they share a bias to action. This is not online or onsite training; rather, it is practical learning that builds competencies and is focused around solving problems, creating visions, seeking goals, or leveraging strengths.[26]

Typically, participants in action learning are assembled to work on a practical, real-world problem.[27] They may be chosen based on their individual abilities that will contribute to the issue that brings the team together and a developmental need to be met. They are asked to collect information about an issue, experiment with solutions or implement them, and learn while they do that.

To use action learning appropriately, organizational leaders must select the right people to put on the right teams. By doing that, individuals learn while doing. And the organization gains a solution to a problem, a clearly conceptualized vision, or a quantum leap in leveraging a strength.

Summary

Promotion from within is an important way to implement succession plans. To that end, the organization should test bench strength, establish an unequivocal internal promotion policy to ensure internal promotion when appropriate, prepare individual development plans (IDPs) to close the gap between what individuals presently do and what they must do to qualify for promotion, and use internal development when appropriate to realize the learning objectives established on IDPs.

But internal promotion and internal development are not the only means by which succession planning and management needs can be met. Alternative means, which usually fall outside the realm of succession planning and management, are treated in the next chapter. In these days of business process reengineering and process improvement, those involved in succession planning and management should have some awareness of approaches to meeting work requirements other than traditional succession methods relying on job movements.

CHAPTER 11

ASSESSING ALTERNATIVES TO INTERNAL DEVELOPMENT

The traditional approach is to prepare successors for key positions internally. Some descriptions of succession planning and management (SP&M) treat it as nothing more than a form of replacement planning. In this process, several key assumptions are usually made: (1) key positions will be replaced whenever a vacancy occurs; (2) employees already working in the organization—and often within the function—will be the prime source of replacements; and (3) a key measure of effectiveness is the percentage of key positions that can be filled from within, with minimal delay and uproar, whenever a vacancy occurs. Some organizations add a fourth: the relative racial and sexual diversity of replacements should be enhanced so that protected labor groups are well represented among the qualified replacements for key positions prepared internally.

A systematic approach to SP&M has major advantages, of course. First, it makes succession predictable. Each time a vacancy in a key position occurs, people know precisely what to do: find a replacement. Second, since a high percentage of successors are assumed to be employed by the organization, investments in employee development can be justified to minimize losses in productivity and turnover.

However, when SP&M is treated in this way it can occasionally become a mindless exercise in "filling in the blank name on the organization chart." Concern about that should be sufficient to lead strategists to explore innovative alternatives to the traditional replacement-from-within mentality. This chapter focuses on those alternatives—and on when they should be used instead of the traditional approach to SP&M.

The Need to Manage for "Getting the Work Done" Rather than "Managing Succession"

"The natural response to a problem," writes James L. Adams in *Conceptual Blockbusting*, "seems to be to try to get rid of it by finding an answer—often taking the first answer that occurs and pursuing it because of one's reluctance

257

to spend the time and mental effort needed to conjure up a richer storehouse of alternatives from which to choose. This hit-and-run approach to problem-solving begets all sorts of oddities.''[1]

Succession planning and management can fall victim to the same natural response to which Adams refers: Whenever a vacancy occurs, the organization is confronted with a problem. The "natural response" is to find an immediate replacement. There may also be a tendency to "clone the incumbent"—that is, find someone who resembles the incumbent in order to minimize the need to make adjustments to a new person. But replacement is not always appropriate. Consider a replacement unnecessary when any one of the questions listed below can be answered yes. (Review the flowchart appearing in Exhibit 11-1 as a simplified aid in helping with this decision process.)

Question 1: Is the Key Position No Longer Necessary?

A replacement is not necessary when a key position is no longer worth doing. In that situation, a "key" position is no longer "key." Decision-makers can simply choose not to fill the key position when a vacancy occurs. Of course, if this question is answered no, then a replacement may still have to be found.

Question 2: Can a Key Position Be Rendered Unnecessary by Finding New Ways to Achieve Comparable Results?

A replacement may not be necessary if key work outcomes can be achieved in new ways. In this sense, then, SP&M can be affected by business process reengineering, defined by best-selling authors Michael Hammer and James Champy as "the fundamental rethinking and radical redesign of business processes to achieve dramatic improvements in critical, contemporary measures of performance, such as cost, quality, service, and speed."[2] If the organization can reengineer work processes and thereby eliminate positions that were once key to an old process, then replacing a key job incumbent will be unnecessary. In short, key positions may be reengineered out of existence.

To that end, try applying the model suggested by Rummler and Brache to process improvement[3]:

1. Identify the critical business issue or process that is to be reexamined.
2. Select critical processes related to the issue or subprocesses.
3. Select a leader and members for a process improvement team.
4. Train the team on process improvement methods.
5. Develop "is" maps to show the relationship between where and how work flows into a system, how it is transformed through work methods, and where it goes when the products or services are provided to the "customers."

(text continues on page 265)

Exhibit 11-1. Deciding When Replacing a Key Job Incumbent Is Unnecessary: A Flowchart

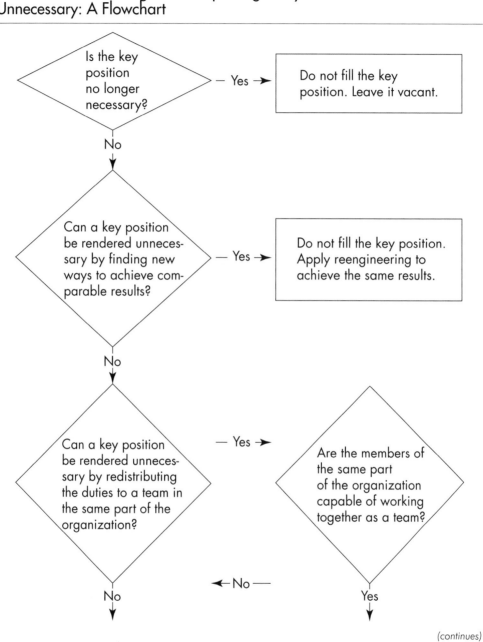

(continues)

Exhibit 11-1. *(continued)*

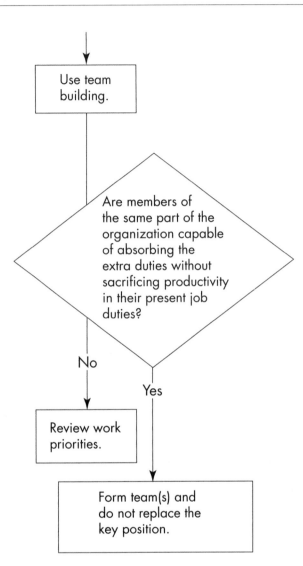

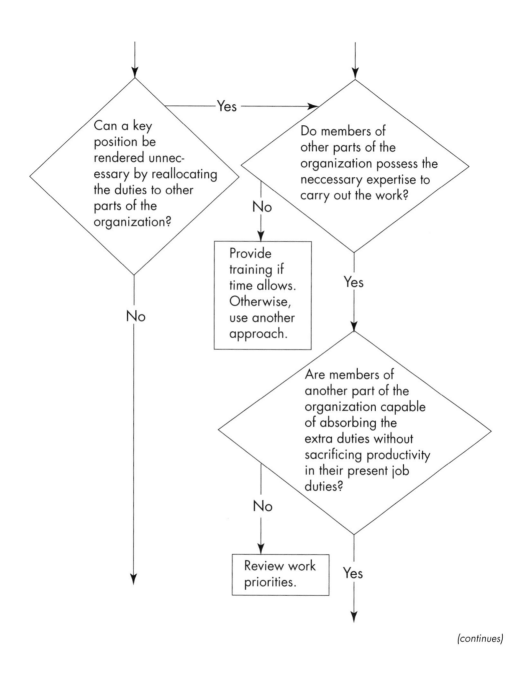

(continues)

Exhibit 11-1. *(continued)*

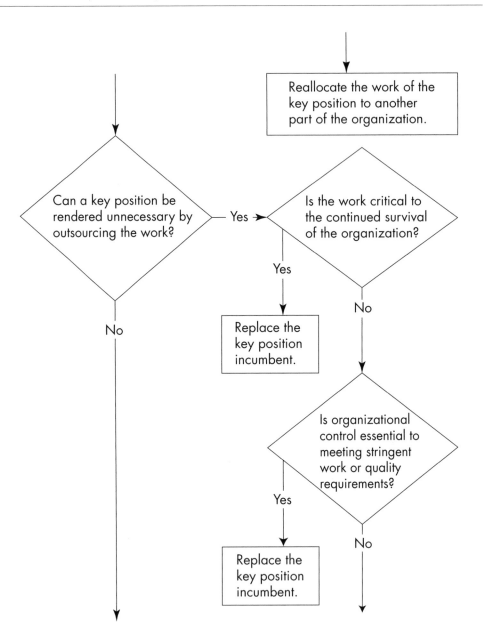

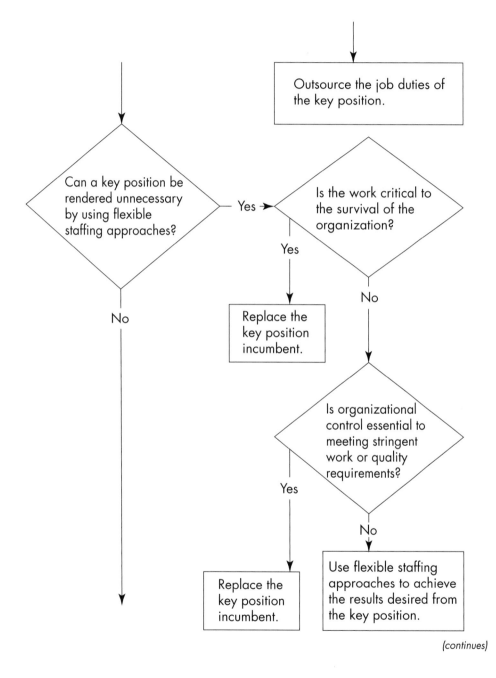

(continues)

Exhibit 11-1. *(continued)*

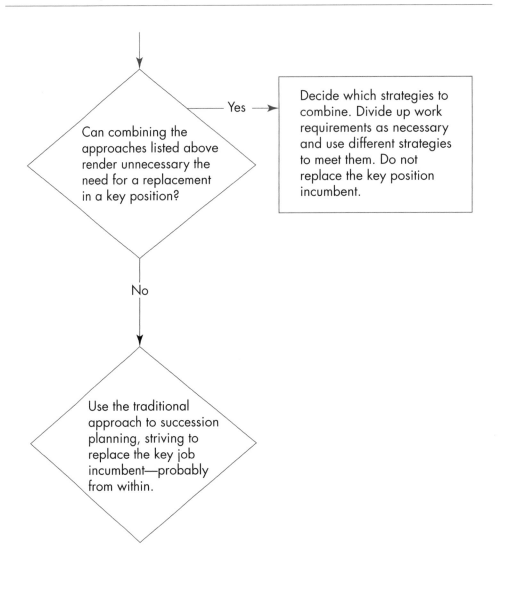

6. Find "disconnects," which are missing, redundant, or illogical factors that could affect the critical business issue or the process.
7. Analyze the disconnects.
8. Develop a "should" map to present a more efficient or effective method of handling the work.
9. Establish measures or standards for what is desired.
10. Recommend changes.
11. Implement the changes.

In essence, the same steps described above can be used to determine whether there are ways to "engineer a key position out of existence." If there is, then no successor will be needed. (However, the work process may be broken up and reallocated, necessitating new competencies for those who absorb the new duties.)

Question 3: Can a Key Position Be Rendered Unnecessary by Redistributing the Duties to a Team?

If the answer is yes, then it should be possible to achieve the same work results by placing responsibility in a team of workers from the same function or work unit. However, two caveats should be considered. First, if the workers have never functioned as a team, then they will probably require team-building and training on team skills to work as a cohesive group. Second, if prospective team members are already working at—or beyond—their individual capacities, then loading additional duties on a team will not be successful.

Question 4: Can a Key Position Be Rendered Unnecessary by Reallocating the Duties to Other Parts of the Organization?

In short, is it possible to avoid filling a key position by reorganizing, moving the work responsibility to another function or organizational unit? If the answer is yes, then replacing a key job incumbent may prove to be unnecessary. But, as in redistributing work to a team in the same part of the organization, assess whether the inheritors of key position duties are trained adequately to perform the work and can do them without sacrificing productivity in their present jobs. If both conditions can be met, consider moving responsibilities to another part of the organization to avoid replacing a key job incumbent.

Question 5: Can a Key Position Be Rendered Unnecessary by Outsourcing the Work?

If the answer is yes, then replacing a key job incumbent may be unnecessary. The same results may be achieved more cost-effectively than by replacing a key job incumbent. Pay particular attention to two key issues when answering the question: *criticality* and *control*. If the work is critical to the continued survival of the organization, then outsourcing it may be unwise because that may vest too much influence in an individual or group having little or no stake in the organization's continued survival. If the work must meet stringent, specialized requirements for which few external sources can be found, then outsourcing may also prove to be unwise because controlling the activities of an external contractor may become as time-consuming as performing the work in-house.

Question 6: Can a Key Position Be Rendered Unnecessary by Using Flexible Staffing Approaches?

Can the same results be achieved through the use of permanent part-time or temporary part-time staff, rotating employees, or internships? If the answer is yes, then replacing a key job incumbent may be unnecessary. However, as in outsourcing, pay attention to criticality and control. If the work is critical to the continued survival of the organization, then using innovative staffing approaches may prove to be unwise because that will grant too much influence to an individual or group with little or no stake in the organization's existence. If the work must meet stringent, specialized requirements that require mastery, then part-time talent may not be able to achieve or maintain that mastery.

Question 7: Can Combining the Approaches Listed Above Obviate the Need for a Replacement in a Key Position?

In other words, is it possible to split apart the key results or outcomes desired from the key position and handle them separately—through reengineering, team-based management, organizational redesign, or other means? If that question can be answered yes, then it should be possible to ensure that the organization achieves the same results as those provided by the key job incumbent—but without the need for a replacement. Use the worksheet in Exhibit 11-2 to decide when it is possible to answer yes to any one—or all—of the questions listed above.

Innovative Approaches to Tapping the Retiree Base

Succession planning and management is not an all-or-nothing proposition. It is also possible to meet staffing needs to get the work done by tapping the very group that is causing some of the problems—that is, baby boomers who are nearing retirement. And that is also not an all-or-nothing proposition in the sense that discouraging people from retiring, while one option, is not the only way to tap into the power of those who are eligible to retire.

The word *retire*—taken from the Middle French word *retirer* (which means "to draw back")—is being reinvented now. Much evidence exists to support that.[4] Older workers are delaying their retirement due to a roller-coaster stock market and eroding health insurance coverage, which is (in turn)

Exhibit 11-2. A Worksheet for Identifying Alternatives to the Traditional Approach to Succession Planning and Management

Directions: Use this worksheet to help you identify alternatives to the traditional approach to succession planning—that is, promoting from within the organization and within the function.

In the first space below, identify by title the key position that you are examining. Then answer the questions about it appearing in the left column of the second space below. Write your responses in the right column, making notes about ways by which you can use alternatives to the traditional approach to succession planning. When you finish, share your responses with others in the organization for their thoughts— and, if possible, to compare their comments to yours. Add paper if necessary.

There are no "right" or "wrong" answers to this activity; rather, the aim is to provide you with an aid to creative ways by which to meet succession planning needs.

Space One: What is the key position? (Provide a job title.)

Questions About the Key Position	*Question Responses (Describe ideas to avoid simple replacement from within.)*
Is the key position no longer necessary?	
Can a key position be rendered unnecessary by finding new ways to achieve comparable results?	

(continues)

Exhibit 11-2. (continued)

Questions About the Key Position	Question Responses (Describe ideas to avoid simple replacement from within)
Can a key position be rendered unnecessary by redistributing the duties to a team in the same part of the organization?	
Can a key position be rendered unnecessary by reallocating the duties to other parts of the organization?	
Can a key position be rendered unnecessary by outsourcing the work?	
Can a key position be rendered unnecessary by using flexible staffing approaches?	
Can combining the approaches listed above eliminate the need for a replacement in a key position?	

eroding the value of their pension packages. Some observers of the business scene even doubt that a talent shortage will appear.[5] At the same time, employers do not want to experience the confusion that results from filling tough-to-fill positions with green, off-the-street (or at least untested) hires. One researcher found that only 12 to 16 percent of retirees currently work past retirement but that 80 percent of baby boomers intend to do so.[6]

If you say "reinvent retirement" today to most employers, the first thing that crosses their minds is to discourage experienced workers from exercising their retirement option when eligible or else to call retired people back to full-time work. But many other options exist, and reinventing retirement means tapping the retiree base in creative ways to meet the organization's short-term and long-term talent needs.

There are actually many ways that retirees could be tapped. They can be temps; contingent workers; consultants; teleworkers or telecommuters; assigned to special projects, perhaps at distant (even international) locations; or assigned as coaches or mentors for their successors. Many other options are also possible (see Exhibit 11-3).

Tapping the retiree base will be a challenge for the future. A first step is to establish who wants to do what, who wants to work when and how, and how to find and tap the talents of retirees on demand. That will require creative applications of exit interviews, conducted with retirees, and periodic follow-ups with retirees to see if they have changed their minds about the work options available to them. It will also require better competency or talent inventories to find the competencies that retirees possess and tap them creatively on short notice. It will also require new management approaches, since retirees may have lower tolerance for arbitrary management practices than others.

Deciding What to Do

There is no foolproof way to integrate SP&M with alternatives to replacement from within. The important point is to make sure that alternatives to simple replacement are considered. Often, that responsibility will rest with HR generalists, HRD specialists, SP&M coordinators, and even CEOs or others who bear major responsibility for succession planning and management. A good strategy is to raise the issue at two different—and opportune—times: (1) during review meetings to identify successors; and (2) on the occasions when a vacancy occurs in a key position and permission is sought to fill it.

During the review process, ask operating managers how they plan to meet replacement needs. At that time, raise the alternatives, and ask them to consider other possibilities as well. Be sure that only key positions are being considered in succession planning and management efforts in order to focus attention on areas of critical need.

When a vacancy occurs—or is about to occur—in a key position, raise the

Exhibit 11-3. A Tool for Contemplating Ten Ways to Tap the Retiree Base

Directions: Use this worksheet to guide your thinking on how the retiree base of your organization might be more effectively tapped to shore up talent needs. In any given situation when your organization is facing a talent need or shortage wrought by a retirement, consider each of the strategies listed below. For each way to use the retiree base to solve the problem, indicate whether it might be appropriate to that situation by checking yes, no, or maybe. Make remarks in the right column about whether two or more alternatives might be combined.

	Ways of Tapping the Retiree Base to Meet a Talent Need	Is This Approach Appropriate to the Situation?			Remarks: Can Two or More Alternatives Be Combined?
		Yes ✓	No ✓	Maybe ✓	
	Could the work be accomplished by:				
1	Calling in retirees for full-time employment?	☐	☐	☐	
2	Calling in retirees for "permanent part-time" employment?	☐	☐	☐	
3	Calling retirees "as needed"?	☐	☐	☐	
4	Giving the retirees virtual work to do?	☐	☐	☐	
5	Giving retirees cell phones and putting them "on call" to coach their replacements when needed?	☐	☐	☐	
6	Hiring retirees as coaches for those who are really not ready for the promotions they are given?	☐	☐	☐	
7	Giving retirees computers and having them do virtual coaching by "instant messaging" as needed?	☐	☐	☐	
8	Tapping retirees as onsite or online trainers?	☐	☐	☐	
9	Hiring retirees to document procedures or other information that they know?	☐	☐	☐	
10	Hiring retirees as consultants?	☐	☐	☐	
11	Other (Specify:)	☐	☐	☐	

issue again. Ask operating managers what alternatives to simple replacement they have considered. Briefly review some of them to ensure that succession is driven by work requirements and not by custom, resistance to change, or other issues that may be needlessly costly or inefficient.

Summary

This chapter has reviewed alternatives to traditional replacement from within. Alternatives may be used when any one or all of the following questions may be answered yes:

1. Is the key position no longer necessary?
2. Can a key position be rendered unnecessary by finding new ways to achieve comparable results?
3. Can a key position be rendered unnecessary by redistributing the duties to a team in the same part of the organization?
4. Can a key position be rendered unnecessary by reallocating the duties to other parts of the organization?
5. Can a key position be rendered unnecessary by outsourcing the work?
6. Can a key position be rendered unnecessary by using flexible staffing approaches?
7. Can combining the approaches listed above obviate the need for a replacement in a key position?
8. Can the retiree base be tapped for a qualified replacement?

Pose these questions during review meetings to identify successors and on the occasions when a vacancy occurs in a key position. Be sure that key positions are filled only when absolutely necessary to achieve essential work requirements and to meet the organization's real strategic objectives.

CHAPTER 12

USING TECHNOLOGY TO SUPPORT SUCCESSION PLANNING AND MANAGEMENT PROGRAMS

The Internet and the World Wide Web have profoundly influenced the world. That fact is as true for succession planning and management (SP&M) practices as for anything else. Many organizations are in a competitive race to enter e-commerce, or to consolidate the competitive edge they are already acquiring from it.

Online and high-tech approaches have also had a dramatic impact on succession planning and management practices. This chapter focuses attention on four key questions: (1) How are online and high-tech methods defined? (2) In what areas of succession planning and management can online and high-tech methods be applied? (3) How are online and high-tech applications used? and (4) What specialized competencies are required by succession planning coordinators to use these applications?

Defining Online and High-Tech Methods

An *online method* relies on the Internet, a company or organizational intranet, an extranet, or the World Wide Web. Examples of online methods range from traditional print-based electronic mail to Web-based multimedia productions that integrate print, sound effects, music, animation, still graphics, and video. A *high-tech method* is anything other than an online method that substitutes technology for face-to-face interpersonal interaction. Examples of high-tech methods include videoconferencing or audio-teleconferencing.

One way to conceptualize online and high-tech methods is to think of them as existing on one continuum ranging from simple to complex and on a second continuum ranging from noninteractive to fully interactive, as depicted in Exhibit 12-1. Simple methods are usually easy to design and inexpensive to use. Complex methods are usually difficult to design and are often expensive to design and use. Noninteractive methods do not involve people in real time, while interactive methods require people to participate actively. These distinctions are important when planning and budgeting the use of online and high-tech methods. The most complex or interactive methods often necessitate spe-

Exhibit 12-1. Continua of Online and High-Tech Approaches

	Simple	*Complex*
Noninteractive	△ Electronic mail △ Web-based documents △ Audiotape-based training or instructions △ Videotape-based training or instructions	△ Online help with forms △ Policies, procedures, instructions, forms, or instruments distributed by disk or CD-ROM
Interactive	△ Print surveys sent electronically △ Print surveys completed over the Web △ PC-based audioteleconference △ PC-based videoteleconference	△ Groupware △ Interactive television △ Multimedia training material △ Virtual reality applications

cial skills in the design process and are more expensive and time-consuming to plan and use.

The software to support succession planning and management is becoming increasingly sophisticated. Nontechnical users who are tasked with sourcing the right technology to support the organization's operations in this area face a daunting task. And the information is not necessarily easy to come by. Much time can be spent just trying to find what software is available and compare their features. A good approach is to clarify what your organization plans to do with the software and then find a product that will best meet the needs. Use the rating sheet in Exhibit 12-2 as a starting point to define what is needed.

I have found that some popular vendors on the market are the following (this is not a product endorsement):

- ▲ Talent Management by AIM (see www.aimworld.com/AIMtalent.html)
- ▲ Succession by Business Decisions, Inc. (see www.businessdecisions .com/)
- ▲ HRSoft by Executrack (see www.hrsoft.com/)
- ▲ Click XG Workforce by PeopleClik (see www.peopleclick.com/)
- ▲ Succession Pulse by Pilat (see www.pilat-hr.com/solutions/succession .html)
- ▲ Workforce Performance Management by Success Factors (see www.suc cessfactors.com/index.php)
- ▲ Human Capital Management by Softscape (see www.softscape.com/us/ home.htm)

(text continues on page 277)

Exhibit 12-2. A Starting Point for a Rating Sheet to Assess Vendors for Succession Planning and Management Software

Directions: Use this rating sheet as a starting point to develop your own rating sheet to assess various software vendors for succession planning and management software. Note that there are three sections. The first section asks you to rate the software product. The second section asks you to rate the vendor. The third section allows you to provide any additional comments you wish to provide. For each criterion listed in the left column below, gather sufficient evidence to rate the vendor in the center column according to the following ratings: **0** = Not Applicable; **1** = Not Acceptable; **2** = Somewhat Unacceptable; **3** = Somewhat Acceptable; **4** = Fully Acceptable. In the right column, provide notes to explain your scores. If you rate the vendor as anything less than fully acceptable, provide a justification in the right column.

Part I: The Software

	N/A	Not Acceptable	Somewhat Unacceptable	Somewhat Acceptable	Fully Acceptable	Justification
	0	1	2	3	4	
Is the software:						
1. Compatible with other software that your company uses—or can it be made compatible with relative ease?	0	1	2	3	4	
2. Simple to use?	0	1	2	3	4	
3. Browser-based?	0	1	2	3	4	
4. Capable of giving different levels of access to different types of users?	0	1	2	3	4	

5. Able to provide the kind of reports that you or others will want?	0	1	2	3	4
6. Capable of being customized for individuals, such as your CEO?	0	1	2	3	4
7. Capable of providing the level of security that you want?	0	1	2	3	4
8. Competitively priced?	0	1	2	3	4
9. Priced with upgrades?	0	1	2	3	4
10. Well-matched to the needs your organization plans to meet with it?	0	1	2	3	4

Part II: The Vendor

Does the vendor:

1. Have a good track record with other clients?	0	1	2	3	4
2. Provide the support your organization will need?	0	1	2	3	4
3. Respond to requests?	0	1	2	3	4

(continues)

Exhibit 12-2. *(continued)*

	N/A	Not Acceptable	Somewhat Unacceptable	Somewhat Acceptable	Fully Acceptable	Justification
4. Know enough about succession planning and management to be helpful?	0	1	2	3	4	
5. Provide the level of support your organization needs/wants?	0	1	2	3	4	
6. Provide a range of solutions and avoid a "one-size-fits-all" approach?	0	1	2	3	4	
7. Provide training you or others might need?	0	1	2	3	4	

Now add up the scores.
The higher the score, the more acceptable it is: Total _____

Part III: Your Additional Comments

For additional help, check out the current *Buyer's Guide to Talent Management Systems*, which could be found (at the time this book goes to press) at http://shop.hr.com/products/ICGReport_TalentMS.asp. Of course, many more software packages are out there.

Where to Apply Technology Methods

To state the issue simply, online and high-tech methods can be applied to almost any area of an SP&M program. Such methods may be used in: (1) formulating SP&M program policy, procedures, and action plans; (2) assessing present work or competency requirements; (3) evaluating current employee performance; (4) determining future work or competency requirements; (5) assessing potential; (6) closing developmental gaps; (7) maintaining talent inventories; and (8) evaluating the program. Of course, online and high-tech methods can also be used for communicating details of a succession program and providing training and skill building, or even real-time coaching. They substitute virtual interaction for face-to-face interaction. The maddening thing about them is that they date so quickly. Almost nothing today changes as fast as technological innovations.

How to Evaluate and Use Technology Applications

To use online and high-tech applications in SP&M programs, you can use a hierarchy of applications, such as presented in Exhibit 12-3. The subsections below first describe the hierarchy and then provide specifics about how to apply online and high-tech methods to an SP&M program.

A Hierarchy of Applications

Researching secondary information is the first, and lowest, level of online and high-tech applications for SP&M. You can use the Web—or your organization's human resource information systems (HRIS)—to collect and analyze information that is readily available. Use secondary information of this kind to look for articles, books, or Web sites about best practices and research on succession issues. Surf the Web, using search engines or metasearch engines (see a full list of metasearch engines at www.searchiq.com/directory/multi.htm), around key words or phrases linked to succession planning. Conduct analyses of your organization's workforce using your organizational HR information system about such important issues as the ages of your workers at various levels (executive, managerial, professional, and technical) and their projected retirement ages, their racial or gender composition, performance ratings, turnover rates, absenteeism, and other information. Try to use this information to answer such questions as these:

Exhibit 12-3. A Hierarchy of Online and High-Tech Applications for Succession Planning and Management

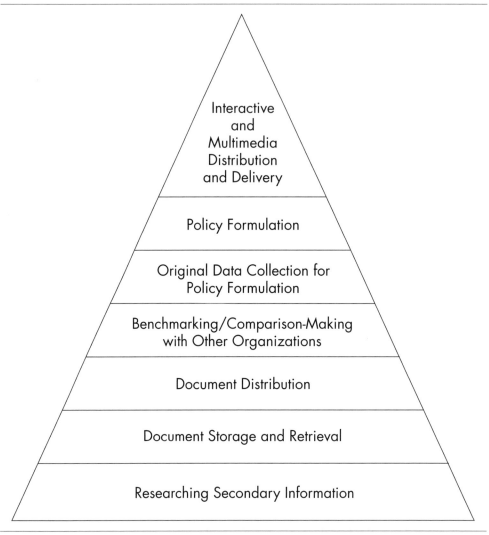

Interactive and Multimedia Distribution and Delivery

Policy Formulation

Original Data Collection for Policy Formulation

Benchmarking/Comparison-Making with Other Organizations

Document Distribution

Document Storage and Retrieval

Researching Secondary Information

▲ How many people exist at each level of the organization and in each important occupational or hierarchical grouping?

▲ When are those people expected to retire?

▲ What percentage of those people fall into protected labor classes?

▲ What is the turnover rate by level?

▲ What is the critical turnover rate by level?

▲ How well are people performing?

▲ How many potential candidates for succession exist at each level, and how many potential candidates may be needed to exist to support the organization's expected growth?

In each case, these questions involve analysis of existing information. This is the lowest level of the hierarchy of applications, and it is also the easiest to use, provided that the necessary records exist and can be manipulated in ways permitting analysis.

Document storage and retrieval is the second level of the hierarchy. On-line methods are often useful for storing and retrieving documents important to SP&M such as job descriptions, competency models, value statements, performance appraisal forms, potential assessments, and replacement charts. As organizations move toward realizing the promise of the paperless office, document storage and retrieval becomes more important. Document imaging permits hard copy to be scanned and kept electronically.

Document distribution is the third level of the hierarchy. This level adds interactivity and permits SP&M coordinators to place documents online. For instance, from company Web sites, users can download documents such as job descriptions, job analysis questionnaires or interview guides, competency models, performance appraisal forms, individual potential assessment forms, individual development plans, and even training for advancement. Additionally, users may even complete the forms online and send them to SP&M coordinators so that the transactions are paperless. Data can then be analyzed directly online. (That also improves data security.)

Benchmarking is the fourth level of the hierarchy. While the third level permits document distribution and analysis within an organization, benchmarking permits information sharing among organizations. For instance, a succession planning coordinator in one organization can send electronic questionnaires—or even sample documents, such as succession planning policies—to consultants, college professors, or SP&M coordinators in other organizations. That permits easy comparisons and discussions of important issues across organizations.

Original data collection for policy formulation is the fifth level of the hierarchy. Using online survey software, for instance, SP&M coordinators can poll managers, workers, and other stakeholders about emerging problems that affect succession planning. For instance, an attitude survey could be conducted periodically online to gather information about employee job satisfaction (which can affect or even help to predict turnover rates), attitudes about existing succession practices, and other relevant issues. This information is valuable in formulating new policies or revising existing policies.

Policy formulation is the sixth level of the hierarchy. Decision-makers can use groupware—software that links individuals virtually for decision making in real time—to formulate new policies on issues affecting SP&M. For instance, during policy formulation, decision-makers can work together on virtual teams to establish a new or revised succession policy, devise a competency model, prepare a job description, plan training to close developmental gaps, carry out potential assessment or performance appraisal, or offer confidential advice on a difficult succession issue.

Interactive and multimedia distribution and delivery is the seventh and highest level of the hierarchy. This is usually the most complex, and often the most expensive, to create. It includes multimedia training prepared and delivered over the Web or over a company intranet. It also includes CD-ROM-based training designed to build competencies to prepare people for advancement and other high-tech methods, such as desktop video, that can link decision-makers in discussions about individual development or about SP&M policy issues.

Use the worksheet in Exhibit 12-4 to brainstorm when and how to use online and high-tech methods according to the hierarchy of applications described in this section.

Formulating Policy, Procedures, and Action Plans

Recall from earlier in this book that an important starting point for any SP&M program is a policy to guide the program, as well as procedures and action plans to implement the program. Lacking those, decision-makers will probably not share the same views about what results are to be achieved, how they are to be achieved, or even why the program exists. The process of formulating SP&M program policy, procedures, and action plans is important because the process is key to gaining stakeholder ownership and understanding.

Online and high-tech methods can be helpful in formulating policy, procedures, and action plans. It is not always necessary, of course, to formulate policies in face-to-face meetings. Some (and on occasion all) of the work can be done online, and some work can be done by virtual teams when decision-makers are geographically scattered.

Groupware can bring stakeholders together to make a decision in real time. (For an example of groupware that can be downloaded for free, see http://teamwave.com/.) Some people can be in the United States; some can be in Europe; some can be in South America; some can be in Australia; and some can be in Asia. But they all assemble online at the same time and focus attention on discussing and reaching conclusions about key issues.

High-tech methods can also be used. Conference calls are probably the simplest of these methods. Users discuss succession policies, procedures, and action plans over the phone. To hold down costs, such calls can be made over personal computers by using software such as netphone (see www.sonoma-systems.com/news/netphone.htm).

With the advent of small and inexpensive video cameras that can be attached to the top of personal computers or even to laptops, and the easy availability of software to link those cameras (such as Microsoft's Netmeeting, available for download at www.microsoft.com/windows/netmeeting/), decision-makers can meet from their desktops from almost anywhere. Netmeeting permits real-time video and audioconferencing, graphics collaboration through a whiteboard feature, text conversations through a chat feature, an Internet directory for reaching others, a file transfer feature to permit document swap-

(text continues on page 283)

Exhibit 12-4. A Worksheet for Brainstorming When and How to Use Online and High-Tech Methods

Directions: Use this worksheet to help you brainstorm when and how to use various online and high-tech methods in your organization's SP&M program. For each area of SP&M listed in the left column below, jot down ideas under the appropriate headers in the right column on ways that your organization may appropriately and effectively use the online and high-tech approaches described. Add paper if necessary.

Area of Succession Planning and Management	Notes on When and How to Use Online and High-Tech Approaches					
	Researching Secondary Information	Document Storage and Retrieval	Document Distribution	Benchmarking	Original Data Collection for Policy Formulation	Policy Formulation	Interactive and Multimedia Distribution and Delivery
1 Formulating SP&M Policy						
2 Assessing Present Work/people Requirements						
3 Evaluating Current Employee Performance						

(continues)

Exhibit 12-4. (*continued*)

4 Determining Future Work/People Require-ments							
5 Assessing Potential							
6 Closing Developmental Gaps							
7 Maintaining Talent Inventories							
8 Evaluating the Program							
9 Others (list below)							

ping in real time, program sharing, and many other features. In short, Net-meeting provides most of the advantages of a face-to-face meeting and some that cannot be obtained in such a meeting.

Experienced videoconferencing users, however, have learned that it is advisable to test the equipment and software before the scheduled meeting time to make sure that it works. They have also learned that a meeting agenda should be sent out beforehand with short questions intended to keep the meeting focused. Meetings should be kept short, since participants find that watching compressed video can be tedious. The number of callers should be kept to a minimum, since multiple sites can be difficult to manage in videoconferencing.

What are some tips to make these meetings most effective? Here are a few:

▲ Make sure the time schedules are clear, especially when callers are located in different time zones.

▲ Open all meetings with introductions so that everyone knows who is there, why they are there, and what they can contribute.

▲ Keep the structure of the meeting simple. If difficult decisions are to be made, provide material in advance and ask people to review it before the meeting.

▲ Send out, by e-mail, sample policies, procedures, and action plans governing succession planning and invite participants to focus their attention on them. Sample documents tend to focus attention faster.

▲ Schedule follow-up discussions to resolve differences of opinion rather than trying to iron them out in a videoconference.

▲ Make sure everyone has contact information for everyone else, such as e-mail addresses, so that people can discuss important issues of interest among themselves later.

Assessing Present Work Requirements

Assessing present work requirements is a second important component of any effective SP&M program. People cannot prepare for the future if they do not know what is expected of them at present.

Traditionally, present work requirements have been assessed in several ways. One way is for the supervisor to write a job description. Another way is for a specialist in the human resources department to interview one or more job incumbents and their supervisors, draft a job description, and then ask for a review by those interviewed. Online and high-tech approaches have added new dimensions to this process. It is now possible to send worksheets or questionnaires for preparing job descriptions as attached documents from one location. Supervisors or HR specialists can then draft job descriptions and send them around electronically for supervisors or HR specialists and job incumbents to review and modify, make corrections, and reach agreement virtually. Alternatively, audioconferences or videoconferences can be substituted for face-to-face meetings.

Additionally, many resources now exist to help the harried HR specialist or supervisor write job descriptions. For instance, supervisors or HR specialists can invest in software such as Descriptions Now! (see www.gneil.com/item .html?s-5040&i-21&pos-2&sessionid-S9nac7q435), which provides draft language for job descriptions and helps the user draft newspaper advertisements to recruit applicants. As an alternative, supervisors or HR specialists can find thousands of free job descriptions on the Web as a starting point for discussion and for ideas in preparing them. As just one example, visit www.stepfour.com/ jobs/ to find 12,741 job descriptions from the *Dictionary of Occupational Titles* arranged in alphabetical order. Also visit ONet, which is the electronic system that is replacing *The Dictionary of Occupational Titles.* Real-time training on the Web is also available to help supervisors or workers learn how to write job descriptions. (See www.siu.edu/~humres/doitright/descrip.html.)

The important point to remember is that no online substitute exists for reaching agreement among supervisors, incumbents, and HR specialists on what are the current work requirements, why they are necessary for success in the job, and how they can be met. In other words, online and high-tech approaches should be used as supplements, not as substitutes, for traditional job analysis, competency identification, and other approaches to assessing present work requirements.

Evaluating Current Employee Performance

A third important component of any effective succession planning program is some means of evaluating current employee performance. As noted earlier in the book, people are rarely considered for promotion—or any other advancement opportunity, for that matter—if they are not performing well in their current jobs. Of course, a good performance appraisal system should measure individual performance as it relates to work requirements, standards, performance targets or expectations, or behavioral indicators tied to job competencies.

Traditionally, the process of evaluating current employee performance has been handled with paper forms that are completed and then followed up on by means of face-to-face interviews between workers and their immediate supervisors. Often, the human resources department is responsible for establishing the process by which individual performance is appraised. The information gathered in this process is, in turn, used in making wage or salary determinations, identifying training or individual development needs, and planning for future improvement.

Online and high-tech approaches have added new dimensions to this process. It is now possible to solicit, through e-mail or Web sites, opinions of other people about an individual's performance. For instance, a performance appraisal form may be sent for input to (among others) an individual's organizational superiors, peers, subordinates, customers, company suppliers, and company distributors.

Additionally, software resources now exist that can help supervisors write performance appraisals. For instance, supervisors or HR specialists can invest in software such as Performance Now! (available at the time this book goes to press at www.gneil.com/item.html?s-5040&i-20&pos-8&sessionid-S9nac7q-435) that supplies draft language for employee performance appraisals and can offer legal advice about what is and is not advisable to put in writing on appraisal forms. Free resources can also be found on the Web to support the formulation of policies on employee performance appraisal (such as, for instance, sample policies available at the time this book goes to press at http://ukcc.uky.edu/~hrinfo/hrp/hrp061.txt, www.tempe.gov/hradmin/docs/Perf--Appr--Inst.htm, and www.infosys.ilstu.edu/ohr/PAexempt.html); complete appraisal systems for a fee (available when this book goes to press at www.performance-appraisal.com/manual/download.htm); and sample forms (available when this book goes to press at http://fcn.state.fl.us/dms/hrm/forms/forms.html and http://ohioline.ag.ohio-state.edu/hrm-fact/0007.html).

Using online and high-tech methods with employee performance appraisal can be beneficial. However, SP&M coordinators should always remember that every useful performance appraisal system comes at a price. This means that, while online aids can be helpful and can offer valuable support, no substitute exists for the laborious process of establishing and measuring the unique performance requirements of people in one organization.

Determining Future Work Requirements

Forecasting or planning for future work requirements is a fourth important component of any effective SP&M program. After all, it is no more likely that work requirements will remain static than it is that the organization itself will remain static. Organizational needs change, and so do work requirements. It is therefore important to engage stakeholders and decision-makers in planning for the expected changes that may occur in the organization and in its work requirements. That is essential if individuals are to be prepared to meet those requirements in the future. Few organizations regularly and systematically forecast future work or competency requirements. However, the need to do that is growing. It is simply not possible to prepare people if future work requirements remain unknown.

Online and high-tech approaches have, however, provided new approaches to job forecasting, scenario planning, and future-oriented competency modeling. *Job forecasting* estimates future job requirements. It may address such questions as these:

▲ What will be the future purpose of the job? How will that be different from the job's present purpose?

▲ What are the expected work duties or responsibilities of the job in the future, and how are they expected to change?

▲ What knowledge, skills, or attitudes are needed by individuals in the future to qualify for those jobs?

▲ How important will be the various duties or responsibilities of those jobs, and which ones will be considered most critical to success in the future?

Answering such questions is the process of job forecasting.

Scenario planning identifies possible alternative futures. Instead of assuming that jobs or work will change in one way, as job forecasting does, scenario planning offers probabilities. Scenarios resemble written stories about the future. They help people plan by giving them clear descriptions of what the future may look like, or different pictures of various futures. Groupware, described in an earlier section, can be useful as an online approach to conducting job scenario planning. It is thus possible to prepare different versions of job descriptions for the future and then use those to stimulate planning among job incumbents and their immediate organizational supervisors.

Another way to carry out scenario planning is to rely on software or Web sites that make it relatively easier than it might otherwise be. One resource for conducting scenario planning is the Web site of the Global Business Network (found at the time this book goes to press at www.gbn.org/public/help/map.htm). This Web site offers member services for conducting scenario planning. While the key emphasis in most scenario planning is business planning and financial analysis, it is possible to find help in doing job scenario planning.

Future-oriented competency modeling projects the future competencies required by departments or job groups. Its focus, unlike traditional competency modeling, is on what will set exemplary performers apart from fully successful performers in the future. It is therefore future-oriented and is sometimes based on trends.

Many resources exist to help SP&M coordinators conduct future-oriented competency modeling. For instance, you can find a list of competencies needed in businesses in the future by consulting http://cithr.cit.cornell.edu/FutComp.html, or a compelling article about organizational core competencies of the future at www.bah.de/viewpoints/insights/cmt_core_comp.html. You can also purchase software for competency modeling, such as The Competence Expert (described at the time this book goes to press at www.kravetz.com/compexpert.html) or the Competency Coach for Windows (described at www.coopercomm.com/ccchfact.htm) One other source is Kenneth Carlton Cooper's *Effective Competency Modeling & Reporting* (AMACOM, 2000), which includes a working model on CD-ROM of Competency Coach for Windows.

Assessing Potential

A fifth important component of any effective succession planning program is some means by which to assess individual potential for the future. What is the individual's potential for advancement to higher levels of responsibility, or to higher levels of technical expertise in his or her specialization? That is the question answered by this component.

One approach that is increasingly used for potential assessment is full-circle, multirater feedback. Described in an earlier chapter, this involves assessing an individual's potential based on the perceptions of those surrounding him or her in the organization. It is important to remember, however, that potential assessment should be conducted in the context of work requirements. In other words, an individual should not just be appraised for his or her current abilities. Instead, he or she should be assessed for meeting future job requirements or future competencies.

Both PC-usable software and Web-based full-circle, multirater assessment instruments are widely available. To find many of them, it is only necessary to type "360 assessment" into a search engine on the Web. But a word of caution is again in order: most full-circle, multirater assessment instruments have been based on competency models from other organizations. That means they are not necessarily useful, applicable, or even appropriate in all corporate cultures. To be most effective, a company-specific competency model must be prepared for every department or every job category (such as supervisor, manager, and executive). Potential assessment is useful only when done in this way. Indeed, rating individual potential on competencies that are not company-specific can lead to major mistakes and miscalculations. Hence, while online and high-tech approaches can be useful, they should be used appropriately to measure individual potential within a unique corporate culture.

Closing Developmental Gaps

Closing developmental gaps is a sixth important component of any effective SP&M program. This component leads to an action plan to help individuals narrow the gap between what they can do now and what they need to do to advance. Individual development planning is the process by which this is accomplished.

Although few software packages exist to support the individual development planning process—in fact, I could find none after an extensive search on the Web—many resources can be found on the Web to assist with the process. For instance, sample forms can be found at the time this book goes to press at www.johnco.cc.ks.us/acad/sd/sdidp.htm, http://www.grc.nasa.gov/WWW/OHR/next6.htm, and www.hr.lanl.gov/CareerDevelopment/IDPs.htm. Sample policies guiding the use of an individual development planning (IDP) form can also be found at the time this book goes to press at www.lerc.nasa.gov/WWW/

ODT/idp.htm and http://ohr.gsfc.nasa.gov/DevGuide/idp.htm, and a sample training plan about individual development planning can be found at http://www.doleta.gov/ohrw2w/volume1/v1md11.htm.

Maintaining Talent Inventories

A seventh important component of any effective SP&M program is some means by which to maintain talent or skill inventories. How can the organization keep track of the knowledge, skills, and competencies of existing staff? That is the question answered by talent or skill inventories. Organizations possessing no means by which to inventory talent will have a difficult time locating qualified people in the organization when vacancies occur in key positions or when emergencies arise. Every organization should have some way to inventory its talent.

Succession planning and management inventories may take two forms: manual or automated. A *manual system* relies on paper files. It consists of individual personnel files or specialized records, assembled especially for SP&M, that take the form of a succession planning and management notebook or Rolodex file. These files contain information relevant to making succession decisions, such as:

▲ Descriptions of individual position duties or competencies (for instance, a current position description)

▲ Individual employee performance appraisals

▲ Statements of individual career goals or career plans

▲ Summaries of individual qualifications (for instance, educational and training records)

▲ Summaries of individual skills (for instance, a personal skill inventory that details previous work experience and languages known)[1]

Of course, other information may be added, such as individual potential assessment forms and replacement planning charts.

A manual inventory will suffice for a small organization having neither specialized expertise available to oversee SP&M activities nor resources available for automated systems. A chief advantage is that most of the information is filed in personnel files anyway, so no monumental effort is necessary to compile information on individual employees. However, a manual inventory can lead to difficulties in handling, storing, cross-referencing, and maintaining security over numerous (and sometimes lengthy) forms. Even in a small organization, these disadvantages can present formidable problems.

Even small organizations, however, can now gain access to relatively inexpensive PC-based software that places much information at a manager's (or HR specialist's) fingertips. One example is People Manager (see www.gneil.com/item.html?s-5040&i-878&pos-5&sessionid-S9nac7q-43 5). A second is People-Trak (see www.gneil.com/item.html?s-5040&i-695&pos-7&sessionid-S9nac7q-

43 5). A third is !Trak-IT HR (see www.gneil.com/item.html?s-5040&i-591&pos-17&sessionid-S9nac7q-4 35). Each software package permits some limited talent inventorying that can be useful even in small businesses.

Automated inventories used in SP&M take any one of three typical forms: (1) simple word processing files; (2) tailored SP&M software; or (3) SP&M software integrated with other personnel records. Simple word processing files are the next step beyond paper files. Special forms (templates) are created for SP&M using a popular word processing program, such as Microsoft Word. Blank forms are placed on disk or CD-ROM. Managers are asked to complete the forms on disk and return them, physically or electronically, to a central location. This approach reduces paper flow and makes handling, storing, and security easier to manage than is possible with paper records. Unfortunately, SP&M information that is inventoried in this manner will usually be troublesome to cross-reference.

Tailored SP&M software is becoming more common. Much of it is now Web-based or suitable for Web applications. Succession planning and management coordinators should review several such packages before purchasing one. The chief advantage of this software is that it is designed specifically for SP&M. Indeed, it can give decision-makers good ideas about desirable features to change, add to, or subtract from the SP&M program. Handling, storing, cross-referencing, and maintaining security over much information is greatly simplified. While software prices were relatively high even a few years ago, they are now affordable to most organizations employing fifty or more people.

The only major disadvantage of this software is that it can present temptations to modify organization needs to satisfy software demands. In other words, software may not provide sufficient flexibility to tailor SP&M forms and procedures to meet the unique needs of one organization. That can be a major drawback. For this reason, SP&M software should be carefully reviewed, in cooperation with the vendor, prior to purchase. Of course, it may be possible for the vendor to modify the software to meet organizational needs at a modest cost.

Succession planning and management software may also be integrated with other personnel systems. In this case—and some large organizations attempt to keep all data in one place, usually in a mainframe system, in an effort to economize the problems inherent in multiple-source data entry and manipulation—SP&M information is included with payroll, training, and other records. Unfortunately, such software is usually of limited value for SP&M applications. To be tailored to a large organization's uses, such software may have to undergo lengthy and large-scale programming projects. A typical—and major—problem with such mainframe HRIS programs is that they provide insufficient storage space for detailed, individualized recordkeeping tailored to unique organizational procedures. When that is the case, it may be easier to use a personal-computer-based system—or else mount a massive, expensive, and probably quickly dated programming effort to modify a mainframe program.

Evaluating the Program

An eighth and final important component of any effective SP&M program is some means by which to evaluate the SP&M program and each of its components. This ensures that continuous program improvement can be made. At this writing, however, no online software currently exists that is specifically tailored to evaluating SP&M programs. Thus SP&M coordinators must prepare their own online and high-tech approaches if they wish to use them for evaluating their programs.

Of course, it should be relatively simple to prepare online questionnaires or other surveys to gather information about the relative value of SP&M programs. Typical evaluation issues that should be addressed will be discussed in the next chapter. Using online methods, however, may increase the speed and ease of response and facilitate data analysis.

Other Applications

There are other online and high-tech applications for SP&M. For instance, you can use software to prepare replacement charts. Best known, and perhaps least expensive, for doing that is probably OrgPlus (found at the time this book goes to press at www.gneil.com/item.html?s-5041&i-601&pos-6&sessionid-S9 nac7q435).

Software can also be purchased to facilitate preparation of forms for succession planning (such as Formtool, described at www.cdromshop.com/cdshop/desc/p.730526347135.html) or online training support to build competencies. Many so-called e-learning sites exist on the Web, and they can be tied to the competencies that individuals need to build to qualify for advancement opportunities.

What Specialized Competencies Do Succession Planning and Management Coordinators Need to Use These Applications?

The specialized competencies required by SP&M program coordinators to use online and high-tech applications in their programs will, of course, vary by the medium or media that they use and their applications. It is not advisable to try to be all things to all people, so it is best to target specific applications of potential value to the organization and spend only the time necessary to master those.

Succession planning and management coordinators can apply online and high-tech methods in essentially three ways. First, they can try to learn it on their own. The competency requirements to do that can be the most daunting. It means mastery of the subject matter—such as, for instance, performance appraisal—and the technical issues associated with the application. As a simple example, putting the company's performance appraisal system on the Web might mean that technical knowledge is required of HTML and JAVA languages. Likewise, preparing Web-based training may require knowledge of the subject matter, instructional design, and the programming languages necessary to place it on the Web.

Second, contractual assistance could be hired to provide help with all or part of the project. That would permit the SP&M coordinator to concentrate on the subject matter and on managing the project. Hence, necessary competencies would focus around the subject area and project management. Technical issues would be handled by a contractor.

Third, the SP&M coordinator could create a team whose members collectively possess the competencies necessary to perform the work. In this case, the coordinator would at least require subject matter competence, project management competence, and facilitation competence to help team members work together. The coordinator may be able to choose team members from within the organization who possess the requisite technical knowledge of the media or medium.

Some competencies are shared no matter which of the three approaches is chosen. First, patience is an essential competency to work with any online or high-tech application. (It is never as easy as it appears to be.) Second, knowledge of the organization's corporate culture and politics is also important. The SP&M coordinator must understand how decisions are made in the organization and be able to work through that process to achieve the desired results. Third and finally, the SP&M coordinator must be able to excite enthusiasm among other people for the project. Without these competencies, it will be difficult to make any application successful.

Summary

As this chapter has pointed out, online and high-tech approaches are having an important impact on succession planning and management practices. The chapter focused attention on four key questions: (1) How are online and high-tech methods defined? (2) In what areas of succession planning and management can online and high-tech methods be applied? (3) How are online and high-tech applications used? and (4) What specialized competencies are required by succession planning and management coordinators to use these applications?

The next chapter focuses on the important issue of evaluating succession planning and management programs. As decision-makers devote more time and other resources to succession issues, they naturally wonder if their efforts are paying off. For that reason, evaluation is becoming more important in succession planning and management.

CHAPTER 13

EVALUATING SUCCESSION PLANNING AND MANAGEMENT PROGRAMS

After a succession planning and management (SP&M) program has been implemented, top managers will eventually ask, "Is this effort worth what it costs? How well is it working? Is it meeting the organization's needs?" Simple answers to these questions will prove to be elusive because an SP&M program will affect many people, and will usually have to satisfy conflicting goals, interests, and priorities. But the questions do underscore the need to establish some way to evaluate the program. This chapter, then, will explore three simple questions: (1) What is evaluation? (2) What should be evaluated in SP&M? and (3) How should an SP&M program be evaluated?

What Is Evaluation?

Evaluation means placing value or determining worth.[1] It is a process of determining how much value is being added to an activity by a program, and it is through evaluation that the need for program improvements is identified and such improvements are eventually made. Evaluation is typically carried out by an evaluator or team of evaluators against a backdrop of client expectations about the program and the need for information on which to make sound decisions.

Interest in Evaluation

The evaluation of human resource programs has been a popular topic of numerous books, articles, and professional presentations.[2] Treatments of it have tended to focus on such bottom-line issues as cost/benefit analysis and return on investment,[3] which should not be surprising since, in view of the perception of HR practitioners, these issues are of chief interest to top managers. Training has figured most prominently in this literature, probably because it continues to enjoy the dubious reputation of being the first HR program to be slashed when an organization falls on hard times.

On the other hand, writers on evaluation have tended to pay far less attention to SP&M than to training. One reason could be that systematic SP&M is less common in organizations than training is. A second reason could be that evaluations of SP&M are informally made on a case-by-case basis whenever a vacancy occurs in a key position: if a successor is "ready, willing, and able" when needed, the SP&M program is given the credit; otherwise, it is blamed. While the value of SP&M should (of course) be judged on more than that basis alone, the reality is often far different.

Key Questions Governing Evaluation

To be performed effectively, evaluation for SP&M should focus on several key questions:

1. Who will use the results?
2. How will the results be used?
3. What do the program's clients expect from it?
4. Who is carrying out the evaluation?

The first question seeks to identify the audience. The second question seeks to clarify what decisions will be made based on evaluation results. The third question grounds evaluation in client expectations and program objectives. Finally, the fourth question provides clues about appropriate evaluation techniques based on the expertise of the chosen evaluator(s).

What Should Be Evaluated?

Some years ago, Donald Kirkpatrick developed a four-level hierarchy of training evaluation that may be usefully modified to help conceptualize what should be evaluated in SP&M.[4]

Kirkpatrick's Hierarchy of Training Evaluation

The four levels of Kirkpatrick's training evaluation hierarchy are reaction, learning, behavior, and organizational outcomes or results. *Reaction* forms the base of the hierarchy and is easiest to measure. It examines customer satisfaction—that is, "How much did participants like what they learned?" *Learning*, the second level on the hierarchy, has to do with immediate change. In other words, "How well did participants master the information or skills they were supposed to learn in training?" The third level of the hierarchy, *behavior*, has to do with on-the-job application. "How much change occurred on the job as a result of learner participation in training?" The highest level of Kirkpatrick's hierarchy, the fourth and final one, is *organizational outcomes*, or results. It is also the most difficult to measure. "How much influence did the results or effects of training have on the organization?"

Modifying Kirkpatrick's Hierarchy

Use Kirkpatrick's Hierarchy of Training Evaluation to provide a conceptual basis for evaluating an SP&M program. (Examine the Hierarchy of Succession Planning and Management Evaluation depicted in Exhibit 13-1.)

Make the first level *customer satisfaction*, which corresponds to Kirkpatrick's reaction level. Pose the following questions:

▲ How satisfied with the SP&M program are its chief customers?

▲ How satisfied are its customers with each program component—such as job descriptions, competency models, performance appraisal processes, individual potential assessment processes, individual development forms, and individual development activities?

▲ How well does SP&M match up to individual career plans? How do employees perceive SP&M?

Make the second level *program progress*, which is meant to correspond to Kirkpatrick's learning level. Pose the following questions:

▲ How well is each part of the SP&M program working compared to stated program objectives?

▲ How well are individuals progressing through their developmental experiences in preparation for future advancement into key positions?

Make the third level *effective placements*, which is meant to correspond to Kirkpatrick's behavior level. Pose these questions:

▲ What percentage of vacancies in key positions is the organization able to fill internally?

▲ How quickly is the organization able to fill vacancies in key positions?

▲ What percentage of vacancies in key positions is the organization able to fill successfully (that is, without avoidable turnover in the first two years in the position)?

▲ How quickly are internal replacements for key positions able to perform at the level required for the organization?

Exhibit 13-1. The Hierarchy of Succession Planning and Management Evaluation

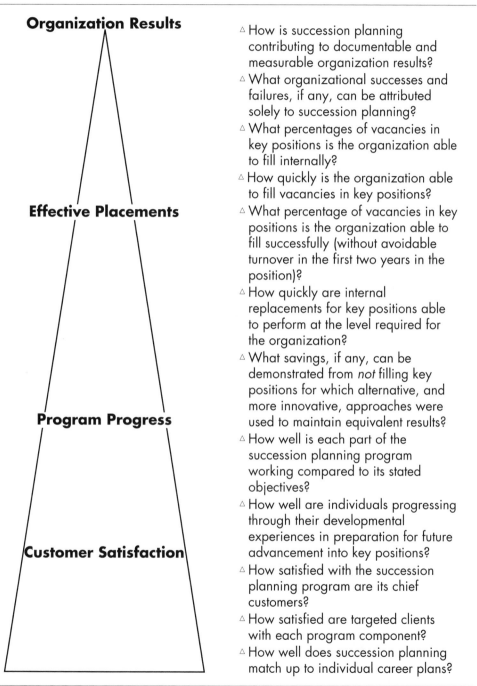

Organization Results

△ How is succession planning contributing to documentable and measurable organization results?

△ What organizational successes and failures, if any, can be attributed solely to succession planning?

△ What percentages of vacancies in key positions is the organization able to fill internally?

△ How quickly is the organization able to fill vacancies in key positions?

Effective Placements

△ What percentage of vacancies in key positions is the organization able to fill successfully (without avoidable turnover in the first two years in the position)?

△ How quickly are internal replacements for key positions able to perform at the level required for the organization?

△ What savings, if any, can be demonstrated from *not* filling key positions for which alternative, and more innovative, approaches were used to maintain equivalent results?

Program Progress

△ How well is each part of the succession planning program working compared to its stated objectives?

△ How well are individuals progressing through their developmental experiences in preparation for future advancement into key positions?

Customer Satisfaction

△ How satisfied with the succession planning program are its chief customers?

△ How satisfied are targeted clients with each program component?

△ How well does succession planning match up to individual career plans?

▲ What savings, if any, can be demonstrated from not filling key positions for which alternative, and more innovative, approaches were used to achieve results?

Make the fourth level *organizational results*, which is meant to correspond to Kirkpatrick's outcomes or results. Direct attention to the impact of SP&M on the organization's ability to compete effectively, which is (admittedly) difficult to do. Consider the following questions:

▲ How is SP&M contributing, if at all, to documentable organizational results?
▲ What successes or failures in organizational strategic plans, if any, can be attributed to SP&M?

Use the guidelines in Exhibit 13-2 and the worksheet in Exhibit 13-3 to consider ways to evaluate SP&M in an organization on each level of the hierarchy. Of course, it is possible to evaluate an SP&M program on all four levels, and when that is done, a *scorecard* for SP&M is created.

How Should Evaluation Be Conducted?

Evaluation may be conducted anecdotally, periodically, or programmatically.

Anecdotal Evaluation

Anecdotal evaluation is akin to using testimonials in evaluating training.[5] It examines the operation of the SP&M program on a case-by-case basis. As vacancies occur in key positions, someone—often the SP&M coordinator—documents in incident reports how they are filled. (See Exhibit 13-4 for an example of an incident report.) The incident reports are eventually brought to the organization's SP&M committee for review and discussion. They provide a solid foundation for troubleshooting problems in SP&M that the organization is confronting. They can then be used as a basis for planning to handle similar problems in the future.

Anecdotal evaluation dramatizes especially good and bad practices. This draws attention to them and provides an impetus for change, a chief advantage of the anecdotal approach. On the other hand, anecdotal evaluation suffers from a lack of research rigor. It is not necessarily representative of typical SP&M practices in the organization. (Indeed, it focuses on so-called special cases, horror stories, and war stories.) It may thus draw attention to unique, even minor, problems with SP&M in the organization.

(text continues on page 301)

Exhibit 13-2. Guidelines for Evaluating the Succession Planning and Management Program

Type/Level	Purpose	Strengths	Weaknesses
Customer Satisfaction	To measure client feelings about the program and its results.	△ Easy to measure. △ Provides immediate feedback on program activities and components.	△ Subjective. △ Provides no objective measurement of program results.
Program Progress	To measure results of each component of the succession planning program.	△ Provides objective data on the effectiveness of the succession planning program.	△ Requires skill in program evaluation. △ Provides no measurement of skills of benefit to the organization.
Effective Placements	To measure the results of the succession decisions made.	△ Provides objective data on impact to the job situation.	△ Requires first-rate employee performance appraisal system.
Organizational Results	To measure impact of the succession planning program on the organization.	△ Provides objective data for cost-benefit analysis and organizational support.	△ Requires high level of evaluation design skills; requires collection of data over a period of time. △ Requires knowledge of the organization's strategy and goals.

(continues)

Exhibit 13-2. (continued)

Type/Level	Examples	Guidelines for Development
Customer Satisfaction	△ "Happiness reports." △ Informal interviews with "clients" at all levels. △ Group discussion in succession planning meetings.	△ Design a survey form that can be easily tabulated. △ Ask questions to provide information about what you need to know: attitudes about each component of the succession planning program. △ Allow for anonymity and allow the respondents the opportunity to provide additional comments.
Program Progress	△ Examine individual movements through the organization.	△ Design an instrument that will provide quantitative data. △ Include "pre" and "post" level of skill/knowledge in design. △ Tie evaluation items directly to program objectives.
Effective Placements	△ Performance checklists. △ Performance appraisals. △ Critical incident analysis. △ Self-appraisal.	△ Base measurement instrument on systematic analysis of key positions. △ Consider the use of a variety of persons to conduct the evaluation.
Organizational Results	△ Organizational analysis. △ Speed of replacement. △ Cost of replacements. △ Cost of nonreplacements. △ Turnover.	△ Involve all necessary levels of the organization. △ Gain commitment to allow access to organization indices and records. △ Use organization business plans and mission statements to compare organizational needs and program results.

Exhibit 13-3. A Worksheet for Identifying Appropriate Ways to Evaluate Succession Planning and Management in an Organization

Directions: Use this worksheet to help you identify appropriate ways to evaluate the SP&M program in your organization.

In column 1 below, indicate the various stakeholder groups (such as top managers, key position incumbents, line managers, and the SP&M coordinator) who will be primarily interested in evaluation results on SP&M in your organization. Then, in column 2, indicate what *levels* of evaluation—customer satisfaction, program progress, effective placements, and organizational results—will probably be of prime interest to each stakeholder group. Then, in column 3, indicate *how* evaluation of SP&M may be carried out in your organization.

Column 1	Column 2	Column 3
Stakeholder Groups for Evaluation	What Levels of Evaluation Will Probably Be of Prime Interest to Each Group?	How Should Evaluation of the SP&M Program Be Carried Out in Your Organization?

Exhibit 13-4. A Sample "Incident Report" for Succession Planning and Management

Directions: The purpose of this "incident report" is to track successor/replacement experiences in your organization.

Answer the questions appearing in the spaces below. Be as truthful as possible because the collective results of many incident reports will be used to identify program improvement initiatives for the succession planning program.

Fill out this report for each position filled from within. (This report should be completed *in addition to* any personnel requisitions/justification forms that you are to complete.) Submit the completed form to (*name*) at (*organization address*) within 3 weeks after filling the vacancy.

Name of Departing Employee _____ Job Title _____

Department _____ Time in Position _____

Reason for Leaving (*if known*)_____

Name of Replacing Employee _____ Job Title _____

Department _____ Work Unit/Team _____

Time in Position _____ Today's Date _____

1. Describe how this position is being replaced (internally/externally).

2. Was there an identifiable "successor" who had been prepared to assume this position previously? If so, briefly explain who and how the individual was being prepared; if not, briefly explain reasons for not preparing a successor.

3. Who was selected for the position, and why was he/she selected?

4. If an individual other than an identifiable successor was chosen for the position, explain why.

_____ Approval _____

Management Employee _____ Title _____
                      (*Signature*)

Periodic Evaluation

Periodic evaluation examines components of SP&M at different times, focusing attention on program operations at present or in the recent past. Rather than evaluate critical incidents (as anecdotal evaluation does) or all program components (as programmatic evaluation does), periodic evaluation examines isolated program components. For instance, the SP&M coordinator may direct attention to:

▲ The Program Mission Statement
▲ Program Objectives, Policy, and Philosophy
▲ Methods of Determining Work Requirements for Key Positions
▲ Employee Performance Appraisal
▲ Employee Potential Assessment
▲ Individual Development Planning
▲ Individual Development Activities

Periodic evaluation may be conducted during regular SP&M meetings and/or in SP&M committee meetings. Alternatively, the organization's decision-makers may wish to establish a task force, create a subcommittee of the SP&M committee, or even involve a committee of the board of directors in this evaluation process.

A chief advantage of periodic evaluation is that it provides occasional, formal monitoring of the SP&M program. That process can build involvement, and thus ownership, of key stakeholders while simultaneously surfacing important problems in the operation of the SP&M program. A chief disadvantage of periodic evaluation is that it makes the improvement of SP&M an incremental rather than a continuous effort. Problems may be left to fester for too long before they are targeted for investigation.

Programmatic Evaluation

Programmatic evaluation examines the SP&M program comprehensively against its stated mission, objectives, and activities. It is an in-depth program review and resembles the human resources audit that may be conducted of all HR activities.[6]

Programmatic evaluation is usually carried out by a formally appointed committee or by an external consultant. The SP&M coordinator is usually a member of a committee. Representatives of key line management areas—and the CEO or members of the corporate board of directors—may also be members.

Examine the steps in Exhibit 13-5 and the checklist in Exhibit 13-6 as starting points for conducting a program evaluation of SP&M in an organization.

(text continues on page 307)

Exhibit 13-5. Steps for Completing a Program Evaluation of a Succession Planning and Management Program

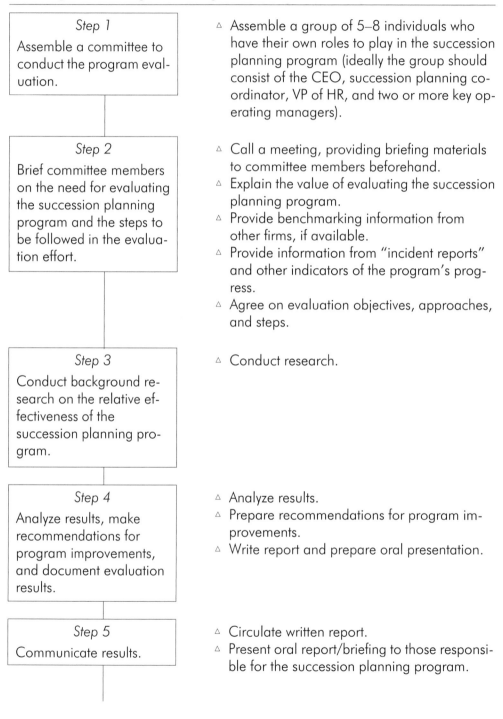

Step 1	
Assemble a committee to conduct the program evaluation.	△ Assemble a group of 5–8 individuals who have their own roles to play in the succession planning program (ideally the group should consist of the CEO, succession planning coordinator, VP of HR, and two or more key operating managers).

Step 2	
Brief committee members on the need for evaluating the succession planning program and the steps to be followed in the evaluation effort.	△ Call a meeting, providing briefing materials to committee members beforehand. △ Explain the value of evaluating the succession planning program. △ Provide benchmarking information from other firms, if available. △ Provide information from "incident reports" and other indicators of the program's progress. △ Agree on evaluation objectives, approaches, and steps.

Step 3	
Conduct background research on the relative effectiveness of the succession planning program.	△ Conduct research.

Step 4	
Analyze results, make recommendations for program improvements, and document evaluation results.	△ Analyze results. △ Prepare recommendations for program improvements. △ Write report and prepare oral presentation.

Step 5	
Communicate results.	△ Circulate written report. △ Present oral report/briefing to those responsible for the succession planning program.

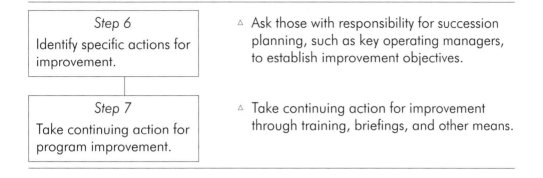

| Step 6 | △ Ask those with responsibility for succession |
| Identify specific actions for improvement. | planning, such as key operating managers, to establish improvement objectives. |

| Step 7 | △ Take continuing action for improvement |
| Take continuing action for program improvement. | through training, briefings, and other means. |

Exhibit 13-6. A Checksheet for Conducting a Program Evaluation for the Succession Planning and Management Program

Directions: Use this checksheet as a starting point for deciding what to evaluate in your organization's succession planning program. Ask members of a program evaluation committee to complete the following checksheet, compare notes, and then use the results as the basis for recommending improvements to the succession planning program. Add, delete, or modify characteristics in the left column as appropriate.

Characteristics of Effective Programs	*Does your organization's succession planning program have this characteristic?*		*How important do you believe this characteristic to be for an effective succession planning program?*				
For the succession planning program, has your organization:	*YES* (√)	*NO* (√)	*Not Important* 1	2	3	*Very Important* 4	5
1. Tied the succession planning program to organizational strategic plans?	( )	( )	1	2	3	4	5
2. Tied the succession planning program to individual career plans?	( )	( )	1	2	3	4	5
3. Tied the succession planning program to training programs?	( )	( )	1	2	3	4	5
4. Prepared a written program purpose statement?	( )	( )	1	2	3	4	5
5. Prepared written program goals to indicate what results the succession planning program should achieve?	( )	( )	1	2	3	4	5
6. Established *measurable* objectives for program operation (such as number of positions replaced per year)?	( )	( )	1	2	3	4	5
7. Identified what groups are to be served by the program, in priority order?	( )	( )	1	2	3	4	5

8. Established a written policy statement to guide the program? ( ) ( ) 1 2 3 4 5

9. Articulated a written philosophy about the program? ( ) ( ) 1 2 3 4 5

10. Established a program action plan? ( ) ( ) 1 2 3 4 5

11. Established a schedule of program events based on the action plan? ( ) ( ) 1 2 3 4 5

12. Fixed responsibility for organizational oversight of the program? ( ) ( ) 1 2 3 4 5

13. Fixed responsibility of each participant in the program? ( ) ( ) 1 2 3 4 5

14. Established incentives/rewards for identified successors in the succession planning program? ( ) ( ) 1 2 3 4 5

15. Established incentives/rewards for managers with identified successors? ( ) ( ) 1 2 3 4 5

16. Developed a means to budget for a succession planning program? ( ) ( ) 1 2 3 4 5

17. Devised a means to keep records for individuals who are designated as successors? ( ) ( ) 1 2 3 4 5

18. Created workshops to train management employees about the succession planning program? ( ) ( ) 1 2 3 4 5

19. Created workshops to train individuals about career planning? ( ) ( ) 1 2 3 4 5

20. Established a means to clarify *present position responsibilities*? ( ) ( ) 1 2 3 4 5

(continues)

Exhibit 13-6. *(continued)*

Characteristics of Effective Programs	Does your organization's succession planning program have this characteristic?		How important do you believe this characteristic to be for an effective succession planning program?				
For the succession planning program, has your organization:	YES (√)	NO (√)	Not Important 1	2	3	Very Important 4	5
21. Established a means to clarify *future position responsibilities?*	( )	( )	1	2	3	4	5
22. Established a means to appraise individual performance?	( )	( )	1	2	3	4	5
23. Established a means to compare individual skills to the requirements of a future position (potential assessment)?	( )	( )	1	2	3	4	5
24. Established a way to review organizational talent at least annually?	( )	( )	1	2	3	4	5
25. Established a way to forecast future talent needs?	( )	( )	1	2	3	4	5
26. Established a way to plan for meeting succession planning needs through individual development plans?	( )	( )	1	2	3	4	5
27. Established a means to track development activities to prepare successors for eventual advancement?	( )	( )	1	2	3	4	5
28. Established a means to evaluate the results of the succession planning program?	( )	( )	1	2	3	4	5

(Compare Exhibit 13-6 to the survey responses appearing in Exhibit 2-1 as a means of evaluating your organization's SP&M program against others.)

Summary

This chapter addressed three simple questions: (1) What is evaluation? (2) What should be evaluated in succession planning and management? and (3) How should a succession planning and management program be evaluated? *Evaluation* was defined as the process of placing value or determining worth. It is through evaluation that the need for improvements is identified and such improvements are eventually made to the succession planning and management program. Evaluation should focus on several key questions: (1) Who will use the results? (2) How will the results be used? (3) What do the program's clients expect from it? and (4) Who is carrying out the evaluation?

The evaluation of succession planning and management was focused on four levels, comparable to those devised by Donald Kirkpatrick to describe training evaluation. Those four levels are customer satisfaction, program progress, effective placements, and organizational results. One conducts evaluation anecdotally, periodically, or programmatically. Anecdotal evaluation is akin to using testimonials in evaluating training. Periodic evaluation examines isolated components of the succession planning and management program at different times, focusing attention on program operations at present or in the recent past. Programmatic evaluation examines the succession planning and management program comprehensively against its stated mission, objectives, and activities.

CHAPTER 14

THE FUTURE OF SUCCESSION PLANNING AND MANAGEMENT

No organization is immune to changing external environmental conditions. However, what external conditions will affect an organization varies, depending on such factors as the organization's industry, size, and relative market dominance. Moreover, how those conditions affect an organization depends on the ways in which its leaders and workers choose to address them. These principles hold as true for succession planning and management (SP&M) programs as for strategic planning.

Examining trends is a popular HR activity. Much has been written in recent years about trends affecting HR generally,[1] functional areas within HR specifically,[2] and SP&M efforts.[3] A cursory glance at the writing in the field yields many topics concerning outsourcing HR, cutting HR (and particularly benefits) costs, transforming HR into a strategic partner, building bench strength and talent pools, enhancing work and life balance, maintaining employee security in the wake of increasing violence in the workplace and threats of terrorism outside the workplace,[4] and using technology to leverage HR productivity.

In this final chapter, I gaze into the crystal ball and offer predictions for the future of SP&M that are likely to arise from changing external environmental conditions. While some predictions remain unchanged from the last edition of this book, I add some additional ones. SP&M needs will:

▲ Prompt efforts by decision-makers to find a flexible range of strategies to address organizational talent needs.

▲ Lead to integrated retention policies and procedures that seek the early identification of high-potential talent, efforts to retain that talent, and efforts to retain older high-potential workers.

▲ Have a global impact.

▲ Be influenced increasingly by real-time technological innovations.

▲ Become an issue in government agencies, academic institutions, and nonprofit organizations in a way never before seen. Businesses will not be the only organizations interested in succession issues.

▲ Lead to increasing organizational openness about possible successors.

▲ Increasingly seek to integrate effective succession issues with career-development issues.

▲ Be heavily influenced by concerns about work/family balance and spirituality issues.

▲ Focus increasingly on real-time talent-development efforts as well as strategic efforts, which center on the role of managers in daily work with their reports.

▲ Center as much on ethical and value-oriented issues as on competency-based issues.

▲ Become more fully integrated with selection decisions.

▲ Focus on leveraging talent as well as developing it.

▲ Include alternatives to one-hire-at-a-time approaches, such as mergers, acquisitions, or takeovers for the purpose of rapid and broad-based talent acquisition.

▲ Become closely linked to risk management and concerns about security.

▲ Become associated with more than management succession.

Before you read about these predictions, use the worksheet in Exhibit 14-1 to structure your thinking (and that of decision-makers in your organization).

The Fifteen Predictions

Prediction 1: Decision-Makers Will Seek Flexible Strategies to Address Future Organizational Talent Needs

In the future, decision-makers will not view succession issues as one problem requiring only one solution. Instead, they will seek a range of strategies to address future organizational talent needs that will include, but will go beyond, SP&M programs. In other words, succession problems will be solved using many possible solutions. The choice of a solution will be made on a case-by-case basis, but with a strategic view that seeks an integration of approaches.

Think about it for a minute. In how many ways can an organization's talent needs be met through approaches other than an SP&M program that is designed to build in-house bench strength over time? Consider at least fifteen possible alternative approaches. Each approach should be reviewed at the time decision-makers plan for succession needs. Decision-makers should begin by clarifying what talent they require, why their organization has that need, and how the need might be met.

The first alternative approach to SP&M is to hire from the outside. In fact, this is probably the most obvious way to meet a talent need other than through internal promotion or development. It is sometimes chosen before internal

(text continues on page 312)

Exhibit 14-1. A Worksheet to Structure Your Thinking About Predictions for Succession Planning and Management in the Future

Directions: Use this worksheet to structure your thinking about possible predictions that may influence SP&M programs in the future. For each prediction listed in Column 1 below, indicate in Column 2 whether you believe that the prediction is true. Then describe under Column 3 what you believe the prediction means in your organization and under Column 4 how much impact that prediction will have in your organization. Finally, under Column 5, offer suggestions about what your organization should do about the prediction. There are no "right" or "wrong" approaches to addressing these predictions. Instead, use this worksheet to do some brainstorming about predictions affecting SP&M in your organization in the future. Add paper if necessary.

	Column 1 What is the prediction?	**Column 2** *Do you believe the prediction is true?*		**Column 3** *What does the prediction mean in your organization?*	**Column 4** *How much impact will that prediction have in your organization?*	**Column 5** *What actions should your organization take to address the prediction?*
		Yes	No			
	Succession planning and management will:	☒	☒			
1	Prompt efforts by decision-makers to find a flexible range of strategies to address organizational talent needs.	☐	☐			
2	Lead to integrated retention policies and procedures that seek the early identification of high-potential talent, efforts to retain that talent, and efforts to retain older high-potential workers.	☐	☐			

3	Have a global impact.	☐	☐		
4	Be influenced increasingly by real-time technological innovations.	☐	☐		
5	Become an issue in government agencies, academic institutions, and nonprofit organizations in a way never before seen. Businesses will not be the only organizations interested in succession issues.	☐	☐		
6	Lead to increasing organizational openness about possible successors.	☐	☐		
7	Increasingly seek to integrate effective succession issues with career development issues.	☐	☐		
8	Be heavily influenced by concerns about work/family balance and spirituality issues.	☐	☐		

replacements are considered. A key advantage of this approach is that it prevents inbreeding, since newcomers often bring with them fresh solutions to old organizational problems. A key disadvantage of this approach is that the cycle time required to fill a vacancy can be agonizingly long—and there is no guarantee that someone chosen from outside the organization will successfully adapt to its unique corporate culture.

A second approach is to reorganize. Take just one example: If the vice president of human resources retires, dies, or leaves the organization, the CEO may choose to meet the need by assigning the HR function to another manager. That is just one example of how to solve a talent need by reorganizing. The same approach can be used to meet talent needs in other key positions. Of course, this approach only works if someone qualified is available—and has sufficient interest, motivation, and ability to assume more responsibility.

A third approach is to outsource the work. If this approach is chosen, the challenge is to find a suitable outsourcing partner. That cannot always be done, but it is one option. A disadvantage is that this approach should be used only with activities not directly related to the organization's core competence—the key strategic strength that sets an organization apart from competitors. It is, after all, unwise to outsource the essence of what makes an organization competitive, since that path can lead to bankruptcy or to a takeover.

A fourth approach is to insource the work. If this approach is used, decision-makers seek to find synergy between two functions. Of course, this assumes that some excess capacity—that is, people or resources—exists somewhere in the organization. Suppose, for instance, that a vacancy for a key position exists in one industrial plant. That need could be met by insourcing the work to another plant operated by the same company. An external partner is not sought. Instead, the function is performed internally. This approach differs from reorganization because the insourcing partner does not permanently assume the duties of the new function but performs them only temporarily.

A fifth approach is to hire, on contract, a temporary replacement for a key position.. Some firms specialize in supplying temporary help, even for positions such as CEO, with which temps have not been historically associated.

A sixth approach is to bring in a consultant to help. While similar to using a temp, this approach differs in that a consultant is usually not on site every day to perform the work, as temps generally are. The consultant, in short, performs the work on a project-to-project basis and may even telecommute. This can reduce costs but may also diminish the impact of the key position on the organization.

A seventh approach is to transfer someone from another part of the organization, temporarily or permanently, to meet a succession need. Of course, it is usually assumed that an individual who is transferred meets at least the basic entry-level requirements for the job. Internal transfers, however, have the disadvantage of touching off a *domino effect* (sometimes called a *musical chairs effect*), in which the movement of one person can prompt movements by many others.

An eighth approach is to acquire another organization that possesses the needed talent. In the past, mergers, acquisitions, purchases, and takeovers were sought to realize savings from economies of scale, a desire for higher executive salaries resulting from correlations between senior executive pay and organizational size, and the pursuit of improved integration with such key groups as suppliers, distributors, and even competitors. In the future, however, CEOs will regard mergers, acquisitions, purchases, and takeovers as one means to address talent shortages.[5] (That is an issue treated at greater length below.) Organizations with well-known core competencies will become acquisition targets for other firms that are cash rich but are experiencing talent shortages. Instead of struggling to fill one vacancy at a time, organizations will look for other firms to absorb outright to achieve a massive infusion of new talent.

The ninth approach is to reduce or eliminate the work completely. In other words, the work performed by an otherwise critically important function or position could be reduced or eliminated to solve a succession problem. As one way to do that, the CEO can choose to spin off or sell the business or function.

A tenth approach is to delegate the work up to a high potential in the organization. This is, of course, a form of reorganization. But instead of giving responsibility to another manager when the organization experiences a loss of talent, the work is absorbed by the immediate organizational superior.

An eleventh approach is to delegate the work down. As with the tenth approach, it is a form of reorganization. The work of a high-potential employee is absorbed by one or more of his or her subordinates, without promotion. A variation of this approach is to form a team and delegate the work to that group.

A twelfth approach is to form a strategic alliance with another organization to meet succession needs. This usually means arranging a short-term partnership. While strategic alliances have often been formed in product manufacturing, they could also be formed to meet succession needs. However, this approach is potentially useful on a short-term basis only, since few organizations want to lose high-potential talent forever.

A thirteenth approach is to trade needed talent, temporarily or permanently, with other organizations. Similar to a strategic alliance, this approach tends to be even shorter term. Some organizations provide "loaned executives," for instance, to build the competencies of their high potentials. However, few organizations want to lose their high potentials for an extended time.

A fourteenth approach is to recruit globally rather than domestically, targeting individuals with needed talent outside the United States. Multinational corporations especially may be able to trade talent from one part of the world to another and thereby treat succession issues as moves on a global chessboard.

A fifteenth approach is to hire back managers or other talent. As the U.S. population ages, this approach is already being used by many organizations, such as is the case of Deloitte's Senior Leaders Program, launched to preserve the knowledge and experience of its talent after the traditional retirement age.[6]

Use the worksheet in Exhibit 14-2 to structure your thinking about ways to meet succession needs based on the approaches described above. Whenever a talent need arises in your organization, use the worksheet to contemplate possibilities for meeting that need. Also use the worksheet to integrate the strategies so that your organization is not dependent on only one strategy.

Prediction 2: Decision-Makers Will Seek Integrated Retention Policies and Procedures

Employers in the United States may face a growing problem in finding and keeping talent. As this book goes to press, employment levels are at record lows. While that means that talent is plentiful at the moment, employers can no longer safely assume that the future will be like the present. It is likely they will be competing with many other employers, and this competition is especially intense for high-potential workers with proven track records.

To address this problem, employers should formulate and implement policies and procedures to identify the high-potential talent earlier and to retain that talent longer. Employers will thus need to take such steps as these:

▲ Develop early tracking systems to find new hires having special promise. That can be done with potential assessments performed within the first few months of employment.

▲ Track the reasons for "quits" generally and the reasons for the departure of high-potential talent specifically. That may require revamped exit interviews to capture information about why people (and especially high potentials) leave, where they go, and what they believe could have prompted them to stay. Exit interview systems beg to be reinvented.

▲ Use attitude surveys on a continuing basis to predict turnover and measure job satisfaction. That can be done simply by asking workers on a survey whether they plan to quit within the next year and then supplying questions to uncover chief sources of dissatisfaction. The results can be cross-tabulated, and provide useful information for improving retention and making accurate predictions of turnover.

▲ Track voluntary turnover and critical turnover by department and examine increases in each department for trends or patterns. Then act to address problems in these hot spots.

▲ Provide incentives for people to remain with the organization. (Do not assume that all incentives are financial.) Find out what people need to encourage them to remain with the employer.

By taking these and similar actions, employers can devise an integrated retention strategy to reduce turnover and thereby improve retention.

(text continues on page 318)

Exhibit 14-2. A Worksheet to Structure Your Thinking About Alternative Approaches to Meeting Succession Needs

Directions: Use this worksheet to structure your thinking about alternative approaches to meeting succession needs. First, describe the succession need in the space below and indicate how important it is to the organization, why it is important, and when action needs to be taken to meet the need. Then, rate possible alternatives to internal succession. Then rate each alternative approach, using the following scale:

1 = Not at All Effective
2 = It May Be Somewhat Useful
3 = It Will Be Useful
4 = It Will Be Very Useful

What is the succession need? (*Describe the need. Then answer these questions: (1) How important is this succession need to the organization? (2) Why is it important? and (3) When does action need to be taken to meet the need?*)

	Approach How well can the succession need be met by:	Rating of the Approach				Notes
		Not at All Effective	It May Be Somewhat Useful	It Will Be Useful	It Will Be Very Useful	
1	Hiring from the outside?	1	2	3	4	
2	Reorganizing?	1	2	3	4	
3	Outsourcing the work?	1	2	3	4	
4	Insourcing the work?	1	2	3	4	
5	Hiring a temporary replacement on contract?	1	2	3	4	

(continues)

Exhibit 14-2. (continued)

Approach How well can the succession need be met by:	Rating of the Approach				Notes
	Not at All Effective	It May Be Somewhat Useful	It Will Be Useful	It Will Be Very Useful	
6 Bringing in a consultant to help?	1	2	3	4	
7 Transferring someone from another part of the organization, temporarily or permanently, to meet the succession need?	1	2	3	4	
8 Acquiring another organization that possesses the needed talent?	1	2	3	4	
9 Reducing or eliminating the work completely?	1	2	3	4	
10 Delegating the work up in the organization?	1	2	3	4	
11 Delegating the work down in the organization?	1	2	3	4	
12 Forming a strategic alliance with another organization to meet the need?	1	2	3	4	

		1	2	3	4	
13	Trading needed talent, temporarily or permanently, with other organizations?	1	2	3	4	
14	Recruiting globally rather than domestically, targeting individuals with needed talent outside the borders of the United States?	1	2	3	4	
15	Hiring back needed managers or other talent after they have departed from the organization?	1	2	3	4	
16	What other alternative approaches can you think of, and how effective are they? *(List them below.)*	1	2	3	4	

Prediction 3: Succession Planning and Management Issues Will Have a Global Impact

Succession issues have emerged as front-burner topics in the United States because of the well-known demographic trends for retirement in future years. (See Exhibit 14-3 for the projected U.S. population breakdown in the year 2025.) Indeed, the number of people between the ages of fifty-five and sixty-four is expected to increase by 54 percent between 1996 and 2006.[7] At the same time, there will be a decrease of 8.8 percent in the number of people expected to enter the workforce in the traditional entry-level ages of twenty-five to thirty-four.[8]

What is not so well known is that trends elsewhere in the world also point toward growing numbers of older people as a greater proportion of the population. For instance, consider Exhibits 14-4, 14-5, and 14-6. These exhibits depict the projected populations in China, the United Kingdom, and France, respectively, in the year 2025. Note the numbers of people in the traditional postretirement categories in each nation. Government attempts to control overpopulation (such as the "one child per couple" policy in China) and preferences for smaller families elsewhere point toward growth in the number of elder citizens and fewer young people to take their place. As there are more elderly people living longer in the world, succession issues will emerge as a global concern.

Based on these demographic projections, I predict that SP&M issues will be a challenge to many nations by the year 2025. Many organizations, both large and small, will need to devote attention to succession issues in a way they have not traditionally done. Also influential will be national policies that encourage the employment of older citizens. Expect that many nations will

Exhibit 14-3. Age Distribution of the U.S. Population in 2025

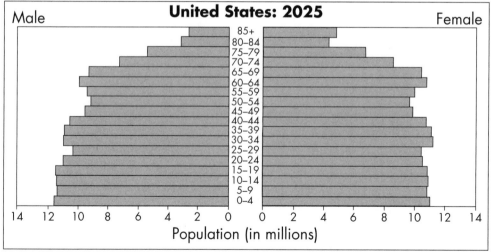

Source: U.S. Census Bureau (2000). Population pyramid summary for the U.S. http://www.census.gov/egi-bin/ipc/idbpyrs ..pl?cty = IN&out = s&ymax = 250.

Exhibit 14-4. Age Distribution of the Chinese Population in 2025

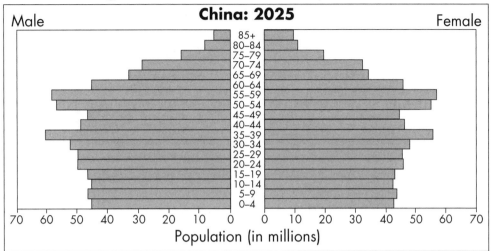

Source: U.S. Census Bureau (2000). Population pyramid summary for China. http://www.census.gov/egi-bin/ipc/idbpyrs ..pl?cty = IN&out = s&ymax = 250.

Exhibit 14-5. Age Distribution of the Population in the United Kingdom in 2025

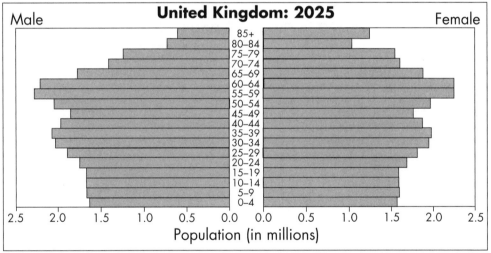

Source: U.S. Census Bureau (2000). Population pyramid summary for the United Kingdom. http://www.census.gov/egi-bin/ipc/idbpyrs..pl?cty = IN&out = s&ymax = 250.

begin to focus on older workers and institute policies to encourage people to retire later. These older workers will represent an important political group, exerting influence directly or indirectly on government policymakers.

Although managers in the United States are often tempted to think only in terms of domestic talent, the fact remains that SP&M issues have a global impact and may require a global solution. At one time, many companies relied heavily on expatriate labor forces to meet succession needs globally. In other

Exhibit 14-6. Age Distribution of the French Population in 2025

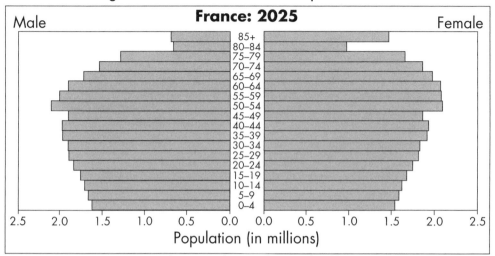

Source: U.S. Census Bureau (2000). Population pyramid summary for France. http://www.census.gov/egi-bin/ipc/idbpyrs
..pl?cty = IN&out = s&ymax = 250.

words, when they needed specialized skills not available in the developing world, they simply exported talent from the developed world. But this strategy is less frequently used as decision-makers pursue localization strategies designed to identify and accelerate the development of high-potential local talent.[9]

A localization strategy has many advantages. One such advantage is that it builds the bench strength across the corporation, serving as a rising tide that lifts all boats. In other words, the corporation builds bench strength everywhere rather than relying on exported talent. A second advantage is that local talent faces no problems adapting to the local culture the way expatriates do. A third advantage is that local talent is not resented, as expatriates often are, for the higher wages and better benefit packages they receive. A fourth advantage is that a localization strategy provides political and public relations advantages, since the organizations are seen as building the local economy rather than exploiting it.

In the future, localization efforts will increase. Government policymakers may even require it. Additionally, forward-thinking corporations will find ways to hitchhike on the talent they have internationally by using online and other virtual methods to encourage "sharing," telecommuting, videocommuting, concurrent work (prepared in one nation but used in another), and idea generation across borders. These developments have profound implications for SP&M, since they can build competencies at the same time as the work is performed.

The challenge for SP&M program coordinators will be to find ways to carry so-called *soft skills technologies*—such as management and HR practices—across cultures. That may require special programs to encourage information-sharing and skill building across cultures, through either online or face-to-face approaches.

Prediction 4: Succession Issues Will Be Influenced by Real-Time Technological Innovations

As Chapter 12 showed, technological innovation is already exerting a major influence on succession issues. This trend will continue. Right now, many organizations are using online methods for recruitment. In the future, online methods will be used in real time to conduct competency modeling, potential assessment, performance appraisal, individual development planning, and individual coaching.

The challenge for SP&M program coordinators will be to find and apply these approaches. One major goal, of course, is to slash cycle time for filling key positions and sourcing talent. Another major goal is to lower geographical barriers, making it possible to access—and develop—talent anywhere and at any time.

Prediction 5: Succession Planning and Management Will Emerge as an Issue in Government Agencies, Academic Institutions, and Nonprofit Enterprises

Traditionally, sectors of the economy other than business have been slow to adopt effective SP&M practices. Government agencies, academic institutions, and nonprofit enterprises have not typically attempted to identify replacements for key positions and have often relied on a talent-pool approach, which is more consistent with the laws, rules, regulations, political realities, and organizational cultures found in these economic sectors. Additionally, government agencies and academic institutions in particular have found systematic succession approaches difficult to use because of institutional policies or civil service regulations that require competitive searches, job posting, and preferences based on factors other than individual performance. Efforts to groom individuals in these settings have sometimes been prohibited rather than encouraged. One result has been long lead times between the appearance of a vacancy and the appointment of a successor.

However, as a direct result of increasing turnover, increasing retirement rates, lagging salary and performance bonuses, and the greater rewards in a private-sector economy that makes the (relative) security of government service and academic appointments less appealing than they once were, I predict that government agencies and academic institutions will be forced to adopt more systematic succession practices. It is no longer effective to follow the business-as-usual approach of "calling for the list" of qualified individuals who have taken civil service exams or "conducting a national search" for each academic appointment by simply placing one advertisement in the *Chronicle of Higher Education*. The reason? There are few, if any, candidates on the civil service "list" and few, if any, applicants sending in material to *Chronicle* advertisements for academic positions. This problem is particularly acute at senior levels in government and in educational institutions, where people do not want or need to move.

It is important to understand that these problems take different shapes in government, educational institutions, and nonprofit organizations; hence, they require different solution strategies. Within each economic sector, differences in procedures also exist. For example, in government, human resource practices have not been the same among local, state, and federal agencies. In academic institutions, human resource practices have differed among government-supported and privately funded colleges and universities. In nonprofit enterprises, unlike in government agencies and academic institutions, the intrinsic satisfaction of the work has mediated the need to pay competitive salaries or provide competitive benefits.

However, these three economic sectors do share similar challenges. Indeed, the key challenge is to find better ways to recruit, retain, motivate, and cultivate talent without sacrificing existing civil service laws and rules and without sacrificing merit-based employment in favor of political patronage, nepotism, or unlawful discrimination. There are no simple answers, and each institution needs to form a task force and focus attention on improving succession within the framework of its existing policies, procedures, and governmental laws, rules, and regulations. The challenge for SP&M program coordinators will be to find ways to adapt the approaches recommended in this book to the unique settings of government agencies, academic institutions, and nonprofit enterprises.

Prediction 6: Succession Planning and Management Will Lead to an Increasing Policy of Organizational Openness

Many organizations still do not share information about openings with the prospective successors for key positions. Some executives worry that such openness might lead to problems such as "greenmail" or the "crown prince dilemma." *Greenmail* occurs when designated successors attract lucrative offers from other employers and then leverage them to achieve counteroffers from their current employers. The *crown prince dilemma* occurs when designated successors believe they are guaranteed advancement, rest on their laurels, and let their performance decline.

Despite these potential problems, however, I predict that organizations will be forced to become more open about naming future successors. If they do not, they risk losing their high potentials to employers that are more open, make promises, and are forthcoming in offering attractive employment packages that include professional development opportunities.

Prediction 7: Succession Planning and Management Will Increasingly Be Integrated with Career Development

Career planning and management programs are usually planned by individuals. They are thus planned from the bottom up. Succession planning and management programs are usually planned by senior executives, and are thus planned from the top down. As described elsewhere in the book, the two work together and should be integrated.

In the future, decision-makers will recognize how important it is to have both. Their synergistic power is greater than the sum of their individual parts. For that reason, organizations will revive company-sponsored career-planning and management programs to empower individuals with greater responsibility to prepare themselves for the future. This also serves as a double-check on, and verification of, replacement and succession plans.

The challenge for SP&M program coordinators will be to find ways to integrate career and succession programs. Exhibit 14-7 lists some important characteristics of career planning and management programs. Exhibit 14-8 provides an assessment sheet for you to structure your thinking about ways to integrate career planning and management programs with SP&M programs.

Prediction 8: Succession Planning and Management Will Be Heavily Influenced by Concerns about Work/Family Balance and Spirituality

A competitive economy has led many managers to devote more time to their work. In fact, the average number of hours per week that managers work has been on the rise. The same may well be true of other groups. That, in turn, has prompted many people to question their priorities. There is more to life than work, and they know it. Some seek more time with their families or others in their lives. Some look for religion or a deeper feeling about the meaning of life. These desires to balance work and life or achieve a greater sense of spirituality are major drivers for change. I predict that these will become issues of growing importance to organizational decision-makers. They will find that high potentials refuse additional responsibility if that responsibility requires too much personal sacrifice. This situation includes job assignments that prompt upheavals in their personal lives.

The challenge for SP&M program coordinators will be to find ways to help high potentials balance their work responsibilities and their personal lives. This may require using time off as an incentive or giving people time away from work so they can balance work and personal life or pursue their spirituality.

Prediction 9: Succession Planning and Management Will Focus Increasingly on Real-Time Talent-Development Efforts as Well as Strategic Efforts

The manager has a role in developing talent. That is a daily responsibility, not a one-time-a-year-effort to be discussed, and managed, in a talent show.

(text continues on page 328)

Exhibit 14-7. Important Characteristics of Career Planning and Management Programs

Directions: Use this worksheet to rate your organization on how well it addresses important issues in career planning and management. For each characteristic of an effective career planning and management program listed in the left column below, rate how well you believe your organization rates on that characteristic in the right column. Use the following scale:

1 = Not at All Effective
2 = Somewhat Ineffective
3 = Somewhat Effective
4 = Effective

Characteristic of a Career Planning and Management Program *The career planning and management program is:*	*Rating*			
	Not at All Effective *1*	*Somewhat Ineffective* *2*	*Somewhat Effective* *3*	*Effective* *4*
1 Focused on meeting specific business needs or issues of the organization.	1	2	3	4
2 Targeted on specific groups in the organization.	1	2	3	4
3 Responsive to the organization's unique corporate culture and "ways of doing things."	1	2	3	4
4 Organized around a unified model that can be easily and readily explained to such stakeholders as managers and workers.	1	2	3	4
5 Based on a comprehensive approach that goes well beyond a "one-shot" approach to addressing career planning in the organization.	1	2	3	4

6	Involves, and thereby commands the ownership of, all key stakeholder groups (such as executives, managers, HR specialists, and workers).	1	2	3	4
7	Well publicized to stakeholders.	1	2	3	4
8	Evaluated both on how well it helps individuals achieve their goals and the organization achieves its goals.	1	2	3	4
Score		Add up the numbers in the column above and place the sum in the box below:			

Interpretation of the Score

Score 1–8	Your organization does not have a career planning and management program—or, if your organization does possess such a program, it is regarded as singularly ineffective. Grade it as an F.
Score 9–16	Your organization possesses a career planning and management program, but it is not regarded as effective or useful; only as somewhat so. Grade it as a C.
Score 17–24	Your organization's career planning and management program is regarded as generally effective. Grade it a B.
Score 25+	Your organization's career planning and management program is regarded as highly successful and effective. Grade it an A.

Exhibit 14-8. An Assessment Sheet for Integrating Career Planning and Management Programs with Succession Planning and Management Programs

Directions: Use this worksheet to assess how well your organization's career planning and management program is integrated with your SP&M program. For each characteristic of effective career and succession programs listed in the left column below, rate how well you believe your organization has integrated them in the right columns. Use the following scale:

   1 = Not at All Integrated
   2 = Somewhat Integrated—but Not Enough
   3 = Well Integrated
   4 = Very Well Integrated

Characteristics of Effective Career and Succession Programs Both the career planning and management program and the SP&M program:	Rating			
	Not at All Integrated 1	Somewhat Integrated —but Not Enough 2	Well Integrated 3	Very Well Integrated 4
1 Are focused on meeting specific business needs.	1	2	3	4
2 Are guided by program objectives that have been compared and integrated.	1	2	3	4
3 Use work requirements or competencies as common denominators.	1	2	3	4
4 Identify gaps between what people know or can do now and what they need to know.	1	2	3	4
5 Clarify what career goals are sought by individuals.	1	2	3	4

6	Can, and often do, use full-circle, multirater assessments.	1	2	3	4
7	Rely on individual development plans to narrow individual developmental gaps.	1	2	3	4
8	Are evaluated.	1	2	3	4
Score		*Add up the numbers in the column above and place the sum in the box below:*			

Interpretation of the Score

Score 1–8	Your organization has not integrated career planning and management with SP&M.
Score 9–16	Your organization has somewhat integrated career planning and management with SP&M. However, they are not perceived as sufficiently integrated.
Score 17–24	Your organization has effectively integrated career planning and management with SP&M.
Score 25+	Your organization has succeeded in achieving a very good integration between career planning and management with SP&M.

Organizational leaders can encourage that practice by rewarding managers for talent development, establishing mentoring programs (see the CD-ROM that comes with this book for a briefing on mentoring programs), and clarifying their role as managers in cultivating talent (see the CD-ROM that comes with this book for a briefing on the manager's role in succession planning and management).

Most development occurs on the job. The kinds of assignments that managers give their workers build their competencies. That is why experience is prized in organizations. That experience can be managed in such a way that workers can build their capabilities while meeting the real-time requirements of the organization. Managing that situation on a daily basis is the manager's job. I predict that, in the future, organizational leaders will do a better job of building managers' abilities to develop their workers' talents in real time.

Prediction 10: Succession Planning and Management Will Center as Much on Ethical and Value-Oriented Issues as on Competency-Based Issues

Earlier in the book, I explained that, as a result of the Enron and other corporate scandals, leaders have recognized that performance cannot be gained at any price. It must be constrained by legal, moral, and ethical considerations. I predict that potential assessment will increasingly survey how well individuals comply with corporate codes of conduct, as well as meet other ethical, moral, and legal standards. Indeed, the mere appearance of impropriety can lead to onerous new regulations; consequently, organizational leaders will insist that individuals being considered for more management responsibility—or more demanding professional and technical responsibility—be measured against ethical, moral, and legal standards as well as competency-based (productivity) standards.

Prediction 11: Succession Planning and Management Will Become More Fully Integrated with Selection Decisions

Some competencies can be developed, but others must be selected for. As a result, it is essential that development and selection efforts be integrated. During competency identification efforts, HR professionals and others may need to pinpoint which competencies can be developed and which must be selected for.

Prediction 12: Succession Planning and Management Will Focus on Leveraging Talent as Well as Developing It

It is not enough to develop talent. Since some people are more productive or creative than others, the challenge is to leverage that ability to mentor, coach, and build the competencies of others. A challenge for organizational leaders is to find ways to match those who possess unique talents and strengths with those who can stand to develop those competencies. Mentoring can occur between peers and not just between an individual and those at higher levels of the corporate hierarchy.

Prediction 13: Succession Planning and Management Includes Alternatives to One-Hire-at-a-Time Approaches, Such as Mergers, Acquisitions, or Takeovers, for the Purpose of Rapid and Broad-Based Talent Acquisition

Organizations can acquire talent in more than one way, and one way to acquire talent is to hire it. A second way is to develop it. But there are alternatives.

For example, yet another approach is to merge, acquire, or take over other organizations that enjoy talent that may be otherwise lacking in the organization. Think of it as a blood transfusion. A merger, acquisition, or takeover can inject a lot of talent at once into the organization.

Of course, great care should be exercised in such ventures. If the corporate cultures of the two organizations are not compatible, talent will vanish through attrition. For that reason, organizational leaders should take steps to reassure the talented people in an organization being merged, acquired, or taken over that their futures are not in jeopardy. Without such due diligence, the high potentials may leave quickly, rendering the whole change effort a failure.

Prediction 14: Succession Planning and Management Will Become Closely Linked to Risk Management and Concerns About Security

The unexpected loss of talent can occur in more than one way. Accidents happen, but if the organization's leaders take steps to minimize the impact of such accidents, they are acting prudently with the talent of the organization. It is for this reason that some organizations limit how many executives may travel on the same plane, in the same automobile, on the same bus, or in any other vehicle.

Another issue to consider is what to do in the event of the sudden loss of an entire facility. It is no longer unthinkable that a whole city could be lost. Will the organization be able to function if the corporate headquarters is destroyed, as happened to several companies when the World Trade Center towers collapsed? Organizational leaders should thus do scenario planning to prepare for such catastrophic losses of human as well as physical assets.

Prediction 15: Succession Planning and Management Will Become Associated with More than Management Succession

Most people have traditionally associated succession planning and management with management succession. Moving up the organization chart has been a traditional focus, as has finding those who can be groomed for such advancement. But advancement can mean more than management succession. For example, it can also mean advancement along a horizontal continuum of professional competence.[10]

Summary

This chapter has offered fifteen predictions about succession planning and management. In the future, succession planning and management will: (1) Prompt efforts by decision-makers to find flexible strategies to address future organizational talent needs; (2) lead to integrated retention policies and procedures that are intended to identify high-potential talent earlier, retain that talent, and preserve older high-potential workers; (3) have a global impact; (4) be influenced increasingly by real-time technological innovations; (5) become an issue in government agencies, academic institutions, and nonprofit enterprises in a way never before seen; (6) lead to increasing organizational openness about possible successors; (7) increasingly be integrated with career-development issues; (8) be heavily influenced in the future by concerns about work/family balance and spirituality; (9) focus increasingly on real-time talent-development efforts as well as strategic efforts, which center around the role of managers in daily work with their reports; (10) center as much around ethical and value-oriented issues as around competency-based issues; (11) become more fully integrated with selection decisions; (12) focus on leveraging talent as well as developing it; (13) include alternatives to one-hire-at-a-time approaches, such as mergers, acquisitions, or takeovers for the purpose of rapid and broad-based talent acquisition; (14) become closely linked to risk management and concerns about security; and (15) become associated with more than management succession.

FREQUENTLY ASKED QUESTIONS (FAQs) ABOUT SUCCESSION PLANNING AND MANAGEMENT

1. What is succession planning?

Simply stated, succession planning is a process of developing talent to meet the needs of the organization now and in the future. Every time a manager makes a work assignment, he or she is preparing someone for the future because he or she is building that worker's ability. Work experience builds competence, and different kinds of work experience build different kinds of competence.

2. How is succession planning different from replacement planning?

Replacement planning is about finding backups to fill vacancies on an organization chart. But succession planning is about grooming the talent needed for the future. They are related but different activities.

3. Why is succession planning needed?

Organizational leaders need to think about aligning their staffing and leadership needs with the organization's future strategic objectives. If they do not take action to establish an effective succession planning and management program, they are likely to fall victim to the so-called *like me* problem. That is the dilemma in which people are biased to pick other people like themselves, viewing them more favorably. It is not intentional discrimination but, rather, human nature—to see the world through our own lenses. For that reason, men tend to prefer men, women prefer women, engineers prefer engineers, and so forth. The more ways that you are like your boss, the more likely your boss is to regard you favorably. Since there is a tendency to want to "clone" job incumbents for successors, organizations must take steps to counteract that built-in bias, for the simple reason that the job incumbent of today, while perhaps perfectly suited for the business environment now, may not be suitable for the business environment of the future. For that reason, organizational leaders must take steps to determine how many and what kind of people are needed for the future so that succession plans can pick winners who can help the organization realize its strategic objectives.

4. Why are organizational leaders interested in succession planning and management now?

Many organizations are experiencing the effects of aging workforces that are putting them at risk of losing their most experienced workers to retirement. At the same time, concerns about terrorism have raised the stakes on prudent planning to ensure that leaders, and other key workers, have backups in case they are needed. Finally, years of downsizing and other cost-cutting measures have reduced the internal bench strength of many organizations so that it is more difficult to find internal replacements. Since most managers do not want to wait a long time to fill critical positions, and organizations have downsized such that external talent is not readily available, many organizational leaders are taking steps now to "grow their own talent," particularly for those hard-to-fill internal positions that require extensive, unique knowledge of "the way we do things here."

5. What are the essential components of a succession planning program?

Think about the following:

▲ *The Purpose of the Program*. Why do you need it? (Do *not* assume that all executives of the organization will just naturally share the same objectives. They will not. Some will want some things; others will want others. But confused goals will not lead to effective results.)

▲ *The Measurable Objectives of the Program*. What measurable results are desired from it over time?

▲ *The Competencies Needed for Success Now*. What kind of person is needed to be a successful performer in every department and at every organizational level?

▲ *The Way Those Competencies Are Measured*. How well is the organization's performance management system measuring present competencies? (That is needed because we only want to promote those who are succeeding in their current jobs.)

▲ *The Competencies Needed for Success in the Future*. What kind of person is needed to be a successful performer in every department, and at every organizational level in the future, if the organization is to realize its strategic objectives?

▲ *The Way the Organization Assesses Potential.* How do we know that someone can succeed at a future, higher level of responsibility if we have never seen him or her perform it? (Think of this as measuring performance against future, as yet unperformed, job challenges.)

▲ *Narrowing Gaps.* How do we narrow gaps between the person's present job requirements and present performance and his or her future targets or possible future levels and what he or she needs to know or do to be ready for that higher-level or more difficult responsibility?

▲ *Evaluating Results.* How do we know that our efforts to narrow gaps are working and that the succession program is achieving its mission and accomplishing its measurable objectives?

6. How does an organization get started establishing and implementing a succession planning and management program if it has not had one before?

Start by "making the business case," which means "showing a compelling business need to establish and implement a succession program." (Some people say "find a burning platform.") Based on that case, establish the goals to be addressed by the program. How exactly do you make the business case? Here are some possibilities:

▲ Conduct a study of the projected retirements in your organization by going to your payroll system and asking for a report that shows the projected retirement dates of everyone on the payroll. Then dig deeper to see projected retirement dates by job level (position on the organization chart), geographical location, department, job code, and any other specifics that may be important to your organization. Then do the same work by examining projected retirement dates over rolling three-year periods. Remember that some people will not retire when they are eligible, but you are simply assessing risks.

▲ Ask executives what would happen if the whole senior team was wiped out at once in a plane crash, car accident, or bombing of corporate headquarters.

▲ Ask each manager how he or she would advise handling his or her sudden loss due to death, disability, or accident. Who is the backup, and how did he or she determine that person?

Of course, you may be able to come up with some other ways to build a business case, depending on the unique business conditions that your organization faces. But start with a persuasive argument, since succession planning is one of those things like buying burial plots that everyone knows should be done but wants to put off doing. (In fact, the old joke is that succession is something we are too busy to do when business is good and too expensive to do when business is bad. The result is that we never do it.)

7. What's the return-on-investment for succession planning and management programs?

Nobody knows the average ROI for succession planning and management programs. Even best-in-class companies have not effectively measured it. (By the way, what is the ROI of your accounting department?) Determine ROI by starting with the measurable objectives to be achieved by the program. Find out what it costs—and how long it takes—to fill vacancies today. Then find out what it costs—and how long it takes—to fill vacancies after the succession planning and management program is up and running. Use these figures to show the costs and benefits of an SP&M program.

8. What are the most common problems that organizations experience in getting started on a succession planning and management program?

Common problems in getting started on a succession planning and management program include:

▲ Defining it as an HR problem rather than as a responsibility shared by the board of directors, senior leadership team, managers at all levels of the organization, and even individual workers. Everyone has some responsibility to groom talent to meet the organization's future needs.

▲ Understaffing the effort. A good succession program requires time and effort. Someone must coordinate that. It cannot be "completely outsourced." Consultants can help, but they cannot "do it for you." Managers cannot abdicate responsibility—or accountability.

▲ Establishing confused or overly ambitious goals. If the organization's leaders do not focus the succession effort on specific, and measurable, objectives to be achieved, the succession program will lack goal clarity and resources will be wasted in pursuing many confusing, overlapping, and perhaps conflicting goals. You have to be clear about what you want before a program can be established to accomplish it.

▲ Failing to hold people accountable. This is perhaps the biggest problem facing all succession programs. What happens if this year's individual development plans are not met by an individual? What happens if the senior executive in charge of a division does not meet measurable talent-development objectives for his or her division? These questions center on accountability. Different organizations solve the problem in different ways, depending on corporate culture. But the real question is, "How do we arrange consequences for building talent or failing to build talent?" "How does talent development stack up against meeting the numbers for this week, month, quarter, or year, and what do we do if we are making profits or sales but not grooming people for the future?"

9. What are the biggest benefits that organizations experience from a succession planning and management program?

If an organization has established an effective succession planning program, organizational leaders should expect that:

▲ It will take less time and expense to source talent to fill vacancies because the talent has already been identified and prepared.

▲ People-development efforts have been aligned with the organization's strategic objectives so that the right people will be available at the right times and in the right places to meet the right objectives.

▲ The organization is prepared to deal with sudden, catastrophic losses of key people.

10. What is the role of the corporate board in a succession planning and management program? CEO in a succession planning and management program? What is the senior management team's role? What is the HR department's role? What is the individual's role?

▲ The board should ensure that an effective succession planning and management program exists and is actually working effectively.

▲ The CEO is personally responsible for ensuring that an effective succession planning and management program exists and works effectively. If he or she does not, it is like a pilot who is not flying the airplane. If the plane crashes, who is responsible?

▲ Senior managers are like the co-pilots of the airplane. Each is responsible for establishing talent development objectives for his or her own division or department and then meeting those objectives.

▲ The HR department provides support for the effort by arranging for the policies, procedures, technology, and other support to help ensure that the "plane flies in the right direction." Think of the HR vice president's role as akin to the navigator of the plane. He or she gives advice to the pilot where and how to fly and provides on-the-spot advice about how to deal with unique problems, situations, or challenges.

▲ Department managers are responsible for attracting, identifying, developing, and retaining talent for their respective departments. They should realize that they are responsible—and accountable—for both "making the numbers" *and* "grooming talent to meet the organization's future requirements."

▲ Individuals are responsible for knowing what they want out of life, their careers, and the organization. They are also responsible for developing themselves for the future. While there is nothing wrong with individuals "wanting to stay where they are"—particularly if that stems from a work/life balance decision—individuals have a responsibility to let people know what their objectives are so long as it does not hurt their own interests and possible future employability.

CASE STUDIES ON SUCCESSION PLANNING AND MANAGEMENT

The case studies in this Appendix are meant to represent a broad range of succession planning and management programs drawn from previously published accounts. They represent both best-practice and typical-practice cases. Read them and note the similarities—and the differences—that exist in succession planning and management efforts across a spectrum of organizations.

Case 1: How Business Plans for Succession:
Matching Talent with Tasks

With 61,000 workers in more than ninety countries, Dole Food Company Inc. has talent all over the world. Only a few hundred of those employees are in top management at the 151-year-old company headquartered in Westlake Village, California, which produces and markets fruits, vegetables, and flowers. Trouble is, Dole doesn't have comprehensive knowledge of who these managers are or what they can do.

To be sure, business-unit leaders know their own direct reports well—their strengths, weaknesses, experience, and career goals. The problem is, these leaders have no way to share that knowledge with other business units. If a key job opens up in North America, the business-unit leader wouldn't know if the perfect candidate worked in another Dole unit in South America. Dole has no way to match its top managerial talent with its executive needs.

But that is changing. The highly decentralized company is launching a succession planning process, supported by Web-based software, through which Dole executives hope to rectify their inability to promote the best and the brightest across the corporation.

"We are looking to execute an organized process where we will identify weaknesses and strengths of our people and build plans to deal with that," says George Horne, Dole's vice president of administration and support operations.

Source: Bill Roberts, "Matching Talents with Tasks," *HR Magazine* 47:11 (2002), 91–93. Used with permission of *HR Magazine.*

337

"We also want to identify areas where we will need to bring in some people from outside to fill some gaps at the top."

Knowing Your People

Succession planning used to mean that a company president hoped his oldest child would join the family business and replace Dad someday. If not the oldest, then any child would do. Today, succession planning—also called workforce planning *or* progression planning—means having the right person in the right place at the right time for the right job, says Ren Nardoni, senior vice president at Pilat NAI, a Lebanon, New Jersey, subsidiary of Pilat Technologies International Ltd. of London. It means knowing your people; knowing their strengths, experience, and career goals; and knowing where they need development. Succession planning helps HR and managers know what to do if a position becomes vacant. "You're looking for the vulnerabilities of the organization," he says.

Succession planning has grown more important since the 1980s and picked up steam in the 1990s. These days, experts say, most Fortune 500 companies take succession planning seriously, and many smaller companies embrace it. Marc Kaiser, a consultant with Hewitt Associates in Lincolnshire, Illinois, says savvy companies recognize that they must be prepared to tackle the leadership gap created by retiring baby boomers. The ability to easily automate succession planning using the Web also drives interest. "It is easier now, and that's one reason people are doing it," he says.

Most companies that adopt succession planning automate it with software. Nardoni estimates that 50 percent to 60 percent of the Fortune 500 and 30 percent of the largest 2,500 U.S. companies have installed succession planning systems, either stand-alone software or the succession-planning module in their HR management system (HRMS). "Our average client starts with succession planning for between 150 and 250 positions. The minute you get above 50 to 75 positions, it becomes a pain in the butt on paper," he says.

Government agencies, such as the Federal Aviation Administration, also embrace succession planning, Nardoni says, because they have to plan for people moving in and out and retiring. However, the government's succession planning initiatives don't have the same intensity as those of the Fortune 500, he adds.

Succession planning correlates positively with the bottom line, says Nardoni.

Kaiser points to a 2002 Hewitt study, "Top 20 Companies for Leaders," that shows that companies with reputations as good places to work have stronger succession planning and commit more resources to it, including the CEO's time. Hewitt surveyed some 348 HR executives and CEOs at 240 publicly held companies on various leadership topics, identifying companies that succeed in attracting, developing, and retaining leaders, and noting the practices that influenced their success.

Dole's Culture Change

Succession planning was one of several corporate-wide initiatives Dole launched in the past 18 months to decrease decentralization in an attempt to improve the bottom line, Horne says. The company was No. 353 in the Fortune 500 in 2002 with revenues of more than $4.6 billion.

Historically, Horne explains, Dole's seven business units were so autonomous that corporate wasn't much more than a holding company. When Larry Kern became president in February 2001, he set out to keep as much decentralization as made sense while adding some corporatewide accountability and processes.

Succession planning (Dole calls it progression planning) was one such change. The process itself would require a change of culture and could become an agent for further culture change. "The idea of succession planning is contrary to being highly decentralized," says Sue Hagen, vice president of HR for North American operations, who led the effort.

Although Dole's annual turnover rate among top management is less than 10 percent, succession planning was on its radar screen for years, says Hagen. "Talent is scarce. Time and cost to ramp someone up in our business is difficult and costly. It makes going outside more difficult."

Hagen talked informally to all corporate executives, and the leaders and staffs of each business unit, to generate consensus for succession planning for corporate positions—corporate officers, business unit presidents and their direct reports. The initial group would be about 100, she says. Next year, another few hundred will be included.

The reaction was mostly positive, Hagen says. "We got a range of responses. It was more an issue of education, especially for the businesses based outside the United States. We had to educate them to what the objectives were going to be and why we do it centrally rather than decentralized."

Senior management approved the project, and Kern is especially enthusiastic, Hagen says. "He wants us to maximize the internal talent we have."

Defining the Processes

Hagen's next step was to hold a series of in-depth interviews with the executives to determine which succession planning processes were needed and how often they should be conducted. The goal was to reflect as much of their thinking as possible. "One division wanted to review succession plans on their people six times a year. Another didn't want to do it at all," she says. Hagen compromised: Succession planning will be conducted twice a year. She also identified four competencies on which everyone would be evaluated: accountability, business acumen, multifunctionality (cross-training), and vision/originality.

Kaiser and another Hewitt consultant, Lisa Labat, assisted Hagen with the Dole project. "One of the first questions we ask organizations is, 'What are the business needs?'" says Labat. They also ask, "What is your business today and where are you going to be taking it? What does that mean for the talent you need in place, especially at the top?"

Hagen did not want software to dictate the process, nor did she want to create a process and then search for software that exactly fit. Instead, she started to look at software while developing the process itself, looking for a package that is flexible, needs little customization, and is easy to learn. The Hewitt consultants pointed her toward several products but did not participate in the selection. Hagen also networked with other HR professionals who had adopted succession-planning software.

Many HRMS software suites have an optional succession-planning module, but neither Dole nor its business units have an HRMS. Since most employees are farm or factory workers, there is not much need for the detailed information an HRMS provides, says Hagen. "It would be overkill." In a way, the succession planning software Dole adopted will become a mini-HRMS for top personnel, she adds.

Hagen also wanted an application service provider (ASP) model. Outsourcing, including payroll, is common at Dole. Hagen didn't want to own and support technology, and she didn't want the small corporate information technology staff to have to work on it.

About 20 percent of the requests for proposals that Pilat NAI sees request an ASP model, and 50 percent want information about that option, Nardoni says. He expects 25 percent or more of his business to be ASP-based in the next two years.

Hagen identified products from nine companies and asked for presentations from four. She chose Pilat NAI's succession planning software because it was cost-effective and flexible. The inner workings of the system are invisible to Dole.

Pilat NAI runs the software on one of its servers for a monthly fee based on the number of users who will be system administrators plus a flat fee for the first 1,000 records stored on the software. Hagen serves as vendor manager, and a coworker handles day-to-day contact with Pilat NAI regarding development, troubleshooting, and user issues. The contract spells out confidentiality and fire-wall protection for the data.

Hagen began the project in March, selected the software in April, and began installing in May. The project began to roll out in September, and Dole expects to produce the first reports for management by the end of this year.

A Plan for Each Manager

Installation required less than 10 percent customization and did not require the full-time involvement of anyone at Dole. One HR person pulled data from the payroll system and fed it into the succession-planning database, but that was a onetime task. The basic data gives users a starting point.

The users—top managers—access the program from the Web with a password. They fill out a resume, including career interests, and note any mobility restrictions. They assess themselves on the four competencies. When they are done, the system automatically notifies their manager, who does an assessment and indicates whether he or she thinks the individual could be promoted. The manager also assesses overall potential and the risk of losing the user. This assessment then goes automatically to the division head, then the divisional HR director, then Hagen.

All assessments will be pulled together in a report, to be reviewed by Kern, Horne, legal counsel, and the chief financial officer. Hagen will use the information to create a career development plan for each individual, including seminars she'll organize. She'll also direct business unit leaders to potential candidates in other units when they have appropriate openings.

"The beauty is, for the first time we'll have a database that ties together these talent metrics and can serve as a clearinghouse for people available for opportunities," Hagen says. The system will also help Dole identify where it has talent gaps so it can better recruit from outside, adds Horne.

Dole's corporate management hopes all business units will eventually adopt similar succession planning processes and software, Hagen says. "I view this as a pilot, a very visible pilot," she says. "To get the buy-in of individual business units, we'll show them that this was adopted by their senior management and that it works."

Case 2: How Government Plans for Succession:
Public-Sector Succession—A Strategic Approach to Sustaining Innovation

In the public and private sectors alike, demand for change is the one constant. There is a loud call for leaders who can accommodate change personally and who can initiate and drive broad changes in their organizations. These demands make sense but raise a troubling issue. By relentlessly insisting on change, are we risking the loss of innovations recently realized? This is a particularly salient question for public-sector agencies, which are currently under attack from all sides.

In this article, I assert that while change must be on the agenda of any public agency for its very survival as well as for the public good, it is just as important to ensure that gains achieved in one administration be given a fair assessment and not be jettisoned, without review, to the god of change. Indeed, the importance of "sustained innovation"—essentially keeping change alive—is an increasing challenge for public agencies.[1]

Will innovative programs created as a response to social problems be allowed to live out their "natural" lives, or will they be killed off before their time, independent of performance and outcomes? This issue is particularly acute in the transition between elected or appointed government officials—especially in a highly politicized environment that limits government's capacity to continue efforts across administrations. Moreover, one critical tool available to the private sector, succession planning, is rarely used by public agencies because the executive's fortunes are generally tied to a particular administration. Many public-sector leaders have devised strategies for continuing efforts across administrations.

Source: Ellen Schall, "Public-Sector Succession: A Strategic Approach to Sustaining Innovation," *Public Administration Review* 57:1 (1997), 4–10. Used with permission of *Public Administration Review*.

Some establish support beyond the government, for example, from the business community or other local "elites"; some obtain early bipartisan political support. Still others avoid program demise by identifying a champion linked to the incoming administration so as to have a voice "inside," or by creating wide support within the agency (and other agencies) so that the new governor or mayor hears a consistent message. Finally, some administrators have succeeded in winning national recognition for their innovations so that discontinuing them is a perceived political risk.

As important as these approaches are, innovations also can be sustained by cabinet secretaries or agency heads engaging in succession planning, even though these people are as vulnerable to shifting political winds as their superiors. In fact, this level, where so much actual and potential innovation resides, represents a real opportunity for both preserving innovations and transferring them to subsequent regimes—provided the agency heads can, and will, extend their strategic vision beyond their own tenure. It is no longer sufficient to achieve change, difficult as it may be. The public-sector leader must learn to consider not only what can be but what will be, how what is achieved can be sustained. This requires future-oriented strategic thinking, which I argue must include attention to succession planning. Succession planning done well involves preparing the agency for a change in leadership, but it also includes assessing what has been valuable and how that can be preserved and transferred to the subsequent regime. It is this strategic, sustaining innovation aspect of succession planning that I focus on in this article.

First, I shall look at how research on succession in the private sector is both helpful and hindering for public-sector succession planning, especially in the realm of sustaining innovation. I will also examine the research that exists in the public sector and its relevance. I describe a series of constraints or barriers that must be overcome if succession is to be taken seriously in public-sector organizations.

I present a case study drawn from my experience as Commissioner of the New York City Department of Juvenile Justice, where I served for seven years and managed my succession in a way that enabled the innovations that had been put in place to be retained and further innovations based on these to be created. I discuss the four interconnected strategies devised to implement this succession and show how they can help both in overcoming barriers to taking succession seriously and in shaping the legacy of a public-sector organization.

Succession and Succession Planning: A Brief Review of the Literature

Most articles on succession and succession planning begin with a familiar lament: executive-level transition merits more attention than it gets in the literature (Rainey and Wechsler, 1988; Greenblatt, 1983; Gordon and Rosen, 1981; Austin and Gilmore, 1993). The relatively few authors who address the issue in the context of the public sector point out the even more serious gap on that side. The National Academy of Public Administration (NAPA), anticipating significant retirements in the Federal Senior Executive Service beginning in 1994, began a serious look at succession planning in the early 1990s (NAPA, 1992). The NAPA researchers also remarked on the lack of attention to public-sector transitions. In an article written in 1993, although published later, Farquhar refers to the "rapidly expanding" literature on succession (Farquhar, 1996), and in 1995, she edited a special edition of *Human Resource Management* on the topic of leadership transitions (Farquhar, 1995).

Both the problem in the public sector and its consequences have been described by Rainey and Wechsler (1988), who argue, "Whether one adopts a broad or more specific approach to organizational performance and productivity, effective transition management is essential to achieving positive results." At the same time, the authors characterize executive transitions at all levels of government as "marked by serious deficiencies in preparation, orientation, and communication" (p. 45). However, while noting that some research exists on the political management of transition at the presidential and gubernatorial levels, the authors do not make use of the broader literature on transition and executive succession that would help guide an analysis of transition and change at the agency level—particularly within, not between, administrations.

Various frameworks help conceptualize transition generally and the issues that surround it. The most useful begin before the actual succession event (Rainey and Wechsler, 1988; Greenblatt, 1983; Gordon and Rosen, 1981) and draw attention to what Rainey and Wechsler call the objective as well as subjective domains. But there is something missing even here. Greenblatt, for example, begins with what he terms the "anticipatory" stage but fails to capture the opportunity for a strategic view of this moment. Gordon and Rosen point out the need to attend to the time before the new leader arrives, but they still start with the new leader's being chosen. Rainey and Wechsler describe transition as a major "strategy influencing" event. This stops short of grasping transition's full potential to make, not just influence, strategy. They write as if the departing leader has no role in shaping the transition.

Although the literature gives some attention to the person leaving (Kets de Vries, 1988), more is given to the new leader and his or her dilemmas (Gouldner, 1950; Greenblatt, 1983; Gilmore and Ronchi, 1995). In a particularly interesting article on leadership during interregna, Farquhar (1991) examines 43 Legal Service Corporations and analyzes the dynamics and impact of interim administrations.

Other research distinguishes the important dimensions in which cases differ, arguably the most significant being the reason for departure. Not all CEO successions are equally interesting for theorists. Fredrickson, Hambrick, and Baumrin (1988) suggest that firings and voluntary departures offer the most meat because only then are real choices made; their work focuses on dismissals. Austin and Gilmore (1993) also highlight the importance of the reason for transition. They outline various reasons and cite previous works on each—retirement, term expiration, protest, reassignment, illness, or death—but select for case analysis the leader who chooses to move on to a new opportunity. They are especially helpful in suggesting explicit strategies the departing leader can use to manage the exit process. On the topic of contemplating one's successor, Austin and Gilmore (1993, p. 52) comment, "It is striking how many executives have known that they will be leaving within a year or two and have not found a way either to focus on leadership succession or to expand the talent to help the organization cope with a change."

This is the territory that my article attempts to plumb further: the voluntary decision to leave, planned and discussed in advance, as opposed to the sudden and traumatic leaving that Farquhar (1996) has written about and strategically framed.

Taking Succession Seriously

It is a serious matter that succession planning in the public sector, especially below the presidential level, has not, until recently, received much attention in the literature. However, a more critical issue is that it has not received much attention in the actual world of public service. This omission, in part, reflects the fact that leaders in the public sector have themselves not taken the issue of succession planning seriously, except for obvious concerns like elections and mandates. Doing strategic executive searches in the public sector is difficult, but that is a secondary factor. What is primary, I suggest, is changing public-sector culture so that focusing on succession and beyond becomes a hallmark of strategic leadership. The public-sector executive must begin to consider the end right at the beginning. The pull to get consumed by the demands of the present is strong but must be resisted. Creating a picture of what the leader wants to leave behind will actually help focus strategic choices as well as direct the leader's attention to often overlooked strengths of the existing organization.

Public-sector leaders must surmount four types of barriers to taking succession seriously: (1) The leader's reluctance to take up the succession "task"; (2) The assumption that succession issues are beyond the scope of the leader's work; (3) Confusion about how the succession task should be framed—is it a matter of replacing oneself or of strategic "positioning?" and (4) Lack of information about how to take up the task—how to plan for succession in the midst of a shifting political environment and given regulatory and political constraints.

Reluctance to "Deal" with Succession

In *The Hero's Farewell*, a study of 50 prominent, retired, private-sector CEOs, Jeffrey Sonnenfeld (1988) discusses the "heroic self-concept of the departing leader" (p. 3) as having a great influence on succession. Part of that self-concept is a "sense of heroic mission, a feeling that one has a unique role to fill and that only the hero is capable of carrying out the responsibilities of the job." Sonnenfeld describes this attitude as "a barrier to the hero's exit" (p. 62). The greater the frustration with the heroic mission, and the more attached to the "heroic stature" of the office (another aspect of the heroic self-concept), the longer the CEOs Sonnenfeld studied stayed on the job (p. 69).

Sonnenfeld groups CEO attitudes toward departure into four categories ranging from complete reluctance to willingness. *Monarchs* will not leave voluntarily and either die in office or are overthrown. *Generals* leave with great reluctance and then plot comebacks. *Ambassadors* leave gracefully and maintain amicable ties to their old organizations. *Governors* are pleased to serve only a limited time and then leave to do something else, maintaining little contact with the company. Monarchs and generals are clearly the most averse to acknowledging that the end draws nigh, and that factor affects the likelihood of a succession planning process occurring at all.

Manfred F. R. Kets de Vries (1988) also writes about the reluctance of corporate CEOs to tackle succession planning. As does Sonnenfeld, he focuses on the retirement-age CEO in the private sector who has to overcome the "hidden fears that plague us all" (p. 57) to face stepping down.

Drawing direct parallels between public- and private-sector research on succession must be done carefully. Because the public sector has more short-term leaders than institution builders, one must take particular care in using the categories Sonnenfeld has illuminated. Nevertheless, the public sector has its share of reluctant-to-leave leaders. Certainly there are generals who believe, against all evidence, that there is some chance they can survive even an unfriendly transition of mayor or governor and thus are averse to planning for a succession they do not want to happen. One also finds monarchs who are so imbued with their heroic sense of mission that they find it unthinkable that they ever would be forced to depart, no matter how unreasonable that belief may be. They therefore resist any attempt to broach the idea of succession, much less the planning for it.

The public sector has more than its fair share of governors, too. They seem an unlikely group on whom to depend for succession planning. Their investment in the agency is often minimal, as is the agency's in them. The hope for planning must lie with the ambassadors, primarily by encouraging them to enlarge the scope of their vision to include the task of succession planning.

Assuming That Succession Is Beyond the Scope of the Leader's Work
Beyond personal reluctance lies the power of the group norm. The public sector is focused on the here-and-now, and authority is thought to be given, not taken up.

Both the private and not-for-profit sectors have a clearer focus on the future. While the American business community is sometimes criticized for attending too much to the short term, as compared to the Japanese, for example, it is clear that there are mechanisms and institutionalized roles within the private sector to carry the perspective of the future: the stockholders and the board of directors, if not the CEO. Regina Herzlinger (1994) has argued that this focus on the future and "intergenerational equity" is among the most significant responsibilities of the not-for-profit board. These future-oriented mechanisms and roles are weak or nonexistent in the public sector, certainly at the agency level. Those outside government often call mayors and governors to task for budget wizardry that risks future crisis for present peace. If agency heads are held accountable at all, it is for their management of day-to-day problems, not their investment in the future.

The literature's lack of attention to accountability for the future both underlines and reinforces the current situation. As more researchers turn their attention to this issue, it is possible there may be some shift in the public's expectations. It is likely, though, that it will need some greater push than that. Teaching in both graduate school and executive education programs can have a great impact. Just as faculty try to set a standard that expects strategic leadership from public-sector executives and discourages a narrow focus on fighting fires, teachers can extend their understanding of what it takes to be strategic. Faculty can "raise the bar" and draw a new picture of what excellence in the public sector demands: an attention to the future as well as to the present.

Confusion About the Succession "Frame"

Succession planning, even in the private sector, has all too often been regarded as a replacement issue, not a strategic responsibility to be shared among the organization's stakeholders (National Academy of Public Administration, 1992; Kets de Vries, 1988). That is, the intent is to replace X by Y, who has similar skills and training. What is missing is the link between the vacancy, or the forthcoming vacancy, and the organization's strategic needs (Gratton and Syrett, 1990)—particularly those related to preserving the innovations it has achieved. Unprecedented global competition is forcing companies in the private sector to rethink succession planning in this strategic light, and those failing to do so are increasingly being "punished" by either the market or their competition, and usually by both. I would argue that the need for such strategic thinking is equally acute in the public sector, albeit motivated by different factors. The approach, however, seems long in coming. Although some states have moved toward a more strategic view of executive recruitment, this effort has generally been initiated only after the leader has resigned or been terminated.[2]

Difficulty of Managing Succession in a Turbulent Environment

There are actually two challenges to managing succession: technology and turbulence. Public-sector leaders have limited access to search technology and search firms; they may not even understand the steps in a strategic search process. The literature is thin on the subject and offers few clues about how to proceed. Turbulence now exists in all three sectors. It is not just in the public sector that strategic planning must somehow be both short- and long-term. The source of turbulence differs by sector (competition versus election, for example), but the swirling confused winds that each produces can make the process more complicated anywhere. What separates the sectors is their reaction to turbulence.

Public-sector leaders too often allow the turbulence to limit their scope of action ("there will be a new mayor so I have no control"), whereas private-sector leaders are expected to "manage" the turbulence ("how can we move into this new market and fast?"). Elections need not doom the process of executive succession. If the first three barriers could be overcome and leaders had the will—were expected to plan for succession and saw it as a strategic task—the technology could be acquired and the turbulence acknowledged but not succumbed to. Keeping these barriers in mind, we turn to an example of how a public-sector succession can be managed successfully and how hard-won innovations can survive the transition.

Managing a Public-Sector Transition: A Case Study

The New York City Department of Juvenile Justice was created as a separate executive-branch agency in 1979. I served as its commissioner for seven years, from 1983 to 1990. During my tenure, the department accomplished two major goals. We revitalized a bureaucracy that had originally been part of a "mega-agency" and had lost all sense of purpose and efficiency before being reincarnated as a separate department in 1979 (Gilmore and Schall, 1986). We developed a clear mission and role for juvenile detention. Overall, we created an innovative organization, and believed that sustaining our innovations and the impetus to innovate were critically important.[3] The executive staff of the Juvenile Justice Department had become a team in Katzenbach and Smith's (1993) sense. We had moved from being preoccupied with handling an endless supply of short-term issues toward building the capacity for and the pattern of looking ahead. Crucial to this focus was creating the notion of case management as a way to make real our newly defined mission of custody and care and to explore its implications for the children we served and the staff attending to them. Although I was offered opportunities to leave the department early on, I determined that two additional goals had to be reached before I felt "finished" enough to depart. The first involved institutionalizing our case management program throughout the agency. The second was receiving final city approval of our plans to replace a much maligned secure detention facility with two new, smaller, community-based facilities.

By early 1988, these goals were well on their way toward accomplishment, and I believed the time for new leadership was nearing. I discussed my role in the transition process with Tom Gilmore, an organizational consultant to the department and author of *Making a Leadership Change* (Gilmore, 1988). It is to his thinking and framework that we owe much of the work that followed, beginning with a retreat, in the fall of 1988, for the executive staff.

Launching the "Finishing Up" Phase

During this multiday retreat, we began by discussing how our group was currently faring and what work each unit in the agency would be undertaking in the next two years. Then, each executive staff member outlined what his or her own time horizon was likely to be, and how that did or did not dovetail with the work to be accomplished. In essence, we acknowledged we were launching a "finishing up" phase, with all that implied: pride in achievement, exhaustion from the effort, disappointment about unrealized goals, and full doses of the irritation and affection built up over the years. I announced my intention to leave at this time but did not actually leave for 18 months.

We then turned to issues of both legacy and succession: legacy to ensure that our innovations would survive and succession as a major strategy. As to succession, we determined that we preferred someone from our own ranks. By the end of the retreat, not only had we "chosen" our candidate, the assistant commissioner for secure detention, she had begun to see herself as a possible successor. But how could we ensure that our legacy would be preserved? We invented four questions for ourselves, which we attempted to address simultaneously during the retreat and for the next year and more. We saw these challenges, in fact, as a set of Russian dolls, each nested in another:

▲ How could we get our candidate appointed as the next commissioner of the Juvenile Justice Department?
▲ If this failed, how could we get someone else who would continue our innovations and our vision?
▲ If this too failed, and a nonsupporter was appointed, how could we keep successful innovations alive?
▲ If all else failed, could we leave a "treasure map" so a future supportive commissioner could rediscover what we had done?

We tackled these questions simultaneously by scenario-playing, by anticipating pitfalls, and by creating alternative paths—what Bardach (1977) calls the work of "dirty-minded implementors." Our strategies are discussed below in reverse order from the list of questions.

Designing a Treasure Map

The idea was, if all else had failed, to provide the next supportive commissioner with a series of clues about our efforts—our treasures. We decided, for example, to leave behind the following:

▲ Traces of each of our innovative programs, rather than cutting any one (in the face of significant budget cuts) to spare the rest
▲ At least one staff person for each program so it could be fairly easily resurrected
▲ A good written record in files and public documents about our accomplishments
▲ Champions for each major initiative

More generally, we knew we were leaving behind a staff imbued with a vision of innovation and excellence.

Our support and acknowledgment of the staff's good work had been a hallmark of our administration, and we counted on their enhanced capacity to carry forward much of the innovation.

We were not naive enough to believe that, if discovered, our treasures would get resurrected under the same names and exactly in the same way. That was not the goal. We were not looking for eternal life; rather, we hoped that the clues might somehow provoke new ideas to sustain our momentum and direction.

Keeping Successful Innovations Alive

The two new tactics we pursued were preparing people and "hardwiring" the system. We also took advantage of previous strategic decisions to help preserve our legacy of innovative programs.

Preparing People

By early 1989 the executive staff began identifying talent at the next level down within each unit. Determining the criteria for such identification was not a simple matter, however, and provoked heated debates about overall skills, vision, agency mission, managerial ability, and other factors. Nevertheless, we compiled a list of about 30 people and then assessed each person's strengths and weaknesses and the likelihood of the individual's staying on with the agency. We specified what each needed for professional development and began connecting her or him with appropriate opportunities—pledging that we would watch out for each other's staff and help them along the way. From this review, for example, we drew upon the talent of a staff assistant with the potential of developing managerial capacity and targeted a heretofore overlooked senior operational manager for more cross-agency work and exposure to the overall system. As we grew to understand who would be leaving, we discussed who could be groomed to take over.

Compiling this list helped immensely in focusing our training resources. As we learned of various city-wide programs, for example, we referred to our list so people on it could be offered these opportunities.

Hardwiring

Some things in organizations have a life of their own; they go on against almost all efforts to change them. At the Juvenile Justice Department those things included the forms used to process kids. I remember two years into my tenure finding forms in use that predated the 1979 creation of the department as a separate agency. This infuriated me then. Later, it intrigued me. What about those forms made them survive despite our efforts to create new systems? They seemed almost like permanent fixtures of the agency; they were hardwired. In a deliberate effort to create an equivalent method with equal sticking power, we turned our attention to what we hoped might be our version of those old forms: the department's newly developed case-management computer-tracking system. We put a great deal of energy into moving that ahead. We believed that if a system was in place, hardwired, which in effect systematized the case management of individual children and reported data, it would carry a great deal of weight. We knew that weight could easily become inertia: it would take an effort of significant proportion to shift away from it.

Our focus on hardwiring also extended to the department's external relationships, particularly in the realm of oversight. "Blessed" with multiple agencies overseeing our work, we figured that if they became accustomed to receiving certain data, reported in certain ways, they would be likely to request that information and format subsequently and exert some pressure toward our case management approach and system to receive it.

Strategic Decisions

Earlier, we had decided to run a community-based aftercare program ourselves rather than contract it out; doing so involved tremendous effort, including establishing new civil service positions. We felt that in an (inevitable) financial crisis, it would be easier for the city to cancel contracts than to authorize layoffs, and we were right. We experienced successive rounds of budget cuts but were able to hold on to at least a core of staff. Also, our intensive home-based program, Family Ties, an alternative to costly state placement, was positioned as a revenue-enhancer: each staff person should not be charged to our budget as a cost, we insisted, but instead counted as saving the state and city together $70,000 per child placed with Family Ties. As a result, the Juvenile Justice Department actually added positions in the program when the overall budget was cut.

Finding a Successor Who Would Continue Our Efforts

Because New York City was facing a mayoral campaign (between David Dinkins and Rudolph Giuliani) as we were devising our legacy and succession strategies, we designed scenarios for each candidate based on whom he might want as commissioner of the Juvenile Justice Department. We brainstormed a range of issues including values, ethnicity, and gender and considered people fitting various profiles. We wanted to be able to present a list of real candidates if someone asked—and to present that list even if no one did. We then went on to think about who would likely be influential in the new mayor's decision-making process and whether we knew them or knew someone who did.

Getting Our Candidate Appointed

David Dinkins was elected, and his approach to appointing commissioners was decentralized, bordering on the chaotic. Committees named for each agency were asked to interview candidates and make recommendations to the mayor. I knew the person chairing the Juvenile Justice group and talked with her directly. Along with others, our candidate was interviewed; she was recommended and ultimately selected to be the new commissioner.

Managing the Feelings

Although the decision to leave the Department of Juvenile Justice was strictly my own, and I strongly attempted to ensure that the transition was smooth, the process was hardly easy. Indeed, years after, when I began writing this article, I thought that I had announced my intention to leave six months prior to my departure—only after checking notes did I realize it actually had been 18 months. This confusion reflects the difficulties involved. There were issues of authority, over hiring, for example, and the natural tension each of us felt between being ready to move on and reluctant to leave. Managing one's own succession is not a simple affair, which is why, in the public and private sector, the issue of succession itself and the process of seeking a successor are so often badly handled.

Yet I believe that when a team has invested as much as we had in creating and innovating organization, the work is unfinished if you have not attempted to think strategically about its continuation. Today, the department's case-management system and the Aftercare and Family Ties programs are all in place, although reduced by budget cuts. While my successor remained committed to the agenda we had developed together, she took the agency in new directions with a focus on prevention. She remained at Juvenile Justice for four years and her successor has worked hard to keep the basic programs in place and move the agency forward.

Moving Forward

How can we persuade public-sector leaders to take up the task of succession? Sector does not matter when it comes to the leader's dark side; the wish to believe in one's own immortality and to stay in control (Kets de Vries, 1988) can be found in leaders across sectors. Although leaders in all sectors confront relentless demands on their time and energies, private-sector cultures work more powerfully to stress the need to plan ahead. We will have to cultivate that emphasis in the public sector if we seek it. We can begin by searching for stories or case examples of successful and strategic public-sector transitions. We can attempt to set the expectation through education, solidify it through public attention, and seek to attract ambassadors to the work of the public sector.

This is not the easiest of times to build a focus on the long term, however. There is a serious disconnect between the demands on, and expectations of, public-sector leaders and their lengths of stay. Perhaps the "connect" is all too clear: as citizens we ask a lot, offer little in terms of understanding and support (let alone compensation), blame easily, and reward infrequently. In any event, the average tenure of public-sector agency heads is less than two years. Given the impact of such a brief tenure on expected results, advice is being offered about how to shorten the learning curve or reach full speed more quickly. These observations, while well intentioned, seem inevitably to fall short. Public-sector leaders need to stay longer and focus more on the future to ensure the quality of government we need.

Democracies offer citizens an opportunity, through elections, to signal their preferences, and elected officials have the right to create new directions and change course. Yet both citizens and elected officials must avoid "change for change's sake." Not only can that attitude slide all too easily into simple-minded government-bashing, with the public increasingly losing respect for any government programs and any government worker; it also severely constrains government's capacity to go forward and build on the best of its efforts—in other words, its capacity to sustain innovation.

Both the public and those in the government need to learn to honor the past and build upon it. We must begin creating the expectation that the public sector can, and should, focus on the longer term. As I have suggested in this article, senior officials, whether elected or appointed, must not only think strategically during their tenure but also be oriented beyond their tenure. Developing the willingness and ability to devise an effective approach to succession planning is a crucial step in that process.

Acknowledgment

The author wishes to thank Bob Behn and the participants in the 1994 Duke University Faculty Seminar on Organizational Innovation in State and Local Government, sponsored by the Ford Foundation, for their reactions and assistance in working through issues of public-sector succession. Katherine Farquhar demonstrated extraordinary generosity in offering a thorough and thoughtful critique of an earlier version of this article. The comments of the anonymous reviewers are also very much appreciated. Finally, Tom Gilmore's earlier assistance and continuous support deserve acknowledgment here.

Notes

1. See Yin (1979) for an early discussion of the routinization of innovations.

2. In the early 1980s, the Edna McConnell Clark Foundation funded what was then the executive search firm of Isaacson, Ford, Webb to be available to governors looking for new commissioners of correction. And the National Governors Association, with funding from the Robert Wood Johnson Foundation, began a State Health Recruitment Center in the early 1990s that lasted no more than two years. Individual governors and mayors have turned to search firms from time to time, but most rely on a narrow pool of people they know.

3. The Department of Juvenile Justice won the Ford Foundation/Kennedy School of Government Innovation Award in State and Local Government in 1986, the first year of the awards program, for its case-management program for at-risk youth. The department was also recognized in the Public Broadcasting System documentary, "Excellence in the Public Sector with Tom Peters." Additional program innovations included creating an Aftercare Program and adapting Home Builders to the juvenile justice system in a program we called Family Ties.

References

Austin, Michael J. and Thomas N. Gilmore. 1993. "Executive Exit: Multiple Perspectives on Managing the Leadership Transition." *Administration in Social Work*, vol. 17 (1): 47–60.

Bardach, Eugene.1977. *The Implementation Game: What Happens After a Bill Becomes a Law*. Cambridge, MA: MIT Press.

Farquhar, Katherine. 1991. "Leadership in Limbo: Organization Dynamics During Interim Administrations." *Public Administration Review*, vol. 51 (3): 210.

Farquhar, Katherine. 1996. "A Tough Act to Follow: Traumatic Executive Departure and the Post-Transformational Context." *International Journal of Public Administration*, December.

Farquhar, Katherine, guest editor. 1995. *Human Resource Management*, vol. 34 (spring).

Fredrickson, James W., Donald C. Hambrick, and Sara Baumrin. 1988. "A Model of CEO Dismissal." *Academy of Management Review*, vol. 13 (2): 255–270.

Gilmore, Thomas N. and Don Ronchi. 1995. "Managing Predecessors' Shadows in Executive Transitions." *Human Resource Management*, vol. 34 (1): ll-26.

Gilmore, Thomas N. 1988. *Making a Leadership Change: How Organizations and Leaders Can Handle Leadership Transitions Successfully*. San Francisco: Jossey-Bass.

Gilmore, Thomas N. and Ellen Schall. 1986. "The Use of Case Management as a Revitalizing Theme in a Juvenile Justice Agency." *Public Administration Review*, vol. 46 (3): 267–274.

Gordon, Gil E. and Ned Rosen, 1981. "Critical Factors in Leadership Succession." *Organizational Behavior and Human Performance*, vol. 27, 227–254.

Gouldner, Alvin W. 1950. "The Problem of Succession and Bureaucracy." In A. W. Gouldner, ed., *Studies in Leadership*. New York: Harper & Brothers, pp. 644–662.

Gratton, Lynda and Michel Syrett. 1990. "Heirs Apparent: Succession Strategies for the Future." *Personnel Management,* January, pp. 34–38.

Greenblatt, Milton. 1983. "Management Succession: Some Major Parameters." *Human Science Press*.

Herzlinger, Regina. 1994. "Effective Oversight: A Guide for Non profit Directors." *Harvard Business Review*, July-August, pp. 52–60.

Katzenbach, Jon R. and Douglas K Smith. 1993. *The Wisdom of Teams: Creating the High Performance Organization*. Boston: Harvard Business School Press.

Kets de Vries, Manfred F. R. 1988. "The Dark Side of CEO Succession." *Harvard Business Review*, vol. 88 (1): 56–60.

National Academy of Public Administration. 1992. *Paths to Leadership: Executive Succession Planning in the Federal Government*. Washington, D.C.: National Academy of Public Administration.

Rainey, Hal G. and Barton Wechsler. 1988. "Executive-Level Transition: Toward a Conceptual Framework." *Public Productivity Review*, vol. 13 (1).

Rainey, Hal G. and Barton Wechsler. 1992. "Study of Succession Planning and Executive Selection: Preliminary Research Results." *Literature Review and Annotated Bibliography*, June.

Sonnenfeld, Jeffrey A. 1988. *The Hero's Farewell: What Happens When CEO's Retire*. New York: Oxford University Press.

Yin, Robert K. 1979. *Changing Urban Bureaucracies: How New Practices Become Routinized.* Lexington, MA: Lexington Books.

Case 3: How a Nonprofit Organization Plans for Succession: Next in Line

Elaine's Perspective

When my husband retired, I realized that the day was approaching when I would no longer work for the Greensboro Regional Realtors Association (GRRA). Having worked diligently to turn the association into a good-to-great organization—a Jim Collins concept explored in his book by the same name (2001, HarperCollins)—I made a deliberate decision that given the opportunity I would help the association continue on its path to excellence no matter who led the organization.

In the fall of 2000, I contacted the incoming board president and president-elect to discuss my decision to leave the association at the end of 2002. I informed them that I had identified one employee as my potential successor—Michael Barr, GRRA's chief operating officer. Having worked closely with Michael for a little more than a year, I saw in him several qualities that exemplified leadership:

▲ Humility

▲ A professional willingness to do what had to be done

▲ The willingness to channel energy into the association rather than into himself

▲ The ability to credit staff and volunteers, when appropriate

▲ A desire to develop both personally and professionally

Based on my recommendation to consider an internal candidate for my position, the incoming president and president-elect both felt that a succession plan was in order. The next decision was whether I or a consultant should put the plan together.

Shortly after my conversation with the president and president-elect, the full executive committee met and decided that I should create the succession plan. The committee believed that my knowledge of the association, its mission, and its needs—as well as my 10 years in its top staff position—gave me the insight required to create a thorough plan. Additionally, the committee expressed complete trust in me and my ability to not compromise the association. In total, the committee felt that a solid management plan for succession would be an important part of the association's efforts to develop talent, meet organizational needs, and improve the association's overall results on behalf of members.

Using my job description, a list of things that I did that were not in my official

Source: Elaine H. Ernest and Michael P. Barr, "Next in Line," *Association Management*, 55:10 (2003), 42. Used with permission of *Association Management.*

job description, knowledge gained from scanning literature on CEO skill sets, and my understanding of the association's strategic plan, I drafted a work plan that defined the responsibilities and challenges of the executive position and outlined the areas in which I would coach and mentor Michael. It was early March 2001 when I submitted this draft succession plan to the executive committee. The committee accepted the plan in mid-March, and Michael and I began discussions about his long-range career plans. I asked him questions such as:

▲ Are you interested in obtaining the Certified Association Executive (CAE) designation?

▲ Are you interested in expanding your responsibilities in the association and the community?

▲ Are you willing to travel with me to additional professional development seminars?

▲ Are you willing to work with me as your mentor for an opportunity to become a CEO? (No promises were made, of course.)

His affirmative answers noted, we started working through the actual plan outline.

Because Michael was COO, all staff reported to him. To free up time for him to work through the succession plan, we diverted some of his day-to-day responsibilities to other staff members. Job descriptions for senior managers were reworked to lessen Michael's workload. To explain this shift in activities, we informed staff that the executive committee wanted Michael to be more involved with the overall operations and mission of the association. While this was true, we did not apprise staff that Michael was being groomed as my potential replacement.

For the next 15 months, Michael and I spent a few hours each week reviewing the plan, setting priorities for the next month, making adjustments when necessary, and reporting to the executive committee on a quarterly basis. The committee left the decisions of progress, needed training, and adjustments to me, with input from Michael.

Here are a few things that I learned from this experience.

1. Every CEO is capable of doing succession planning if he or she cares about the organization.
2. Succession planning is not an easy task. Little research is available about it, especially for the not-for-profit sector.
3. Succession planning is an excellent way to assess the organization, look at trends, peek at what is coming down the road, and realize your strengths and weaknesses as an executive.

Working through this plan with leadership and another high-level manager, it was easy to see what habits made the association successful and what areas needed more attention. It also solidified the organization's core values and made it clear what was important to continue.

Michael's Perspective

After I agreed to and signed the work plan outline, I really got busy. I'd like to say the task ahead of me looked simple, but it didn't. At times I felt as though I was pledging a fraternity all over again. However, Elaine was a wonderful coach and mentor. Whether this adventure would turn out as suggested was anyone's guess. My focus was on learning as much as I could about association management, qualifying to sit for and passing the CAE exam, accomplishing the items detailed in the work plan, building a network of colleagues, and enjoying the experience. The plan was specific and intense. It outlined nine major components of the executive position and specified several competencies in each area. Following are the components of the work plan and some of my prominent accomplishments in each area.

Essential Management Responsibilities

This area included nine components such as financial oversight, office administration, and understanding the parallel structures of the association. Accomplishments:

▲ Worked with and advised association volunteer groups, task forces, committees, directors, officers, and presidents.

▲ Supervised staff; evaluated job descriptions, performance, salary administration, and work processes to provide high-quality and efficient services to the membership.

▲ Developed a three-year budget model and new reports for the board of directors on nondues revenue sources.

▲ Developed a new member benefits program that included affiliating with a local credit union and offering members discounts on local products and services.

Essential Administrative Responsibilities

This component was primarily composed of human resources management issues such as employee performance, oversight of employee benefits plans, and compensation planning. Accomplishments:

▲ Coordinated employee searches that included position marketing, resume evaluations, telephone and on-site interviews, compensation negotiations, and follow-up correspondence.

▲ Researched and presented a new 401(k) retirement program and an employee education assistance program, which the board approved.

Research and Statistics

Among other things, this area dealt with member demographics, trends in the profession, and industry demographics. Accomplishments:

▲ Collaborated with a local university economist to provide our membership with local and regional market reports.
▲ Collaborated with a local university professor to produce an unbiased survey for the association membership.

Information Technology

This area included competencies such as keeping members up to date with industry technology trends and continual analysis and implementation of the membership's technology needs. Accomplishments:

▲ Developed and implemented a technology infrastructure plan that included replacing the phone system, upgrading computer software, and adapting wireless technology.
▲ Developed a new Web site that allows the membership to pay association bills online and provides segmented information according to members' preferences.
▲ Provided the membership with various technology-training opportunities, which had been requested through membership surveys.

Facilities Management

This area covered everything from the HVAC system to aesthetics and landscaping. Accomplishments:

▲ Managed and supervised the association's banquet facility renovations and grounds beautification.
▲ Managed and supervised the association's building maintenance contractors and banquet facility operations.

Strategic Planning

True competency in this area was defined by the ability to keep staff focused on the vision of the association, continually evaluate the association's operations, and commit and adhere to the strategic objective of the organization. Accomplishments:

▲ Participated in the research and preparation of the strategic planning board retreat, including negotiating with consultants, preparatory work with consultants, and execution of retreat, followed by the development and yearly refinement of the plan.
▲ Focused staff on association priorities to accomplish the strategic goals of the association within the set timeline.

Internal and External Relations
Government affairs, coalition building, and public relations were the bedrocks of this component. Accomplishments:

▲ Attended local, state, and National Realtor Association board of director meetings.

▲ Represented the association at the Triad Real Estate and Building Industry Coalition and at other regional coalitions.

▲ Continually represented the association at community events, local government meetings, and association events.

▲ Networked with the leaders of the local and state associations.

Continuing Education
One of the key thrusts of this area was attaining the CAE designation, showing a commitment to association management, and continual learning. Accomplishments:

▲ Attended numerous coaching and training seminars offered by ASAE, the National Association of Realtors, the North Carolina Association of Realtors, and GRRA on various subjects.

▲ Earned my CAE designation.

General Working Knowledge
The final component focused on understanding industry-specific processes, our bylaws, and the financial aspects of the association. Accomplishments:

▲ Trained to administer the association's professional standards and arbitration process.

▲ Studied and enforced multiple listing service rules and regulations and association bylaws and rules and regulations.

▲ Acted as chapter administrator for 360-member North Carolina Certified Commercial Investment Members, which the association manages.

After working through each component of the succession plan, I submitted a letter to the executive committee expressing my interest in the CEO position. At this point it was May 2002, and I was able to include a detailed description of how I had accomplished the work set out in the plan.

Coming to the Conclusion
A month later, the full board of directors met. The president informed the directors that Elaine was leaving her position as CEO of GRRA at year's end. Copies of the completed work plan and Michael's letter of interest were distributed. Discus-

sion ensued about the succession process and whether the job opening should be taken outside the organization.

A minority of board members felt that if Michael were truly qualified, he would win out in an extensive search. The majority of the directors, however, felt comfortable that the plan was comprehensive and that the executive committee had been sufficiently involved through its receipt of progress reports. An open search, in their opinion, would cost the association time and money. After taking a vote, the executive committee was granted permission to interview Michael for the position. If the committee was not satisfied with the interview, the search would be opened, and a selection committee appointed.

"Ten of eleven good-to-great CEOs came from inside the company," says Jim Collins in his book *Good to Great.* The Greensboro Regional Realtors Association found that to be the case after Michael's successful interview for the chief staff executive position. In mid-July 2002, more than a year after the draft succession plan was submitted, GRRA's board president started contract negotiations for the association's new president. Michael took over the top spot on January 1, 2003.

Mentoring Magic

Since Michael P. Barr, CAE, took over as executive vice president of the Greensboro Regional Realtors Association, North Carolina, in January, he has started his own mentoring program with senior staff. Read what he has to say on the subject.

Association Management: Why did you start the program?

Michael P. Barr, CAE: Being a product of mentoring, I saw the value in developing staff to their fullest and helping them with their career goals. Essentially that's what Elaine did for me. It's a win-win for both the association and the employees.

Association Management: What's involved?

Barr: I meet regularly with staff. We consistently go over both their work goals and professional goals. It's individualized according to their preferences, because we're trying to help them achieve their professional best. I take them to conferences, send them to workshops, and help them achieve the designation of their choosing. Basically, I go over their goals and objectives and help them get the education they need to obtain their goals. The board thinks that this is so important that it has increased the budget line item for staff development.

Association Management: Who can participate?

Barr: It's open to anyone who has expressed an interest in association management. Obviously, it has to be tied to the job. Senior staff is really taking advantage of it.

Association Management: How's it been received so far?

Barr: I have full participation. Those who have expressed an interest in learning what the top job entails, what running an association entails, are really receptive to learning. Empowering them to take on projects and responsibility has been a big plus in the operation of the association.

Association Management: What advice would you give to staffers?

Barr. Approach mentoring with the best attitude possible. It's a win no matter what happens. You're going to do a lot of extra work, but it's good preparation for executive-level positions. Get ready for long hours.

Resources
Articles
"Executive Selection: A Systematic, Team-Based Approach," *Executive IdeaLink,* July 2001.

"What If You Were Gone," *Association Management,* August 2000.

"Mentoring: A Tool for Learning and Development," *Association Educator,* October 1999.

Books
Knowdell, Richard L. *Building a Career Development Program: Nine Steps for Effective Implementation.* Consulting Psychologists Press, 1996.

Rothwell, William J. *Effective Succession Planning: Ensuring Leadership Continuity and Building Talent From Within.* AMACOM, 2000.

Byham, William C., Audrey B. Smith, and Matthew J. Paese. *Grow Your Own Leaders: How to Identify, Develop, and Retain Leadership Talent.* Financial Times, Prentice-Hall, 2002.

Wolfe, Rebecca Luhn. *Systematic Succession Planning: Building Leadership From Within.* 1996, Crisp Publications, 1996.

Web Site
Succession Planning Library (www.managementhelp.org/staffing /planning/sccs_pln/sccs_pln.htm)

Case 4: Small Business Case:
Passing the Torch

Jim Gibney, president of Warren Pike Associates, says he grew up in the business. "I was always drawn to mechanical things," says Gibney, whose family-owned power transmission and motion control business is headquartered in Needham, Massachusetts "As a child, I became interested in the business. During the school vacations, I would go in to the business and help out. There I got to learn from one of the best salesmen there is, my father."

Gibney characterizes his father as a master salesman and as a leader. He recounts his father's career at Warner Electric before purchasing Warren Pike Associates followed by the purchases of W.M. Steele Co. and Cohen Machinery Co. to form J.G. Industries, Inc. Gibney says his siblings were drawn to other interests and have pursued other successful careers, but that he followed his

Source: Richard Trombly, "Passing the Torch," *Industrial Distribution,* 90:4(2001), 69–72. Used with permission from *Industrial Distribution.*

father's footsteps from the beginning. He says that wasn't always a simple path. "My father was a hard worker and that was one of the values he instilled in me," says Gibney. "I worked my way up through the ranks. I've been in shipping and receiving, inside sales and outside sales before taking on a role in management."

His father still remains active in the company and retains the title of CEO, but after years of working hard for the company, he is able to work on something else—his golf game down in Florida. Meanwhile, Gibney has taken on the role of president.

"It was an easy transition," says Gibney. "I have been in upper management for so long and was already very familiar with the business. My siblings had never been involved with the business, so they weren't concerned with the process of succession. My father and I had discussed it over the years and we knew I would take over when the time was right." Gibney said they did very little in the way of formal succession planning.

"After some internal planning and adjustments," says Gibney, "we realized that the end of year 2000 would be the right time."

Gibney admits that part of the success of the transition relies upon keeping open channels of communication. While nothing was formalized in their planning, the details of succession were discussed and understood by all parties, including JG Industries' 17 employees. "Communication is key," says Gibney. "We have a family atmosphere and we involve the employees in the business. People usually resist change and that can make succession difficult, but we involved them in the process. I think, by being included in this way, they are now excited by new opportunities in a rapidly changing industry."

Will his own children take over the family business? Gibney says his children are between the ages of seven and 13, so it is a little too soon to tell if they will be involved. "Perhaps, down the road," speculates Gibney.

Not all children grow into their parents' roles and not all successions occur so simply and with such positive results, points out Robert Middleton, a partner with the Chicago law firm of Nisen & Elliot.

"In most cases there are some hard truths," says Middleton. "Many entrepreneurs spend their entire lives sacrificing time and energy only to have the whole organization fall apart and maybe tear the family apart in the process."

Marc Silverman, president of Providence, Rhode Island-based consulting firm Strategic Initiatives Inc., says that when he counsels a family business, the first thing is to try to separate the family from the business.

"Then we can decide what we want for the family and what we want for the business," says Silverman. "By looking at the family and the business, we can determine what they both need to be successful."

Silverman advises a team approach by getting all of the family involved. He suggests a family council to assist in planning for the business's future and in choosing a leader that will be best suited to the business—as well as resolving issues of the siblings that are not groomed for succession.

Outsiders can be an enormous amount of help, says Silverman, though he admits that can be difficult for entrepreneurs who are used to doing things in an autocratic style. It is hard to be objective and many of these issues are closely tied to the psychological issues of aging. He suggests bringing in a consultant early in the process if any obstacles develop.

"It is like tooth decay," says Silverman. "The problem gets bigger the longer you wait." Jefferey Gallant, a partner with Goodkind, Labaton, Rudoff & Sucharow, also suggests that businesses have an advisory board. It may be made up of family members, management, or outside professionals. Gallant says a board can decide on the important issues of who should lead and what their services are worth.

Gallant says he is usually brought in for estate planning and has to bring up the topic of succession. He helps decide what makes the most sense as far as tax options and retirement, as well as for the business.

"The next step is to get all the parties involved to buy in to it," says Gallant. "It is so much easier when the owner is involved rather than handling these issues as part of an estate."

Case 5: Family Business Succession:
The Seeds of a Smooth Transition

A month before Christmas, the garden center at Shiloh Nurseries Inc. in Emigsville, Pennsylvania, looks like a scene from a Norman Rockwell painting, with decorations and holiday greens at every door and window. Along the path leading to the side entrance, flowering cabbages are in full bloom.

Inside, Michael Stebbins, 47, is busy getting ready for a Christmas selling season that will be short because of the late arrival of Thanksgiving. After 27 years as co-owner of the nursery and landscaping business with his partner, Carl Jacobs, Stebbins knows exactly how he wants everything to look.

He also knows exactly what he wants to happen to the company when he and Jacobs retire. Both want Shiloh Nurseries to remain a thriving business.

That almost didn't happen for the family that owned the company before them. When its founder died with no estate plan, his wife and son discovered they were unable to work together. The son left to form his own nursery business, taking many of Shiloh's employees with him, and his mother was forced to sell the firm, which was tallying a modest $55,000 in annual sales. Today, Stebbins and Jacobs employ 25 full-time workers and about 40 more seasonal employees, and they expect to post sales of about $3 million this year.

The two owners have six children between them but none who wants to take over the business—they've had their fill of nursery life during high school and summers home from college. Nonetheless, Stebbins and Jacobs do have two longtime, highly valued employees—their top salesman and landscape architect,

Source: "The Seeds of a Smooth Transition," *Nation's Business*, 85:4 (1997), 25. Used with permission from *Nation's Business*.

and their landscape supervisor—who would like to run a nursery and landscaping business someday.

Stebbins and Jacobs liked the idea of them running Shiloh, so they set up a buy/sell agreement with the pair under which the two employees will begin to buy the company over two consecutive five-year periods. Each employee will purchase 12 percent of the company's stock during the first five years and another 12 percent during the second, at a fixed price of two times book value (with book value being recalculated annually). Payments will be made on an installment plan bearing interest at the prime rate plus 1.5 percent.

After 10 years, the four principals will decide how to proceed. Jacobs, now 53, is likely to retire then, but Stebbins hasn't decided what he will do. Possible options include having the two employees purchase the remaining 52 percent of the company at that time or allowing a small number of other key employees to purchase some of that stock.

Either way, Stebbins and Jacobs are glad that the salesman and the landscape supervisor are becoming part owners, because they will be positioned to take over the business when necessary. Shiloh has taken out life-insurance policies on each of the four shareholding partners; the insurance is in amounts sufficient to ensure that if any of the partners dies before the buy/sell agreement is completed, the other partners will be able to meet their obligations under the agreement.

To come up with their plan, Stebbins and Jacobs drew on the advice of an estate-planning firm, Estate Archetypes Inc., in nearby York, Pennsylvania., and on Gordon Porter, a CPA and small-business consultant in Dover, Pennsylvania., before approaching their lawyer to draft the necessary documents.

"One of the reasons I'm inclined to be so sure we're doing things right is because I'm proud of the fact that we took a small business and grew it successfully," Stebbins says. "This is the company's 60th-anniversary year, and I'd like to see it be here for another 60 years."

Case 6: CEO Succession Planning Case:
Do You Have a CEO Succession Plan?

Jim Lumpkin's first move as interim chief executive officer (CEO) for U.S.–Agencies Credit Union was to eliminate the position he'd just vacated. "The credit union was top heavy," recalls Lumpkin, CEO of the Portland, Oregon, credit union. "At the time, we were spending too much money on management positions. We needed a CEO who could handle both jobs."

Then he insisted that the board undertake a detailed search, both inside and outside the credit union, for CEO candidates. "Our last CEO felt he was named by default. The board never did a full search so there never was that buy-in that

Source: Bill Merrick, "Do You Have a CEO Succession Plan?," *Credit Union Magazine* 67:7 (2001), 52. Used with permission from *Credit Union Magazine*.

they had the right person," Lumpkin explains. "I stipulated that I wouldn't apply for the job unless the board went through a full search process and really looked for who they wanted. That way there wouldn't be any second-guessing."

The board named Lumpkin CEO after a five-month search, and he has served in that capacity for four years. But watching the board struggle through the process made him recognize the need for a detailed succession plan outlining steps the board should take in case of CEO turnover—whether by resignation, termination, or death.

The credit union's recently completed succession plan details planning and preparation, general board guidelines, steps for emergency succession (broken down by the first day, week, and month), recruiting and hiring, desired qualifications and attributes, and other information. "We're a smaller company and we look at our CEO as more of an operational CEO," Lumpkin notes. "So the CEO needs to know which areas he or she would be responsible for—accounting, asset/liability management, compliance issues, examination processes, human resource administration, and investments. If the CEO leaves, board members might wonder who else will leave and how they'll run the credit union. I wanted to identify skill sets and experiences they should look for."

Among other information, the plan lists nine basic steps for CEO replacement:

1. The board hopes for 90 to 120 days' notice of intent to leave so it can have an orderly transition. The board would like to hire the new CEO at least 30 days before the departure of the current CEO. It would be preferable to allow 60 days for this transition.

2. The board will appoint a search committee to monitor the plan and recommend final candidates to the full board. The board's executive committee will make up the search committee in part or in whole. It's recommended that the committee consist of three to five individuals. It's advisable that the current CEO not be a member of the search committee.

3. The board will decide whether the search committee will conduct the full search process or whether to use an outside consulting firm. If the board hires an outside firm, determine the company's responsibilities and cost, and specify details in a signed, written contract. Use a firm that's familiar with credit union needs and philosophy.

4. The executive committee, with the assistance of the interim CEO and management team, will update the existing CEO job description, organizational chart, and other information, and provide it to the search committee and/or consulting firm.

5. Advertising for the CEO position will appear in local and industry trade publications.

6. All resumes will be reviewed for basic qualities and experience. Interviews will be limited to three to five candidates. The search committee or consulting firm will present the best candidate to the board. If the board

doesn't accept this candidate, the search committee or consulting firm will present the second choice.

7. Verification of candidate credentials and employability may include, but isn't limited to, educational transcripts, reference checks, credit bureau reports, CUMIS bond check, medical assessment as allowed by law, psychological appraisal, and chemical dependency testing.

8. Notification of the new CEO will be provided to the Oregon Department of Consumer and Business Services, National Credit Union Administration, Credit Union Association of Oregon, CUMIS Insurance Group, and credit union attorneys.

9. Publish articles in the quarterly newsletter to announce the current CEO's departure and introduce the new CEO.

"Having a plan makes the board and our state regulator feel better," Lumpkin says. "Also, staff knows that if something happens, the board will find a match that will fit members' needs, internal staffing needs, and the credit union's culture. It builds confidence throughout the credit union and reduces uncertainty."

NOTES

Preface

1. Warren Bennis and Burt Nanus, *Leaders: The Strategies for Taking Charge* (New York: Harper and Row, 1985), p. 2.

2. Bradley Agle, "Understanding Research on Values in Business," *Business & Society*, September 1999, 326–387. See also Ken Hultman and Bill Gellerman, *Balancing Individual and Organizational Values: Walking the Tightrope to Success* (San Francisco: Pfeiffer, 2002).

3. Charlene Marmer Solomon, "The Loyalty Factor," *Personnel Journal*, September 1992, 52–62.

4. Shari Caudron, "The Looming Leadership Crisis," *Workforce*, September 1999, 72–79.

5. Arthur Deegan, *Succession Planning: Key to Corporate Excellence* (New York: Wiley-Interscience, 1986), p. 5. [This book, while out of print, is a classic.]

6. As quoted in Harper W. Moulton and Arthur A. Fickel, *Executive Development: Preparing for the 21st Century* (New York: Oxford University Press, 1993), p. 29.

7. E. Zajac, "CEO Selection, Succession, Compensation and Firm Performance: A Theoretical Integration and Empirical Analysis," *Strategic Management Journal* 11:3 (1990), 228. See also William Rothwell, "What's Special About CEO Succession?" *Global CEO Magazine* [India], March 2004, Special Issue, 15–20.

8. R. Sahl, "Succession Planning Drives Plant Turnaround," *Personnel Journal* 71:9 (1992), 67–70.

9. "Long-Term Business Success Can Hinge on Succession Planning," *Training Directors' Forum Newsletter* 5:4 (1989), 1.

10. Dirk Dreux, "Succession Planning and Exit Strategies," *CPA Journal* 69:9 (1999), 30–35; Oliver Esman, "Succession Planning in Small and Medium-Sized Companies," *HR Horizons* 103 (1991), 15–19; Barton C. Francis, "Family Business Succession Planning," *Journal of Accountancy* 176:2 (1993), 49–51; John O'Connell, "Triple-Tax Threat in Succession Planning," *National Underwriter* 102:40 (1998), 11, 19; T. Roger Peay and W. Gibb Dyer, Jr., "Power Orientations of Entrepreneurs and Succession Planning," *Journal of Small Business Management* 27:1 (1989), 47–52; Michael J. Sales, "Succession Planning in the Family Business," *Small Business Reports* 15:2 (1990), 31–40.

Chapter 1

1. Henry Fayol, *Administration Industrielle et Generale* (Paris: Société de l'Industrie Minerale, 1916).

2. Norman H. Carter, "Guaranteeing Management's Future Through Succession Planning," *Journal of Information Systems Management* 3:3 (1986), 13–14.

3. See the classic article, Michael Leibman, "Succession Management: The Next Generation of Succession Planning," *Human Resource Planning* 19:3 (1996), 16–29. See also Ram Charan, Stephen Drotter, and James Noel, *The Leadership Pipeline: How to Build the Leadership-Powered Company* (San Francisco: Jossey-Bass, 2001).

4. Richard Hansen and Richard H. Wexler, "Effective Succession Planning," *Employment Relations Today* 15:1 (1989), 19.

5. See Chris Argyris and Donald Schön, *Organizational Learning: A Theory of Action Perspective* (Reading, Mass.: Addison-Wesley, 1978); Peter Senge, *The Fifth Discipline: The Art and Practice of the Learning Organization* (New York: Doubleday/Currency, 1990).

6. Thomas P. Bechet, *Strategic Staffing: A Practical Toolkit for Workforce Planning* (New York: AMACOM, 2002).

7. David E. Hartley, "Tools for Talent," *T + D* 58:4 (2004): 20–22.

8. Ibid., p. 21.

9. William J. Rothwell and H. C. Kazanas, *The Strategic Development of Talent* (Amherst, Mass.: HRD Press, 2003).

10. Downloaded from http://news.ft.com/servlet/ContentServer?pagename = FT.com/Page/GenericPage2 &c = Page&cid = 1079420675546 on 18 July 2004.

11. Stephen Overell, "A Meeting of Minds Brings HR into Focus," downloaded on 18 July 2004 from http://news.ft.com/servlet/ContentServer?pagename = FT.com/StoryFT/FullStory&c = StoryFT&cid = 1079420676509&p = 10 79420675546

12. *The Human Capital Challenge* (Alexandria, Va.: ASTD, 2003).

13. J. Christopher Mihm, *Human Capital: Succession Planning and Management Is Critical Driver of Organizational Transformation* (Washington, D.C.: U.S. General Accounting Office, 2003).

14. Walter R. Mahler and Stephen J. Drotter, *The Succession Planning Handbook for the Chief Executive* (Midland Park, N.J.: Mahler Publishing Co., 1986), p. 1.

15. "Long-Term Business Success Can Hinge on Succession Planning," *Training Directors' Forum Newsletter* 5:4 (1989), 1.

16. Wilbur Moore, *The Conduct of the Corporation* (New York: Random House, 1962), p. 109.

17. Rosabeth Moss Kanter, *The Men and Women of the Corporation* (New York: Basic Books, 1977), p. 48.

18. Norman H. Carter, "Guaranteeing Management's Future Through Succession Planning," *Journal of Information Systems Management* 3:3 (1986), 13–14.

19. Thomas Gilmore, *Making a Leadership Change: How Organizations and Leaders Can Handle Leadership Transitions Successfully* (San Francisco: Jossey-Bass, 1988), p. 19.

20. William J. Rothwell and H. C. Kazanas, *The Strategic Development of Talent* (Amherst, Mass.: HRD Press, 2003).

21. Lynda Gratton and Michel Syrett, "Heirs Apparent: Succession Strategies for the Future," *Personnel Management* 22:1 (1990), 34.

22. A. Walker, "The Newest Job in Personnel: Human Resource Data Administrator," *Personnel Journal* 61:12 (1982), 5.

23. William J. Rothwell and H. C. Kazanas, *Planning and Managing Human Resources: Strategic Planning for Personnel Management*, 2nd. ed. (Amherst, Mass.: HRD Press, 2003).

24. Andrew O. Manzini and John D. Gridley, *Integrating Human Resources and Strategic Business Planning* (New York: AMACOM, 1986), p. 3.

25. Peter Capelli, "A Market-Driven Approach to Retaining Talent," *Harvard Business Review* 78:1 (2000), 103–111; Joanne Cole, "De-Stressing the Workplace," *HR Focus* 76:10 (1999), 1, 10–11; Robert Leo, "Career Counseling Works for Employers Too," *HR Focus* 76:9 (1999), 6.

26. "The Numbers Game," *Time*, 142:21 (1993), 14–15.

27. Ann Morrison, *The New Leaders: Guidelines on Leadership Diversity in America* (San Francisco: Jossey-Bass, 1992), p. 1.

28. Ibid., p. 7.

29. Arthur Sherman, George Bohlander, and Herbert Chruden, *Managing Human Resources*, 8th ed. (Cincinnati: South-Western Publishing Co., 1988), p. 226.

30. Warren Boroson and Linda Burgess, "Survivors' Syndrome," *Across the Board* 29:11 (1992), 41–45.

31. Gilmore, *Making a Leadership Change*, p. 10.

32. Morrison, *The New Leaders*, p. 1.

33. See, for instance, Robert M. Fulmer, "Choose Tomorrow's Leaders Today: Succession Planning Grooms Firms for Success." Downloaded on 19 July 2004 from http://gbr.pepperdine.edu/021/succession.html; W. Rothwell (Ed.), *Effective Succession Management: Building Winning Systems for Identifying and Developing Key Talent*, 2nd ed. [See http://www.cfor.org/News/article.asp?id=4.] (Lexington, Mass.: The Center for Organizational Research [A division of Linkage, Inc.], 2004); "Succession Management: Filling the Leadership Pipeline," *Chief Executive*, April 2004, 1, 4.

34. M. Haire, "Approach to an Integrated Personnel Policy," *Industrial Relations*, 1968, 107–117.

35. J. Stuller, "Why Not 'Inplacement?'" *Training* 30:6 (1993), 37–44.

36. William J. Rothwell, H. C. Kazanas, and Darla Haines, "Issues and Prac-

tices in Management Job Rotation Programs as Perceived by HRD Profession-als," *Performance Improvement Quarterly* 5:1 (1992), 49–69. [This article is the only existing research-based article on management job rotations that the author can find.]

37. William J. Rothwell, "Go Beyond Replacing Executives and Manage Your Work and Values." In D. Ulrich, L. Carter, M. Goldsmith, J. Bolt, & N. Smallwood (Eds.), *The Change Champion's Fieldguide* (Waltham, Mass.: Best Practice Publications, 2003), pp. 192–204.

38. Matt Hennecke, "Toward the Change-Sensitive Organization," *Training,* May 1991, 58.

39. D. Ancona and D. Nadler, "Top Hats and Executive Tales: Designing the Senior Team," *Sloan Management Review* 3:1 (1989), 19–28.

40. Ken Dychtwald, Tamara Erickson, and Bob Morison, "It's Time to Re-tire Retirement," *Harvard Business Review,* March 2004, downloaded from the online version on 3 May 2004.

Chapter 2

1. See William J. Rothwell, "Trends in Succession Management," *The Link-age, Inc.* eNewsletter, 2/15/00 (2000), presented on the Web at www.linkage inc.com/newsletter26/research.htm.

2. See the now classic article, Michael Leibman, "Succession Management: The Next Generation of Succession Planning," *Human Resource Planning* 19:3 (1996), 16–29.

3. William J. Rothwell, Robert K. Prescott, and Maria Taylor, *Strategic Human Resource Leader: How to Help Your Organization Manage the 6 Trends Affecting the Workforce* (Palo Alto, Calif.: Davies-Black Publishing, 1998).

4. Ibid.

5. P. Smith and D. Reinertsen, *Developing Products in Half the Time* (New York: Van Nostrand Reinhold, 1991).

6. See Jac Fitz-Enz, *How to Measure Human Resources Management* (New York: McGraw-Hill, 1984).

7. "The Aging Baby Boomers," *Workplace Visions,* Sept.-Oct. 1996, found at www.shrm.org/issues/0996wv01.htm.

8. "Cross-Generational Approaches," *Workforce Strategies* 17:11 (1999), WS63–WS64.

9. Shari Caudron, "The Looming Leadership Crisis," *Workforce,* Septem-ber 1999, 72–79.

10. "The Aging Baby Boomers."

11. "Gap Between Rich and Poor Keeps Widening," *The CCPA Monitor,* 1995, presented at http://infoweb.magi.com/ccpa/articles/article21t.html [Un-fortunately this site is restricted.]

12. Peter Cappelli, "A Market-Driven Approach to Retaining Talent," *Harvard Business Review,* Jan.-Feb. 2000, 103–111; Joseph Dobrian, "Amenities Gain Ground as Recruiting/Retention Tools," *HR Focus,* November 1999, 11–12.

13. Charlene Marmer Solomon, "The Loyalty Factor," *Personnel Journal,* September 1992, 52–62.

14. David L. Stum, "Five Ingredients for an Employee Retention Formula," *HR Focus,* September 1998, S9–S10.

15. Lynn E. Densford, "Corporate Universities Add Value by Helping Recruit, Retain Talent," *Corporate University Review* 7:2 (1999), 8–12.

16. See, for instance, Thomas A. Stewart, "Have You Got What It Takes," *Fortune* 140:7 (1999), 318–322.

17. Richard McDermott, "Why Information Technology Inspired but Cannot Deliver Knowledge Management," *California Management Review* 41:4 (1999), 103–117.

18. Dawn Anfuso, "Core Values Shape W. L. Gore's Innovative Culture," *Workforce* 78:3 (1999), 48–53; Donald Tosti, "Global Fluency," *Performance Improvement* 38:2 (1999), 49–54.

19. William J. Rothwell and John Lindholm, "Competency Identification, Modelling and Assessment in the USA," *International Journal of Training and Development* 3:2 (1999), 90–105. For quality control in using competencies for assessment, see: Harm Tillema, "Auditing Assessment Practices in Organizations: Establishing Quality Criteria for Appraising Competencies," *International Journal of Human Resources Development and Management,* 3:4 (2003): 359.

20. Rothwell, Prescott, and Taylor, *Strategic Human Resource Leader.*

21. Bradley Agle, "Understanding Research on Values in Business," *Business and Society* 38:3 (1999), 326–387. See also K. Blanchard and M. O'Connor, *Managing by Values* (San Francisco: Berrett-Koehler, 1997); Ken Hultman with Bill Gellerman, *Balancing Individual and Organizational Values: Walking the Tightrope to Success* (San Francisco: Pfeiffer, 2002). The classic book on values is still, of course, Milton Rokeach, *The Nature of Human Values* (New York: The Free Press, 1973).

22. W. Davidson, C., Nemec, D., Worrell, and J. Lin, "Industrial Origin of CEOs in Outside Succession: Board Preference and Stockholder Reaction," *Journal of Management and Governance,* 6 (2002): 4.

23. Linda Bushrod, "Sorting Out Succession," *European Venture Capital Journal,* February 1, 2004, p. 1; Herbert Neubauer, "The Dynamics of Succession in Family Businesses in Western European Countries," *Family Business Review* 16:4 (2003), 269–282; Slimane Haddadj, "Organization Change and the Complexity of Succession: A Longitudinal Case Study from France," *Journal of Organizational Change Management* 15:2 (2003), 135–154.

24. Wendi J. Everton, "Growing Your Company's Leaders: How Great Organizations Use Succession Management to Sustain Competitive Advantage," *The Academy of Management Executive,* 18:1 (Feb. 2004), 137.

25. Sarah McBride, "Gray Area: In Corporate Asia, A Looming Crisis Over Succession; As Empire Founders Age, Many Fail to Lay Proper Plans; 'You Want to Get Rid of Me'; Daesung's Three Heads," *Wall Street Journal*, August 7 2003, A1.

26. Barry Came, "The Succession Question," *MacLean's* 112:8 (2003), 44–45. [However, admittedly, this article is about national leadership succession rather than company succession.]

27. Matthew Bellingham and Dione Schick, "Succession Planning-Issues for New Zealand Chartered Accountants," *Chartered Accountants Journal of New Zealand* 82:10 (2003), 24.

28. Will Hickey, "A Survey of MNC Succession Planning Effectiveness in China, Summer 2001," *Performance Improvement Quarterly* 15:4 (2002), 20.

29. William J. Rothwell, "Succession Planning and Management in Government: Dreaming the Impossible Dream," *IPMA-HR News* 69:10 (2003), 1, 7–9.

30. William J. Rothwell, "Start Assessing Retiring University Officials at Your University," *HR on Campus* 5:8 (2002), 5.

31. James Olan Hutcheson, "Triple Header: For Succession Planning to Succeed, Retiring Business Owners Need Life-Planning Skills as Well as Financial Advice," *Financial Planning*, April 1, 2004, 1; Khai Sheang Lee, Guan Hua Lim, and Wei Shi Lim, "Family Business Succession: Appropriation Risk and Choice of Successor," *The Academy of Management Review* 28:4 (October 2003), 657; William S. White, Timothy D. Krinke, and David L. Geller, "Family Business Succession Planning: Devising an Overall Strategy," *Journal of Financial Service Professionals* 58:3 (2004), 67–86.

32. William S. White, Timothy D. Krinke, and David L. Geller, "Family Business Succession Planning: Devising an Overall Strategy," *Journal of Financial Service Professionals* 58:3 (2004), 67.

33. D. Carey and D. Ogden, *CEO Succession: A Window On How Boards Can Get It Right When Choosing A New Chief Executive* (New York: Oxford University Press, 2000).

34. A classic article that summarizes much succession research is I. Kesner and T. Sebora, "Executive Succession: Past, Present and Future," *Journal of Management* 20:2 (1994), 327–372.

35. S. Haddadj, "Organization Change and the Complexity of Succession: A Longitudinal Case Study from France," *Journal of Organizational Change Management* 16:2 (2003), 135–153.

36. "Global CEO Turnover at Record Highs," *Financial Executive* 19:5 (2003), 10.

37. D. Gabriel, "Lost Leaders," *Telephony* 243:10 (2002), 44.

38. "PPG Industries Speeds, Refines Succession Preparation Process," *Workforce Strategies* 17:10 (1999), WS57–WS58.

Chapter 3

1. This paragraph is based on information in C. Derr, C. Jones, and E. Toomey, "Managing High-Potential Employees: Current Practices in Thirty-three U.S. Corporations," *Human Resource Management* 27:3 (1988), 278. For more recent information, see also William J. Rothwell and H. C. Kazanas, *Building In-House Leadership and Management Development Programs* (Westport, Conn.: Quorum, 1999), and David D. Dubois and William J. Rothwell, *The Competency Toolkit*, 2 vols. (Amherst, Mass.: HRD Press, 2000). For more recent thinking on high-potential workers, see Morgan W. McCall, Jr., *High Flyers: Developing the Next Generation of Leaders* (Boston: Harvard Business School Press, 1998).

2. See William J. Rothwell, *The Action Learning Guidebook: A Real-Time Strategy for Problem-Solving, Training Design, and Employee Development* (San Francisco: Pfeiffer, 1999).

3. See S. Cunningham, "Coaching Today's Executive," *Public Utilities Fortnightly* 128:2 (1991), 22–25; Steven J. Stowell and Matt Starcevich, *The Coach: Creating Partnerships for a Competitive Edge* (Salt Lake City: The Center for Management and Organization Effectiveness, 1987).

4. Charles E. Watson, *Management Development Through Training* (Reading, Mass.: Addison-Wesley, 1979).

5. Manuel London and Stephen A. Stumpf, *Managing Careers* (Reading, Mass.: Addison-Wesley, 1982), p. 274.

6. James E. McElwain, "Succession Plans Designed to Manage Change," *HR Magazine* 36:2 (1991), 67.

7. James Fraze, "Succession Planning Should Be a Priority for HR Professionals," *Resource*, June 1988, 4.

8. Ibid.

9. Ibid.

10. Ibid.

11. Thomas North Gilmore, *Making a Leadership Change: How Organizations Can Handle Leadership Transitions Successfully* (San Francisco: Jossey-Bass, 1988), p. 10.

12. Fraze, "Succession Planning Should Be a Priority," 4.

13. David W. Rhodes, "Succession Planning—Overweight and Underperforming," *The Journal of Business Strategy* 9:6 (1988), 62.

14. Ibid.

15. Ibid.

16. See Roland Sullivan, Linda Fairburn, and William J. Rothwell, "The Whole System Transformation Conference: Fast Change for the 21st Century." In S. Herman, ed., *Rewiring Organizations for the Networked Economy: Organizing, Managing, and Leading in the Information Age* (San Francisco: Pfeiffer, 2002), p. 117.

17. See Jane Magruder Watkins and Bernard J. Mohr, *Appreciative Inquiry: Change at the Speed of Imagination* (San Francisco: Pfeiffer, 2001).

18. See Diana Whitney, Amanda Trosten-Bloom, and David Cooperrider, *The Power of Appreciative Inquiry: A Practical Guide to Positive Change* (San Francisco: Berrett-Koehler, 2003).

Chapter 4

1. See R. White, "Motivation Reconsidered: The Concept of Competence," *Psychological Review* 66 (1959), 279–333.

2. David C. McClelland, "Testing for Competence Rather Than for 'Intelligence,'" *American Psychologist,* January 1973, 1–14.

3. See J. C. Flanagan, "The Critical Incident Technique," *Psychological Bulletin*, April 1954, 327–358; J. Hayes, "A New Look at Managerial Competence: The AMA Model for Worthy Performance," *Management Review*, November 1979, 2–3; Patricia McLagan, "Competency Models," *Training and Development Journal*, December 1980, 23; L. Spencer & S. Spencer, *Competence at Work: Models for Superior Performance* (New York: John Wiley & Sons, 1993).

4. A. R. Boyatzis, *The Competent Manager: A Model for Effective Performance* (New York: John Wiley & Sons, 1982), pp. 20–21.

5. David D. Dubois and William J. Rothwell, *The Competency Toolkit*, 2 vols. (Amherst, Mass.: HRD Press, 2000).

6. Ibid.

7. Ibid.

8. See David D. Dubois, *The Executive's Guide to Competency-Based Performance Improvement* (Amherst, Mass.: HRD Press, 1996); D. D. Dubois, Ed., *The Competency Case Book: Twelve Studies in Competency-Based Performance Improvement* (Amherst, Mass.: HRD Press and the International Society for Performance Improvement, 1998); David D. Dubois and William J. Rothwell, *The Competency Toolkit*, 2 volumes (Amherst, Mass.: HRD Press, 2000); David D. Dubois and William J. Rothwell, *Competency-Based Human Resource Management* (Palo Alto, Calif.: Davies-Black, 2004); Jeffrey S. Shippman, Ronald A. Ash, Linda Carr, Beryl Hesketh, Kenneth Pearlman, Mariangela Battista, Lorraine D. Eyde, Jerry Kehoe, Erich Prien, and Juan Sanchez, "The Practice of Competency Modeling," *Personnel Psychology* 53:3 (2000), 703–740.

9. T. R. Athey and M. S. Orth, "Emerging Competency Methods for the Future," *Human Resource Management* 38:3 (1999), 215–226. See also Jay A. Conger and Douglas A. Ready, "Rethinking Leadership Competencies," *Leader to Leader*, Spring 2004, 41–47.

10. David D. Dubois and William J. Rothwell, *Competency-Based Human Resource Management* (Palo Alto, Calif.: Davies-Black, 2004).

11. Danny G. Langdon and Anne F. Marrelli, "A New Model for Systematic

Competency Identification," *Performance Improvement* 41:4 (2002), 14–21. If you want to see a case study online for developing a competency model (but on a secure site open only to ASTD members), check out Karen Elizabeth Tabet, "Implementing a Competency Model: A Short Case Study," *In Practice*, 2004. It was found at the time this book goes to press at http://www.astd.org/astd/Publications/ASTD_Links/April2004/InPractice_Ap ri l04_Tabet.htm

12. See, for instance, Susan H. Gebelein, *Successful Manager's Handbook: Development Suggestions for Today's Managers*, 6th ed. (Minneapolis: Epredix, 2001).

13. Bradley Agle, "Understanding Research on Values in Business," *Business & Society*, September 1999, 326–387.

14. W. G. Lee, "A Conversation with Herb Kelleher," *Organizational Dynamics* 23:2 (1994), 64–74.

15. A. Farnham, "State Your Values, Hold the Hot Air," *Fortune*, August 1993, 117–124.

16. See, for instance, William J. Pfeiffer, Ed., *The Encyclopedia of Group Activities* (San Diego: University Associates, 1989); and Barbara Singer and Kathleen Von Buren, *Work Values: Facilitation Guide for Managers, Teams & Trainers* (Durango, Colo.: Self-Management Institute, 1995).

17. Michael Hickins, "A Day at the Races," *Management Review* 88:5 (1999), 56–61.

18. W. Rothwell, "Go beyond replacing executives and manage your work and values," in D. Ulrich, L. Carter, M. Goldsmith, J. Bolt, and N. Smallwood (eds.), *The Change Champion's Filedguide* (Waltham, Mass.: Best Practice Publications, 2003), pp. 192–204.

Chapter 5

1. Jac Fitz-Enz, *How to Measure Human Resources Management* (New York: McGraw-Hill, 1984), p. 48. See also Jac Fitz-Enz, *The ROI of Human Capital* (New York: AMACOM, 2000).

2. Fitz-Enz, *How to Measure*, p. 48.

3. Particularly good articles on this topic include: Paul Brauchle, "Costing Out the Value of Training," *Technical and Skills Training* 3:4 (1992), 35–40; J. Hassett, "Simplifying ROI," *Training*, September 1992; J. Phillips, "Measuring the Return on HRD," *Employment Relations Today*, August 1991.

4. For example, see especially the classic but dated C. Derr, C. Jones, and E. Toomey, "Managing High-Potential Employees: Current Practices in Thirty-three U.S. Corporations," *Human Resource Management* 27:3 (1988), 273–290; O. Esman, "Succession Planning in Small and Medium-Sized Corporations," *HR Horizons* 91:103 (1991), 15–19; *The Identification and Development of High Potential Managers* (Palatine, Ill.: Executive Knowledgeworks, 1987); Meg Kerr, *Succession Planning in America's Corporations* (Palatine,

Ill.: Anthony J. Fresina and Associates and Executive Knowledgeworks, 1987); and E. Zajac, "CEO Selection, Succession, Compensation and Firm Performance: A Theoretical Integration and Empirical Analysis," *Strategic Management Journal* 11:3 (1990), 217–230.

5. P. Linkow, "HRD at the Roots of Corporate Strategy," *Training and Development Journal* 39:5 (1985), 85–87; William J. Rothwell, ed., *In Action: Linking HRD and Organizational Strategy* (Alexandria, Va.: The American Society for Training and Development, 1998).

6. Karen A. Golden and Vasudevan Ramanujam, "Between a Dream and a Nightmare: On the Integration of the Human Resource Management and Strategic Business Planning Processes," *Human Resource Management* 24:4 (1985), 429.

7. William J. Rothwell and H. C. Kazanas, *The Strategic Development of Talent* (Amherst, Mass.: HRD Press, 2003).

8. See William J. Rothwell and H. C. Kazanas, "Training: Key to Strategic Management," *Performance Improvement Quarterly* 3:1 (1990), 42–56; and William J. Rothwell and H. C. Kazanas, *Planning and Managing Human Resources: Strategic Planning for Personnel Management,* 2nd ed. (Amherst, Mass.: HRD Press, 2003).

9. Robert C. Camp, *Benchmarking: The Search for Industry Best Practices That Lead to Superior Performance* (Milwaukee, Wisc.: Quality Press/American Society for Quality Control; White Plains, N.Y.: Quality Resources, 1989), p. 3. See also Michael J. Spendolini, *The Benchmarking Book* (New York: AMACOM, 1992).

10. Ibid., p. 17.

11. Diane Dormant, "The ABCDs of Managing Change," in M. Smith, Ed., *Introduction to Performance Technology* (Washington, D.C.: The National Society for Performance and Instruction, 1986), pp. 238–256.

12. Ibid., p. 239.

13. Ibid., p. 241.

14. Jack Welch and John A. Byrne, *Jack: Straight from the Gut* (New York: Warner Business Books, 2001).

15. "Business: The King Lear Syndrome: Succession Planning," *The Economist* 369:8354 (2003), 75.

Chapter 6

1. James L. Gibson, John M. Ivancevich, and James H. Donnelly, Jr., *Organizations: Behavior, Structure, Processes,* 5th ed. (Plano, Tex.: Business Publications, 1985), p. 280.

2. Walter R. Mahler and Stephen J. Drotter, *The Succession Planning Handbook for the Chief Executive* (Midland Park, N.J.: Mahler Publishing, 1986), p. 8.

3. "Choosing Your Successor," *Chief Executive Magazine,* May/June 1988, 48–63; Jeffrey Sonnenfeld, *The Hero's Farewell: What Happens When CEOs Retire* (New York: Oxford University Press, 1988); Richard F. Vancil, *Passing the Baton: Managing the Process of CEO Succession* (Boston: Harvard Business School Press, 1987); E. Zajac, "CEO Selection, Succession, Compensation and Firm Performance: A Theoretical Integration and Empirical Analysis," *Strategic Management Journal* 11:3 (1990), 217–230. See also D. Carey and D. Ogden, *CEO Succession: A Window On How Boards Can Get It Right When Choosing A New Chief Executive* (New York: Oxford University Press, 2000) and

4. "Global CEO Turnover at Record Highs," *Financial Executive* 19:5 (2003), 10.

Chapter 7

1. Allen Kraut, Patricia Pedigo, Douglas McKenna, and Marvin Dunnette, "The Role of the Manager: What's Really Important in Different Management Jobs," *Academy of Management Executive* 3:4 (1989), 287.

2. See, for instance, R. Smither, "The Return of the Authoritarian Manager," *Training* 28:11 (1991), 40–44.

Chapter 8

1. M. Pastin, "The Fallacy of Long-Range Thinking," *Training* 23:5 (1986), 47–53.

2. B. Staw, "Knee-Deep in the Big Muddy," *Organizational Behavior and Human Performance* 16:1 (1976), 27–44.

3. Karen Stephenson and Valdis Krebs, "A More Accurate Way to Measure Diversity," *Personnel Journal* 72:10 (1993), 66–72, 74.

4. Rosabeth Moss Kanter, *The Men and Women of the Corporation* (New York: Basic Books, 1977), p. 48.

5. Ibid.

6. Glenn E. Baker, A. Grubbs, and Thomas Ahern, "Triangulation: Strengthening Your Best Guess," *Performance Improvement Quarterly* 3:3 (1990), 27–35.

7. Arthur W. Sherman, Jr., George W. Bohlander, and Herbert Chruden, *Managing Human Resources*, 8th ed. (Cincinnati: South-Western Publishing Co., 1988), pp. 95–96.

8. For one excellent approach, see Roger J. Plachy and Sandra J. Plachy, *Results-Oriented Job Descriptions* (New York: AMACOM, 1993). See also *Model Job Descriptions for Business* (N.p.: Local Government Institute, 1997).

9. W. Barlow and E. Hane, "A Practical Guide to the Americans with Disabilities Act," *Personnel Journal* 71:6 (1992), 54.

10. Kenneth E. Carlisle, *Analyzing Jobs and Tasks* (Englewood Cliffs, N.J.: Educational Technology Publications, 1986), p. 5.

11. See Barlow and Hane, "A Practical Guide," 53–60; M. Chalker, "Tooling Up for ADA," *HR Magazine,* December 1991, 61–63, 65; and J. Kohl and P. Greenlaw, "The Americans with Disabilities Act of 1990: Implications for Managers," *Sloan Management Review* 33:3 (1992), 87–90.

12. See, for instance, Roger J. Plachy and Sandra J. Plachy, *Results-Oriented Job Descriptions* (New York: AMACOM, 1993).

13. William J. Rothwell, "HRD and the Americans with Disabilities Act," *Training and Development* 45:8 (1991), 45–47.

14. Richard Boyatzis, *The Competent Manager: A Model for Effective Performance* (New York: John Wiley & Sons, 1982).

15. David Dubois, *Competency-Based Performance Improvement: A Strategy for Organizational Change* (Amherst, Mass.: HRD Press, 1993), p. 9.

16. Ibid.

17. R. Norton, *Dacum Handbook* (Columbus, Ohio: The National Center for Research in Vocational Education, The Ohio State University, 1985). See also D. Faber, E. Fangman, and J. Low, "DACUM: A Collaborative Tool for Workforce Development," *Journal of Studies in Technical Careers* 13:2 (1991), 145–159.

18. Ibid., pp. 1–2.

19. See A. Osborn, *Applied Imagination*, 3rd ed. (New York: Scribner, 1963); A. Van Gundy, *Techniques of Structured Problem Solving* (New York: Van Nostrand Reinhold, 1981); Michael Michalko, *Thinkertoys: A Handbook of Business Creativity for the 90s* (Berkeley, Calif.: Ten Speed Press, 1991); Dario Nardi, *Multiple Intelligences and Personality Type: Tools and Strategies for Developing Human Potential* (Huntington Beach, Calif.: Telos Publications, 2001); Pamela Meyer, *Quantum Creativity* (New York: McGraw-Hill, 2000).

20. A. Van Gundy, *Techniques of Structured Problem Solving.*

21. G. Huet-Cox, T. M. Nielsen, and E. Sundstrom, "Get the Most From 360-Degree Feedback: Put It on the Internet," *HR Magazine* 44:5 (1999), 92–103; "Finding Leaders: How Ameritech Feeds Its Pipeline," *Training Directors' Forum Newsletter* 15:5 (1999), 4.

22. Leanne Atwater and David Waldman, "Accountability in 360-Degree Feedback," *HR Magazine* 43:6 (1998), 96–104. The article asserts that over 90 percent of Fortune 1000 companies use some form of multisource assessment. For more information on full-circle, multirater assessment, see David D. Dubois and William J. Rothwell, *The Competency Toolkit*, 2 vols. (Amherst, Mass.: HRD Press, 2000); Keith Morical, "A Product Review: 360 Assessments," *Training and Development* 53:4 (1999), 43–47; Kenneth Nowack, Jeanne Hartley, and William Bradley, "How to Evaluate Your 360-Feedback Efforts," *Training & Development* 53:4 (1999), 48–53; David Waldman and David E. Bowen, "The Acceptability of 360-Degree Appraisals: A Customer-Supplier Relation-

ship Perspective," *Human Resource Management* 37:2 (1998), 117–129. Other recent writings on 360-degree assessment include Anne Freedman, "The Evolution of 360s," *Human Resource Executive*, 16:17 (2002), 47–51; Marnie E. Green, "Ensuring the Organization's Future: A Leadership Development Case Study," *Public Personnel Management* 31:4 (2002), 431–439; Fred Luthans and Suzanne J. Peterson, "360-Degree Feedback with Systematic Coaching: Empirical Analysis Suggests a Winning Combination," *Human Resource Management* 42:3 (2003), 243–256; Bruce Pfau and Ira Kay, "Does 360-Degree Feedback Negatively Affect Company Performance?", *HR Magazine* 47:6 (2002), 54–59; Scott Wimer, "The Dark Side of 360-Degree Feedback," *T + D* 56:9 (2002), 37–42.

23. See, for instance, Paul J. Taylor and Jon L. Pierce, "Effects of Introducing a Performance Management System on Employees' Subsequent Attitudes and Effort," *Public Personnel Management* 28:3 (1999), 423–452.

24. See, for instance, *Performance Appraisals: The Ongoing Legal Nightmare* (Ramsey, N.J.: Alexander Hamilton Institute, 1993).

25. Mary Walton, *The Deming Management Method* (New York: Perigee Books, 1986), p. 91.

26. See, for instance, S. Cunningham, "Coaching Today's Executive," *Public Utilities Fortnightly* 128:2 (1991), 22–25; David L. Dotlich and Peter C. Cairo, *Action Coaching: How to Leverage Individual Performance for Company Success* (San Francisco: Jossey-Bass, 1999); Steven J. Stowell and Matt Starcevich, *The Coach: Creating Partnerships for a Competitive Edge* (Salt Lake City: The Center for Management and Organization Effectiveness, 1987).

27. *BLR Encyclopedia of Performance Appraisal* (Madison, Conn.: Business and Legal Reports, 1985). See also Richard C. Grote, *The Complete Guide to Performance Appraisal* (New York: AMACOM, 1996).

28. David D. Dubois and William J. Rothwell, *Competency-Based Human Resource Management* (Palo Alto, Calif.: Davies-Black, 2004).

29. Paul Kaihla, "Getting Inside the Boss's Head," *Business 2.0* 4:10 (2003), 49.

30. Scott Highhouse, "Assessing the Candidate as a Whole: A Historical and Critical Analysis of Individual Psychological Assessment for Personnel Decision-Making," *Personnel Psychology* 55:2 (2002), 363–396.

Chapter 9

1. See William J. Rothwell and H. C. Kazanas, *Planning and Managing Human Resources: Strategic Planning for Personnel Management*, 2nd ed. (Amherst, Mass.: HRD Press, 2003).

2. William J. Rothwell and H. C. Kazanas, "Developing Management Employees to Cope with the Moving Target Effect," *Performance and Instruction* 32:8 (1993), 1–5.

3. See, for instance, Newman S. Peery, Jr., and Mahmoud Salem, "Strategic Management of Emerging Human Resource Issues," *Human Resource Development Quarterly* 4:1 (1993), 81–95; Raynold A. Svenson and Monica J. Rinderer, *The Training and Development Strategic Plan Workbook* (Englewood Cliffs, N.J.: Prentice-Hall, 1992). For works specifically on environmental scanning, see F. Aguilar, *Scanning the Business Environment* (New York: Macmillan, 1967); Patrick Callan, Ed., *Environmental Scanning for Strategic Leadership* (San Francisco: Jossey-Bass, 1986); L. Fahey, W. King, and V. Narayanan, "Environmental Scanning and Forecasting in Strategic Planning—The State of the Art," *Long Range Planning* 14:1 (1981), 32–39; R. Heath and Associates, *Strategic Issues Management: How Organizations Influence and Respond to Public Interests and Policies* (San Francisco: Jossey-Bass, 1988).

4. Harry Levinson, *Organizational Diagnosis* (Cambridge, Mass.: Harvard University Press, 1972); A. O. Manzini, *Organizational Diagnosis* (New York: AMACOM, 1988); and Marvin Weisbord, *Organizational Diagnosis: A Workbook of Theory and Practice* (Reading, Mass.: Addison-Wesley, 1978).

5. This is an issue of classic debate: Does structure affect strategy or does strategy affect structure? The first discussion appears in A. Chandler, *Strategy and Structure: Chapters in the History of American Industrial Enterprise* (Cambridge, Mass.: Massachusetts Institute of Technology, 1962). Other authors are not sure that strategy always affects structure. See, for instance, J. Galbraith and D. Nathanson, "The Role of Organizational Structure and Process in Strategy Implementation," in D. Schendel and C. Hofer, Eds., *Strategic Management* (Boston: Little, Brown and Co., 1979).

6. See Kees Van Der Heijden, *Scenarios: The Art of Strategic Conversation* (New York: John Wiley & Sons, 1996); and William J. Rothwell and H. C. Kazanas, *The Strategic Development of Talent* (Amherst, Mass.: HRD Press, 2003).

7. See, for instance, the classic article by J. Wissema, A. Brand, and H. Van Der Pol, "The Incorporation of Management Development in Strategic Management," *Strategic Management Journal* 2 (1981), 361–377.

8. See remarks in Larry Davis and E. McCallon, *Planning, Conducting, Evaluating Workshops* (Austin, Tex.: Learning Concepts, 1974).

9. Rothwell and Kazanas, "Developing Management Employees," 1–5.

10. See Rothwell and Kazanas, *Planning and Managing Human Resources*.

11. Melvin Sorcher, *Predicting Executive Success: What It Takes to Make It Into Senior Management* (New York: John Wiley & Sons, 1985), p. 2.

12. William J. Rothwell and H. C. Kazanas, *Building In-House Leadership and Management Development Programs* (Westport, Conn.: Quorum Books, 1999).

13. Ibid.

14. See the classic study: E. Lindsey, V. Homes, and M. McCall, *Key Events in Executives' Lives* (Greensboro, N.C.: The Center for Creative Leadership, 1987).

15. This approach is described at length in George S. Odiorne, *Strategic*

Management of Human Resources: A Portfolio Approach (San Francisco: Jossey-Bass, 1984).

16. Ibid.

17. Ibid.

18. Ibid.

19. Ibid.

20. Rose Mary Wentling, "Women in Middle Management: Their Career Development and Aspirations," *Business Horizons* (January-February 1992), 47–54.

21. "Assessment Centres Show Signs of Growth" (2004, February 24), 47.

22. Cam Caldwell, George C. Thornton III, and Melissa L Gruys. "Ten Classic Assessment Center Errors: Challenges to Selection Validity." *Public Personnel Management* 32:1 (2003), 73–88.

23. For more on assessment centers, see: International Task Force on Assessment Center Guidelines, "Guidelines and Ethical Considerations for Assessment Center Operations: International Task Force on Assessment Center Guidelines," *Public Personnel Management* 29:3 (2000), 315–331; P. G. Jansen and B. A. M. Stoop, "The Dynamics of Assessment Center Validity: Results of a 7-Year Study," *Journal of Applied Psychology* 86:4 (2001), 741–753; G. C. Thornton, *Assessment Centers in Human Resource Management* (Reading, Mass.: Addison-Wesley, 1992); A. Tziner, S. Ronen, and D. Hacohen, "A Four-year Validation Study of an Assessment Center in a Financial Corporation," *Journal of Organizational Behavior* 14 (1993), 225–237.

Chapter 10

1. Walter R. Mahler and Stephen J. Drotter, *The Succession Planning Handbook for the Chief Executive* (Midland Park, N.J.: Mahler Publishing Co., 1986).

2. Peter F. Drucker, "How to Make People Decisions," *Harvard Business Review* 63:4 (1985), 22–26.

3. Lawrence S. Kleiman and Kimberly J. Clark, "User's Satisfaction with Job Posting," *Personnel Administrator* 29:9 (1984), 104–108.

4. Lawrence S. Kleiman and Kimberly J. Clark, "An Effective Job Posting System," *Personnel Journal* 63:2 (1984), 20–25.

5. Malcolm Knowles, *Using Learning Contracts: Practical Approaches to Individualizing and Structuring Learning* (San Francisco: Jossey-Bass, 1986), pp. 28–32.

6. R. Fritz, *Personal Performance Contracts: The Key to Job Success* (Los Altos, Calif.: Crisp, 1987).

7. Arthur X. Deegan II, *Succession Planning: Key to Corporate Excellence* (New York: Wiley-Interscience, 1986), p. 167.

8. Robert F. Mager, *Preparing Instructional Objectives*, 2nd ed. (Belmont, Calif.: Lear-Siegler, 1975).

9. M. Lombardo and R. Eichinger, *Eighty-eight Assignments for Development in Place: Enhancing the Developmental Challenge of Existing Jobs* (Greensboro, N.C.: The Center for Creative Leadership, 1989).

10. A. Huczynski, *Encyclopedia of Management Development Methods* (London: Gower, 1983).

11. See, for instance, Paul R. Yost and Mary Mannion Plunkett, "Turn Business Strategy Into Leadership Development," *T + D* 56:3 (2002), 48–51.

12. See, for instance, William J. Rothwell and H. C. Kazanas, *Building In-House Leadership and Management Development Programs* (Westport, Conn.: Quorum, 1999) and Marshall Tarley, "Leadership Development for Small Organizations," *T + D* 56:3 (2002), 52–55.

13. Maryse Dubouloy, "The Transitional Space and Self-Recovery: A Psychoanalytical Approach to High-Potential Managers' Training," *Human Relations* 57:4 (2004), 467–496; "A Formal Coaching Program," *Sales and Marketing Management,* 156:7 (2004), 14; Stephen Hrop, "Coaching Across Cultures: New Tools for Leveraging National, Corporate, and Professional Differences," *Personnel Psychology* 57:1 (2004), 220–223; Leigh Rivenbark, "Adaptive Coaching," *HR Magazine* 49:5 (2004), 128–129; Mark Rotella, Sarah F Gold, Lynn Andriani, Michael Scharf, and Emily Chenoweth, "Leverage Your Best, Ditch The Rest: The Coaching Secrets Top Executives Depend On," *Publishers Weekly* 251:20 (2004), 45.

14. Chris Bones, "Coaching? It's What Managers Are For," *Human Resources,* June 2004, 14.

15. James M. Hunt and Joseph R. Weintraub, *The Coaching Manager: Developing Top Talent in Business* (Thousand Oaks, Calif.: Sage Publications, 2002).

16. See the Coaching Federation of Canada Web site (http://www.coach.ca/e/nccp/) and an ERIC Web site with a list of them available, at least on 17 July 2004, at http://www.ericdigests.org/pre-9212/coaching.htm

17. See, for instance, http://www.coachfederation.org/credentialing/en/core.htm. [That is the Web site of the International Coaching Federation, which has a competency model for coaching on the Web in downloadable format.]

18. Heather Johnson, "The Ins and Outs of Executive Coaching," *Training* 41:5 (2004), 36–41.

19. See, for instance, the Worldwide Association of Business Coaches at http://www.wabccoaches.com/.

20. See, for an example, http://mycoach.com/ethics_abeta.shtml

21. See http://www.execcoach.net/Competences.htm

22. Edgar Schein, *Process Consultation Revisited: Building the Helping Relationship* (Reading, Mass.: Addison-Wesley, 1998).

23. S. J. Armstrong, C. W. Allinson, and J. Hayes, "Formal Mentoring Systems: An Examination of the Effects of Mentor/Protégé Cognitive Styles on the

Mentoring Process," *The Journal of Management Studies* 39 (December 2002), 1111–1137; N. Bozionelos, "Mentoring Provided: Relation to Mentor's Career Success, Personality, and Mentoring Received," *Journal of Vocational Behavior* 64 (February 2004), 24–46; C. Conway, *Strategies for Mentoring: A Blueprint for Successful Organizational Development* (New York: John Wiley & Sons, 1998); V. M. Godshalk and J. J. Sosik, "Does Mentor-Protégé Agreement on Mentor Leadership Behavior Influence the Quality of a Mentoring Relationship?" *Group and Organization Management* 25 (September 2000), 291–317; B.A. Hamilton and T. A. Scandura, "E-Mentoring: Implications for Organizational Learning and Development in a Wired World," *Organizational Dynamics* 31:4 (2003), 388–402.

24. Reg Revans, *Developing Effective Managers* (New York: Praeger, 1971).

25. David L. Dotlich and James L. Noel, *Action Learning : How the World's Top Companies are Re-Creating Their Leaders and Themselves* (San Francisco: Jossey-Bass, 1998); Ian McGill and Liz Beaty, *Action Learning: A Guide for Professional, Management & Educational Development*, 2nd ed. (New York: Taylor and Francis, 2001); Michael Marquardt, *Action Learning in Action: Transforming Problems and People for World-Class Organizational Learning* (Palo Alto, Calif.: Davies-Black, 1999); Michael Marquardt, *Optimizing the Power of Action Learning: Solving Problems and Building Leaders in Real Time* (Palo Alto, Calif.: Davies-Black, 2004).

26. Michael Marquardt, "Harnessing the Power of Action Learning," *T + D* 58:6 (2004), 26–32.

27. William J. Rothwell, *The Action Learning Guidebook: A Real-Time Strategy for Problem-Solving, Training Design, and Employee Development* (San Francisco: Jossey-Bass/Pfeiffer, 1999).

Chapter 11

1. James L. Adams, *Conceptual Blockbusting: A Guide to Better Ideas*, 3rd ed. (Reading, Mass.: Addison-Wesley, 1986), p. 7.

2. Michael Hammer and James Champy, *Reengineering the Corporation: A Manifesto for Business Revolution* (New York: HarperBusiness, 1993), p. 32.

3. G. Rummler and A. Brache, "Managing the White Space," *Training* 28:1 (1991), 55–70.

4. See Eva Kaplan-Leiserson, "Aged to Perfection," *T+D* 55:10 (2001), 16–17; and Neil Lebovits, "Seniors Returning to the Accounting Workforce: Supply Meets Demand," *The CPA Journal*, 73:11 (2003), 14.

5. Anne Freedman, "What Shortage?" *Human Resource Executive* 18:4 (2004), 26–28.

6. Dayton Fandray, "Gray Matters," *Workforce* 79:7 (2000), 26–32.

Chapter 12

1. For assistance in conceptualizing a skill inventory and/or a recordkeeping system for that purpose, see D. Gould, *Personnel Skills Inventory Skill Study* (Madison, Conn.: Business and Legal Reports, 1986).

Chapter 13

1. William J. Rothwell and Henry J. Sredl, *The American Society for Training and Development Reference Guide to Workplace Learning and Performance*, 3rd ed., 2 vols. (Amherst, Mass.: HRD Press, 2000).

2. See Nancy Dixon, *Evaluation: A Tool for Improving HRD Quality* (Alexandria, Va.: The American Society for Training and Development, 1990); Jack Phillips, *Handbook of Training Evaluation and Measurement Methods*, 2nd ed. (Houston: Gulf Publishing, 1991); Leslie Rae, *How to Measure Training Effectiveness* (Brookfield, Vt.: Gower Publishing, 1991); William J. Rothwell, Ed., *Creating, Measuring and Documenting Service Impact: A Capacity Building Resource: Rationales, Models, Activities, Methods, Techniques, Instruments* (Columbus, Ohio: The Enterprise Ohio Network, 1998).

3. Paul Brauchle, "Costing Out the Value of Training," *Technical and Skills Training* 3:4 (1992), 35–40; W. Cascio, *Costing Human Resources: The Financial Impact of Behavior in Organizations*, 2nd ed. (Boston: PWS-Kent Publishing, 1987); C. Fauber, "Use of Improvement (Learning) Curves to Predict Learning Costs," *Production and Inventory Management* 30:3 (1989), 57–60; T. Jackson, *Evaluation: Relating Training to Business Performance* (San Diego: Pfeiffer and Company, 1989); L. Spencer, *Calculating Human Resource Costs and Benefits* (Somerset, N.J.: John Wiley and Sons, 1986); Richard Swanson and Deane Gradous, *Forecasting Financial Benefits of Human Resource Development* (San Francisco: Jossey-Bass, 1988).

4. See Donald Kirkpatrick, "Techniques for Evaluating Training Programs," *Journal of the American Society for Training and Development* [now called *T + D*] 14:1 (1960), 13–18.

5. R. Brinkerhoff, "The Success Case: A Low-Cost High-Yield Evaluation," *Training and Development Journal* 37:8 (1983), 58–61. See also Rothwell, Ed., *Creating, Measuring and Documenting Service Impact*.

6. See William J. Rothwell and H. C. Kazanas, *Planning and Managing Human Resources: Strategic Planning for Personnel Management*, 2nd ed. (Amherst, Mass.: HRD Press, 2003).

Chapter 14

1. See Pamela Babcock, "Slicing Off Pieces of HR," *HR Magazine* 49:7 (2004), 70; Karen Colteryahn and Patty Davis, "8 Trends You Need to Know Now," *T + D* 58:1 (2004), 28–36; Simon Kent, "When Is Enough, Enough?"

Personnel Today, June 15, 2004, 7; James F. Orr, "Outsourcing Human Resources," *Chief Executive,* June 2004, 16; Sara L. Rynes, "'Where Do We Go From Here?' Imagining New Roles for Human Resources," *Journal of Management Inquiry* 13:3 (2004), 203–213; William B. Scott and Carole Hedden, "People Issues: Good Leaders, Ethics, Growth Opportunities Rank High on Employee Preference Lists," *Aviation Week and Space Technology* 160:18 (2004), 61; Uyen Vu, "HR Responds to Cost Crunch with Workforce Cuts: Survey," *Canadian HR Reporter* 17:11 (2004), 1–2; Joe Willmore, "The Future of Performance," *T + D,* August 2004, 26–31, 49, 53; Ron Zemke, "The Confidence Crisis," *Training* 41:6 (2004), 22–27.

2. Anonymous, "An HR Outsourcing Report," *Employee Benefit Plan Review* 59:1 (2004), 5–6; "The Return of Work/Life Plans," *HR Focus* 81:4 (2004), 1–3; Damon Cline, "Companies Seeking 'Right' Candidates Increasingly Turn to Personality Tests," *Knight Ridder Tribune Business News,* March 9, 2004, 1; Kristine Ellis, "Top Training Strategies," *Training* 40:7 (2003), 30–36; Brandon Hall, "Time to Outsource?", *Training* 41:6 (2004), 14; Fay Hansen, "Currents in Compensation and Benefits," *Compensation and Benefits Review* 36:3 (2004), 6–25.

3. Craig E. Aronoff and Christopher J. Eckrich, "Trends in Family-Business Transitions," *Nation's Business* 87:5 (1999), 62–63; John Beeson, "Succession Planning," *Across the Board* 37:2 (2000), 38–41; Ram Charan and Geoffrey Colvin, "The Right Fit," *Fortune* 141:8 (2000), 226–233; Robert J. Grossman, "HR On the Board," *HR Magazine* 49:6 (2004), 56–63; William J. Rothwell, "What's Special about CEO Succession?" *Global CEO Magazine,* March 2004, 15–20; William J. Rothwell, "Knowledge Transfer: 12 Strategies For Succession Management," *IPMA-HR News,* July 2004, 10–12; William J. Rothwell, "Competency-Based Succession Planning: Do I Fit In? The Individual's Role in Succession Planning," *Career Planning and Adult Development Journal* 18:4 (2003), 120–135; William J. Rothwell, "Succession Planning and Management in Government: Dreaming the Impossible Dream," *IPMA-HR News* 69:10 (2003), 1, 7—9; William J. Rothwell and Christopher Faust, "Managing the Quiet Crisis: The Impact of an Effective Succession Plan: Leveraging Web-Based Human Capital Management Systems to Plan for the Future and Manage the Talent Pool Today," Published online at http://www.softscape.com/white papers/whitepapers.htm.; William J. Rothwell "Beyond Succession Management: New Directions and Fresh Approaches," *Linkage Link and Learn Newsletter,* published at http://www.linkageinc.com/newsletter/archives/leadership/ beyond_succession erothwell.shtml.; William J. Rothwell, "Go Beyond Replacing Executives and Manage Your Work and Values," in D. Ulrich, L. Carter, M. Goldsmith, J. Bolt & N. Smallwood (Eds.), *The Change Champion's Fieldguide* (pp. 192–204). (Waltham, Mass.: Best Practice Publications, 2003); George B. Yancey, "Succession Planning Creates Quality Leadership," *Credit Union Executive Journal* 41:6 (2001), 24–27.

4. Susan Ladika, "Executive Protection: Terror Alerts and Corporate Board

Liability Are Focusing New Attention on Security Issues for Top Company Offi-cers," *HR Magazine* 49:10 (2004), 105–106, 108–109.

5. See Thomas Hoffman, "Labor Gap May Drive Mergers," *Online News,* July 13, 1998, at http://www.idg.net/crd[lh.5,p6]it[lh.5,p6]9–65593.html.

6. Jennifer Reingold and Diane Brady, "Brain Drain," *Business Week,* September 20, 1999, 112–115, 118, 120, 124, 126.

7. Ibid.

8. Ibid.

9. Leslie Gross Klaff, "Thinning the Ranks of the 'Career Expats,'" *Workforce Management* 83:10 (2004), 84–84, 86–87.

10. W. Rothwell and S. Poduch, "Introducing Technical (Not Managerial) Succession Planning," *Personnel Management, 33*(4), 2004, pp. 405–420.

WHAT'S ON THE CD?

Selected Worksheets and Resources from the Book

Exhibit 2-1. An Assessment Questionnaire: How Well Is Your Organization Managing the Consequences of Trends Influencing Succession Planning and Management?

Exhibit 3-2. Assessment Questionnaire for Effective Succession Planning and Management

Exhibit 3-3. A Simple Exercise to Dramatize the Need for Succession Planning and Management

Exhibit 5-4. A Questionnaire for Assessing the Status of Succession Planning and Management in an Organization

Exhibit 5-5. A Worksheet for Demonstrating the Need for Succession Planning and Management

Exhibit 5-6. An Interview Guide for Determining the Requirements for a Succession Planning and Management Program

Exhibit 5-7. An Interview Guide for Benchmarking Succession Planning and Management Practices

Exhibit 6-3. A Worksheet to Formulate a Mission Statement for Succession Planning and Management

Exhibit 6-4. A Sample Succession Planning and Management Policy

Exhibit 6-6. An Activity for Identifying Initial Targets for Succession Planning and Management Activities

Exhibit 6-7. An Activity for Establishing Program Priorities in Succession Planning and Management

Exhibit 6-8. Handout: U.S. Labor Laws

Exhibit 7-1. A Worksheet for Preparing an Action Plan to Establish the Succession Planning and Management Program

Exhibit 8-1. A Worksheet for Writing a Key Position Description

Exhibit 8-2. A Worksheet for Considering Key Issues in Full-Circle, Multirater Assessments

Exhibit 8-5. A Worksheet for Developing an Employee Performance Appraisal Linked to a Position Description

Exhibit 9-1. A Worksheet for Environmental Scanning

Also:

- ▲ Effective Succession Planning: A Fully Customizable Leader Guide for The Manager's Role in Succession Planning
- ▲ Effective Succession Planning: A Fully Customizable Participant Guide for The Manager's Role in Succession Planning
- ▲ PowerPoint Slides to Accompany The Manager's Role in Succession Planning
- ▲ Assessment Instrument for Use with The Manager's Role in Succession Planning
- ▲ Executive Assessment Instrument for Use with The Manager's Role in Succession Planning
- ▲ PowerPoint Slides to Accompany Executive Briefing on Succession Planning
- ▲ Frequently-Asked Questions About Succession Planning (from the Book) for Use with the Executive Briefing on Succession Planning
- ▲ Effective Succession Planning: A Fully Customizable Leader Guide for Mentoring from A to Z
- ▲ Effective Succession Planning: A Fully Customizable Participant Guide for Mentoring from A to Z
- ▲ PowerPoint Slides to Accompany Mentoring from A to Z

INDEX

ABOUT THE AUTHOR

William J. Rothwell is Professor-in-Charge of Workforce Education and Development in the Department of Learning and Performance Systems in the College of Education on the University Park campus of The Pennsylvania State University. He leads a graduate emphasis in workplace learning and performance. He is also President of Rothwell & Associates, Inc. (see www.rothwell-associates.com), a full-service private consulting firm that specializes in all facets of succession planning and management and related HR issues.

Rothwell completed a B.A. in English at Illinois State University, an M.A. (and all courses for the doctorate) in English at the University of Illinois at Urbana-Champaign, an M.B.A. at the University of Illinois at Springfield, and a Ph.D. degree with a specialization in employee training at the University of Illinois at Urbana-Champaign. He holds life accreditation as a Senior Professional of Human Resources (SPHR) and was the first U.S. citizen awarded trainer certification (CTDP) by the Canadian Society for Training and Development (CSTD).

Before entering academe in 1993, Rothwell had twenty years of experience as an HR practitioner, serving first as Training Director for the Illinois Office of Auditor General and later as Assistant Vice President and Management Development Director for The Franklin Life Insurance Company, at that time a wholly owned subsidiary of a Fortune 50 multinational company.

Best-known for his extensive and high-profile work in succession management, Rothwell is a frequent speaker or keynoter at conferences and seminars around the world. He has authored, coauthored, edited, or coedited numerous books, book chapters, and articles. Among his most recent publications are *Beyond Training and Development*, 2nd ed. (AMACOM, 2005), *Practicing Organization Development*, 2nd ed. (Pfeiffer, 2005), the current ASTD competency study to define the workplace learning and performance field entitled *Mapping the Future* (with P. Bernthal and others, ASTD, 2004), *Competency-Based Human Resource Management* (with D. Dubois, Davies-Black, 2004), *Linking Training to Performance* (with P. Gerity and E. Gaertner, American Association of Community Colleges, 2004), *The Strategic Development of Talent* (with H. Kazanas, HRD Press, 2004), *Mastering the Instructional Design Process*, 3rd ed. (with H. Kazanas, Pfefifer, 2004), *Improving On-The-Job Train-*

ing, 2nd ed. (with H. Kazanas, Pfeiffer, 2004), *What CEOs Expect from Corporate Training: Building Workplace Learning and Performance Initiatives That Advance Organizational Goals* (with J. Lindholm and W. Wallick, AMACOM, 2003), *Planning and Managing Human Resources*, 2nd ed. (with H.C. Kazanas, HRD Press, 2003), *Creating Sales Training and Development Programs: A Competency-Based Approach to Building Sales Ability* (with W. Donahue and J. Park, Greenwood Press, 2002), *The Workplace Learner: How to Align Training Initiatives with Individual Learning Competencies* (AMACOM, 2002), and *Building Effective Technical Training: How to Develop Hard Skills Within Organizations* (with J. Benkowski, Pfeiffer, 2002).

Rothwell is the U.S. editor of the *International Journal of Training and Development* (Blackwell's), an academic journal on which he works with editorial counterparts in Europe and Asia. He is also a book series coeditor, with Roland Sullivan and Kris Quade, of the Wiley/Jossey-Bass/Pfeiffer book series *Practicing Organization Change and Development*; a book series coeditor, with Rita Richey and Tim Spannaus, of the Wiley/Jossey-Bass/Pfeiffer book series *Using Technology in Training and Learning*; and a book series coeditor, with Victoria Marsick and Andrea Ellinger, of the AMACOM book series *Adult Learning Theory*.